Notice to the Reader

On April 7, 1993, when *Lost Tycoon* had already been printed and was awaiting shipment, the publisher, who had met with Donald Trump and his lawyers on March 3, received the following communication from Donald Trump's lawyers. The statement by Ivana Trump does not contradict or invalidate any information contained in this book, and it is included here only to give full expression to differing points of view on an important event.

STATEMENT OF IVANA TRUMP

During a deposition given by me in connection with my matrimonial case, I stated that my husband had raped me.

I wish to say that on one occasion during 1989, Mr. Trump and I had marital relations in which he behaved very differently toward me than he had during our marriage. As a woman, I felt violated, as the love and tenderness, which he normally exhibited toward me, was absent. I referred to this as a "rape," but I do not want my words to be interpreted in a literal or criminal sense.

Any contrary conclusion would be an incorrect and most unfortunate interpretation of my statement which I do not want to be interpreted in a speculative fashion and I do not want the press or media to misconstrue any of the facts set forth above. All I wish is for this matter to be put to rest.

This statement can only be released and used in its entirety.
Approved: Ivana M. Trump
Date: April 6, 1993

LOST
TYCOON

LOST
TYCOON

.

The many
lives of
Donald J. Trump

■

HARRY HURT III

W·W·Norton & Company New York London

Printed in the United States of America.

First Edition.

The text of this book is composed in Baskerville,
with the display set in latin condensed.
Composition and manufacturing by The Maple-Vail Book
Manufacturing Group.
Book design by Guenet Abraham.

Portions of this book appeared in a previous form in
Esquire magazine.

Library of Congress Cataloging-in-Publication Data

Hurt, Harry.
The lost tycoon : the rise and demise of Donald J. Trump /
by Harry Hurt III.
p.   cm.
1. Trump, Donald 1946–   . 2. Businessmen—United States—
Biography. 3. Real estate developers—United States—Biography.
I. Title.
HC102.5.T78H87   1993
333.33′092—dc20
[B]   92-37043

ISBN 0-393-03029-6

W. W. Norton & Company, Inc., 500 Fifth Avenue, New York, N.Y. 10110

W. W. Norton & Company Ltd., 10 Coptic Street, London WC1A 1PU

1 2 3 4 5 6 7 8 9 0

CONTENTS

PART ONE: THE CRASH

PART TWO: THE ART OF THE SPIEL

PART THREE: BEST SEX EVER HAD

There are no second acts in American lives.
—F. Scott Fitzgerald, *The Last Tycoon* (1941)

Part one

THE CRASH

■ DONALD J. TRUMP wakes up in the middle of a bad dream and sees a band of baby angels hovering above his head. It's 6:00 A.M. on Tuesday, October 10, 1989. Donald has just spent another fitful night in the sixty-seventh- floor master bedroom of his Trump Tower triplex. As usual, he's allowed himself only four hours' sleep. That is maybe sixty to ninety minutes less than the bare minimum most medical experts say is necessary to maintain normal mental health. But Donald J. Trump isn't interested in normal mental health.

Still dressed in a T-shirt and undershorts, Donald tosses off the covers and stares at the winged cherubs painted on the ceiling over the bed. He's a great believer in his almost sadomasochistic practice of enforced insomnia. He thinks it is one of the secrets behind his stunning success. As he's just told *Playboy* magazine in an exclusive interview, it's all part of the unique psychosis that inspired a braggadocian kid from Queens to become a self-made mythic American billionaire by the age of forty-three.

"I've never met a successful man who wasn't neurotic," Donald confided to *Playboy* interviewer Glenn Plaskin just a few days before. "It's not a terrible thing—it's controlled neurosis. . . . Controlled neurosis means having a tremendous energy level, an abundance of discontent that often isn't visible. It's also not oversleeping. I don't sleep more than four hours a night. I have friends who need twelve hours a night and I tell them they're at a major disadvantage in terms of playing the game."

Donald swings his legs to the floor and stands up in the disquieting darkness he's come to know so well. His forty-year-old Czech-born wife, Ivana Maria Zelnicekova Winklmayr Trump, the mother of their three children, does not stir. She and Donald still share the same bed after almost thirteen years of marriage, but they haven't had sex in nearly sixteen months. And considering the way things are going in Donald's secret affair with Marla Ann Maples, a twenty-six-year-old former Georgia beauty queen turned actress-model, it doesn't look as if he and Ivana will have sex again anytime soon.

"What is marriage to you?" Glenn Plaskin had the nerve to ask Donald in the exclusive interview for *Playboy*. "Is it monogamous?"

"I don't have to answer that," Donald rejoined. "I never speak about my wife—which is one of the advantages of not being a politician. My marriage is and should be a personal thing."

"But you do enjoy flirtations?" Plaskin pressed.

"I think any man enjoys flirtations," Donald replied, oblivious to the possibility that his comment might come back to haunt him when the interview is published early in 1990, "and if he said he didn't, he'd be lying or he'd be a politician trying to get the extra four votes. I think everybody likes knowing he's well responded to. Especially as you get into a certain strata where there is an ego involved and a high level of success, it's important. People really like the idea that other people respond to them well."

Donald shuffles toward the bedroom door, marveling at his flirtation with interior design. When he and Ivana first moved into the apartment back in 1983, he delegated responsibility for decorating the family domicile to her. With the help of designer Angelo Donghia, she furnished the apartment with cute, cozy overstuffed chairs and ladylike silken drapes. But in 1985, after a visit to Adnan Khashoggi's sensational and even more spacious pad in Olympic Tower, Donald had decided to embark on a major enlargement and redecoration that took more than three years to complete. He was assisted by California designer Henry Conversano, who, not incidentally, specialized in doing the interiors of casinos in Las Vegas and Atlantic City.

The Trump Tower triplex now looks like the ultimate high-roller suite. The newly expanded interior space occupies the better part of three floors (the sixty-sixth, sixty-seventh, and sixty-eighth) and encompasses at least fifty rooms. The master bedroom typifies the decor. It has floor-to-ceiling windows facing a facade of fake Greek columns. Twenty-four-carat gold leaf drips from the moldings, the trimmings, and the bases and capitals of the columns. There is a gold canopied king-size bed with the heavenly mural dome Donald sees upon waking, a pair of matching antique night tables of uncertain provenance, and, in a nod to his wife's native country, an enormous wedding cake-shaped chandelier made of crystal imported from Czechoslovakia.

The rest of the triplex picks up where the master bedroom leaves off. The dining room has floor-to-ceiling windows that rise a full two stories. Another enormous crystal chandelier from Czechoslovakia illuminates a gilt-edged table surrounded by chairs dripping with more gold leaf. The living room is eighty feet long and paved with honey-colored marble. The walls are covered with custom-made reproductions of European tapestries, and the front door is made of sixteen panels of solid bronze. But the living room's most eye-catching appointment is a twelve-foot waterfall that pours into a fountain sparkling beneath an elliptically shaped Czech crystal chandelier.

"I have the largest living room in New York City," Donald likes to brag, often hastening to add, "And I have the most incredible view."

He also has a secret stash in his Trump Tower triplex: a safe that reportedly holds at least $100,000 cash. According to a high-ranking employee, whose account Donald denies, Donald loves to accumulate this "off-the-books" cash by making personal side deals on his real estate transactions. Many of these side deals have allegedly been made in the course of leasing the retail spaces on the lower floors of Trump Tower.

Even so, as Donald traverses the catwalk between the master bedroom and his private bathroom, he realizes, once again, that all this is not enough. Ever since he was a little boy, his father, Fred C. Trump, Sr., has been hammering the same lines into his head: "You are a killer. . . . You are a king. . . . You are a killer. . . . You are a king. . . ." Donald believes he can't be one without being the other. As his father has pointed out over and over again, most people are weaklings. Only the strong survive. You have to be a killer if you want to be a king. A case in point was Donald's late older brother Fred Trump,

Jr., a former airline pilot who ultimately drank himself to death after being emotionally crucified for not having joined the family real estate business.

"When somebody tries to push me around, when they're after my ass, I push back a hell of alot harder than I was pushed in the first place," Donald informed *Playboy*. "If somebody tries to push me around, he's going to pay a price." As if to prove that his machismo comes with a social conscience, Donald has recently taken out an advertisement in the *New York Times* demanding the death penalty for a gang of black youths accused of raping a female jogger in Central Park.

"BRING BACK OUR POLICE . . . BRING BACK THE DEATH PENALTY . . . MAKE NEW YORK CITY SAFE AGAIN," the advertisement implores.

Donald strips down in front of a brown onyx-topped vanity, showers, and puts on one of his trademark blue Brioni suits. He stands just under six feet two inches tall, and he weighs over two hundred pounds. With his boyishly long dirty gold locks, silvery blue eyes, spider-webbed brows, pouty bee-stung lips, and almost invisible jawline, he has a rakishly romantic and slightly menacing look that is variously compared by both friends and foes with the visages of the late rock star Elvis Presley and the devil Mephistopheles. And yet, as if to confound both impressions, his body exudes the exquisite aroma of Fendi cologne and a charismatic intensity of purpose that is far more important to his wheeling and dealing than his sometimes fuzzy head for figures.

"I think what attracts us so much together is not only the love and all that stuff, it's the energy . . . that fabulous energy," his wife, Ivana, told an interviewer in happier times. "You see people who are doers, they have this energy, this life, this spark. It's a part of Donald that that energy gets from one person to another. He's just a great leader, the way he motivates people."

Donald is not impressed, however, with what he sees in the looking glass. In a few weeks he is slated to pose for a cover photograph for the March 1990 issue of *Playboy*, in which his interview with Glenn Plaskin will run. Donald will be the first male to appear on the magazine's cover in nearly twenty years, a distinction certain to enhance his carefully cultivated image as a business-suited sex symbol. But

Donald is so embarrassed by the sorry state of his physique that he wears undershorts and a T-shirt even when he is in bed. Thanks to a diet of junk foods and an aversion to exercise, his waist, thighs, and buttocks have swollen as thick and spongy as giant doughnuts. And most disconcerting of all, as far as he's concerned, he is losing the hair on the crown of his head.

Donald is determined to counteract the encroachments of middle age at almost all costs. In the past he tried to control his weight with prescription diet pills supplied by a physician whose office is just a few short blocks from Trump Tower. But the diet pills, whose pharmacologic activity is similar to that of amphetamines, made the already frenetic Manhattan mogul a holy terror both at home and at the office. Donald is now mulling a new approach to weight control: having a doctor remove his fat by means of liposuction. He is also thinking about undergoing an even more radical-sounding procedure called scalp reduction, supplemented by a hair transplant, to cover his bald spot.

"The worst thing a man can do is go bald," he has warned one of his top executives. "Never let yourself go bald."

Donald strides toward the front door. It is one of those fabulous fall mornings in New York, New York, the city he and most other late twentieth-century robber barons believe to be the socioeconomic center of the universe. The temperature is climbing toward a high of sixty-two degrees, and though the forecast calls for an afternoon of increasing cloudiness, the rising sun is shining like a big bronze amulet amid the velveteen smog enshrouding the world's most famous skyline. As the rush-hour traffic honks above the crack-infested infrastructure, an innocent newcomer could easily mistake this dazzling, decaying urban cacophony to be Donald J. Trump's own private province.

He can see his name everywhere. In the air. On the water. And especially on the land. Up above the Triborough Bridge, gleaming 727 commercial passenger jets with "Trump" emblazoned on their fuselages in bold red block letters shuttle in and out of La Guardia Airport. At a mooring down the Atlantic seaboard a pearl white 282-foot-long yacht christened *Trump Princess* rocks and rolls with the waves. And around the corner of Fifth Avenue and Fifty-seventh Street, a commercial crossroads that may well be the very epicenter of the universe, the eponymous monuments to his greatness tower over the steel and brownstone edifices of midtown Manhattan.

Trump Tower is, of course, the crown jewel. A sawtooth-shaped office-commercial-residential complex constructed of reinforced concrete and bronzed glass, it rises fifty-eight stories, though with typical hyperbole Donald claims the building to be ten stories higher and has renumbered the floors accordingly. Trump Tower features, among other amenities, a six-story retail atrium with a gurgling waterfall and a gold-framed front door monogrammed with golden *T*'s. More important, Trump Tower occupies what Donald calls "the Tiffany location," a prime site next door to the flagship store of the renowned Tiffany jewelry chain at the corner of Fifty-seventh and Fifth. Trump Tower's neighbors include some of the most prestigious names in American capitalism and modern retailing: General Motors, Avon, F. A. O. Schwarz, Bergdorf Goodman, Henri Bendel, Bulgari, Van Cleef & Arpels, Steuben, Harry Winston, and Doubleday.

North, south, east, and west of Trump Tower there are more of Donald's so-called trophy properties. Along the Hudson River between Sixtieth and Seventy-second streets lie the seventy-acre West Side yards, the largest undeveloped real estate parcel in Manhattan, also known as the future site of "Trump City" and/or "TV City." Across town on Third Avenue stand Trump Plaza, a thirty-nine-story luxury apartment building, and Trump Palace, an even more luxurious fifty-five-story apartment complex due to open in 1991. Along Central Park South there are Trump Parc, a gold-crowned art deco condominium; Trump Parc East, an embattled rent-controlled apartment building; the fan-shaped expanse of Wollman Rink, a city-owned ice skating facility in Central Park that to great public acclaim Donald has restored; and the green-gabled roof of his latest and potentially greatest real estate acquisition, the landmark Plaza Hotel. Fifteen blocks to the south, nestled behind Grand Central Terminal, is Donald's first Manhattan real estate development, the chrome-columned Grand Hyatt Hotel.

Incredibly enough, Donald's sprawling portfolio of New York real estate properties amounts to little more than half his total domain. In Atlantic City, New Jersey, the northeastern capital of legalized gambling, he owns a noncasino hotel, Trump Regency, and three casino hotels, Trump Plaza, Trump Castle, and the still-uncompleted Trump Taj Mahal, a fantastical structure projected to be fully twice as large as any other gaming hall in town. In Florida he owns a twin-towered condominium development, called Trump Plaza of the Palm Beaches, and a truly palatial estate, Mar-a-Lago, the former residence of the late breakfast cereal heiress Marjorie Merriweather Post. He owns a waterfront weekend estate in Greenwich, Connecticut, and, in addition to the Trump Shuttle commuter airline and the Trump Air helicopter service, a Boeing 727 jet and a Super Puma helicopter for his own private use.

But Donald's most valuable property—at least as far as he is concerned—is his name. He boasts time and again that he can instantly add value to any property or project simply by adding "Trump" to it. Along with gracing the facades of most of his real estate properties, the Trump name is branded on a Monopoly-style board game called Trump, a television game show called "Trump Card," a Brazilian horse called the Trump Cup, a bicycle race called Tour de Trump, and a new custom-manufactured Cadillac limousine called the Trump Cadillac. It is in the title of his first book, *Trump: The Art of the Deal* (Random House, 1987), which remained atop the *New York Times* best-seller list for almost one full year. It will also be in the title of his second book, now in progress, *Trump: Surviving at the Top,* and in the title of a movie script in progress to be called *The Donald Trump Story.*

"I believe I've added show business to the real estate business," Donald told *Playboy,* "and that's been a positive for my properties and in my life."

Thanks in no small part to Donald J. Trump's talent for inventing and reinventing himself and the media influence afforded by a $30 million casino advertising budget, the Trump name has in fact become the signature for an entire decade in U.S. history, the age of acquisitiveness. The October 23, 1989, issue of *Forbes,* which is already going to press, duly lists Donald on its roster of the four hundred richest Americans. According to *Forbes,* he has a net worth of $1.7 billion, which earns him nineteenth place in the pecking order of U.S. billionaires. That puts Donald far below media magnate John W. Kluge ($5.2 billion), stock market investment wizard Warren E. Buffett ($4.2 billion), and corporate raider Ronald O. Perelman ($2.75 billion), but well above Texas oil heir Ray L. Hunt ($1.4 billion), publishing mogul Walter H. Annenberg ($1.4 billion), and even recently indicted financial wizard Michael R. Milken ($1.27 billion).

Donald is now on the hunt for even larger game. Just six days before, on October 4, he announced a $7.5 billion tender for AMR, the parent company of American Airlines. The bid, which translates to an offering price of $120 a share, has caused AMR stock to soar from $83 a share to over $104 a share in less than a week. Besides claiming that American Airlines would be a perfect complement to his Trump Shuttle commuter airline, Donald claims that he'll have no problem raising the funds necessary to make good on his multi-billion tender. But many members of the Wall Street community wonder if his bid for AMR is merely a ploy to boost the stock and/or attempt to collect some greenmail, the corporate raider's equivalent of a payoff, for dropping the takeover attempt.

"Nope," Donald insisted in his exclusive interview with *Playboy,* "I want it."

Donald slips out of the triplex and takes the elevator down to the Trump Organization headquarters on the twenty-sixth floor. He employs upwards of twelve thousand people, counting all the members of his real estate development and hotel enterprises, the Trump Shuttle, his existing casino operations, and the work force expected to staff the Trump Taj Mahal. But his management structure is still entrepreneurial, rather than corporate, in size and style. His Trump Organization headquarters staff consists of fewer than forty people. The highest-ranking executives besides himself are a cadre of six executive vice-presidents, including his wife, Ivana, and his younger brother, Robert.

Donald likes to give the impression that he is in total control at all times. That, however, is a false impression. Although he brags that he personally signs every check, unpaid bills and past-due invoices pile up on his desk for months at a time. He has a notoriously short attention span, the duration of which a top-ranking former employee measures at "twenty-six seconds." And even though he claims years of experience and expertise in real estate development, another longtime Trump Organization executive claims that he cannot even read blueprints. "Donald starts one project after another, but he has no idea how any of them work or what it takes to make them a success," complains one insider. "It's like he deliberately messes things up and expects us to fix them for him."

Donald exits the twenty-sixth-floor elevator bank and pushes through a set of plate glass doors demarcating his headquarters suite. If the decor of the Trump family apartment resembles that of an Atlantic City high-roller suite, the decor of the Trump Organization nerve center has the look of an elaborate casino counting room. The reception area is trimmed with brown Formica, which Donald claims is burl wood, and sports a sign that says THE TRUMP ORGANIZATION in billboard-size bronze letters. By 8:00 A.M. a gaggle of attractive young female assistants will be scurrying about the beige-carpeted hallways in short skirts and high heels. At one point Donald tried—unsuccessfully—to convince *Playboy* magazine to run a spread on the "Girls of Trump," for which some of his staffers would supposedly agree to pose in the nude.

Donald pushes through a second set of plate glass doors leading from the reception area to his personal domain. His private quarters consist of a brown-and-beige-carpeted office enclosed on three sides by floor-to-ceiling picture windows. The single solid wall is paneled with gold-framed magazine covers featuring his photograph. A scale model of a Trump Shuttle jet rests on a nearby windowsill. In the far corner adjacent to the office door, a second door opens into a private bathroom with black onyx bowls similar to those in his dressing room upstairs in the family triplex.

The centerpiece of Donald's office, however, is a gull-winged red desk surrounded by overstuffed burgundy armchairs. He sometimes claims that the desk is made of Brazilian rosewood; according to an informed staff member, it is actually made of heavily lacquered wood supplied by an Italian furniture maker. Although Donald employs a personal security force consisting of a burly limousine driver and up to a dozen even burlier armed bodyguards, he keeps a .38-caliber pistol locked in his desk and a second pistol locked in a box upstairs in the family triplex. The desk is also equipped with a system for surreptitiously tape recording business meetings. But the interoffice paging system is decidedly low tech.

"Norma! Norma!" Donald shrieks when he hears another person entering the Trump inner sanctum.

Norma Foerderer, his executive assistant, hurries in from a cubicle across the hall. A hazel-eyed, auburn-haired divorcée in her early sixties, she wears bangle earrings, designer business suits, and a matronly expression. Fluent in French, she once worked in the State Department as an assistant to the U.S. ambassador to Tunisia. She got her job with the Trump Organization by answering an advertisement Ivana Trump placed in the *New York Times* and has stayed with the organization for nearly a decade. Far more than an ordinary secretary, Norma is Donald's special confidante, surrogate mother, and public spokesperson. She even has the exclusive assignment of bringing him his daily doses of Diet Coke, which has to be chilled with a specified amount of ice and served in a glass gripped only around the base so that germs will not rub off on the lip.

Norma instructs like a schoolmarm not to forget that he is due at the Plaza Hotel for a press conference at ten o'clock.

Donald scowls his trademark scowl as Norma returns to her cubicle across the hall. The press conference at the Plaza Hotel that morning has been called by the newly formed Trump Sports and Entertainment (TSE). TSE's main function is to promote boxing matches at Trump casinos in Atlantic City and market the rights to network or cable television. The first TSE-sponsored main event is a bout between two allegedly washed-up former lightweight champions, Hector ("Macho Man") Camacho and Vinny Pazienza. The bout is scheduled to be held on February 3, 1990, at the Trump Plaza casino in Atlantic City. Donald, however, has already caused a minor crisis within his executive ranks by announcing that he does not want to attend the Plaza Hotel press conference.

"It's not going to be a big fight," he declared a few days before. "The public doesn't care about this. I'm not coming. I can't be attending every shitty little press conference. It's not dignified."

Donald has reason to be concerned about his dignity, for his vaunted public image has been coming under vicious attack from several quarters. New York Mayor Ed Koch, an alienated potential ally turned archnemesis, has dubbed him and his ambitious development plans for the city "greedy, greedy, greedy." *Time* magazine has scored him for failing to reverse the continuing socioeconomic blight of Atlantic City even as his casinos appear to prosper. *Spy* magazine is scorning him as a "short fingered vulgarian." And cartoonist G. B. Trudeau is lampooning him in the comic strip *Doonesbury* as a tasteless megalo-maniac.

"Call my lawyers and tell them I want to legally rename myself," Trudeau has his Donald J. Trump caricature proclaiming in one installment.

"After yourself, sir?" asks an attending character.

"Trump T. Trump!" affirms the Donald J. Trump caricature. "I like it! It screams quality!"

Donald claims not to understand the humor of Trudeau's cartoon, but to his obvious delight, the general public still seems to believe in him. Earlier this month a group of Connecticut schoolchildren wrote to him as if he were a real-life Santa Claus, asking him to save a 1927 vintage carousel from the scrap heap. "Dear Mr. Trumps [*sic*]," wrote third grader Melissa Plancon, a student at Goodwin Elementary School in Old Saybrook, Connecticut, "Please buy the carousel. We need it bad. All the kids like it. You are the riches [*sic*] one in the country." Norma Foerderer has promised the children that her boss will review their request.

Donald and the highest-ranking members of the Trump Organi-zation—with the notable exception of Ivana—know full well that he has been fooling the adult world about his business acumen and financial strength much as he might fool the Connecticut schoolchil-dren. But the only indication he has given to anyone outside his financial inner circle that things are not as rosy as he makes them seem came one day earlier in the fall, when he and Marla Maples were watching the Trump helicopter take off from Atlantic City.

"Can you believe that I own that? Can you believe that's my name on the side?" Donald bubbled like a little boy amazed at the magnifi-cence of his own toys. Then he added cryptically: "You know all of this could go away tomorrow."

That may be one of the reasons Donald decides to change his mind about skipping the TSE press conference. He is simply too supersti-tious to depart from what he believes to be his proved formula for success. He wears the same dark blue suits and the same complement of bold red and bright pink ties day in and day out because he believes these are his lucky colors. He seldom trims his shaggy eyebrows because he believes they add to his intimidating presence in one-on-one negotiations. And he is, above all else, incurably addicted to self-glorifying publicity.

"Norma! Norma!" he screams from behind his red-lacquered gull-winged desk.

Norma Foerderer rushes back into his office with pad and pen in hand. He instructs her to contact the Trump gaming division executives in charge of the TSE press conference at the Plaza Hotel later that morning, and inform them that he will attend after all.

Ivana Trump has been standing with a pair of binoculars in the dining room of the Trump Tower triplex, peeking at a target two blocks up Fifth Avenue. Her diamond-encrusted Cartier watch is ticking toward nine o'clock on the morning of October 10, 1989. Ivana has dressed in typical workday attire: a black, white, and blue checked Chanel suit and a pair of black crocodile pumps by Charles Jourdan. But her thoughts have been on the grave of a beloved former boyfriend thousands of miles away in Czechoslovakia, where she has sent a memorial wreath, as she does this time every year, with a card that reads: "In loving memory of George."

Ivana pans the binoculars from the giant gold statue of General William Tecumseh Sherman on the corner of Fifth Avenue and Fifty-ninth Street straight across the Pulitzer Fountain in Grand Army Plaza until she can train her lenses directly on the Plaza Hotel. As she focuses on the bustle of activity taking place beneath the hotel's flag-draped front entrance, the loving memory of George gives way to the not-so-loving memory of one of The Donald's more infamous one-liners. Shortly after he named Ivana the new chief executive of the Plaza in the spring of 1988, a reporter asked how, if at all, he was going to compensate her for her services.

"I pay her a salary of one dollar a year and all the dresses she can buy," The Donald had joked.

Haunted by that double-edged remark, Ivana has been striving to earn her keep and keep her self-esteem. Besides overseeing the Plaza's daily operations, she is in charge of supervising a major renovation of the hotel. Over the past year and a half she has reportedly spent upwards of $60 million on top of the nearly $400 million her husband paid to acquire the property, in an effort to restore the circa 1907 landmark to its former glory. Even though she thinks of herself first and foremost as wife and mother, she regards her duties at the Plaza as crucial to her self-image—and to the survival of her marriage.

"If Donald were married to a lady who didn't work and make certain contributions," she told *Time* magazine in a January 1989 cover story about her husband, "he would be gone."

Ivana has been every bit as perfectionist as The Donald, if not more so. She has been coming into her office at the Plaza Hotel from nine to five every day without fail. No detail escapes her notice, no matter how small. After issuing specific instructions to the housekeeping staff advising that every towel should be folded exactly the same way in all 814 rooms of the hotel, she pulled up the hem of her designer skirt and got down on her hands and knees to demonstrate how the bathroom floors should be scrubbed. With the moral fervor of her Czechoslovakian Catholic upbringing, she considers any breach of decorum or lapse in cleanliness as tantamount to mortal sin, and she has let it be known that there will be hell to pay if her standards are not met.

"I run my operations like a family business," Ivana informed *Time*. "I sign every check, every receipt. I'm not tough, but I am strong. You can't be a pussycat."

Whatever the Plaza's twelve hundred employees have been thinking of Ivana, none of them has ever accused her of being a pussycat. During her reign as queen of the Trump Castle casino hotel in Atlantic City, she monitored the comings and goings of her staff via a television camera mounted in the parking garage. Since taking over management of the Plaza, she has been using binoculars to spy on the performance of the hotel's front-door crew, proving that even Big Brother is no match for Big Mother. One morning, for example, she spied a batch of newspapers that had blown up against the side of the hotel from across the street. She picked up the telephone and dialed the front desk in a fury.

"Who is responsible for this?" she demanded. "I'll fire their fucking ass!"

This was not an idle threat. The previous Thanksgiving two mischievous Plaza staffers had forged a memo on hotel stationery announcing that Ivana would be giving away free turkeys for the holidays. She responded by directing Trump security to trace the memo back to the typewriter on which it was composed. Once the guilty parties were identified, Ivana fired them both on the spot, even though one was an electrical engineer who had put in twenty-eight years at the hotel. "This time it was a turkey," she told the *New York Post* in defense of her action, "but next time someone might get hurt."

Lest the Plaza's employees conclude their boss was lacking in the holiday spirit, Ivana tried to make at least partial amends for the Thanksgiving Day massacre. She had never intended to send out free turkeys prior to the circulation of the forged memo. But the incident prompted her to reconsider. In the end she wound up sending complimentary birds to the twelve hundred Plaza employees. "That's the difference between Ivana and Donald," one Ivana loyalist maintained. "She has a heart." And yet, as another Plaza staffer observed in the wake of the turkey turnaround, Ivana's schizophrenic symbiosis of wicked witch and fairy godmother made her "seem almost like two people."

In fact, Ivana has been at least two people: Ivana before and Ivana after. Like the Plaza Hotel, she, too, has undergone a dramatic physical transformation. Five feet eight inches tall, she is, at the age of forty, still a scrupulously trim 110 pounds. She still wears her gold-tinctured tresses straight down and parted to one side with wispy bangs in front. She still speaks in deep, seductive whispers with a thick Slavic accent that has her inserting "the" in front of nouns and proper names (as in "The Donald") and substituting *z* sounds for *th* sounds.

But after nearly thirteen years as Mrs. Donald J. Trump, Ivana was starting to show her age and the toll taken by her dual roles as wife and businesswoman. For a brief time she seemed to be turning into a flat-chested, pumpkin-faced Moravian matron with deeply creased jowls, crow's-feet around her hazel eyes, and lips so thin they resembled a bathtub ring. She quickly put a stop to that with the help of modern medical science and The Donald's munificence.

"I never intend to look a day over 28," she told *New York Daily News* gossip columnist Liz Smith, "but it's going to cost Donald a lot of money."

Ivana's renovation turned out to be relatively inexpensive by comparison to the restoration of the Plaza. It cost in the neighborhood of $25,000 to $35,000, and it was performed by Los Angeles-based plastic surgeon Dr. Steven Hoefflin in April 1989. Hoefflin, who first won fame for treating the burn injuries of singing star Michael Jackson, resculpted her cheekbones, injected collagen in her lips, and amply implanted her breasts. Ivana's outward appearance now bears a striking resemblance to that of the French movie actress Brigitte Bardot. But her soul is being tortured by the same obsession with success that causes The Donald's nightly insomnia.

"In fifty years . . ." she recently informed a reporter from the *San Diego Union,* "we will be the Rockefellers."

Along the way Ivana has even coined a phrase that aptly characterizes what The Donald—and she herself—are all about. "He's off scheming and beaming," she informed The Donald's younger brother, Robert, one day. "You mean wheeling and dealing," Robert politely corrected. "Wheeling and dealing, scheming and beaming," Ivana returned. "It is all the same thing, no?"

Ivana folds her binoculars and walks out the big bronze-paneled front door of the triplex. She takes the elevator down to the hotel-style lobby of the building's residential entrance on Fifty-sixth Street, where she is met by a six-foot-tall Italian-American bodyguard-chauffeur with a square jaw and combed-back brown hair. Ivana's bodyguard-chauffeur ushers her into a black Mercedes sedan and drives her on a four-block route to her job site.

Upon arriving in front of the Plaza, Ivana slips out of the Mercedes and quickly inspects the hotel's eighteen-story French Renaissance facade with its cream-colored brick turrets hopelessly smudged by urban grime and its gabled copper-covered roof green with age. Then the bodyguard escorts her up the red-carpeted front steps, past the five bulbed antique brass lamps illuminating the brass-framed revolving doors, and into the lobby.

"Lions and fawns may once again walk the halls of New York City's Plaza Hotel if Ivana Trump has her way," *Fortune* magazine predicted in an article on American billionaires in the fall of 1988. "Very rich ladies used to bring such exotic pets when they stayed there. But the carriage trade snubbed the place long ago, especially after the Plaza joined the Westin chain in 1975. Ivana is determined to bring back the old money set."

In truth, Ivana's ambitions have a literary rather than a zoological bent. Like many of her New York-born friends, she is a fan of *Eloise*, the 1955 best-selling children's novel by Kay Thompson that describes the mischievous antics of a six-year-old girl living in the hotel. "I want to revive the Eloise cult," Ivana proclaimed early on. Unfortunately she had to revise her plans when Thompson refused to cooperate. Ivana has finally settled on a pseudo-European look distinguished by homages to the Louis XIV, XV, and XVI periods and influences from the Trump casinos, such as the shiny new marble tiles in the hotel bathrooms.

The Plaza's lobby now displays Ivana's nouveau classical taste throughout. She has ripped up the green carpet installed under the former management of the Westin hotel chain and replaced it with a rich burgundy-colored carpet laced with golds, greens, and blues. She has covered the walls with specially commissioned reproductions of antique French tapestries similar to those hanging in the Louvre. She has gilded the moldings and the bases and tops of the decorative columns with gobs of gold leaf and illuminated the ceiling with enormous Strass crystal chandeliers from her native Czechoslovakia. Finally she has set two big marble-topped entry hall tables inherited from the Westin regime with peach-colored flowers, nicknamed Ivana roses, which have become tourist attractions in their own right.

Ivana marches quickly across the lobby, turning heads in her direction with each step she takes. If The Donald bursts with as much energy as the sun itself, he has nothing on her. Ivana absolutely glows, and not merely with the reflected glory of a female moon. Since taking over the Plaza, she has become a shining star in her own firmament, an international celebrity socialite who also has a serious head for business on her shoulders. In fact, it is her scintillating presence even more than the hotel's expensive face-lift that has catapulted the Plaza back to the pinnacle of prominence among New York City's power elite.

Undaunted by the eyes following her every move, Ivana goes directly to her second-floor executive offices. In sharp contrast with The Donald's domain on the twenty-sixth floor of Trump Tower, Ivana's L-shaped suite exudes the warmth of the traditional living room. The burgundy-carpeted main wing is furnished with a fireplace, a pair of matching mahogany bookcases, a square glass coffee table surrounded by Queen Anne chairs covered in pink damask, and a leather-topped banker's desk. The wall beside the main entrance is covered with beige-and-pink-striped silk and dominated by a portrait of The Donald. The facing wall, which is covered in a pink floral fabric, opens into an adjoining conference room.

Ivana's office has been further distinguished from The Donald's by three special features. Unlike her teetotaling husband, Ivana loves to drink Cristal champagne. She has made sure that her inner sanctum at the Plaza includes a fully stocked minibar, which his office lacks. Also unlike The Donald, Ivana is an avid gardener. She insists on filling her office with green plants and fresh-cut flowers of every description. Finally, and perhaps most tellingly, the windowsill behind Ivana's banker's desk is crowded with framed photographs of the Trumps' three children and other close relatives. Although an entire wall in The Donald's office is paneled with photographs of him, there are no visibly displayed pictures of his family supposedly because he fears that some nefarious visitor might spot them and know whom to kidnap.

In almost every other important way, however, Ivana Trump has become Donald Trump's female clone and alter ego or, as she likes to put it in her fractured English, his "wife-twin." Since their marriage in the spring of 1977 she has remained faithfully, some might even say aggressively, by his side on both the business and domestic fronts. She has helped design the interiors of the Grand Hyatt, Trump Tower, Trump Plaza in New York, and Trump Plaza casino in Atlantic City. In 1985 she took over management of Trump Castle (then known as Trump's Castle), her husband's first wholly owned casino, and steered it from seventh place in citywide gross revenues to a brief pinnacle as number one.

Besides adding a feminine touch to the Trump testosterone, Ivana has been adding what passes in New York City social-climbing circles as a touch of class. She has spearheaded the Trumps' move into philanthropy, volunteering to work for and later chairing such charity affairs as the United Cerebral Palsy and the March of Dimes gala balls. Ivana also loves fraternizing with fashion designers such as Arnold Scaasi, and socialites such as Nina Griscom, the stepdaughter of fabled New York City financier Felix Rohatyn; Jerome ("Jerry") Zipkin, best known as the escort of former First Lady Nancy Reagan;

designer Carolyne Roehm, wife of corporate raider Henry Kravis; perfume company founder Georgette Mosbacher, the wife of Secretary of Commerce Robert Mosbacher; and *Vogue* staffer Shirley Lord Rosenthal, wife of *New York Times* executive A. M. ("Abe") Rosenthal. Although The Donald has disparaged such highfalutin types as members of "the Lucky Sperm Club," the Trumps' social gambits have garnered what he craves most—more publicity.

Ivana, in turn, has helped perpetuate the larger-than-life myths The Donald has manufactured about her, including the false claim that she was a member of the Czechoslovakian Olympic ski team. She has no intention of setting the record straight partly because she fears that telling the truth might embarrass The Donald. "I always stand by the man, never contradict Donald, even though I might think it's silly," she proclaimed to the *New York Daily News.* "I'm a very traditional European wife, and I don't mind that Donald is the boss. I like it that way. I have to have a strong man, not someone I can just ride over. This is my upbringing. This is why most feminists aren't married, and have no children. I like to have both. They're never going to get married because they can't find a husband. A man is not going to put up with that nonsense. I'm a normal woman."

At the same time Ivana has been beginning to realize that many, if not most, outsiders regard her as anything but a "normal woman." Like The Donald, she has recently come under attack in the media for a laundry list of alleged sins and faux pas. The feminist press, specifically *Savvy* and *New Woman,* has scored her for the very thing she takes pride in: standing by her man at all costs. The social set has been snickering at the ostentatiousness of her taste and sniping at her for not staying in her place on the home front. Some of the most unkindest cuts of all came from the May 1989 issue of *Spy* magazine, which ran an extremely unflattering close-up photograph of Ivana on its full-color cover. The story inside by writer Jonathan Van Meter portrayed Ivana as a foulmouthed "wicked witch," a "Bengal tiger," and a "madwoman."

"I think it's upsetting to people that Donald and I have it all," Ivana later told a writer from *Vanity Fair* magazine.

Ivana is now finding herself temporarily preoccupied with matters only indirectly related to The Donald. Her working day begins as usual with a briefing from her executive assistant, Lisa Calandra. Often described as "an Ivana look-alike," Lisa is a thirty-year-old Italian Catholic from a working-class family in Queens. Like Ivana, she has bottle blond hair and a notoriously sharp tongue, and she drives a black Mercedes. Lisa also has a far more shapely figure than her boss, a fact that has not gone unnoticed by The Donald, who originally hired her as a temporary secretary shortly before she graduated from Fordham University. ("Lisa can't type and I can't speak English," Ivana remarked, "so will make good team.") Over the years Lisa has become Ivana's counterpart to The Donald's assistant Norma Foerderer: an all-around girl Friday, confidante, and surrogate mother figure.

"Ivana, you have a full schedule this afternoon," Lisa announces. "You are having lunch in the hotel at noon, and you have an interview with a writer from *Esquire* at three."

Ivana assures Lisa she will keep both the appointments. The luncheon is with her friend Lauren Veronis, wife of investment banker John Veronis. Ivana is looking forward to trading gossip and girl talk in the Plaza's ornately appointed Edwardian Room. The *Esquire* interview ranks only slightly lower on Ivana's list of priorities. Magazine writer Judy Jones is researching a feature story on the city's celebrated "trophy" wives, of whom Ivana is certainly one of the most prominent. The interview offers a perfect opportunity to counteract the bad publicity Ivana received in *Spy*.

Even so, Ivana cannot get over the fact that The Donald himself has been making even more disparaging remarks about her than the most vicious members of the media. Prior to Ivana's visit to her Los Angeles-based plastic surgeon, he repeatedly complained, "Your tits are too small. . . . You're too skinny. . . . Your tits are too small. . . . You're too skinny. . . ." When Ivana emerged from surgery, The Donald was sufficiently impressed to ask her doctor about undergoing some cosmetic procedures himself. Yet despite the fact that Ivana had greatly enlarged her bosoms with implants, he was turned off, rather than turned on, by her new look. "I can't stand to touch those plastic breasts!" he screamed.

Ivana has been hearing rumors of The Donald's alleged infidelity with increasing frequency in recent months. But in the wake of The Donald's disingenuous denials, Ivana has dismissed the rumors out of hand. She has been attributing the sexual dysfunction in their marriage to "male menopause." But Ivana is going to be finding out

the truth sooner than she imagines. For at this very moment the rival
who is causing at least some of The Donald's disaffection with her is
hiding out in the castle Ivana once ruled.

Marla Ann Maples is limping across her cramped little complimentary hotel suite on the twenty-sixth floor of Trump Castle with the
telephone clutched between her neck and chin. It's not too early on
the morning of October 10, 1989, in the glitzy casino gambling mecca
of Atlantic City, New Jersey. But Marla looks none the worse for
wear. Thanks to a foot injury sustained during a jealous temper tantrum in the hotel bar, she has crutches under both arms, and she is
sobbing into the telephone.

"I just know the guy's in love with me, Tom," Marla cries into the
phone. "I just know it."

She pauses to listen to the reassuring voice on the other end of the
line, arching her darkened brows and parting her reddened lips in
the perpetual half-smile of a professional Georgia Peach. Although
she will celebrate her twenty-sixth birthday in a few short weeks, Marla
is hardly over the hill. At five feet eight inches and 125 pounds, she
now boasts an even more titillating figure (37-25-37) than she had
back in her beauty pageant days, when she was slightly more busty
but beset with unbecoming baby fat. She's also improved her touched-
up blond hairstyle, dropping the old Farrah Fawcett shag for a more
sophisticated straight-to-the-shoulders look. But there's not much she
can do with her pouty overshot jaw and facial features so perfectly
plain vanilla they appear to be plaster of paris.

Besides being a former beauty queen, Marla is a former model.
She has posed mostly for print and billboard advertisements, such as
the ones she did for Delta Airlines and Miracle ceramic tile adhesive.
Her true ambition, however, is to be a movie actress. So far she's only
had small parts, such as "The Second Woman" in *Maximum Overdrive,*
a 1986 Stephen King horror film in which her character was crushed
to death by a load of watermelons, and a tennis player in *The Secret of
My Success,* a 1987 film starring Michael J. Fox. But she recently signed
on with the prestigious Ford agency in New York, so she's hoping for
bigger and better jobs in both modeling and acting really soon.

In the meantime, Marla has much more important things to worry about. She happens to be talking to Tom Fitzsimmons, an ex-boy-friend and continuing confidant who often acts as her official escort or "beard." But Marla is not upset about the love lost from her relationship with Tom. She is pining over her current boyfriend, Donald J. Trump, who, like Fitzsimmons, is 125 miles away in New York City.

"Tom, I know he doesn't love Ivana," Marla insists. "He loves me."

Marla hangs up the phone and stares out the window of her suite at a dismal patch of swampy coastal lowland. She does not exactly have a great view. Supposedly glamorous Atlantic City is nothing but a ham bone-shaped barrier island a little more than eight miles long and no more than a mile or so wide, battered by winds in the winter and baked by the sun in the summer. The town's fanciest and most popular neighborhoods are the two gaming zones: the Boardwalk along the oceanfront and the marina district around the hump of the ham bone, where all the flashy new high-rise hotels and casinos are located. Most of the rest of the place, where the city's thirty-thousand predominantly black year-round residents huddle in little wood-shingle bungalows and burned-out brick tenement buildings, is a slum.

Trump Castle, where Ivana once reigned and Marla now stays, is a twin-towered fortress of mustard-colored brick out by the boat basin. Its only neighbor, and closest competitor, is Harrah's, which also overlooks the Atlantic City marina. Marla's suite faces to the north, away from the Boardwalk and most of the action. It is probably just as well. If Marla's suite faced in the opposite direction, she would be constantly reminded of the man she misses. For as the giant red neon signs shining atop one-quarter of the local casino hotels confirm, Atlantic City has become Trumpland.

The first thing everyone sees after crossing the causeway connecting Atlantic City to the mainland is the name Trump. It is also the second, third, and often the fourth thing as well. Trump's flagship casino hotel, Trump Plaza, with its shimmering thirty-one story glass tower, hunkers at the foot of the causeway in the middle of the Boardwalk between Caesar's Palace and the hump-roofed Atlantic City Convention Center, home of the Miss America Pageant. On the other side of the convention center, flanked by pyramidal condominiums and the flashing neon signs of Tropworld, Bally's Grand, Bally's Park Place, the Claridge, and the Sands, there is Trump's noncasino hotel, Trump Regency. Less than half a mile up the Boardwalk, sandwiched between Merv Griffin's resorts and Showboat, is the bustling construction site of the Trump Taj Mahal.

But for the mistress of such a big man, Marla has wound up with a pretty small suite. If the Trump Tower triplex looks like a first-class high-roller suite, Marla's little hideaway looks decidedly second-rate. There is a dash of marble near the front door, a tiny wet bar, two bedrooms, a television set, and an L-shaped couch covered with a tan and brown slip. Marla has always hated that couch and that hideous slipcover. She keeps asking Donald to replace it. She knows he won't, even though he says he will, but she keeps on asking anyway.

Marla's mother, Ann Locklear Maples Ogletree, has also been complaining about her daughter's accommodations.

"If Donald's so rich," she asked Marla one day, "how come he puts you up in such a cheap-looking place?"

"I'm not with him for his money." Marla sighed.

That's not to say that Marla doesn't enjoy the pleasures of Donald's playland when she gets the chance. Her favorite suite at Trump Castle is on the sixth floor of the new Crystal Tower, which was built at the end of Ivana's regime. That suite has a pink marble hot tub and lots of snowy white carpeting. She also likes the suites at Trump Plaza, where she used to hang out when Ivana was at the Castle. She has free access to the beauty parlors, the manicurists, the pedicurists, the masseuses, and all the little shops and boutiques. She can go see all the shows and concerts she wants to see. And she can order up oodles of champagne and trayfuls of her favorite seafood.

There are at least three other good things Marla can say about her current suite at Trump Castle. Number one, it's free. Number two, it has a cute and comfy bedroom with a canopied bed. And number three, it has a very convenient location. Back when Ivana was working in Atlantic City, Marla often had to stay at the Trump-owned St. Moritz Hotel on Central Park South. Her suite at Trump Castle is right down the hall from Donald and Ivana's. The Trumps have a duplex with two bedrooms and two wet bars. Donald uses the upstairs part for an office. He has a nice big desk that overlooks the ocean and a crystal chandelier hanging from the ceiling.

Of course, Donald's suite has some drawbacks of its own. The main one, as far as Marla is concerned, is that Donald has photographs of Ivana all over the place. Marla hates that. She has been to Donald's office in Trump Tower plenty of times. She knows he does not have photos of Ivana plastered all over the walls back there. But he loves to take her through his Trump Castle duplex just so he can show her the pictures of Ivana and throw them in her face. Whenever he does that, she feels like throwing the pictures right back at him.

The last time Ivana came to town was back in September, when Trump Castle was sponsoring a big powerboat race not far from the marina. The powerboat racers were just the kind of people Marla longed to meet. One of them was the movie star Don Johnson; another was Stefano Casiraghi, the husband of Princess Caroline of Monaco. That night there was a party for the racers on the *Trump Princess,* but Donald refused to let Marla attend. Marla was so enraged at being swept under the rug once again that she went down to Viva's lounge in Trump Castle with a contingent of Trump bodyguards, got rip-roaring drunk, and smashed her foot against a heavy barstool.

Unfortunately for Marla, her foot-fracturing performance did not make the intended impression on Donald. He is getting worried that the outside world is going to find out about their illicit affair. He has good reason to fret. Back in July 1988 the *New York Post* ran an unbylined item reporting that a certain "shapely blonde" had been seeing "one of New York's biggest tycoons, a married man," and that the said "shapely blonde supposedly goes around to all the stores in Trump Tower saying, 'Charge it to Donald.' " Marla knows that *Post* gossip columnist Richard Johnson is on the verge of breaking the story wide open, for her own agent-publicist, Chuck Jones, has been working overtime to throw Johnson off the trail.

Besides her mother and Chuck Jones, Marla really has only two people she can turn to for help in time of romantic troubles. One of them is her friend and live-in companion, Kim Knapp, a freckle-faced strawberry blonde whom she met while attending college at the University of Georgia. Kim shares Marla's fascination with New Age spirituality. Both women are devotees of *Emmanuel's Book,* in which an "entity" named Seth communicates or "channels" an occult philosopher's theories on "the limitless power of love." Emmanuel's teachings on the subject of monogamy have a special relevance to Marla's relationship with Donald Trump and his relationship with Ivana.

"Love is the only spiritual way," Emmanuel maintains. "There is no rule that says if a heart has moved, if a consciousness has grown, the human being must remain faithful to something that no longer holds them in the name of society's definition of the meaning of love."

But with all due respect to Kim, Marla's most faithful friend, in need and in deed, is her fortyish ex-beau Tom Fitzsimmons. Six feet two inches tall with thick brown hair, brown eyes, and an easygoing Irish Catholic disposition, Tom is a former New York City cop. He and his twin brother, who is also a former cop, used to deliver babies for welfare mothers between street busts in the Fort Apache section of the Bronx. ("There are probably half a dozen Puerto Rican kids running around town with the middle name Fitzsimmons" Tom likes to joke.) Tom now longs to be a Hollywood actor and screenwriter. He has already written a full-length feature script entitled *Blue Gemini*. The story draws directly from his own experiences and stars a pair of semiestranged twin brothers like him and Bobby Fitzsimmons who reunite to solve a big caper.

If Donald Trump sometimes seems to Marla to be the personification of the Antichrist, Tom Fitzsimmons, the struggling screenwriter, is, if not completely Christ-like, every bit the "anti-Donald." Tom and Marla met through a mutual friend in early 1986, not long after Marla decided to move from Georgia to New York City to pursue her career. Marla immediately moved into Tom's two-bedroom apartment in a high rise at Third Avenue and Ninety-first Street and became his lover and would-be partner in conquering Hollywood. Against all odds, Tom and Marla became better friends after she moved out in the summer of 1987. He helped her get modeling jobs and introduced her to Chuck Jones. He even agreed to put her up in an apartment he owns in midtown Manhattan until she could get on her feet careerwise.

It so happens that Tom and Donald were friends long before either met Marla. They met back in the early seventies, when Donald was still making the rounds on the so-called bachelor circuit of bars on the Upper East Side of Manhattan, at the same night spot where Donald later met Ivana for the first time. Besides trading locker-room talk about fast women with loose morals, Tom and Donald often dreamed aloud about going to Hollywood. Donald had fantasies of becoming a movie producer someday. Tom, in turn, hoped Donald

might finance *Blue Gemini* or another of his screen projects in progress. Although Donald never actually came up with any cash advances,
he began to regard Tom as a kind of alter ego. Much as Marla wished
she could exchange roles with Ivana, so Donald wished he could change
places with Tom.

"Tom, I just wish I was you!" Donald often exclaimed. "You've got
all the women you could ever want, and you haven't got a care in the
world."

Tom nevertheless keeps playing the no-win role of the man in the
middle. Donald often asks him to escort Marla to functions in public
places where he cannot risk being seen on the arm of someone other
than Ivana. Tom almost always obliges. When Marla shows up in
Atlantic City for extended visits at one of the Trump casinos, Donald
will have her registered in under the name Fitzsimmons. Tom takes
that in stride as well, joking that such episodes have inspired the title
for a new screenplay to be called *Use My Name, Everybody Else Does.*

As the morning of October 10, 1989, is almost half over, Marla
picks up the telephone to call Tom again. While he may not lust after
her anymore, she knows that Donald cannot stop talking about what
a great lover she is. According to Tom, Donald keeps saying that sex
with her is the best sex he has ever had. Marla, in turn, has let it be
known that Donald is a real animal in bed. Even more endearingly,
as far as she is concerned, when she and Donald are alone together,
he shows her a sensitive, childlike side that few other people ever see.

Marla smiles at the thought. The funny thing is, there's a side of
Donald that not even she has seen. She has never seen him completely naked—at least almost never—because he won't let her.
Whenever they're about to have sex, he makes her go into the bathroom while he gets undressed. As soon as he takes off his clothes, he
jumps into the bed and pulls up the covers. She knows that he's
ashamed to show her what a flabby old body he has. He has no idea
that just makes him seem cuter and more cuddly to her.

"I don't know why people say such bad things about Donald," she
whines to Tom. "Most of the time when he's with me, he acts so shy
and vulnerable and wounded, just like a sweet little boy."

Marla is getting more than a little anxious to see this side—or, for
that matter, any side—of Donald J. Trump as soon as possible. Before
the day is out, she will get her wish. But despite her New Age spiri-

tuality and the teachings of her occult philosopher Emmanuel, she does not have the slightest premonition that the circumstances destined to bring Donald back to town will have nothing to do with his love for her.

chapter two
LIFE IS CHEAP

■ AT THE STROKE of 10:00 A.M. Donald J. Trump bolts out of the gold-framed front doors of Trump Tower with a pair of bodyguards in tow. He strides up Fifth Avenue, cuts left around the Pulitzer Fountain in Grand Army Plaza, and makes a beeline for the Plaza Hotel, still grousing about all the valuable time he is wasting doing favors for his corporate hirelings by attending the "shitty little press conference" for the Camacho-Pazienza fight.

Donald is met on the red-carpeted front steps of the Plaza by his Atlantic City gaming division chief Stephen Hyde and Trump Sports and Entertainment president Mark Grossinger Etess.

"These two guys are my experts," Donald recently told an interviewer. "With them, I don't need anybody else."

Steve Hyde leads the way inside the hotel to the TSE prefight press conference. Like his boss, Hyde is forty-three years old, but in every other way he is Donald's diametric opposite. A round-faced and rotund former accountant, Hyde is a devout Mormon with eight children, a love of the natural wilderness, and a low-key personal style. He has earned his professional spurs as a top executive at the Golden Nugget casino owned by Donald's archrival Steve Wynn and later as president of the Trump Plaza casino, which he has steered to first place in citywide gross revenues.

Hyde is no friend of Plaza Hotel chief executive Ivana Trump. They warred openly during her tenure as chief executive of Trump Castle. Donald took obvious delight in inflaming their rivalry whenever he could. In the months following Ivana's return to New York,

Hyde has performed the unenviable task of supervising the covert care and feeding of Donald's mistress, Marla Maples, during her extended visits to Atlantic City. Even so, Hyde has not been spared the boss's vitriolic outbursts. He is the one who has to answer to Donald every time something goes awry with the construction of the Trump Taj Mahal, Donald's pet project.

For these and other reasons, Hyde has privately been talking about early retirement. He has just returned from a two-week vacation during which he went bow hunting on horseback in British Columbia. He has lost some weight and gained a ruddier complexion. He has told a top associate back in Atlantic City that he dreams of opening a horse farm someday, adding, "I just hope I'm still young and healthy enough to enjoy the outdoors."

Until that day comes, however, Hyde still has to handle such mundane duties as assisting with the Camacho-Pazienza fight promotion for Trump Sports and Entertainment. He has reminded Donald that Trump Plaza is paying $3.5 million for the boxers' purses and the television rights to the bout. As Hyde sees it, that investment alone is enough to merit Donald's attendance at the TSE press conference.

Mark Grossinger Etess, age thirty-eight, is Steve Hyde's professional protégé, a fellow veteran of the Golden Nugget. The tall, handsome, dark-haired scion of a famous Catskills resort family, Etess has an undergraduate degree from Columbia, a graduate degree from Cornell's School of Hotel Administration, an attractive wife named Lauren, two school-age children, and an impish, winning smile. In addition to his role as president of TSE, Etess is president and chief executive officer of Trump Taj Mahal Associates. Along with Hyde, he is responsible for overseeing the long-awaited completion of what Donald boasts will be the world's biggest and, of course, best casino.

"Donald Trump, Steve Hyde and I all think alike—that our business is to rejuvenate Atlantic City, bring it back to its former glory," Etess recently told an interviewer. "If we do that, our casino hotels will prosper, too."

Mark Etess is one of the few people Donald treats like a true friend. More than a mere business associate, he is almost a surrogate son. The two men talk on the phone at least once a day, often several times a day. Like Donald, Etess has a genuine love of boxing. He also has a similar flair for promotion, complemented by a much more

natural aptitude for customer relations honed during his apprenticeship at the Grossinger family resort. Etess has pointed out that what
Donald calls a "shitty little press conference" has unique importance
if only because it heralds the first boxing match sponsored by their
newly formed Trump Sports and Entertainment venture.

Lest Donald doubt their own personal commitment to the success
of all his business interests, both Hyde and Etess have flown up from
Atlantic City earlier that morning aboard a Trump Air helicopter.
Trump Plaza executive vice-president Jon Benenav, a dark-haired
and mustached thirty-three-year-old Cornell graduate in charge of a
recent hundred-million-dollar renovation of Donald's former flagship casino hotel, has come with them. The only top-ranking Trump
gaming division official who did not make the trip is Trump Plaza
president John R. O'Donnell. An avid amateur athlete, O'Donnell
has excused himself from the press conference in order to take a
previously scheduled vacation in Hawaii, where he plans to compete
in the Iron Man triathlon.

To Donald's surprise, the TSE press conference turns out to be
more than marginally productive after all. The credit is due mainly
to Mark Etess. When the assembled reporters finish interviewing
boxers Hector Camacho and Vinny Pazienza about their upcoming
fight at Trump Plaza, Etess uses the press conference as a forum to
boast about the progress being made toward completing the Taj Mahal.
He then makes an unexpected announcement. He says that he is
finalizing plans to build a family-style amusement park on the pier
just across Atlantic City's fabled Boardwalk from the Taj Mahal.

"I can't wait to bring back the rides," Etess tells the media. "The
family aspect of Atlantic City has been lost for much too long. It'll be
great when we finally get it going again."

When the press conference is over, all three visiting Trump casino
executives are anxious to get back to Atlantic City. Steve Hyde, the
avid outdoorsman, objects in principle to spending any more time in
New York than is absolutely necessary. Besides, both he and Mark
Etess have pressing duties at the Taj Mahal construction site. Hyde
has also promised to cut a $250,000 check that afternoon to pay for
a racehorse he is buying from Robert LiButti, a faithful Trump Plaza

casino customer known as the ultimate high roller. Jon Benenav has
a 2:00 P.M. business appointment. More important, Benenav has just
purchased an engagement ring for his girl friend and is planning to
propose to her upon his return.

But Donald does not seem to care what appointments his gaming
division executives have made for the afternoon. Rather than bid the
trio farewell, he insists on summoning them to an unscheduled meeting in Trump Tower. By the time the meeting commences, it is already
too late for the three gaming division executives to catch the noon
return flight of the Trump Air Sikorsky S-76 helicopter they chartered that morning.

Hyde and his cohorts do not ask for—nor does Donald offer—the
use of the lavishly appointed Super Puma that Donald reserves as his
own private helicopter. They know that the exorbitant cost of flying
the fuel-guzzling Super Puma back to Atlantic City would be billed
to one of the casinos they manage, cutting into their operating profits. Instead Hyde directs Trump Plaza's local marketing office to find
them a cheaper charter helicopter. They are told there is a 1:00 P.M.
flight from the East Sixtieth Street helipad on an Agusta A-109 operated by a non-Trump–owned helicopter service. They book three
seats.

"Donald, we've got to run now. We've got to catch a helicopter,"
Hyde says shortly before one o'clock.

Donald looks up as Hyde, Etess, and Benenav get up to leave and
says nonchalantly, "I'll see you guys over the weekend."

Then he turns his attention to the piles of financial reports spread
across the top of his desk.

At 1:00 P.M. the Agusta A-109 lifts off from the East Sixtieth Street
helipad with Hyde, Etess, and Benenav aboard. A sleek Italian-made
twin-engine craft designed for corporate use, the 1984-model helicopter measures forty-two feet long and seats six passengers in addition to the pilot and copilot. The Agusta is owned by Paramount
Aviation, a charter service that happens to be one of the few Hyde
and his men have never used before. Paramount boasts a flight record
unblemished by fatal accidents of any kind. But unbeknownst to Hyde
and his men, Paramount has gotten reports of some mysterious
vibrations in the front rotor of the chopper they are flying in that
afternoon.

At approximately 1:40 P.M., as the Agusta A-109 comes within a thirty-mile radius of Atlantic City, a lone camper on the ground named Thomas Murray hears "a big bang" overhead. National Transportation and Safety Board investigators later conclude that an aluminum spar inside the front rotor blade was scratched during the manufacture of the helicopter; that defect, which was the source of the previously reported vibrations, causes the rotor to break off and slice through the cockpit. Murray, who has driven down to New Jersey from his home in Providence, Rhode Island, looks up just in time to see the Agusta A-109 split apart in midair. Then he sees the shattered fuselage of the helicopter plunge twenty-eight hundred feet downward toward the northbound lanes of the Garden State Parkway. Murray later tells reporters that "it seemed like an eternity watching it fall."

At two o'clock on the afternoon of October 10, 1989, Donald gets an urgent telephone call from Steve Hyde's secretary, Jeri Hasse. It is nearly a half hour after the three casino executives were due to land at Bader Field in Atlantic City, but their limousine driver still has not seen or heard from them. Donald figures there is merely some kind of mix-up because of the eleventh-hour change in helicopter charter. In all likelihood, he reasons, Paramount Aviation has flown Hyde, Etess, and Benenav to another airport nearby.

Hasse calls back fifteen minutes later. She says Paramount Aviation has told her that the helicopter has gone down but cannot provide further details. Hasse is getting worried.

Donald remains calm. He's flown back and forth between New York and Atlantic City by helicopter hundreds of times. Though his trips have so far been without serious incident, he knows how temperamental choppers can be. He suspects that the helicopter pilots must have detected some minor mechanical problem and decided to make an unscheduled landing for safety's sake.

At 2:30 P.M. Donald gets a telephone call from a CBS News reporter. Before the reporter can state the purpose of the call, Donald asks if he has heard anything about a helicopter going down near Atlantic City.

"Five dead, Mr. Trump," the reporter replies. "Any comment?"

"What?" Donald blurts.

"Five dead. All in body bags. Any comment?"

Donald later claims not to remember what he says to the CBS News reporter. But those with him in Trump Tower on this fateful afternoon will never forget how distraught he looks upon hearing the news that Hyde, Etess, and Benenav are dead. "He was visibly stunned," a close associate recalls afterward. "I've never seen him look so pale or shaken up by anything."

Donald soon learns more grim facts. It turns out that the debris from the falling helicopter miraculously missed all the motorists passing by on the Garden State Parkway. That is the only good news. When the emergency crews arrive on the scene, they find pilot Robert Kent and copilot Lawrence Diener crushed inside the cockpit. The bodies of Hyde, Etess, and Benenav, who were evidently thrown from or struggling out of their seats on impact, lie strewn on the ground about ten feet away from the cabin wreckage.

Donald is still sitting in his office commiserating with some of his staff when he gets a call from yet another reporter. He switches on the speakerphone so that he can hear what the reporter is saying but puts on the mute button so the reporter cannot hear what is being said in the Trump Tower office.

"Mr. Trump, I know this must be horrible for you," says the voice on the other end of the line. "I know it must be terrible for you to lose your three top casino executives all in the same day. I'm so sorry about what happened. . . . I guess the only thing that could have been worse is if you had been on the helicopter with them."

Donald glances across his desk at one of his vice-presidents. "You're going to hate me for this," he says. "But I just can't resist. I can get some publicity out of this."

Then Donald releases the mute button on his speakerphone and informs the reporter, "You know, I was going to go with them on that helicopter. . . ." Donald goes on to confide that for some unexplained reason he changed his mind and decided not to go. The next morning Donald's "revelation" will appear in a caption on the front page of the *New York Daily News* beneath photographs of the three dead men: "Trump decided not to go at the last minute."

The news that Donald barely escaped sudden death seems almost as startling as the crash itself. But according to half a dozen bona fide sources close to Trump, his revelation is a barefaced lie. Donald never planned to accompany Hyde, Etess, and Benenav to Atlantic City. In fact, he had a meeting scheduled for two that afternoon in Trump Tower.

Nearly a year later, when Donald publishes his second autobiography, he will temper his claims, though only slightly. "For an instant, as they were walking out, I thought of going with [Hyde, Etess, and Benenav]," Donald will write, backpedaling on his assertion that he had planned to go with them all along. "But there was just to much to do at the office that day. As quickly as the idea popped into my head, I decided not to go. Instead, I just said good-bye and went back to reading reports and making phone calls."

Donald will then wax philosophical about the meaning of the helicopter crash. The accident has made him more acutely aware of his own mortality than at any time since the death of his older brother, Fred, eight years before. "Life is fragile," he will observe. "It doesn't matter who you are, how good you are at what you do, how many beautiful buildings you put up, or how many people know your name. No one on earth can be totally secure, because nothing can completely protect you from life's tragedies and the relentless passage of time."

That observation is merely a postscript to the kind of remarks Donald makes in the immediate aftermath of the crash. In the view of many Trump employees, some of the things he says are as tasteless, if not quite as devious, as his claim that he planned to join Hyde, Etess, and Benenav on the helicopter flight. Donald's general thrust is not simply to mourn the deaths of three key executives, two of whom qualified as the closest he had to true friends. Instead he fixates on the impact the accident has on Donald J. Trump. In one typically self-centered postmortem, he declares: "It cheapened life to me, unfortunately. These were three incredibly vibrant guys. It tends to cheapen life when you see quality like that going for no reason. It's truly a horrible experience."

That night Donald climbs aboard his Super Puma and flies down to Atlantic City. Ivana does not accompany him. She has already telephoned Donna Hyde and Lauren Etess, the two grieving widows, to express her condolences. But in light of the day's events, she is reluctant to risk another helicopter ride, even one she has taken dozens of times before. Donald, for once, understands. He has instructed Norma Foerderer to have the Trump private jet on standby so that his wife, his father and mother, and his brother, Robert, and his wife can fly down for the funeral services two days hence.

By the time Donald lands in Atlantic City, the sun has long since set, and the roofs of his casino hotels are aglow with the red-lettered neon signs flashing the name Trump. A limousine picks him up at the helipad and takes him directly to the home of the late Mark Etess in suburban Margate. When Donald enters the house, he hugs Lauren Etess sympathetically. Then he blurts, "Can you believe they rode back in a rented helicopter?"

Even though he never really intended to accompany Hyde, Etess, and Benenav to Atlantic City, Donald worries out loud that the crash may not have been an accident but part of a plot directed against him. Weeks later the National Transportation Safety Board official will determine that there was no evidence of "foul play." The last-minute manner in which the charter flight was booked supports the conclusion that even the most murderous Trump enemy would not have had enough advance warning to tamper with the helicopter. But in the hours after the crash, Donald keeps spouting his conspiracy theory.

"Boy, wouldn't the competition love to hurt me in this way," he muses to Jack O'Donnell.

On Wednesday, October 11, 1989, the day after the helicopter accident, there is another kind of crash on Wall Street. Various individual and institutional investors unload an estimated two million shares of stock in AMR Corporation, the parent of American Airlines. In his $7.5 billion takeover attempt launched on October 4, Donald bid $120 a share. By the end of trading on October 11, the price of AMR stock has fallen from a Monday high of $104 a share to just over $97 a share. Donald reportedly owns three million shares, or roughly 4.9 percent of AMR. The downward price swing translates to a paper loss of $21 million in the value of his personal holdings.

That afternoon Donald convenes a meeting of the surviving members of his Atlantic City gaming division management. The meeting is held in a conference room at Trump Plaza. Donald is still reeling from the one-two punch of losing three top men the previous after-noon and then losing on Wall Street that morning.

"This has been a horrible experience . . . a terrible, terrible thing," Donald tells the assembled casino executives. "I'm still in shock. These were three incredibly vibrant guys. And great friends. To see quality like that go for no reason, it's just a tragic waste. . . . But we're going to do something marvelous for them, a statue here in the building, a monument, something just incredible. I don't know what yet, but it will be incredible."

Donald then divides his house of cards within itself. Instead of attempting to replace Hyde and Etess on a man-for-man basis, he apportions their former responsibilities among several successors. Jack O'Donnell, the thirty-five-year-old newly appointed president of Trump Plaza, is at this point one of the most senior members of the Trump gaming division hierarchy. O'Donnell later claims that he believes Donald intended to pass the torch of top leadership to him. That is not the case. Donald appoints Robert Trump, his younger, some would say more handsome, and far more gregarious forty-one-year-old look-alike brother, to oversee the completion of the Taj Mahal, a responsibility formerly shared by Hyde and Etess. He names the former Trump Plaza financial vice-president Walter Haybert the new president of the Taj. And he promotes Ed Tracy, the thirty-six-year-old executive vice-president of Trump Castle, to the post of Castle president.

For the time being, Donald leaves vacant Hyde's old post as head of all three properties in the gaming division. This is not merely an oversight. Donald is still undecided on who should fill the post. To find out, he is harking back to the ploy he used in the days when Ivana ruled the Castle and Hyde ran Trump Plaza. He will pit the leading candidates against each other in an internecine rivalry remi-niscent of the sibling rivalry between himself and his late older brother, Fred C. Trump, Jr. It will be a case of survival of the fittest, winner take all.

On Thursday, October 12, a convoy of black limousines pulls up in front of Temple Beth Israel, a contemporary-style synagogue in

Northfield, New Jersey, a mainland suburb of Atlantic City. A pair
of Trump bodyguards ushers Donald and Ivana out of the lead limo.
They have come to attend funeral services for the late Mark Etess.
So have a thousand other mourners. But there is an unsettling air
about the gathering unrelated to the grief they share.

Donald is clearly on edge. He has agreed to be one of the pallbear-
ers. Lauren Etess has also asked him to speak at the service. But he
has had to beg off. He claims he is simply too overcome with grief to
handle himself in front of a large crowd. As a result, the task of
delivering the funeral oration falls to Mark's brother Mitchell. Though
he gives an eloquent and moving tribute, Mitchell's voice finally cracks
toward the end of his remarks, and he breaks into sobs. Donald reacts
with another expression of self-centered amazement.

"God, that was an incredible thing that Mitchell did!" he exclaims
to Trump Plaza president Jack O'Donnell. "This is really some kid. I
could just never get up in front of people and look like such an asshole. I could never let that happen to myself."

But Donald is immediately distracted by more pressing concerns.
Marla Maples, still propped up on crutches, is standing near the back
of the temple next to her friend Kim Knapp. It is a dicey situation,
ripe for confrontation and mutual embarrassment. Marla cannot help
but have expected that Ivana would be at Etess's service. But she later
insists that she had every right to attend. After all, over the past year
and a half, Marla came to know—and like—all three deceased Trump
executives far better than Ivana did.

Marla's presence is not the only source of consternation for Donald. He and his minions notice that there is a contingent of dark-
suited male strangers in attendance as well. Although they could pass
for bodyguards, the men are not members of the Trump security
force. They are officials from the Division of Gaming Enforcement
(DGE), the investigative arm of the New Jersey Casino Control Commission. Their mysterious presence gives the service the look and feel
of a Mafia funeral.

As it turns out, the DGE men are not on hand simply to pay their
respects to Mark Etess. Part of the division's mandate is to monitor
the operating expenses of the twelve Atlantic City casinos. In addition to wages paid to casino employees, these expenses include so-
called comps, the industry term for complimentary benefits provided

to favored gambling customers in the form of free hotel rooms, free trips, free concert tickets, free champagne, free hairstyling, and the like.

Donald's operatives have gotten word that the DGE has spotted the names Marla Maples and Kim Knapp on the comp lists of Trump Castle. Although neither woman is an active gambler, both have been afforded fairly lavish accommodations over an extended period of time. The DGE wants to know the answers to three basic questions: Who are Marla Maples and Kim Knapp? What is their relationship to Donald Trump? And why are they being so heavily comped when they do not risk any money on the casino floor?

If the DGE men lurking about the funeral services get the right answers, they will have to report the facts to the Casino Control Commission. The commission, in turn, may decide to release the DGE report to the public. And that would cause enormous embarrassment to Donald, not to mention Ivana, Marla, and Kim. It could also prompt more tangible repercussions such as a lawsuit by Trump Castle bondholders charging financial malfeasance and fines, administrative action, or even license review by the state gaming authorities.

Donald knows better than to let himself get caught between his mistress and the state gaming authorities. When the funeral service is over, he escorts his wife out of the temple without stopping to acknowledge either Marla or the DGE. He and Ivana climb into a limousine waiting beside the curb. Then Donald orders the driver to get them the hell out of there.

On Friday, the thirteenth, another convoy of limousines pulls up in front of the Riverside Memorial Chapel, a red-brick funeral parlor in Mount Vernon, New York. Donald and all the other principals in the postcrash drama have reconvened for Jon Benenav's funeral service. The dark-suited contingent from the DGE is there. So is Marla Maples, who is crying uncontrollably on her crutches in the back of the chapel. Standing next to Marla is her ex-boyfriend, Tom Fitzsimmons.

Fitzsimmons can't believe that Marla has the audacity to show up. But Marla does not care who sees her. She feels particularly close to Benenav. In addition to looking after her during her previous stays in Atlantic City, Benenav was assigned to prepare a suite in the Trump Regency noncasino hotel that she could occupy on a more permanent basis. But Marla has more on her mind than grieving over Jon Benenav. She is racked with jealousy over seeing Donald arm and arm with Ivana.

"He doesn't love Ivana," Marla sobs to Fitzsimmons. "He loves me."

When the service is over, Donald and Ivana start down the aisle behind the other mourners. Marla positions herself right beside the door. Fitzsimmons immediately sees trouble in the offing. So do the members of the Trump security detail.

"Hey, Tom," whispers one of the bodyguards who recognizes Fitzsimmons from previous visits to Atlantic City, "can you get her out of here?"

"Are you crazy?" Fitzsimmons replies. "She'll smack me with those crutches."

Marla stares right at Donald and Ivana as they file out the door. Then she hitches up her crutches and follows them.

"Hey, Marla," Fitzsimmons pleads, "we better not do this."

Marla does not listen. By the time she makes her way down the steps, the Trumps have already climbed back inside a waiting limousine. But because of the traffic jam in front of the chapel, the limousine cannot move. Marla hobbles over to the curb, tears streaming down her face, and glares into the darkened windows of the limo until the traffic jam breaks up and Donald and Ivana can finally pull away.

Later that same afternoon Donald flies back down to Atlantic City to attend a service for Steve Hyde. In keeping with the wishes of the family, Hyde will be buried in his hometown of Kaysville, Utah, on the following Monday. But there will be a viewing of Hyde's closed coffin that night in Northfield, New Jersey, for his local friends and former employees.

Ivana, who still rankles over the bitterness she felt toward Hyde during her tenure at Trump Castle, has decided to remain in New York. But Donald is worried that Marla will show up at the funeral parlor and cause another scene. He calls Tom Fitzsimmons, who has also flown to Atlantic City to attend Hyde's service, in hope of initiating preemptive action.

"Tom, you've got to help me get rid of her," Donald begs. "Marla and I are over, finished, kaput."

Fitzsimmons heaves a sigh. "You're always telling me that it's over, finished, kaput. And you're always asking me to help. What is it you want me to do?"

Donald will not be specific. "Just help me get rid of her."

Fitzsimmons concludes that once again the best part of valor is simply to disregard Donald's rantings. That evening he goes to Trump Castle to pick up Marla and escort her to the funeral parlor. But as soon as he sets foot in the lobby, he is intercepted by a Trump bodyguard who has instructions concerning Marla.

"She thinks she's going to the service," the bodyguard informs Fitzsimmons. "but she's not going."

"Why not?" Fitzsimmons asks.

"Donald doesn't want her to go," the bodyguard replies, adding, "He wants you to tell her."

Fitzsimmons rolls his eyes in disbelief. He promises to do his best. But when he arrives at Marla's suite, he wishes for the umpteenth time that he has never allowed himself to get caught between Donald and his ex-girl friend. Marla already knows that Donald does not want her to go to Hyde's service. She is bawling like a spoiled brat. As she reminds Fitzsimmons, she had even more affection for Hyde, especially in light of his open antipathy toward Ivana, than she had for Etess or Benenav.

"It's just not fair, Tom," Marla cries. "I was so close to him."

Fitzsimmons immediately sympathizes with Donald. It is obvious why he wants Marla out of the picture, at least until after Hyde's service.

"What you did at Benenav's funeral was not cool. If you're not careful, you're really going to fuck this guy up," he scolds Marla. Then he turns and walks out of the suite.

Upon arriving at the funeral parlor, Fitzsimmons discovers that Donald has left nothing to chance. Lynwood Smith, his Atlantic City security chief, is stationed on the front steps along with another burly bodyguard. They have been ordered to be on the lookout for Marla and to hustle her away if she dares show up. Fitzsimmons can't resist the chance to test their nerves.

"There she is!" he blurts without warning.

"Where? Where?" Smith demands, reaching inside his coat as if to pull out a pistol. "I'll shoot her on the spot."

Fitzsimmons grins sheepishly. "Just kidding," he says.

That night Donald is gnashing his teeth. The reason has nothing to do with Marla Maples. Friday, the thirteenth, has turned out to be Black Friday on Wall Street. A panic in the bond market that morning quickly has sparked a parallel panic in the stock market. The Dow Jones Average has fallen 190 points, one of the largest single-day losses on record. That plunge, in turn, translates into a loss of $200 billion in the value of publicly traded corporate equities.

Donald has much more at stake than the average investor. His pending tender for AMR, the parent of American Airlines, is pegged at $120 a share. After seesawing up and down all day, the price of AMR stock closed at $98 a share. But in after-hours trading on the London exchange, the price of AMR has fallen to $81 a share, or nearly $40 a share below Donald's offering price, which means that following through on his tender would be financial insanity. One stock market analyst describes the general mood back on the New York Stock Exchange in words that apply to the mood of the man who wants to take over American Airlines: "total emotional and psychological chaos."

Donald's state of mind does not improve during the days immediately following the funerals of his three fallen gaming division executives. Neither does the outlook for his $7.5 billion takeover bid to take over American Airlines. The collapse of previously launched bids for United Air Lines and the Allied and Federated department store chains has scared institutional investors to the sidelines. Even the normally vulturous stock market arbitrageurs, who feast on the price swings attendant to takeover offers, have pulled in their talons.

To make matters worse, Donald's bid for AMR has been igniting a political controversy like the ones previously sparked by Texas Air chief Frank Lorenzo, the man who sold him the Eastern Shuttle, since renamed Trump Shuttle. Fearing the onslaught of another job-cutting union buster, the American Airlines baggage handlers have begun stenciling anti-Trump graffiti on company property visible to the flying public. In Congress a bipartisan coalition of Trump opponents led by Representative John Dingell of Michigan is charging that a bank-financed takeover of American would cripple the airline with debt and create an air safety hazard.

On Monday, October 16, the first New York Stock Exchange trading day after Black Friday, the AMR board of directors is scheduled to meet to consider Donald's $7.5 billion tender. But shortly before 1:00 P.M. Donald fires off a letter to the AMR chairman, Robert Crandall, stating that he is formally withdrawing his takeover bid. "I am currently reviewing all my options with respect to AMR," he informs Crandall, "including making another offer at a lower price, increasing my existing position in AMR, selling my AMR stock, or taking any other actions that I may deem appropriate."

The Wall Street community has no trouble reading between the lines. Donald's bid for AMR is dead. The rumor is that he cannot secure sufficient bank financing to do the deal. Following the announcement that he is withdrawing his tender, the price of AMR stock falls to the $76-a-share range. There are reports circulating among Trump insiders that Donald has already unloaded most of his stock in AMR. Even so, it looks as if the recent market collapse may have cost him as much as $12 million in personal losses on his AMR investment. There are also rumors that certain unidentified members of the Trump family, who reportedly held on to their stock as he sold out, may have suffered even greater per share losses.

Donald knows that the fizzling of his bid for AMR is just the first of the ripple effects of the Black Friday stock market crash. The worst may be yet to come. The crash has prompted a nationwide credit crunch that affects both the junk bond market and the commercial banks. The credit crunch, in turn, threatens Donald's financial survival. For the last several years he has been making most of his money not by operating the trophy properties he buys but by shaving fees and points off the refinancing of those deals and by borrowing more money to make more deals. He has used the proceeds to pay the interest and debt service on money-losing properties such as the Plaza

Hotel. Without more credit, he cannot make more big deals or secure more refinancing. That means his entire empire is vulnerable to a dominolike collapse.

With the specter of the helicopter crash looming over his past, present, and future, Donald decides it is time to take a new attitude toward his business and toward himself. Life, as he recently informed *Playboy*, is merely what you do while you're waiting to die. That being the case, Donald determines that he will spend the rest of his life doing exactly what he wants to do, no more and no less. It is a question of regaining his focus. In terms of business, that means getting his house of cards in order. In terms of his personal affairs, it means, among other things, creating a new and improved Donald J. Trump.

One afternoon in late October the Trump limousine cruises north on Park Avenue past the mid-rise apartment buildings owned by the city's richest and most powerful people and turns left on Eighty-fifth Street, the corner occupied by the elite Park Avenue Christian Church. The neighborhood is a veritable nest of high-priced physicians, internists, urologists, obstetricians, gynecologists, and most especially plastic surgeons. The Trump limo pulls to a stop in front of a black steel door buttressed with black steel crossbars. It is the service entrance for 45 East Eighty-fifth Street, which happens to be the address of the Reed Center for plastic surgery.

Donald J. Trump slips out of the limo and steals inside. He is greeted by Dr. Steven Hoefflin, the handlebar-mustached plastic surgeon from Los Angeles who transformed the face and figure of Ivana Trump earlier in the year. Hoefflin is now prepared to improve Donald's look. The operations in question will cost much less than the cosmetic procedures performed on Ivana, about $10,000 to $15,000 versus $25,000 to $35,000. But both Trumps will pay a heavy price not calculated in monetary terms.

According to Ivana's account, which Donald denies, Hoefflin first removes the fat bulging around Donald's waist and chin. This he does by means of liposuction. The procedure, which takes a little more than two hours, is similar to coring Swiss cheese. Hoefflin has his patient lie down on the operating table, puts him under a general anesthesia, and marks the areas to be treated with concentric circles similar to those of a topographical map. He then makes a series of quarter-inch incisions with a scalpel at appropriate points on Donald's body map. He is now ready to go to work on Donald's waist with a fourteen-inch-long hollow tube called a cannula. One end of the cannula is attached to a fat-collection canister hooked up to a high-suction vacuum pump; the other end can be fitted with a variety of bullet-shaped tips, the most popular of which is called the Mercedes tip because it has struts resembling the hood ornament of a Mercedes.

Hoefflin turns on the high-suction vacuum pump, which shatters the quiet of the operating room with a mechanical hum. Then he inserts the cannula into the deep subcutaneous plane where Donald's fatty tissue is located. Using radially directed strokes, he moves the cannula back and forth several times, creating small tunnels that allow globs of fatty tissue to flow up through the Mercedes tip. Once the fat has accumulated in the tubing of the cannula, it starts to ooze slowly down into the collection canister. Hoefflin then applies the so-called sausage roll technique, pinching Donald's midsection between his fingers to draw out more fat. He repeats the same basic procedure on Donald's chin. By the time he is finished, he has removed approximately fifteen hundred cubic centimeters of tissue, the equivalent of about three pounds, and created a network of Swiss cheese types of tunnels in Donald's waist and chin.

Hoefflin essentially lets nature do the rest. Over time the tissue remaining around Donald's waist and chin will slowly compress upon itself, thereby reducing the size of the unsightly bulges. In order to speed along the natural process, however, Hoefflin will provide Donald with an abdominal binder, which looks like a girdle without the pants section. When Donald wakes up with the abdominal binder around his girth, he will feel painfully bruised and sore. It will take a minimum of two weeks for the bruising to disappear. After that Donald will continue to feel a combination of numbness and hypersensitivity, soreness and lumpiness for at least several more days.

Hoefflin's second chore (also denied by Donald) is to cover the bald spot on the back of his head by a scalp reduction operation. Donald will discover to his dismay that scalp reduction is, as its name implies, a modern medical version of head shrinking. The basic procedure is similar to that used to remove a mole. In this case, however, the mole is Donald's bald spot. According to standard procedure, the surgeon simply slices out a part of the bald spot and sews up the skin. As the scar heals, the hair-bearing skin around it stretches closer together. Typically, the identical procedure will be performed at least one or two more times until all or most of the bald spot disappears.

Hoefflin hopes to avoid the need for repeating the scalp reduction operation by supplementing it with a second procedure: medical-grade tattooing. After shearing off a section of Donald's scalp and closing the wound, he attempts to cover most of the remaining bald spot by stamping dye dispensed from a tattooing machine that looks something like a domestic-grade sewing machine. At first glance the tattooing dye appears to be several shades darker than Donald's own hair. But if applied properly, the tattooing dye will eventually fade to a matching shade.

Following the operation, Donald retreats to his waterfront estate in Greenwich, Connecticut, to convalesce. It is not a pleasant experience. Like many other scalp reduction patients, he finds himself suffering nagging headaches caused by the shrinking of the scalp, the stretching of the skin, and the pain of the initial incision. He is also upset that the color of the tattoo on the back of his head does not yet match the color of his hair and concludes that Hoefflin must have used the wrong color dye. The painful aftereffects of the scalp reduction operation and the discovery of Hoefflin's supposed error enrage Donald, who reacts like a wounded elephant. He telephones Hoefflin, informs him that he is not going to pay the bill for the operations, and threatens bloody revenge.

"I'm going to kill you!" Donald cries. "I'm going to sue you. I'm going to cost you so much money, I'm going to destroy your practice."

Then Donald vents his rage on the person who allegedly got him into this mess in the first place—his wife.

Ivana Trump has been relaxing in the master bedroom of the Trump Tower triplex thinking about the trip she will be going to take to Tahiti. The trip will not be just for a vacation. It has do with The Donald's business. Lauren Etess, the widow of the late Trump gaming division executive Mark Etess, will be going with her. Ivana has been hoping the trip will help them get over the tragedy of the helicopter crash.

Suddenly, according to Ivana, The Donald storms into the room. He is looking very angry, and he is cursing out loud.

"Your fucking doctor has ruined me!" he screams.

The Donald flings Ivana down onto the bed. Then he pins back her arms and grabs her by the hair. The part of her head he is grabbing corresponds to the spot on his head where the scalp reduction operation has been done. The Donald starts ripping out Ivana's hair by the handful, as if he is trying to make her feel the same kind of pain that he is feeling.

Ivana starts crying and screaming. The entire bed is being covered with strands of her golden locks. But The Donald is not finished. He rips off her clothes and unzips his pants. Then he jams his penis inside her for the first time in more than sixteen months.

Ivana is terrified. This is not lovemaking. This is not romantic sex. It is a violent assault. She later describes what The Donald is doing to her in no uncertain terms. According to the versions she repeats to some of her closest confidantes, "He raped me."

When The Donald finally pulls out, Ivana jumps up from the bed. Then she runs upstairs to her mother's room. She locks the door and stays there crying for the rest of the night.

The next morning Ivana musters up the courage to return to the master bedroom. The Donald is there waiting for her. He leaves no doubt that he knows exactly what he did to her the night before. As she looks in horror at the ripped-out hair scattered all over the bed, he glares at her and asks with menacing casualness: "Does it hurt?"

Marla Maples is feeling no pain as the Trump limousine arrives in front of the Taj Mahal construction site. It is a cloudless afternoon in Atlantic City a few weeks after the helicopter crash. Although Marla's right foot is still bandaged, she doesn't need her crutches as much anymore. But what really makes her happy is that Donald is being real nice for a change.

"Come on, Marla," he shouts. "It's show time."

As Donald and Marla climb out of the limousine, all the construction workers stop what they're doing and turn around to look. Marla feels a thousand male eyes on her. Donald cradles Marla in his arms and sweeps her off her feet. Then he carries her gingerly over the surrounding dirt and debris into the front entrance of the Taj.

"All right, Mr. Trump!" shouts someone on a nearby scaffolding. The entire construction site erupts in applause.

Marla is beaming. She and Donald have been together in public places dozens of times in the past two years, but this is the first time that Donald has really shown her off for all the world to see. It looks as if her days of playing hide-and-seek may finally be over.

"I love you, Donald," she purrs.

Donald flashes a wolfish grin as he tours the Taj Mahal construction site. He realizes that his grandstanding with Marla is an act of reckless abandon. He doesn't care. Ivana and the DGE can be damned. The impact of the helicopter crash has changed his outlook. He is going to be open about his relationship with Marla and everything else, or at least as open as he pleases, especially if showing off Marla has the effect of boosting his workers' morale.

Donald needs to play every card in his hand. Having lost three of his top casino executives, he is on his own in Atlantic City for the first time. Although he has appointed his brother to oversee completion of the Taj, Robert does not have the killer instinct or intimidating presence that he has. Donald knows he will have to pay much more personal attention to the Taj to get it done right. And as he inspects the construction site with Marla, he does not like what he sees.

The Taj Mahal is supposed to represent the realization of Donald's grandest dreams and visions. The complex features a forty-seven-story hotel tower, a special-events arena with five thousand seats, and a casino floor encompassing 120,000 square feet, or more than twice the area of any other gambling hall in town. There are supposed to be rainbow-colored onion domes and spiraling minarets on top of the casino roof and a herd of elephants guarding the main entrance. But none of these adornments is yet in place. The opening of the Taj has already been postponed from the fall of 1989 to early 1990. With the deaths of Hyde and Etess, it is highly unlikely that construction will be finished before the spring of 1990. Worse, the project is awash in alleged cost overruns from "operational changes" that eventually total an estimated $23 million.

Donald is starting to change his opinion of Hyde and Etess. He always thought they were first-class operators. Now he is beginning to think they were taking him for a ride. By his reckoning, there is no way the Taj Mahal should be this far behind schedule and this much over budget if those guys were doing their jobs.

In truth, most of the Taj Mahal's problems are Donald's own fault. He has been paying more attention to Marla and his bald spot than he has to minding the store. Prior to the helicopter crash, he rarely toured the Taj construction sites except on weekends, when he would fly down from New York, round up Hyde and Etess, and set out on an impromptu walking tour, listening to advice offered by everyone from the electricians to the sanitation crews.

That kind of unsystematic information gathering often prompted Donald to issue expensive change orders that further disrupted the construction site and strained the budget. So did his penchant for spendthrift extravagance. Among his more costly indulgences has been his decision to furnish the lobby and casino floor of the Taj with $14 million worth of crystal chandeliers.

Even so, Donald keeps finding fault with the deeds of his dead gaming division executives that go beyond foul-ups at the Taj. One particular bone of contention involves the Rolling Stones. Back in the summer of 1989 Mark Etess commenced negotiations with the Stones and BCI Entertainment to stage three concerts in the rock and roll group's Steel Wheels tour at Trump Plaza. The negotiations broke down when Etess rejected the Stones' demand for a $9 million site fee. The talks resumed after Etess's death at the request of the Stones, who ultimately reduced their site fee demand to $3 million.

Trump Plaza president O'Donnell later claims that he told Donald the site fee was still too high. By O'Donnell's calculations, Trump Plaza stood to lose $800,000, But Donald reportedly told him, "Do the deal. Whatever it takes, just do it."

O'Donnell faithfully followed his instructions. As he predicted, however, it now looks as if none of the three concerts will sell out and that Trump Plaza will indeed lose $800,000. When O'Donnell later reminds his boss that accepting the Stones' site fee demand was his idea, Donald summarily blows his stack.

"Are you telling me I let that deal happen?" he will fume. "I don't believe I'm hearing this. That was Mark's deal. I should have known better."

Ironically, even as Donald is chastising his deceased executives, he is making good on his promises to memorialize them. He does not, as he originally suggested, erect statues in their honor. But he does rename the marina in front of Trump Castle after Steve Hyde. He names the special-events arena at the Taj Mahal after Mark Etess. And he puts Jon Benenav's name on a plaque at Trump Plaza. Donald also looks after Donna Hyde and Lauren Etess. He offers them jobs in the Trump casinos and encourages them to join Trump Taj Mahal Associates in filing lawsuits against the manufacturer and operator of the ill-fated helicopter.

Donald feels he has almost as much at stake in the litigation as the two widows. Since he did not carry "keyman" insurance on his executives, a lawsuit is his only chance of financial recovery. But it seems likely that his suit will drag on for years. The widows and their attorneys do not want to wait. Lauren Etess ultimately settles her claim for a reported $6 million. Donna Hyde reportedly settles her claim for a like amount. As if to show he harbors no ill will over their quick settlements, Donald directs Ivana to go ahead with her plans to take Lauren Etess on an all-expenses-paid trip to Tahiti.

But if Donald feels any remorse about what he did to his wife in Trump Tower the previous month, he does not show it. In fact, while Ivana is out of town, he starts being even more open about his affair with Marla Maples. Evidently hoping to pursue a career in Hollywood, Marla has arranged to rent an apartment in Los Angeles starting in January 1990. In the interim she has moved out of one of the apartments Donald helped her find in New York City. Her new temporary residence is apartment 63C in Trump Tower, a unit located just four floors below the Trump family triplex.

On December 17, 1989, Donald takes Marla to a press conference for the Rolling Stones concert at Trump Plaza. He appears to be in a good mood. So does Marla, who is sporting a new full-length fur coat. But Donald's humor quickly sours when one of the Stones' representatives tells him the group refuses to appear until he leaves the conference room.

"Fuck that," Donald explodes. "I'm paying three million dollars for this. It's my press conference. I'll fucking be anywhere I want to be."

But the Stones refuse to budge. Donald finally leaves the room in

a huff with Marla on his heels. In his second book he describes the
Stones as "a bunch of major jerks."

Even so, Donald shows up at the concert that night in the Atlantic
City Convention Center next door to Trump Plaza. He makes a grand
entrance behind a wedge of burly bodyguards. Marla Maples follows
a few feet behind. Tom Fitzsimmons and his date, and Robert Trump
and his wife, Blaine, no friend of Ivana's, bring up the rear. Donald
and Marla leave the convention center before the concert ends. But
it is clear to all who see them that they are together. For all intents
and purposes, Donald's secret affair is no longer a secret.

Ivana Trump is back in New York City a few days before Christmas. She and Lauren Etess have been having a good time. They have
met the *Trump Princess* in Tahiti and used the yacht to tour the neigh-
boring islands. But Ivana is visibly distressed about something that
has happened on the trip.

"I have lost one of the pieces of the diamonds on my wedding
ring," she confides to her executive assistant, Lisa Calandra.

Lisa does not have to be told how Ivana interprets the loss. She
obviously thinks it is an omen about her marriage to The Donald.

"Don't worry, sweetie," Lisa tries to reassure her. "Everything is
going to work out for the best."

On Christmas Day Ivana joins The Donald and the rest of the
Trump family for the traditional Christmas dinner at his parents'
house in Queens. The next day, December 26, she and the three
Trump children fly off to Aspen for the traditional holiday skiing
vacation. The Donald claims he must stay in New York to work on a
plan to take over the Bloomingdale's department store chain. He
promises to join them in a few days.

On the afternoon of December 27 a Boeing 727 with the name
Trump emblazoned on the fuselage touches down at the airport in
Chattanooga, Tennessee. The airport is about an hour's drive from
Dalton, Georgia, where Marla Maples has spent Christmas with her
family. Donald is on board the plane. He knows that Marla wants to

give him a Christmas party. She thinks it would be a perfect occasion to introduce her kin to the man she aims to marry. Donald has no intention of going through all that. But in a weak moment he has promised to swing by and pick her up on his way to Aspen.

When Donald emerges from the plane, he sees that Marla is waiting on the tarmac. So are Marla's mother and stepfather, her mother's best friend, her aunt and uncle, two first cousins, and her grandfather and grandmother, whom she affectionately refers to as Ding Daddy and Meemaw.

For the next two hours Donald plays host to the down-home folks. He takes them on a guided tour of the Trump jet and hands out autographed copies of *Trump: The Art of the Deal*. Then, just as Donald is signaling the pilots that it is time to go, he lets down his guard.

One of Marla's cousins pulls out a camera. He asks if it is okay to take some photographs. Donald tells him to go right ahead. Then he poses for group shots with his mistress and the members of her extended family.

Marla is surprised and elated. This is the first time he has ever allowed them to be photographed together in public. For Donald the thrill of taking such a risk is its own reward. But he will realize, in retrospect, that he should have known better. As he later admits to a friend who gets word of his detour through Chattanooga, "That trip was one of the worst mistakes of my life."

A few minutes later Donald and Marla say good-bye to her relatives and strap on their seat belts. The Trump plane takes off from Chattanooga and turns to the west, bound for the Rocky Mountains and Aspen, Colorado, where Donald will make an even worse mistake.

What is destined to occur in Aspen will spark the tabloid sex scandal of the late twentieth century. It will turn Donald J. Trump's personal life into an international soap opera, destroying his marriage to Ivana, alienating him from his own children, and tainting the lives and careers of all concerned, most especially Marla Maples. It will prove to be the straw that breaks the overleveraged back of Donald's empire, sending him on a collision course toward bankruptcy that will have dire repercussions for his banks, his bondholders, and thousands of Trump employees. Most severely of all, as far as he is concerned, it will make Donald J. Trump a public laughingstock, thereby devaluing the Trump name and irreparably puncturing the Trump myth.

But Donald's impending catastrophe in Aspen will also have significant symbolic repercussions well beyond his circle of family, friends, and financial associates. It will signal a major turning point in contemporary social and economic life. With the end of the so-called greed decade of the 1980s the American dream will turn nightmarish for millions of citizens who never before gave sudden poverty or downward mobility a second thought. The age of acquisitiveness will give way to the age of contraction and retrenchment. With the dawn of the fin-de-siècle decade of the 1990s will come a gloomy realization that in sharp contrast with years gone by, the years to come will no longer be certain to bring ever-increasing growth and prosperity, perhaps not even lasting peace. And as in the 1980s, Donald J. Trump will personify some of what is good and much of what is bad and ugly about the new era of the 1990s.

Donald will later realize that he should have seen it coming. For the seeds of his sensational demise, like those of his sensational rise, were sown long, long ago in the dubious business deals he made and in the devious extramarital dalliances he pursued. To many, Donald's collapse will seem as inevitable as the rising and setting of the sun. It is as if a not–so–deep-seated part of him always wanted to get caught, sexually and financially. Yet Donald will always know that he could have avoided disaster if he had only listened to his old man's warning and heeded the lessons of the past on which he has always refused to dwell.

Part two

■

THE ART OF THE SPIEL

■

chapter three
QUEENS REX

■ FRED TRUMP CHARGED into his son's twenty-sixth-floor Trump Tower office, muttering under his breath. It was an ominous afternoon in the fall of 1989, just a few weeks after the helicopter crash that claimed the lives of Trump gaming division executives Hyde, Etess, and Benenav. The old man plopped down in one of the overstuffed burgundy armchairs in front of Donald's desk.

"You are a killer! You are a king!" he inveighed, repeating his by-now all-too-familiar litany. Then he added: "But you're acting like a damn asshole!"

At the age of eighty-four Fred Trump still cut an imposing figure. He had stooped a few inches below his formerly robust height of six feet. He had lost part of his jaw to bone cancer, his skin was dotted with pink blotches, and he wore a reddish brown toupee that always seemed slightly askew. But he still had the strongly chiseled features of the cigar store Indians he liked to collect and the bushy Mephistophelian eyebrows that had become a Trump trademark.

Fred Trump was also the family fashion plate. With his thick red mustache, custom-tailored gray suit, gold collar pin, red tie, and matching red pocket square, he still displayed the self-promoting sartorial flair that helped get him on the 1950 Best Dressed List along with future President Dwight D. Eisenhower and New York Yankees shortstop Phil Rizzuto. And much to his son's chagrin, he also had the same fiery-tempered, perfectionist spirit that had driven him to become one of the biggest New York real estate developers of the postwar era.

The old man knew that officials from the New Jersey Division of Gaming Enforcement had been snooping around the funeral services of the three deceased Trump executives. He also knew that the DGE's mission was to gather information about Donald's relationship with one Marla Ann Maples. In his own heyday the elder Trump's alleged extramarital dalliances along the Florida Gold Coast had earned him a reputation as the "King of Miami Beach." But he was furious at Donald for being so indiscreet as to attract the unwelcome scrutiny of the DGE.

"You can have a thousand mistresses if you want," Fred Trump lectured his son, "but you don't have just one. And whatever you do, you never, ever let yourself get caught."

Donald pouted like a spoiled brat. "You don't know what you're talking about," he fumed.

Donald's executive assistant, Norma Foerderer, overheard the exchange and rushed in from her cubicle across the hall in another vain attempt to make peace.

"Donald, don't talk to your father that way," she scolded.

"I don't have to take that from you," the old man growled at Donald. Then he lifted himself out of the chair, turned on his heels, and marched toward the elevator.

Moments later Fred Trump climbed into the back seat of a dark blue Cadillac limousine with personalized license plates bearing the initials FT. Donald had set aside a special apartment for him in Trump Tower, but he had never spent a single night there. And in light of the way his son was behaving, he certainly did not intend to stay in Trump Tower now. The old man ordered his driver to take him back to the outer boroughs on Long Island whence he came.

Walt Whitman observed that Long Island, stretching 120 miles in length with a bulge on its western end and twin forks on its eastern end, resembled a giant whale diving for the southern tip of Manhattan while kicking up its tail fins. The world of Fred Trump lay along the head of the whale (Brooklyn and Queens) and the lower jaw (Coney Island). His homeward route took him across the East River, onto the elevated asphalt of the Brooklyn-Queens Expressway, and onto the Prospect Expressway, which then emptied onto Ocean Parkway, headed south toward the Coney Island seashore.

The neighborhoods along the last leg of the drive were as vastly different from the Tiffany locations of Donald J. Trump's trophy properties as the earth from the sun. Instead of zigzagging through concrete-covered skyscraper canyons, the old man's limousine cruised past block after block of almost all-white middle-class enclaves packed with two-family brick facade row houses with white metal porch railings and white metal sun chairs. Then, near the end of Ocean Parkway, barely a mile north of the Atlantic, the limo veered off on a relatively quiet little lane called Avenue Z.

A few blocks down the street, at 600 Avenue Z, there was a small white rectangular sign shaded by the leaves of a maple tree. The sign read: TRUMP ORGANIZATION. The limousine turned into the driveway next to the sign and deposited the old man in a tiny parking lot inserted between a cluster of musty-looking six-story government-financed brick-facade apartment buildings known collectively by the name Beach Haven. Inside the Beach Haven unit adjacent to the parking lot was Fred Trump's longtime headquarters office, a cloister of cubbyholes decorated with 1950s-style furniture and plastic plants.

Fred Trump had scripted his own role in the epic drama of the American dream. In 1950 he hired a Madison Avenue public relations firm to prepare a press release that boasted of a "success story that parallels the fictional Horatio Alger saga about the boy who parlayed a shoestring into a business empire." But Fred Trump's version of his own story, which his press agents duly planted in several local newspapers, was as much fiction as the Horatio Alger story, for it exaggerated, obfuscated, or simply left out the rough-and-tumble truth about his background and his business triumphs. The elder Trump's love of lily gilding was later passed down to and elaborated on by his favorite son.

"The most important influence on me, growing up, was my father, Fred Trump," Donald wrote in his first book, *Trump: The Art of the Deal*. "I learned a lot from him about toughness in a very tough business. I learned about motivating people, and I learned about competence and efficiency: get in, get it done, get it done right, and get out."

Donald learned several other resonant lessons from his father. He learned how to make money by using other people's money, primarily the taxpaying public's. He learned how to make a name for himself and how to use that name to make himself even more money. He learned how to cultivate the friendship of politicians, political fixers, and big bankers, how to handle mob-connected contractors, and how to impress the opposite sex. He also learned how to best his older brother, Fred Trump, Jr., in a bitter sibling rivalry. Perhaps the only lesson Donald learned from his father that he did not heed was how to get away with it all.

In his first book Donald implied that his paternal ancestors were of Swedish descent. That was another big white lie presumably designed to deceive the many Jewish tenants who occupied Trump-owned apartment complexes. Fred Trump's father, who was also named Fred Trump, was a German born in 1870. He came to the United States in 1885 on the forefront of the great wave of European immigration. According to family myth, the first Fred Trump was a hard-drinking, colorful character who had operated a restaurant in the Klondike, then moved to the New York area to run another moderately successful eating establishment. But his principal business was not restaurants; it was real estate. He lived in a predominantly German neighborhood whose residents had last names like Wentzel, Koehler, and Munch, and he held mortgages on properties owned by the likes of steakhouse proprietor Peter Luger. At his death on May 30, 1918, the first Fred Trump left an estate with a net value of $30,254.99, a sizable nest egg at that time.

Born in the Bronx on October 11, 1905, Frederick Charles Trump was still five months shy of his thirteenth birthday when his father died. As the eldest male child (he had an older sister, Elizabeth, and a younger brother, John) Fred assumed the mantle of family leadership. While his mother toiled as a stenographer and part-time seamstress, he earned extra money whitewashing neighborhood curbstones. In 1923, when he was legally still a minor at eighteen years old, he persuaded his mother, Elizabeth Trump, another German immigrant like his father, to form Elizabeth Trump & Son, a real estate management and development firm. He then hired contract labor to build six houses not far from the family home in the Woodhaven section of Queens. Though his only formal education beyond high school consisted of a few night courses in construction management at Pratt Institute, Fred helped put his younger brother, John, through a doctoral program in physics at the Massachusetts Institute of Technology.

Fred's first great window of opportunity was provided by the same sort of calamity that later catapulted his son Donald to prominence in New York City: a major bankruptcy. In 1934 the House of Lehrenkrauss, a scandal-tarred mortgage servicing company based in Brooklyn, wound up in receivership. Lehrenkrauss held mortgages on some forty thousand houses valued at $26 million. Fred Trump marched into bankruptcy court and offered to pay $1,750 plus $500 for every $250,000 worth of mortgages to take over job of collecting the firm's outstanding loans. His real aim, however, was not to become a home mortgage lender but to use the Lehrenkrauss list of foreclosures to identify distressed (and therefore, cheaply priced) real estate properties ripe for rental, renovation, or new home building.

Although the bankruptcy court eventually approved Fred Trump's proposal, he did not submit the highest bid. These were the days when the parceling out of bankruptcy spoils—and other political plums of all description—was controlled by a network of Democratic clubhouses that operated as the local equivalent of Tammany Hall. Two of the most prominent Brooklyn clubhouses were the Seneca Democratic Club, ruled by Frank V. Kelly, and the Madison Club of veteran power broker John McCooey. The trustee in the Lehrenkrauss bankruptcy belonged to Kelly's organization. One of Fred's main competing bidders, who mysteriously dropped out at the last minute, was allied with the Madison Club.

Fred Trump later became a registered member of the Republican party, but he realized that it was always best to play both sides of the fence. After winning the Lehrenkrauss bidding war, Fred paid his dues to both of the borough's big Democratic clubhouses. In 1935 he started a home building business with a crony of Frank Kelly's. Even more propitiously, he funneled his mortgage servicing company's insurance business to a Brooklyn firm called Consolidated. The attorney for the Consolidated insurance firm was Abraham N. Lindenbaum, a wily Madison Club captain whose wife had nicknamed him Bunny.

Trump's newly formed political alliances provided the springboard for most of his future successes. Bunny Lindenbaum, who served as Fred's attorney for the rest of his life, put Fred in touch with a panoply of other Madison Club members destined to become the leading power brokers in both the state and the city. Among the most prominent were the father-and-son team of Irwin and Stanley Steingut, each of whom served as speaker of the state assembly, and Abraham D. Beame, a lowly accountant who eventually became mayor of New York and one of Trump's most obliging political patrons. Along the way Fred also developed close ties to the City Planning Commission chairman, Robert Moses, the single most powerful man in New York, through a Brooklyn law firm founded by Moses's former Yale roommate, Raymond P. McNulty. The Trump portfolio was eventually passed along to one of the McNulty firm's brightest young associates, future New York Governor Mario Cuomo.

Following World War II, Fred decided to stop building the single-family houses and started building far larger, more profitable, apartment buildings. In 1947 he announced plans to build the 1,344-unit Shore Haven project in Brooklyn with $10.4 million in loans provided by the Federal Housing Administration (FHA). At the time there was a statutory limit of $5 million per project on FHA loans. But Fred shrewdly capitalized on his ties to the shadow government created by the Democratic clubhouse bosses and their mob-connected contracting cronies. With the help of local FHA administrator Tommy Grace, he was permitted to split his financing into three parts, as if he were building three separate projects instead of just one.

Fred then went on to develop the nineteen-hundred-unit Beach Haven apartments, which were financed by another $16 million in FHA-guaranteed loans. William Tomasello, who owned a 25 percent interest in Beach Haven, happened to be Fred's one and only business partner in the postwar era. The reasons for their association were highly suspect. According to federal investigators, Tomasello was partners with members of the Gambino and Genovese crime families in other real estate ventures. Tomasello's principal duty on the Beach Haven project was supervision of the massive bricklaying job required to complete the exteriors of the buildings. He was able to save money for himself and Fred Trump by using nonunion labor hired straight off boats arriving from Italy, a practice that would have inevitably prompted strikes and work stoppages were it not for Tomasello's convenient mob connections.

Unfortunately for Fred, his partnership with Tomasello soon became mired in a major national scandal not even the most well-connected mobster could quash. In the fall of 1954 a federal grand jury heard evidence that former Assistant FHA Commissioner Clyde L. Powell had enabled private developers to reap an estimated $51 million in "windfall" profits on 285 government-financed housing projects. According to FBI reports, Powell approved loans on FHA projects far in excess of actual construction costs. The developers, in turn, provided Powell with kickbacks totaling more than $100,000 and pocketed the rest for themselves.

Fred Trump was accused of some of the most egregious windfall profiteering. He had completed the Shore Haven project for roughly $850,000 less than the amount lent him by the government and had kept the surplus for himself; he had also paid himself another $1.5 million in unauthorized "dividends." On the Beach Haven project, Trump and Tomasello managed to withdraw $4 million in alleged windfall profits from the $16 million advanced by the FHA. As the government investigation widened, it was revealed that a law firm run by the brother of the local FHA administrator Tommy Grace was collecting a $20,000 fee from the funds advanced to Trump for handling his loan application.

Fred countercharged the government with "doing untold damage to my standing and reputation," but his diatribe fell on deaf ears. In July 1955 the FHA office in Washington booted Trump's management from Shore Haven. Fred was blacklisted. Several months later the FHA refused to approve his plans for a $23 million housing development on Coney Island. But with the help of friends such as Robert Moses, Fred was able to sell the Coney Island property to the city for a quick profit and managed to get his name removed from the FHA blacklist in just a few short months.

Not far from Beach Haven, Fred Trump could see several other striking monuments to his original real estate domain. The greatest of these was Trump Village, a towering complex of forty-six hundred apartment units in seven twenty-three-story high-rise buildings. Trump Village was the old man's biggest and most successful apartment venture. The project had boasted full occupancy and a long waiting list of would-be tenants since the day it opened in 1963. Like Beach Haven,

Trump Village had been constructed with government funds, though they were provided by the state rather than by the FHA. But here again the old man's alleged windfall profiteering had sparked twin political scandals that besmirched the Trump name.

The first Trump Village scandal started brewing in 1957, when the nonprofit United Housing Foundation (UHF) attempted to get a city tax abatement for building a moderately priced fifty-two-hundred-unit cooperative apartment project on a blighted site overlooking the Coney Island shore. Fred attacked the tax abatement proposed for the UHF project as "a giveaway." Then he waged a three-year-long battle to carve a site for Trump Village out of the UHF site. His field general, Bunny Lindenbaum, lined up the support of such Madison Club cronies as Mayor Robert Wagner, city Budget Director Abe Beame, and Brooklyn Borough President John Cashmore. Even so, Lindenbaum could not guarantee his client Fred Trump a piece of the UHF pie until he took the matter before Robert Moses.

On May 23, 1960, Moses had resigned his position as chairman of the City Planning Commission to take over stewardship of the 1964 World's Fair. He had no official power over what happened to the disputed site, but he still had enormous unofficial influence. Lindenbaum later told a reporter that Moses "sat and listened to both sides" in the controversy and "suggested" a "split." Under the compromise Moses forged, Fred Trump got two-thirds of the total acreage; on that property he would build forty-six hundred apartment units financed by the state of New York under the Mitchell-Lama Act with tax abatements ranging from 43 percent to 62 percent over twenty years. UHF got the remaining one-third of the site, on which to construct twenty-four hundred units.

Two months after the deal was struck, Mayor Wagner appointed Bunny Lindenbaum to the chairmanship of the City Planning Commission vacated by Robert Moses. The quid pro quo occurred in the fall of 1961, when Wagner attended a campaign fund-raising luncheon at Sakele's restaurant in Brooklyn presided over by Bunny Lindenbaum. The luncheon raised a total of $25,000 in campaign contributions, including $2,500 from Fred Trump. The very next day the fund raiser became a major issue in the 1961 mayoral race. One of Wagner's opponents, state Attorney General Louis J. Lefkowitz, pointed out that several of the contributors had business matters pending with the city. They included Fred Trump, who looked forward to building the $65 million Trump Village project. Lefkowitz labeled the Trump Village / UHF affair "the most blatant scandal of all the scandals of the Wagner administration."

The luncheon at Sakele's proved to be extremely costly for Fred Trump's attorney turned city planning commissioner. On October 2, 1961, Lindenbaum unceremoniously resigned his post, allowing himself to become the sacrificial lamb that prevented the political opposition's howling wolves from going after the mayor or Fred's tax abatement for Trump Village. The following month Wagner won reelection. Abe Beame, who ran on the same ticket, was elected city controller, assuring Fred Trump continued influence at City Hall despite Lindenbaum's resignation.

In 1966, Fred Trump found himself embroiled in a second Trump Village scandal. It turned out to be a virtual replay of the FHA scandal involving Shore Haven and Beach Haven. The New York State Investigations Commission heard allegations that Fred had collected a windfall profit based on overestimated project costs that totaled almost $600,000. That profit came on top of the $4.2 million builder's fee legally provided for under the Mitchell-Lama Act. The commission confronted Fred with allegations that an equipment company he had created had charged the state at least $100,000 in unjustifiable rentals, including $21,000 for a dump truck that could be purchased outright for only $3,600. Fred termed the amounts questioned by the state "peanuts." His high-handed attitude toward bilking state taxpayers incensed investigator Jacob Grumet, but there was little that could be done by way of retribution.

"Is there any way to prevent a man who does business like that from getting another contract with the state?" Grumet asked aloud in the public hearing room.

"I don't think so under our present laws," replied the state auditor, Leo Silverman.

In the meantime, Fred attempted to get even more out of his alleged windfall by introducing some cost-saving techniques to the construction of Trump Village. One of the most important was a new method of pouring concrete. Theretofore the slabs forming the floors of high-rise buildings had been reinforced with steel rods that had to be custom-cut and fitted at the job site. Fred introduced the then-revolutionary technique of using welded wire mesh to replace the rods. According to his structural engineers, the wire mesh, which rolled out in a carpetlike grid, produced a better concrete and greatly reduced the man-hours required for installation. But reducing man-hours on a project raised a nasty problem: the potential of running afoul of the mob-controlled unions. The obvious solution to such a problem was to employ a mob-connected concrete contractor, and that is exactly what Fred did.

Of course, it was almost impossible for any large New York developer not to employ a mob-connected concrete contractor. Federal investigators later identified four interconnected companies with close ties to teamster union officials indicted for racketeering as controlling 70 percent of all public and private concrete contracts in Manhattan. The government charged that the four companies had inflated concrete prices in the city by 105 percent over a three-year period, about twice the average industry price rise in other parts of the country. One of the four firms was Dic Concrete Company, also known as the Dic-Underhill joint venture. Dic Concrete got the contract to pour the wire mesh reinforced slabs for Trump Village. Dic-Underhill later got the concrete contract for Trump Tower.

Ironically, Fred Trump found himself swamped by the sheer size of the Trump Village construction operations. The biggest job he had completed to date was the Beach Haven project, whose buildings were only six stories high. After erecting about fourteen or fifteen stories on each of Trump Village's seven twenty-three-story towers, he decided to turn the job over to a veteran contracting firm called HRH Construction. HRH wound up collecting a $1 million fee that was also charged to the state. Later HRH joined Dic-Underhill in building the first major Manhattan projects of Donald J. Trump.

The old man had built the Trump family manor about a dozen miles northeast of Trump Village in the Jamaica Estates section of Queens, not far from Jamaica Hospital, where Fred had given a pavilion named in his honor. The house stood on a grassy knoll overlooking Midland Parkway, the esplanaded main thoroughfare through the Estates that he had developed back in the thirties and forties. The two-story Georgia colonial brick structure boasted no fewer than twenty-three rooms, making it by far the biggest house on the block. The old man sometimes compared it with Tara, the antebellum mansion in *Gone with the Wind*. It turned out to be a more invidious comparison than Fred Trump ever suspected.

Just as Tara and the surrounding plantations had been devastated by the Civil War, the landscape around the Trump family home had been ravaged by the socioeconomic strife of the post-World War II era. Jamaica Estates itself remained suburban in character, a tree-shaded oasis of Tudor and brick tract houses. But immediately outside the open gated confines of the Estates, the neighborhood abruptly became an urban combat zone populated by working-class blacks, Hispanics, and ethnically diverse homeless people. Its principal activity centers consisted of an Off Track Betting parlor, a McDonald's, some aging discount stores, and the last stop on the subway line linking Queens to Manhattan.

With all five Trump kids long since grown and gone, the family mansion in Jamaica Estates had become the haunt of Fred's wife, Mary MacLeod Trump. A native of Stornoway, Scotland, she had immigrated to America at the age of eighteen, a five-foot-eight raven-haired lass with a gentle disposition. Mary had given birth to two daughters and three sons: Maryanne (1937), Fred C., Jr. (1938), Elizabeth (1942), Donald (1946), and Robert (1948). In days gone by, she drove back and forth between her husband's apartment projects in a Rolls-Royce, collecting coins from the washing machines in the laundry rooms. She still had a Rolls, but she was no longer able to drive by herself. At the age of seventy-seven, she had developed a severe case of osteoporosis that made even routine trips up and down steps a perilous chore.

The old man did not spend much time at the house these days. He never had in the past either. Both his personal and professional lives revolved around his office at 600 Avenue Z in Brooklyn. Though he was effectively semiretired, he still went to the office every morning in his chauffeur-driven Cadillac limousine with the personalized plates and stayed there almost until evening. At precisely quarter past noon every afternoon, he would go to lunch on Coney Island, most often at an Italian restaurant on the boardwalk called Garguilo's usually in the company of a female executive assistant who had been his very close friend for decades.

Even so, Fred Trump had emerged from decades of building and battling in the outer boroughs of New York City a worn and weary man. He had long since decided to pass command of his empire to a rightful heir apparent. But well before the most recent episode involving Marla Maples and the Division of Gaming Enforcement, the old man and his favorite son had been fighting each other like tomcats.

Donald's birth on June 14, 1946, coincided with the period when Fred was about to make his big move into building his first FHA-financed apartment projects. The old man wanted an heir cut from the same mold as himself. As far as he was concerned, Freddy, who was eight years older than Donald, did not fill the bill. Slender, blond, and sensitive, Freddy was a good kid who loved the outdoors, especially going fishing. But he dreamed of being an airplane pilot, not a real estate developer. And nothing Freddy ever did was good enough for his father. Fred Senior constantly badgered and berated Fred, Jr., in front of the other children.

The eldest child, Maryanne, who one day became a federal judge, was almost as self-possessed and driven as her father. But being a girl, Maryanne did not suffer the old man's calumny or pressuring. Elizabeth, the second daughter, seemed more like her mother, not especially bright but extremely sweet-natured and compassionate. Donald, however, did have his father's irrepressible energy, which the old man believed was a genetic gift, and a streak of the devil, which the old man begrudgingly admired, as well. Where Freddy immediately cowed under Fred's reprimands, Donald reacted by clamoring for more attention with incorrigible mischief.

"I used to fight back all the time," he admitted to an interviewer years later. "My father was one tough son-of-a-gun. My father respects me because I stood up to him."

Donald grew into a jealous, rebellious blond pumpkin with big white teeth and a passion for baseball, football, and muddying his shoes on trips to his father's construction sites. At Kew Forest School, where he attended grades one through seven, he was a holy terror, notorious for such crimes as spitballing teachers and spraying sodas at the little girls in the class. At one point he even gave his second-grade music teacher a black eye. Donald's God-fearing mother believed religious training would put the fear of God in him and sent him to confirmation classes at the First Presbyterian Church.

But Donald continued to misbehave like a hellion. He particularly enjoyed bullying his baby brother, Robert. One of the most oft-repeated anecdotes about their formative years was the building blocks story, an incident that foreshadowed the development of Donald's most potent business tool, the "art of the spiel." According to Donald's version of the story, he wanted to build a very tall building but did not have enough wooden blocks of his own to finish the structure. He asked to "borrow" some of Robert's blocks, promising to return them when he was done. But when he finished the building, Donald liked it so much that he decided to glue it together in perpetuity. Robert, needless to say, never got his blocks back.

Finally Fred Trump, Sr., determined to make his unruly number two son "straighten up." In the fall of 1959 thirteen-year-old Donald was sent away to the New York Military Academy in Cornwall-on-Hudson to learn some discipline. Known to students and locals alike by the abbreviation NYMA (pronounced Neema), the school crouched atop a somewhat seedy 325-acre hill on the apron of the Palisades just a few miles up the river from the United States Military Academy. With its fortresslike turreted classroom buildings, boot camp-style barracks, riding stables, and parade grounds, the place looked like, and was, a kind of junior-grade West Point for toy gun-toting boy soldiers. The school's most famous graduates were Les Brown, leader of Les Brown and His Band of Renown; TV star Troy Donahue; the sons of assorted South American dictators; and later John Gotti, the namesake son of the reputed New York Mafia don.

Donald, who was nicknamed DT, suffered his share of military school hazing from upperclassmen. ("I don't think there was anybody in that place that didn't get beaten up once or twice," his ex-roommate Ted Levine recalled.) But Donald quickly found a patron who could help grease the wheels of life at NYMA. His name was Colonel Ted Dobias, and he was a rough-and-tumble former marine drill sergeant who happened to be the baseball coach. As Donald grew from a pudgy little brat of an eighth grader into a six-one, 180-pound senior, he became Dobias's star first baseman, the captain of the team, and the coach's pet. "Donald was a take-charge guy," Dobias observed years later. "His senior year he kind of took over the infield and the outfield. He would move people around instead of me doing it. He kind of took over as coach."

Donald proved only modestly agile in the classroom. Four out of five years he made the honor roll, which required an average of eighty-five or above. In tenth grade he ranked as a Proficient Cadet, which meant that he had an average of eighty or above. One year he won the class geometry medal with a perfect score of one hundred. But he did not graduate among the top ten in his relatively small senior class of under one hundred cadets, nor was he voted Most Likely to Succeed. Appropriately enough, Donald's classmates did vote him Ladies Man. But the rich kid from Queens was not exactly the most popular cadet on campus.

Donald mercilessly bullied his junior-year roommate, Ted Levine, who at five feet one and 120 pounds happened to be the smallest kid in the class. Levine's best friend, however, was the stout-shouldered football captain, Stanley Holuba. One day in the midst of a spirited brawl, Levine smacked Donald over the head with a hanger. Donald retaliated by trying to toss Levine out of a second-floor window. At the last minute Holuba rushed in and saved Levine from a nasty fall.

Levine and Holuba soon had another reason to dislike Donald. In his senior year Donald quit the New York Military Academy football team, a move some of his classmates disparaged as the wimp's way out. "He was pushed out," Levine recalled. "The [football] coach was unjustly picking on him. He still shouldn't have left the team, but he did. His decision was justified, but it wasn't acceptable to the other students. I think that Donald's Achilles' heel may have been Teddy Dobias. Teddy put this aura of protection over Donald, and he never let anybody look at Donald the way he really was."

In the spring of 1964 Donald was batting over .480 on the baseball field and, according to Dobias, attracting the attention of at least one major-league scout. But instead of pursuing a sports career, Donald decided, at his father's urging, to attend Fordham University, a Jesuit-run college in the Bronx. The following fall he switched from military school epaulets to mandatory coat and tie, a uniform he would wear ever after. He tried out for the football team as a punter, hurt his ankle, and quit. He then played a rather undistinguished role on the squash team. But his sights were already set on far grander pursuits. The son of Fred C. Trump, Sr., baron of New York City's outer boroughs, had visions of creating an island empire of his own. As a former college classmate recalled, "Donald was constantly talking about changing the Manhattan skyline."

But before Donald could launch his own campaign to take Manhattan, he had to earn his old man's respect by winning the sibling rivalry with his older brother. When Donald entered Fordham in the fall of 1964, Fred Trump, Jr., then twenty-six years old, had already earned an undergraduate degree from Lehigh University. A slender six-footer with wavy hair, Freddy still dreamed of becoming an airplane pilot, an ambition his father still disdained. But considering what Freddy had witnessed of his old man's alleged pilfering of the public fisc, it was not hard to see why he might find the real estate business distasteful.

Donald had been only eight years old when his father was tarred by the 1954 scandal over windfall profits at the Shore Haven and Beach Haven projects. Freddy had been sixteen. He could not help feeling betrayed and embarrassed by the shame Fred, Sr., had brought to the family name by being identified as one of the kingpins in the FHA affair. By the time he graduated from college, he was also aware of his father's hypocritical double life. The old man had recently transferred his religious affiliation to the Marble Collegiate Church in Manhattan, where he listened rapturously to Dr. Norman Vincent Peale's pop psychological preachings about "The Power of Positive Thinking." But Fred Sr.'s reputation as the King of Miami Beach was no secret to his children.

When Freddy started showing up for work at the Trump offices, the old man immediately stuck him with some of the dirtiest of the dirty work. One of his most loathsome assignments was to close down the Pavilion of Fun, the Barrel of Fun, the Pantomime Theater, and virtually all the other attractions at Steeplechase Park on Coney Island. Fred, Sr., who had purchased the property from the original owners in the summer of 1965, then startled local residents by talking about plans to erect "a modern Miami Beach high-rise apartment dwelling" on the amusement park site. That fall, however, an Upper East Side liberal named John V. Lindsay defeated Trump crony Abe Beame in the New York mayoral race. The Lindsay administration announced its opposition to private development of Steeplechase Park, insisting that the site remain zoned for recreational use. At Fred's behest, Freddy had to defend the old man's double-dealing in public.

"The fact is that the whole of Coney Island needs redoing," he maintained, parroting his father's line. "You and I wouldn't take our kids there. People are afraid to walk on Surf Avenue at night."

The Steeplechase Park conflict was ultimately resolved to the mutual dissatisfaction of almost everyone. In the spring of 1968 the Board of Estimate voted to retain the amusement park zoning. Fred Trump, Sr., wound up selling the property to the city for a $1.5 million profit, a deal made possible by the reelection of former mayoral candidate Abe Beame to the post of city controller. But the city never did allocate the funds necessary to develop an amusement park. Instead, it leased the property to park owner Norman Kaufman, a pal of the ubiquitous Trump attorney and former City Planning Commissioner Bunny Lindenbaum, for just $20,000 a year. Under Kaufman's management, the property lay dormant, a decaying ghost of Coney Island past.

The Trump Village investigation in 1966 permanently soured Freddy's appetite for real estate. Married and soon to be a father, he quit the family business and moved to Florida, where he signed on as a pilot for TWA. "Freddy was probably happiest during that period of his life," Donald later observed in his first autobiography. If so, it was because of the distance he put between himself and home. Whenever Freddy returned to New York, both Fred, Sr., and Donald gave him unmitigated grief about his supposedly inferior station in life. "Come on, Freddy," his younger brother taunted on more than one occasion, "what are you doing? You're wasting your time. There's no difference between what you do and driving a bus."

As Fred, Jr., lapsed into an alcoholic depression that eventually claimed both his marriage and his life, Donald charged full speed ahead, intent on proving himself to be Fred Sr.'s true heir apparent. Like his older brother, Donald could not help feeling the stress and shame resulting from their father's highly publicized real estate scandals. But partly by virtue of his place in the family pecking order, Donald reacted in a diametrically opposite fashion. Unlike Freddy, who turned away from Fred, Sr., in adolescent acts of rebellion, Donald identified and allied with the old man, perceiving him to be the power holder in the family. And by associating himself so completely with both his father's power and his shame, he became, in effect, the old man's alter ego.

In the fall of 1966 Donald transferred from Fordham to the University of Pennsylvania's Wharton School of Finance and Commerce, which offered an undergraduate degree in business. He admittedly would have preferred to enter the real business world, but Fred, Sr., kept insisting that he earn a degree. Surprisingly Donald did not leave much of an impression on the Wharton School or on his fellow students. He did not finish among the top students in his class, as he later claimed (Wharton did not give out class rankings to its students), nor was he known as a party-going playboy, for like the old man, he was both a nonsmoker and a nondrinker.

Donald later claimed that the "turning point" in his life and in his business career came in 1971, when he rented his first apartment in Manhattan. The place was a one-bedroom flat on the seventeenth floor of a building just off Third Avenue at 196 East Seventy-fifth Street. Every morning Donald climbed into his newly purchased white Cadillac convertible and drove back across the river to attend to his duties at Fred Trump Sr.'s office at 600 Avenue Z in Brooklyn. But he spent his nights prowling around the Upper East Side of Manhattan. Besides familiarizing himself with "all the good [real estate] properties," he became, as he put it, "a city guy instead of a kid from the boroughs."

One of Donald's first and, to his mind, most important moves was joining Le Club, a members-only East Side eatery and nightclub with pretensions of becoming one of the most exclusive social enclaves in the city. Le Club's eclectic roster of patrons included scions of the *Social Register* aristocracy, gold-digging former debutantes and would-have-been debutantes, European and Latin American party lovers, and assorted political fixers and gentleman mobsters, most of whom were older than the twenty-five-year-old kid from Queens. Ironically, Le Club's president reportedly made Donald promise that if he gained admission, he would not try to steal the wives of the more senior members.

It was at Le Club that Donald met the man who would temporarily replace his father as the mentor of his business career, attorney Roy M. Cohn. Short and sallow-skinned with deep-set droopy blue eyes and a receding hairline, Cohn was one of the most controversial legal minds of his time. As he himself observed, history would always remember him first and foremost as the tenacious—and widely despised—young chief counsel for Senator Joseph R. McCarthy, the anti-Communist witch-hunter of the 1950s. But Cohn, in later life, was much more than a Red-baiter; he was a world-class political fixer who, to the delight of his many enemies, was ultimately disbarred from the practice of law shortly before dying from AIDS in 1986.

Cohn's list of prominent clients included Ron and Nancy Reagan, media moguls Si Newhouse and Rupert Murdoch, Yankees owner George Steinbrenner, U.S. Senators Jesse Helms and Chic Hecht, Chrysler Chairman Lee Iacocca, and TV journalist Barbara Walters. Along with representing the social elite, Cohn used his town house home office on Sixty-fourth Street as a kind of underground parliament for resolving disputes between the city's leading Mafia families. A notoriously sloppy businessman, he made most of his cash by taking a cut from corruptly mismanaged city parking lots. In his autobiography Cohn bragged about his role in assisting the Mafia in appointing U.S. attorneys in New York, about conducting smear campaigns against Senator Thomas Eagleton and others, about closed-door conferences with jurists ruling on cases he had before their courts. "Don't tell me what the law is," he used to say; "just tell me who the judge is."

Donald Trump appeared to fit Roy Cohn's ideal billing profile to perfection. In October 1973, shortly after the two men met at Le Club, the Justice Department filed a civil rights suit under the Fair Housing Act of 1969 charging Trump-owned projects with racial and sexual discrimination in the renting of apartments. The Trumps weren't the only targets of the federal probe. Samuel LeFrak's organization, which commanded an even larger empire of outer borough apartment buildings, faced similar charges. But the Trumps' alleged civil rights violations were certainly among the most blatant and reportedly resulted from policies set at the top by Fred C. Trump, Sr., and his number two son, which included the discouraging of rentals to black tenants and the coding of rental applications according to race.

With Cohn as their attorney, the Trumps reached a settlement with the Justice Department in the summer of 1975. Its terms required the Trump management to initiate an affirmative action program for the ensuing two years. The Trumps pledged to provide the Urban League with a weekly list of apartment vacancies and to advertise in the Harlem-based *Amsterdam News* as well as in the *New York Times*. They also agreed to receive rental applications from the Urban League for buildings with less than 10 percent black tenancy. Donald gloated that the settlement was to the Trumps' "full satisfaction." He noted in a press release that it contained no admission of guilt on the Trumps' part and that it did not have "any requirements that would compel the Trump organization to accept persons on welfare as tenants."

Donald came to the second major turning point in his life in 1973, just as his battle against the Justice Department commenced. With his stylish liberal image having been tarnished by the city budget crisis, New York Mayor John V. Lindsay decided not to run for a third term. Abe Beame won the race to replace him by a 60 percent majority on November 6, 1973. The following year former Congressman Hugh Carey, another Madison Club protégé, won the governor's race. Carey's biggest campaign donor was his oilman brother Ed. The second-biggest contributor was Donald Trump, who gave the candidate $50,000 and cosigned a $300,000 loan to the campaign. Other Carey contributors included Bunny Lindenbaum and his lawyer son, Sandy Lindenbaum, who provided a $40,000 loan, and the Bronx County Democratic Committee chairman and Beame's deputy mayor, Stanley Friedman, who authorized a $25,000 loan.

Buttressed by unprecedented inside influence on both the state and municipal levels, Donald J. Trump embarked on what proved to be the most impressive series of real estate deals anyone in the postwar baby boom generation had ever made. His opportunity was afforded by the same type of fiscal crisis that had given Fred Trump, Sr., his big boost into real estate back in the 1930s: a major bankruptcy. In this case the bankrupt entity was the Penn Central Transportation Company. Over the preceding hundred years, the once-prosperous railroad had amassed more than thirteen thousand real estate properties across the United States. They included the Commodore Hotel next door to Grand Central Terminal, an abandoned rail yard on Thirty-fourth Street, and a second rail yard located on a hundred-acre site on the West Side between Fifty-ninth Street and Seventy-second Street that happened to be the biggest undeveloped property left in Manhattan.

Donald's original vision for both Penn Central rail yards was a legacy of Fred Trump, Sr. He wanted to develop these midtown Manhattan sites into magnificent minicities of government-subsidized middle-income housing, slightly upscale and significantly larger versions of Trump Village. The ultimate success of Donald's undertaking would depend on his marshaling political support and formal approvals from both the city and the state through the good offices of such cronies as Abe Beame and Hugh Carey. But before he could get any project off the ground, he had to convince Penn Central to sell or option the properties he coveted. That was where the art of the spiel came in.

Donald's initial objective was to get appointments with two key players: Victor Palmieri, whose company Penn Central had contracted to supervise the liquidation of its real estate properties in New York, and Ned Eichler, who was Penn Central's real estate manager. It was important for Donald to make a big impression. But at the time he didn't even have a formal name for his own company. So, as he later admitted, he simply made one up. When he finally managed to finagle an appointment with Palmieri, he began referring to his fledgling real estate development operation as the Trump Organization, a big-sounding name for a one-man operation.

Palmieri was not fooled. He figured that the Trumps' combined net worth was about $25 million, the vast majority of which resided in properties owned by the old man. But Palmieri was duly impressed by Donald's personal drive and intensity and by his father's political connections. So was Ned Eichler. In an exercise intended to put Donald's big talk to the test, Eichler asked the young developer if he could get an audience with Mayor Beame. Donald passed the test with a panache that even made Eichler's head swim. Not only was the Penn Central real estate manager ushered directly into the mayor's office, but he listened to Beame declare, "Whatever Donald and Fred want, they have my complete backing."

On July 30, 1974, Donald J. Trump, age twenty-eight, suddenly burst into public consciousness via the front page of the *New York Times* with the announcement that he had "agreed to purchase" Penn Central's abandoned rail yards "for more than $100 million." The *Times* story was actually the first major demonstration of Donald's budding brilliance as a media manipulator. The story made it appear that Donald was on the verge of buying the properties when he had merely agreed to option them. In fact, the Penn Central options were actually in the name of the Trump Village Construction Corporation, an entity formed by Fred Trump, Sr. More important, Donald's bid was still subject to formal approval by the Penn Central bankruptcy judge in Philadelphia.

Word of Donald's pending option on the Penn Central properties prompted jealous competitors to throw in bids of their own. The biggest competing offer was a $150 million bid that came from Starrett Housing. But Donald had two hole cards. The first was the Trump family's business relationship with Starrett, with which they were partners in a major Brooklyn waterfront development. The second was the Trumps' attorney-client relationship with lawyer David Berger, who was representing Penn Central shareholders and originally opposed Donald's bid as too low. As a result, Donald got the inside track on the Penn Central yards much as his father had done thirty years before in the Lehrenkrauss bankruptcy.

In November 1974, just before a hearing to consider bids for the Penn Central properties, Donald was permitted to revise his proposal to make it more commensurate with those of competing bidders. Starrett suddenly dropped out, and Berger suddenly dropped his objections to Donald's bid. Likewise, a last-minute bid submitted by HRH Construction, the firm that had finished Trump Village for Fred, Sr., mysteriously foundered. Donald eventually walked away with free options on both Penn Central yards, along with a commitment by Penn Central to advance up to $750,000 in predevelopment costs.

The alleged quid pro quo gradually came to light over the months that followed. It turned out that David Berger, the attorney for the Penn Central shareholders, was also spearheading a class-action suit by local landlords charging the major oil companies with overcharging them for heating oil in the wake of the OPEC oil embargo. Berger's fee included one-third of any potential award plus an advance payment of a dollar per apartment unit owned by the complaining landlords. Although the Trumps did not formally join the list of complainants until 1976, Donald allegedly promised Berger they would do so prior to the bankruptcy court ruling on his bid for the Penn Central properties. In the summer of 1979 the Trump-Berger relationship came under scrutiny during a criminal bribery investigation by federal prosecutors in Brooklyn. Donald sent his attorney, Roy Cohn, to discuss the matter with U.S. Attorney Edward R. Korman. Korman, in turn, sent an investigator to interview Donald, who denied any wrongdoing. The criminal investigation then died quietly.

In the interim, Donald found himself in the throes of an ever-deepening economic depression. Following the announcement of his options on the Penn Central yards, the financial condition of New York City went from bad to worse. So did the national economy as the OPEC embargo caused oil prices to go through the roof. In August 1974 Richard M. Nixon became the first American president to resign from office. His successor, Gerald R. Ford, harbored an alleged disdain for New York City's fiscal woes that was later immortalized in the *New York Daily News* headline FORD TO CITY: DROP DEAD. In April 1975 the banks refused to renew New York City's loans. That fall Mayor Beame and state officials suspended the issuance of new government-backed housing contracts.

Donald realized that the banks would hardly be interested in financing the development of Penn Central's rail yards into massive housing projects. He immediately changed tack and began promoting the Thirty-fourth Street yards as the site of a new convention center. At the time rival developer Preston Robert Tisch, a Mayor Lindsay appointee, was heading the Convention Center Development Corporation, which favored a site on Forty-fourth Street. Tisch had hired Bunny Lindenbaum's lawyer son, Sandy Lindenbaum, and public relations man Howard Rubenstein to promote the Forty-fourth Street site. In the fall of 1975 Mayor Beame stopped city payments to Tisch's group and began supporting Donald's proposal.

Donald shrewdly enticed the opposition to come over to his side. He had already hired Lindenbaum and Rubenstein to advance his proposal for a housing development at the Penn Central yards on Fifty-ninth Street, which appeared to be at least temporarily on hold. He now retained their services on behalf of his Thirty-fourth Street convention center proposal. Then, after securing Penn Central's formal approval to change his plan for the Thirty-fourth Street property, he convinced the city, with the unflagging support of Mayor Beame and Governor Carey, to select the Thirty-fourth Street property over competing sites.

When the city finally purchased the Thirty-fourth Street yards from Penn Central for $12 million in the spring of 1978, newly elected Mayor Ed Koch announced that Donald would be allowed to collect a $500,000 brokerage commission. But Koch refused to let Donald develop the site. Donald offered to forgo his commission if the city would name the new convention center after Fred Trump, Sr. Koch rejected the offer. The center was ultimately named after former U.S. Senator Jacob K. Javits.

But even as Donald pursued his revised plans for the Thirty-fourth Street site, he began to focus on the old Commodore Hotel, on Forty-second Street next to Grand Central Station. Penn Central had recently spent $2 million to renovate the Commodore, but the hotel was still racking up substantial annual operating deficits. The surrounding neighborhood had long since degenerated into a garbage-strewn slum pockmarked with massage parlors and boarded-up storefronts. There was a flea market in the hotel lobby, and like Penn Central, the Chrysler Building across the street was in receivership. When Donald told his father that he had a chance to buy the Commodore, the old man had a fit.

"Buying the Commodore at a time when even the Chrysler Building is in receivership is like fighting for a seat on the *Titanic*," stormed Fred Trump, Sr.

The old man's reaction only inflamed Donald's desire to prove himself. It was not enough just to make a good deal for the Commodore. He had to make a great deal that would make his old man and everyone else take notice. He knew, however, that this would require what he later called a "juggling act" of major proportions. It would also require him to demonstrate his gifts as a master illusionist and teller of the big lie.

Donald's first step was to lay claim to the hotel site. In late 1974 he announced that he had negotiated an option to buy the Commodore from Penn Central for $10 million for the purpose of renovating the property into a brand-new luxury hotel. The agreement, which called for a nonrefundable option payment of $250,000, contained "subject to" clauses broad enough for a bulldozer; among other things, the deal was subject to financing, city approvals, and the participation of an experienced hotel partner. What Donald did not tell the public, the press, or the city was that Penn Central had not yet signed the option agreement and would not sign it until his lawyers finished quibbling over the fine print. As Donald later confessed, he would have been hard pressed to come up with $250,000 in cash at the time, especially in light of the old man's well-warranted skepticism.

After he announced his still-mythical option agreement, Donald's next step was to get his vision for the Commodore in a form everyone else could see. To that end he hired an ambitious but little-known architect named Der Scutt to come up with a renovation scheme that would dazzle the city and the banks. He told Scutt that he wanted to cover the crumbling brick of the Commodore with a sleek new skin, preferably made out of bronze or glass, that would "make people stop and take notice" of his hotel. He further instructed Scutt to make it look as if a huge sum had been spent on the drawings, then proceeded to convince the architect to do them at a discount by promising him more lucrative work in the future if the Commodore deal panned out.

On May 4, 1975, Donald and the Hyatt hotel chain chief, Jay Pritzker, held a press conference in New York City to announce they had formed a partnership to develop the Commodore into a first-class hotel. The terms of the deal called for Donald to build the hotel and for Hyatt to manage it. But the agreement also contained a variety of clauses specifying that it was subject to financing and city approvals. This was Donald's second major announcement in less than ten months, and he had still not invested anything more than his time and the design fees he paid to Der Scutt. As skeptical industry elders also noted, he had yet to produce a final contract, much less a finished building. "Trump has a great line of shit," sneered veteran real estater Ben Lambert, who was destined to become a friend, "but he still hasn't put two bricks together."

Donald now encountered what he regarded as a major stumbling block to getting the Commodore Hotel done the way he wanted to do it. He claimed that none of the major banks was willing to lend him the money to renovate the hotel unless he got a tax abatement from the city. And the city was not willing to provide him with a tax abatement until he had his financing in place. Compounding the problem was the fact that the city simply did not have a politically acceptable vehicle for providing Donald with the kind of unprecedented tax relief he sought amid the ongoing municipal budget crisis. But the Beame administration promptly came up with a solution.

In February 1976 Mayor Beame announced the creation of the Business Investment Incentive Program. According to mayoral counsel Michael Bailkin, the administration wanted to "make sure that this [program] was viewed as an upscale project leading to new development in the city, and not as a 'political deal.' " In fact, the program was tailor-made specifically for one developer, Donald J. Trump. Bailkin suggested the way to create the tax abatement incentive Donald wanted so desperately. The plan called for the New York State Urban Development Commission (UDC), a tax-exempt public entity, to take title to the Commodore Hotel property, then lease it back to Donald under favorable terms. That, in turn, would allow the Commodore to be eligible for a city tax abatement that could be worth tens of millions of dollars over the life of the project.

Donald had good reason to believe that the Trump family's long-standing ties to Mayor Beame and Governor Carey would enhance the Commodore project's chances at the UDC. In order to participate in the Commodore renovation, the UDC would have to deem the hotel an "industrial" project and declare Forty-second Street a "substandard" area. But as its part of the obvious political agenda, the state agency was anxious to play a meaningful role in New York City's economic revival. The governor's appointed chairman of the UDC was Richard Ravitch, a respected Manhattan developer whose family happened to own a major interest in HRH Construction, the firm that had finished Trump Village for Fred, Sr.

But like every gambler, Donald wanted even more of an edge if possible. In the spring of 1975 he got it in the frenetic person of lobbyist Louise Sunshine. Reared in a politically well-connected New Jersey real estate family, Sunshine was, at the time, Governor Carey's chief fund raiser and the treasurer of the New York State Democratic party. Although Donald officially hired Sunshine to lobby on behalf of his Thirty-fourth Street convention center project, she soon began using her influence throughout the state Democratic political hierarchy on behalf of the Commodore Hotel project and its application before the Urban Development Corporation.

UDC Chairman Ravitch began receiving telephone calls expressing support for Donald's hotel project from Mayor Beame and Deputy Mayor John Zuccotti. He found himself in an awkward position. As it turned out, his family-owned construction firm, HRH, was to become embroiled in litigation against the city for its alleged default on a loan agreement for the firm's Manhattan Plaza project. Though Ravitch later denied any conflict of interest, he admitted feeling political pressure not to obstruct the mayor's economic initiatives. Ravitch was one of the four UDC board members who voted unanimously for approval. He later called the decision to grant the project such a generous tax break "a mistake."

At this point Donald's friends at City Hall started having second thoughts. They wanted assurances that Donald had a firm deal with Penn Central to acquire the property, and they wanted to make sure that he had his financing in place. Donald responded with a barrage of big lies. To reassure the city about his deal with Penn Central, he sent City Hall a copy of a signed option agreement; no one noticed until years later that the option agreement was signed only by him. Likewise, he insisted that he would get financing from the real estate arm of the Equitable Life Assurance Society even though Equitable had given him only a vague oral commitment. Donald did, however, make good on the city's demand that his father be personally involved in the deal. "I'm going to watch construction and provide financial credibility," Fred Trump, Sr., announced.

Donald next had to win approval of the Board of Estimate, a now-defunct megabureaucracy whose members included the mayor of New York and the presidents of the city's five boroughs. One of the most powerful insiders in his camp was Beame's deputy mayor, Stanley Friedman, who was put in charge of negotiating the Commodore Hotel deal for the city. Nevertheless, the Commodore Hotel scheme encountered spirited opposition from City Council Members Henry Stern and Robert F. Wagner, Jr., who charged that Donald was getting too sweet a deal. Donald's tax abatement proposal also provoked the jealous ire of competing hotel operators, such as Harry Helmsley, who demanded a tax break similar to the one being proposed for the Commodore so they could compete on a level playing field.

Donald then got a decisive boost from his friends at Penn Central. On December 12, 1975, several weeks after the Board of Estimate met to consider the Commodore deal for the first time, the Penn Central workout consultant Victor Palmieri announced that in light of $1.2 million in losses sustained over the preceding year, he planned to close down the Commodore Hotel no later than June 30, 1976. On May 12, 1976, Palmieri announced that the Commodore would close ahead of schedule, just six days hence. The new closing date happened to be one day before the Board of Estimate was scheduled to vote on Donald's tax abatement scheme. The prospect of actually watching another decaying landmark get boarded up seemed to have the intended mortifying effect.

On May 20, 1976, the Board of Estimate voted 8–0 to approve a tax abatement and renovation plan for the Commodore Hotel. Under the terms of the board resolution, Donald would pay $10 million for the property, $6 million of which would immediately go to the city to pay Penn Central's back taxes. The Urban Development Corporation would then take title to the property and lease it back to Donald for ninety-nine years. Donald would pay the city a minimum rent of $250,000 a year; it would also get an escalating profit share rising to 15 percent of the net profit over $1.5 million. In return, the city would grant a forty-year tax abatement, the largest in the city's history, worth no less than $160 million.

There were a host of ironies in this tidy little arrangement, not the least of which was the fact that Donald still had not invested a dime in acquiring the Commodore Hotel site. He would not announce that he finally had financing for the project until December 1976. As it turned out, only $35 million of the $70 million needed to fund the project would come from Equitable. The lion's share of funding, some $45 million, would come from the Bowery Savings Bank. Even then the Penn Central bankruptcy judge did not formally approve the sale of the Commodore Hotel to the partnership Donald formed with the Hyatt chain until March 1977. The actual groundbreaking ceremony did not take place until June 1978, more than two years after the passage of the Board of Estimate resolution.

But by his thirtieth birthday on June 14, 1976, Donald J. Trump the kid from the outer boroughs was well on his way to becoming Donald J. Trump the golden boy of Manhattan real estate developers. He had long since moved out of his one-bedroom apartment on Seventy-fifth Street, which he passed on to his younger brother, Robert, and taken up residence in a thirty-second-floor penthouse apartment in the Phoenix House at 160 East Sixty-fifth Street, which he decorated with earth-toned fabrics and flashy chrome coverings. And more important, he had started to hone his bravura style and his indispensable art of the spiel.

"When he was working on the Commodore, he'd say, 'It is the greatest? It is the best? Isn't it just going to be the best? I'm going to do this, and I'm going to do that,' " insurance executive Neil Walsh, one of his old running buddies, remembered nearly two decades later. "That was a very complicated thing he did for a first deal. But he was very positive-thinking. He never brought up for once the idea that he couldn't talk the city, talk the state, talk the banks, talk the insurance companies, talk Hyatt into helping him do what he wanted to do. He just didn't take no for an answer. He would push and push and push. He's a great salesman, and he convinced all these people he could do it."

Donald could not resist tooting his own horn at every opportunity. He went around bragging that he had been a star baseball player at the New York Military Academy, which was true, and that he had graduated first in his class from the Wharton School, which was far from true. He also encouraged his pals to toot their own horns—and often offered to show them how. Walsh got one of these patented self-promotion seminars when he served as chairman of the mayor's committee to bring the 1976 Democratic National Convention to New York. It took place following Walsh's announcement that the city's economists projected the convention would generate $25 million worth of business for the city. Donald called and urged Walsh to tell the press that the convention would bring in $200 million. Walsh asked how he could justify such a statement.

"Who's going to know?" Donald replied. "Say it."

Then, without advance warning, Fred Trump Sr.'s past came back to haunt his favorite son. One day Donald got an urgent telephone call from Prince Georges County, Maryland. The senior Trump had just been arrested at an FHA-financed housing project he owned, the 504-unit Gregory Estates. He was charged with noncompliance with a notice of violations from the local housing authorities. Along with alleged violations of fire and safety codes, Fred Sr.'s project was plagued by heat and hot-water problems, and a high vacancy rate.

In the past it had always been Donald who ran to his father for help. Now the roles were suddenly reversed. The county sheriff had handcuffed Fred, Sr., and hauled him down to jail, where he had to post a $1,000 bond. It took only $100 in cash to secure the bond, but the old man did not have it on him. Donald had to arrange for someone to go bail his father out. Weeks later Fred, Sr., was dragged into district court, where the judge fined the company that nominally owed the housing project and forced the old man to make some direly needed repairs. The Trumps later sold their Maryland project.

Then one night in August 1976 Donald J. Trump walked into a popular New York City night spot on First Avenue and Sixty-fourth Street called Maxwell's Plum, unaware that he was about to reach yet another major turning point in his seemingly charmed life. Owned by Warner LeRoy, a movie industry scion turned restaurant entrepreneur, Maxwell's Plum had pioneered the so-called singles bar phenomenon. It was a dazzling showplace that featured a stained glass ceiling illuminated by crystal chandeliers, walls flashing with ornately framed mirrors, and an enormous rectangular bar surrounded six deep with primping fashion models, aspiring actresses, and leggy airline stewardesses being ogled by young men on the make.

Maxwell's Plum was one of the main terminals on "the circuit" Donald prowled along with such pals as Neil Walsh, Yankees boss George Steinbrenner, Diners Club executive Bill Fugazy, and attorney Roy Cohn. The other key stops were Le Club, "21," Elaine's, and P. J. Clarke's. But Maxwell's Plum was destined to become a special place for Donald J. Trump. It was where he had met Tom Fitzsimmons, the ex-cop turned actor-model and screenwriter who was to play a unique role in his romantic future. And it was also where he was to meet his future bride.

Unlike Tom Fitzsimmons, who had a dance card filled with sexy blondes, brunettes, and redheads, Donald wasn't as happy playing the sexual field as he liked to let on. He still thought that most of the girls he met "had their heads screwed on wrong." That wasn't surprising. After all, the kinds of women who vamped around places on the circuit were not exactly rocket scientists. At the same time Donald wasn't exactly known as Maxwell's Plum's smoothest operator. While he strove to impress men mostly older than him, many of his peers figured him to be something of a nerd. He was always dressed up in a suit and tie, never in casual clothes. And he was always talking about the only two things that seemed to interest him: himself and his deals.

"Donald didn't spend too much time not talking business," his running buddy Neil Walsh recalled years later. "Business would always be somewhere in the conversation even at night, and it would usually be the next deal he was doing. He was always interested in business number one. Number two was politics and sports. And he had a major interest in girls. My wife and I would double-date with Donald and his girl friend of the minute. He always liked them glamorous—blue-eyed blondes."

On this particular August night at Maxwell's Plum, however, Donald, saw a hazel-eyed blonde waiting for a table. She looked like a model, and she was with three or four other attractive young women who also looked like models. That in itself was no big deal. But for some reason this particular blonde caught Donald's eye. She stood out from the rest of the crowd. There was just something about her, he didn't know quite what. He decided to make a move—a move that changed his life.

chapter four
CZECH MATE

■ IVANA WINKLMAYR DID not like waiting in line for the table at Maxwell's Plum. She had done quite a bit of waiting in lines back in Czechoslovakia. But that had been when she was a brown-haired little girl hoping to ride the ski lifts to the top of the mountains. She had now grown up into a twenty-seven-year-old runway model, five feet seven inches tall with bleached blond hair, a svelte figure, and a deep voice. She had come to New York City from her adopted home in Montreal for a fashion show promoting the 1976 summer Olympic Games, and she was impatient to get on with the program.

"We will probably be waiting for the table for two hours," she grumbled to the three other Montreal models who had gone out with her to Maxwell's Plum that evening.

All of a sudden Ivana felt someone tap her on the shoulder. She turned right around. A tall and handsome American gentleman with blue eyes and blond hair was standing behind her.

"Hello, my name is Donald Trump," he said. "I'm very friendly with the owner. Would you like me to help you get a table?"

Ivana turned to her model friends and started speaking to them in heavily accented English. "The gentleman is wanting to know if we would like him to help us get the table," she whispered. Her friends nodded enthusiastically.

"Well, he is probably going to ask if he can join us at the table," Ivana warned. The other Montreal models shrugged. That sounded far better than standing in line all night.

Moments later Ivana's party was escorted to a nearby table. Then, just as she predicted, Donald Trump did ask to join them. After dinner Donald drove Ivana and her friends to the Americana Hotel, where they were staying. He made sure to get all their names and phone numbers, but he already had his eye on Ivana, whom he figured to be the pick of the litter.

The next day Donald sent Ivana a dozen red roses. When she returned to Montreal, he started calling her on the telephone. A few weeks later he flew up to Canada and appeared unannounced at a fashion show Ivana was doing at the Ritz-Carlton. He said hello, then flew right back to New York.

"My God," Ivana exclaimed, "why does he do these things?"

Though Ivana had no way of knowing it at the time, she was to keep asking herself the same question for the next fourteen years.

Ivana Maria Zelnicekova Winklmayr had been born in pain and bred to be a champion. She arrived six weeks premature on February 20, 1949, in the town of Zlín, Czechoslovakia. Officially renamed Gottwaldov in honor of Czechoslovakia's first Communist-installed president, Zlín (population fifty thousand) was about 135 miles southeast of Prague in the ancient state of Moravia. The surrounding countryside was hilly and tree-covered. The town itself was a quaint but increasingly polluted industrialized hamlet of stucco row houses and Communist-built barracks-style brick apartments that huddled beneath the coal-burning smokestacks of the Bata shoe factory.

Ivana's parents lived relatively well considering the fact that they did not belong to the Communist party. Her mother, Maria, a devout Catholic, dark-haired and plump, was the daughter of grape growers who lived near the Austrian border; she worked as an operator at the telephone collective. Ivana's father, Milos Zelnicek, a tall, muscular, and handsome former swimming and skiing champ, labored as an electrical engineer at the shoe factory. His sister had defected to Canada with the advent of the Communist regime, but thanks to his athletic prowess, Milos had become head of the local sports club, which afforded his family travel and certain other privileges. The Zelniceks resided on the second floor of a two-story semidetached brick-facade housing project. Their flat had four rooms and a tiny garden out back.

Ivana spent the first six months of her life in the Zlín hospital fighting for survival. Her parents were told that she would be their only child. The Zelniceks were so overjoyed that their daughter (who, in keeping with Czech tradition, was given the derivational surname Zelnicekova) had managed to survive the preemie ward that they fairly spoiled her with attention. "Ivana was her daddy's girl," Aja Zanova-Steindler, a Czech-born friend and former ice skating champion, observed years later. "She was always very emotionally dependent on her father."

Milos Zelnicek believed that rigorous sports training would help his daughter overcome her infantile frailty and perhaps provide her with an avenue to a better life beyond the iron curtain. He taught her to swim at the age of two. Not long afterward he put her on baby skis. At the age of six Ivana won the very first ski race she entered. When she reached twelve, he enrolled her in a state-run program for Czech athletes, where she disciplined herself to cope with adversity and intense pain. A self-described "daredevil," she tore down the ski slopes with reckless abandon and ended up breaking her legs at least five times.

Zelnicek made sure that Ivana strove to overachieve in areas besides sports. In the summer of her thirteenth year she came home from school with a decidedly mediocre report card. Instead of allowing her to attend sports training camp, her father determined to teach her a lesson, much as Fred Trump, Sr., had vowed to make Donald "straighten up" by shipping him off to military school. Ivana was sent to work on the assembly line at the Bata shoe factory. She sat at the same bench every day hammering heels into pair after pair of plain leather shoes. When school resumed that fall, ever mindful of the lessons of the assembly line, Ivana hit the books with new zeal.

"I promised myself that I was never—ever—going to do that kind of work again!" she recalled years later.

Ivana grew into a strikingly beautiful young maiden with long brown hair, big brown eyes, and an athletically fit figure. She eventually competed for the Charles University ski team, though she never, as she later claimed repeatedly, represented her country at the 1972 Olympics in Sapporo, Japan, or at the 1976 Olympics in Montreal, Canada. At age eighteen, however, she did manage to latch on to the first of three male friends named Jiri, the Czech equivalent of George, who were to play important roles in her life. Each of the three Georges represented a competing social aspiration and a widely differing political perspective.

George number one, her first serious boyfriend, was a jock. His last name was Syrovatka, and he came from a once-prominent Zlín family whose patriarch had been killed by the Germans in World War II. A tall, dark-haired, and handsome champion ski racer, George Syrovatka was six years older than Ivana and something of a father figure. His own father was an accomplished architect closely allied with reform leader Alexander Dubček, which put the Syrovatkas on the liberal end of the Czech political spectrum. During the so-called Prague Spring of 1968, when Dubček briefly ascended to party leadership, George's father was commissioned to design the Czech Embassy in London.

When Ivana began dating George Syrovatka, he was a student at Charles University in Prague. She still lived back home in Zlín. The couple met on weekends at the ski slopes or at George's grandmother's country house, where they drank beer and hung out around the swimming pool. In the fall of 1967 Ivana enrolled in Charles University, intent on pursuing a career in physical education. Upon arriving in the Czech capital, she met George number two, Jiri Janosek. A former basketball jock turned journalist and film student, Janosek later married the daughter of Communist Prime Minister Lubomir Strogal. Although a mutual friend later claimed that Janosek was "not a Communist at heart," his ties to the hard-line regime were suspiciously convenient, both for him and for Ivana.

"A lot of people were sitting on two chairs then," recalled Czech émigrée Helena Fierlinger in a *Vanity Fair* profile of Ivana. "You didn't know who to trust, because the government was trying very hard to turn people into informers." Ivana later admitted being questioned by the Communists but claimed that she "played dumb." In fact, as subsequent events attested, she was wily as a fox.

In 1971, following the Communist crackdown on the Dubček uprising, Ivana and George Syrovatka reached a crossroads in their love affair. Although she had yet to finish her studies at Charles University, he was anxious to leave the country and start a new life. Unfortunately the borders were closed. It seemed that the only way to get out of Czechoslovakia was to defect, but for those who defected, there would be no possibility of returning. George was willing to take the risk. His family had already left for Canada. Ivana's parents, on the other hand, were still living in Zlín. She cringed at the prospect of never being able to see them again.

The two lovers devised a plan to fool the hard-line authorities: a classic cold war marriage. That fall George and Ivana entered a ski race in Austria. When the race was over, Ivana married an Austrian ski buddy of George's named Alfred Winklmayr. This arranged pretend marriage provided Ivana with a way out of the country and, just as important, a way back in. There would be no need to defect. She now had dual Czech and Austrian citizenship. She could come and go as she pleased. According to all three principals, Ivana's nuptial union with Winklmayr was never sexually consummated. On the night of her wedding she slept with George Syrovatka, who then defected to Canada to join his parents.

In the spring of 1972 Ivana got her master's in physical education from Charles University. Although she could have left the country under the guise of her marriage to Alfred Winklmayr, she was no longer of a mind to join George Syrovatka in Canada. She decided to remain in Czechoslovakia. The reason was her newfound love for the third George in her life, a poet and lyricist named George (Jiri) Staidl. Like George number one, George number three was six years older than Ivana and something of a playboy. At the time he was writing hit songs for Karel Gott, a popular and financially successful singer in the Johnny Mathis / Tony Bennett mold whose band regularly traveled from Czechoslovakia to Germany, Austria, and Switzerland.

Ivana and George Staidl lived together for about a year and a half in Jevany, an upscale artist colony outside Prague. According to one of Ivana's closest female friends, "George Staidl was really the love of her life." Though by no means the most handsome man in Prague, he was, as his brother, Ladislav Staidl, recalled, "a very charming artist with a lust for life"—and plenty of money to spend—who could provide Ivana with "more excitement and glamour" than George Syrovatka could. On August 2, 1973, Ivana was granted an absentee divorce in Los Angeles Superior Court from Alfred Winklmayr, who had moved to California to teach skiing. The reason for the divorce was to clear the way for her to marry George Staidl. But the Staidl family had some serious reservations about Ivana. "She was the type who loved parties, drinking, and meeting high society people," Ladislav Staidl recalled. "Our mother didn't like her because she was too fancy. She wanted George to marry a woman who would cook and clean."

On October 9, 1973, George Staidl ran a red light on the road to Jevany and was killed in a collision with a truck. Ivana later told friends that she had been riding in the car with George and had suffered a broken back. That was a lie. According to Ladislav Staidl, Ivana was trying to cover up the fact that "another girl was in the car with George." Despite her refusal to admit the truth about her dead lover's infidelity, she sent a wreath to Prague every year thereafter with a card inscribed "In loving memory of George."

Shortly after George Staidl's fatal accident, Ivana flew to Canada and promptly rekindled her dormant love affair with George Syrovatka. The couple lived in a three-room apartment on the eleventh floor of a building in the stylish Westmount area. By the time Ivana arrived, George had already opened a ski shop called Top Sports. When not minding the store, he gave lessons and trained for downhill races in Canada and at Jay Peak in Vermont. In 1973, the year Ivana emigrated from Czechoslovakia, he won acclaim as North America's fastest skier with a time of 110.6 mph on the Flying Kilometer run in Cervino, Italy. The dashing downhill racer had also made quite a few "contacts" in the Montreal modeling industry, whom he called upon to help launch a new career for his good-looking Czech girl friend. One of George's contacts, a Czech émigrée named Vali Dubski, offered Ivana a job. She accepted the offer in hopes that Dubski could also help her learn to speak English.

Ivana quickly created a whole new image for herself. She dyed her brown hair blond and started wearing heavy gobs of lipstick and eye liner to affect an aura of cosmopolitan glamour. Her new look did not win unanimously favorable reviews. ("I think she was prettier when she was in Czechoslovakia, when she still had dark hair . . . and a lot less makeup," grumbled George Syrovatka's brother, Michael, who frequently saw her at family gatherings in Montreal.) But Ivana's make-over did serve the lucrative purpose of transforming the sports-crazy country girl from Czechoslovakia into a platinum princess with a regal strut. Before long she graduated from Mrs. Dubski's tutelage and signed on with the Audrey Morris modeling agency. Runway jobs poured in, and Ivana started earning up to $50,000 a year.

Ivana and George began to enjoy a storybook life-style. He drove a BMW. She raced around in a flashy red Austin-Healey. On winter weekends she joined him on the slopes at Jay Peak in Vermont, where she became a part-time ski instructor. At Christmastime the couple flew to Aspen with a group of friends. In the summer they went out to a retreat on Lac Brome owned by George's family, where they swam and played tennis. To the Syrovatka family's chagrin, Ivana soon developed an interest in interior decorating. At one point she decided to cover a wall at the Lac Brome retreat with some fake bricks just for the effect. As soon as she returned to Montreal, the family took the bricks down.

Ivana's allegedly high-handed attitude about such matters of taste further alienated George's brother. "I thought she was spoiled, and I just kind of distanced myself," Michael Syrovatka admitted years later. "I obviously thought she wasn't good enough for George. I always had the impression that she was a spoiled brat. She would want to have her way, and it would be her way or the highway. She would act insulted, or sulk. . . . George is easygoing, and Ivana knew how to manipulate him to get her way. She was the only child, and she was used to it that everything she wanted, she always got."

Yet Ivana longed for something more than merely living out of wedlock with George and said so in so many words. In 1975, about the same time Donald was making his first front-page headlines down in New York City, the *Montreal Gazette* ran a splashy profile bannered THE TWO FACES OF IVANA—MODEL AND SPORTSWOMAN. But Ivana informed the interviewer that neither modeling nor skiing was her ultimate goal. "If modeling becomes a career, there's no time to go to the theater, read books, and go on vacation," she noted. "Modeling is a job to me, not a career. I have my social life, my husband, and my home."

Ivana's mention of a "husband" was actually an exercise in wishful thinking. She was not referring to Alfred Winklmayr, from whom she'd been divorced for two years. She was talking about George Syrovatka. They were living together like a married couple. She thought of him as her husband. She now wanted to make it legal. She wanted a church wedding, and she wanted to have children. George, however, was not in any rush. Then, in the summer of 1976, Ivana took the fateful modeling assignment that brought her to New York City and, eventually, to Maxwell's Plum, where she met Donald J. Trump.

In the weeks following his first surprise visit to Montreal, Donald started calling Ivana every day, sometimes several times a day, pestering her for a formal date. Ivana told him that she had been living with someone in Montreal for almost four years. She added that she and her boyfriend had even talked about getting married. Donald didn't care. Ivana wasn't married yet. He begged her to fly down to New York, he'd pay the fare. Finally she consented.

When Ivana arrived in New York, Donald commenced a whirlwind courtship that would have made almost any young woman's head spin. On their first date he took her to Le Club, which had become his favorite haunt. A short time later he hired a bodyguard named Matthew Calamari, who doubled as his chauffeur, and started shuttling Ivana around town in a flashy silver Cadillac. According to his pal Neil Walsh, he boasted about his new girl friend with exactly the same superlatives he used to trumpet his latest real estate deals.

"Have you ever seen anybody more beautiful?" Donald would chant. "Really, is she the most beautiful? Have you ever seen anybody so smart? You know, she speaks French and Russian and Czech. Do you know that she is the greatest skier in the world? Have you ever seen anybody that's so beautiful and so smart?"

In October 1976, barely two months after their chance encounter in Maxwell's Plum, Donald invited Ivana to move to New York and live with him. In a letter addressed to "Sweetie Pie," he declared, "I love you. I want to be with you. I think you're fabulous." Though Donald's love letter did not mention his invitation to cohabit, he alluded to a decision Ivana had at hand. "If you say yes, you'll never regret your decision," he assured her. He closed by pledging, "I'll always love and protect you."

While Ivana pondered how to respond, her relentless suitor contrived to make a favorable impression with the help of the media. On

November 1, 1976, *New York Times* reporter Judy Klemesrud published what proved to be a precedent-setting puff piece headlined DONALD TRUMP, REAL ESTATE PROMOTER, BUILDS IMAGE AS HE BUYS BUILDINGS. The layout featured photos of Donald sitting in his three-bedroom apartment and getting into his chauffeur-driven silver Cadillac with license plates bearing the initials DJT. The lead paragraph of Klemesrud's article read like a Hollywood press release.

"He is tall, lean, and blond, with dazzling white teeth," Klemesrud wrote, "and he looks ever so much like Robert Redford. . . ." The paragraphs that followed embroidered on the truth with shameless—and totally unsubstantiated—hyperbole. Donald told Klemesrud that he had started working in the family real estate business when he was only twelve years old and that he had gone on to graduate first in his class from the Wharton School. He claimed that was now worth "more than $200 million" and that he had recently made a killing in California, where he owned a Beverly Hills mansion. "I've probably made $14 million there over the last two years," he bragged.

Fred Trump, Sr., went right along with the charade. "Donald is the smartest person I know," the old man told Klemesrud. "I gave Donald free rein. He has great vision, and everything he touches seems to turn to gold. As long as he has this great energy in abundance, I'm glad to let him do it."

When the *New York Times* story traveled over the electronic and oral wires to Montreal, Ivana suddenly found herself cast as a real-life Cinderella. The charming knave so assiduously courting her was actually a multimillionaire prince of property. She had never known anyone so wealthy in Montreal, much less in her native Czechoslovakia. But she still wasn't sure he was the one for her. Donald, on the other hand, was becoming increasingly sure that Ivana was the one for him. He let her know that his intentions were serious when he invited her back down to New York one weekend in the fall of 1976 and took her out to Jamaica Estates to meet his family.

Ivana kept reminding Donald of the obstacles to their romance. One weekend she even invited him up to Montreal to meet George Syrovatka. It was not an event Donald looked forward to, for he half expected that George would shake his hand and then smack him in the mouth. But the confrontation proved to be anticlimactic. The easygoing George and the hard-driving Donald found that they actually liked each other—at least as much as could be expected under the circumstances.

Now Donald started to feel anxious and ill at ease. He knew full well that the *New York Times* article exaggerated his wealth by many times. In 1975 he had reported a net taxable income of $76,210. But he was not a poor boy either. On December 12, 1976, Fred Trump, Sr., created five trusts for his children. Donald's father also gave each unmarried child—i.e., Donald, Robert, Elizabeth, and recently divorced Freddy—$1 million in cash. The puff piece in the *New York Times* rekindled Donald's long-standing fears about being victimized by gold diggers. "I'm positive I'm never going to marry a girl from New York," he informed Ivana's modeling industry friend Yolande Cardinal. "They're only after my money."

Cardinal assured Donald that Ivana was not that type. So did her modeling agency mentor, Audrey Morris.

"Well, I'm either going to make it and make a lot of money," Donald predicted, "or I'm going to fall flat on my face and lose it all overnight."

Shortly before Christmas of 1976 Donald took off for Aspen, Colorado. He knew that Ivana and her friends went there every year, and he planned to meet her during the peak of the social ski season between Christmas and New Year. But first he had to learn to hold his own on the slopes. For two weeks he took private lessons and mastered the rudiments of getting downhill. There was no way Donald could hope to match Ivana's championship-caliber skiing ability in so short a time, but he earned high points with Ivana for making the effort. "She is a very determined woman," Yolande Cardinal observed, "and she definitely likes it when someone else shows determination of the kind she exhibits."

Donald had an even bigger surprise in store. On New Year's Eve 1976 he and Ivana settled down for a romantic evening alone in the Highlands Lodge Condominiums. Then Donald popped the question. "Will you marry me?" he asked. Donald heard Ivana say yes— or thought he did.

Upon returning to New York, Donald went out and bought Ivana a three-carat diamond engagement ring from Tiffany's. Then he telephoned Roy Cohn to tell him the good news. Cohn was profoundly nonplussed. He told Donald that getting married was not a good idea and tried to talk him out of it. But Donald insisted he knew what he was doing. That being the case, Cohn insisted on drawing up a prenuptial contract designed to protect Donald's financial assets in the event that his marriage to Ivana ended in separation or divorce.

Ivana was now having second thoughts of her own. She was further confounded by George Syrovatka's reaction to the news that Donald had proposed. "If you really want to get married," George offered, "I'll marry you." In early February 1977, more than a month after Donald's proposal in Aspen, Ivana decided to take a modeling assignment in Tahiti. She thought that the trip would give her a chance to sort things out. Donald, who considered their engagement a done deal, was furious.

"Don't go," he pleaded. "I don't think it's a great idea for you to go."

"Well," she replied firmly, "I am going to go."

Ivana stayed in Tahiti for more than two weeks. Donald was at his wits' end. He could not talk to her because she could not be reached by telephone. It would take weeks for a letter to get there, if it ever got there at all. Finally he sent her a telegram insisting that she return. Ivana did not reply. She stayed in Tahiti until her modeling assignment was finished.

When Ivana finally returned to Montreal in late February, she had made up her mind. After much soul-searching, she realized that George Syrovatka was just not ready for marriage; he simply wasn't mature enough to accept the responsibility. She told George it was all over. She was going to marry Donald Trump. George was devastated. According to his brother, he became almost suicidal. "I remember driving with him in the car," Michael Syrovatka recalled. "He was driving pretty fast, aggressive, reckless."

Donald, however, was elated. It looked as if things were really starting to take off in his personal and his professional lives. In January 1977 he had signed a fully agreed-upon option contract with Penn Central for the Commodore Hotel property. On March 7, 1977, the bankruptcy court in Philadelphia formally approved the deal, and Donald put down his $250,000 option payment, his first and only out-of-pocket expense on the deal other than Der Scutt's architectural fees.

Donald attempted to finalize his marital plans in much the same way he might try to close a real estate transaction. At Ivana's behest, he wrote a note to Maria Zelnicek on Air Canada stationary formally asking for her daughter's hand in marriage. The wedding date was set for April 9, 1976. As Donald saw it, all that remained on the Ivana project was to get her to sign a prenuptial agreement. Then they would be off to the altar.

But the marriage almost cratered before Donald and Ivana ever made it to the church. Less than a month before their scheduled wedding day, Donald suggested that she hire a lawyer to negotiate their prenuptial agreement. Ivana later claimed that she had never heard of prenuptial agreements in Czechoslovakia.

"Does this mean we are giving up on the marriage before we start?" she asked.

"No, not all," Donald insisted. He explained that he wanted her to sign a prenuptial agreement in order to protect his father and mother, who had worked hard all their lives, and his brothers and sisters, who now shared with him in the newly created family trusts. He claimed he could not allow the entire Trump family's financial future to be tied to his. But as he later admitted, he was also looking out for himself. By this time both his older brother, Freddy, and his older sister, Maryanne, had suffered the woes of divorce. Donald's professors back at the Wharton School had lectured the class on more than one occasion about the way divorce could destroy a business, especially an entrepreneurial one.

Much to her later regret, Ivana did not hire someone outside the Trump sphere of influence. Instead, she allowed Donald's attorney, Roy Cohn, to put her in touch with his friend Lawrence Levner, a domestic relations lawyer who had also handled legal work for Cohn. Levner represented Ivana on this first nuptial agreement and on three subsequent updatings of the agreement. Years later Ivana charged through a new set of attorneys that she did not benefit from truly independent counsel in these negotiations, that Levner was actually a pawn in a wicked chess game manipulated by Roy Cohn, an accusation Donald angrily denied.

The first round of fireworks erupted on March 18, 1977, a little more than three weeks before Donald and Ivana were scheduled to be married. That afternoon Donald, Ivana, Cohn, and Levner met for lunch at a restaurant owned by a Cohn crony to review the first draft of the proposed prenuptial agreement, which had been written by Cohn. What started out as a friendly little conference quickly degenerated into a shouting match. The main point of contention was a "give-back" clause Cohn had slyly inserted in the agreement. The clause stipulated that in the event of divorce Ivana would have to return any and all gifts, including jewelry that Donald might have given her in the course of the marriage.

Ivana was furious at the thought of having to surrender jewelry received as a gift from her husband. She then proceeded to make some demands of her own that infuriated Donald. The first and foremost was that he establish a fund of "rainy day" money in her name. The amount she wanted deposited in this rainy day account was $150,000. After all, as she reminded Donald, she would be giving up a modeling career that provided her with an income of as much as $50,000 a year.

Donald was aghast—and insulted. Although he professed to be a multimillionaire, his assets consisted primarily of real estate. One hundred and fifty thousand dollars in cash was a lot of money, even for him. But what really annoyed him was the fact that Ivana wanted money in exchange for making a marriage vow. When Donald resisted her demand, Ivana got up from the table and left. Donald ran out to the sidewalk, calmed her down, and convinced her to come back inside the restaurant. The parties eventually agreed to resume their negotiations the following day.

The next big confrontation occurred at Roy Cohn's town house office. Cohn greeted his guests in bare feet, wearing only a bathrobe. By this time he had struck the clause requiring Ivana to return gifts of jewelry and such in the event of divorce. But her insistence on a rainy day fund remained a major sticking point. "I'm moving to New York," Ivana pointed out. "I think it's appropriate." Like the luncheon meeting, the conference at Cohn's town house ended acrimoniously.

But on March 22, 1977, just two and a half weeks before the wedding, Donald and Ivana finally came to terms. He agreed to establish a rainy day fund of $100,000 in a bank account of her choosing; evidently mindful of potential gift tax consequences, the prenuptial contract noted that the rainy day fund was "not intended to be con-

strued as a gift." In the event of divorce Donald also agreed to pay
Ivana $20,000 after one year of marriage and amounts gradually
escalating to $90,000 per annum after thirty years of marriage.

In return, Ivana agreed to keep hands off the rest of Donald's
money. The prenuptial contract called for her to waive any claims to
"support, maintenance, or alimony" or any additional share of Donald's estate in the event of divorce or his death. Likewise, it also called
for her to give up her rights "to all property . . . now owned or here-
inafter acquired by Donald." Another clause stipulated that Ivana
would waive her rights to take advantage of any forthcoming changes
in New York marital laws that might "create community property or
forced share or equitable distribution upon the dissolution of a marriage."

After affixing their signatures to the nuptial contract, Donald and
Ivana kissed and made up. Then Ivana determined to show her fiancé
that she was not just a taker. Although she wanted to give Donald
something of value just as he had consented to provide her with a
rainy day fund, she had virtually nothing to her name. Her net worth
consisted almost entirely of her personal belongings, clothes, skis, and
her sports car. So Ivana took out a $1 million life insurance policy
and made Donald the beneficiary.

The wedding preparations underscored the imbalance between
bride and groom. This was going to be a Trump wedding, a large
and lavish affair with more than two hundred invited guests. Donald's family would foot the bill. His mother and sisters would take
responsibility for most of the planning. The vast majority of invitees
would be their friends, including such VIPs as Mayor Abe Beame,
Queens Borough President Donald Manes, State Assembly Speaker
Stanley Steingut, attorneys Bunny and Sandy Lindenbaum, mayoral
counsel Michael Bailkin, architect Der Scutt, attorney Gerald Schrager of Dreyer & Traub, and scores of other Trump family retainers.

Ivana, on the other hand, was unable to invite both her parents to
the wedding. It cost thousands of dollars to fly two people from
Czechoslovakia to New York. Her parents couldn't afford two fares,
and neither could she. Although she would get her rainy day fund
of $100,000 upon marrying Donald, she felt embarrassed about ask-
ing him for a bridge loan after their prenuptial agreement spat. As a
result, only Milos Zelnicek flew over for the wedding; Ivana's mother

stayed behind in Zlín. Besides her father, the only guests of the bride would be Audrey Morris, Yolande Cardinal, and a handful of other friends from Montreal.

When the big day arrived at last, Ivana got a severe case of the jitters. According to Audrey Morris, she was "madly in love" with Donald, but she suddenly felt very alone. "Ivana was nervous because she didn't know anyone," observed Yolande Cardinal. "It was hard on her." There was another reason for Ivana's anxiety. "I remember her being afraid because it was so fast," Cardinal claimed years later. "[Donald] was very much rushing it. She did not chase this man. She was almost reluctant."

Despite such last-minute jitters, Donald and Ivana were married as planned on April 9, 1977, in the Marble Collegiate Church on Fifth Avenue. The ceremony was conducted by the Trump family cleric, Dr. Norman Vincent Peale. It was Easter season, and the church was filled with the perfume of thousands of all-white Easter lilies. Ivana wore a two-piece white chiffon gown, mid-calf length, with a long veil but no train. Donald wore a black tuxedo. His best man was his older brother, Fred, Jr. His sisters, Maryanne and Elizabeth, were brides-maids.

After the ceremony the Trump family hosted a seated dinner at "21." The toastmaster was comedian Joey Adams, husband of *New York Post* gossip columnist Cindy Adams, who, like so many of the other guests, happened to be a close friend of the behind-the-scenes master of ceremonies Roy Cohn. The party lasted until midnight. The next day the newlyweds took off for an extended honeymoon in Acapulco. Both before and after the wedding Donald repeatedly asserted that he wanted to have no fewer than five children so he could be sure that "at least one of them will turn out like me." Ivana allowed that she might bear Donald "two or maybe three children." By the time they returned to New York City, she was already pregnant with their first child.

Donald and Ivana Trump began the first summer of their life together with a tender loving embrace. It was a hot and humid day in June 1977. The Trumps had rented a cozy little shingle-sided cottage near Wainscott, Long Island, one of the chain of prerevolution-ary vintage resort towns collectively known as the Hamptons. The cottage was owned by an ultraliberal defense attorney named Michael

J. Kennedy and his wife, Eleanore, who spent the summer in a much larger saltbox house nearby.

Donald led his bride halfway across a catwalk between the cottage and the beach. As they stood above a humpbacked dune blooming with beach plum and rosa rugosa, their eyes nearly blinded by shimmering white sand and sparkling blue water, he held Ivana in his arms and kissed her on the mouth. Though neither of the Trumps knew it, Michael and Eleanore Kennedy were puttering about outside their house and happened to notice their renters kissing on the catwalk.

"Oh, Michael," Eleanore Kennedy sighed, "we're so lucky to have them rent the cottage. They're so in love."

And for the time being the Trumps stayed in love. It wasn't easy, especially for Ivana. Back in New York the couple lived in a prestigiously located but rather Spartan two-bedroom apartment in Olympic Towers, the home of such celebrity financiers as Saudi Arabian arms trading billionaire Adnan Khashoggi. But it seemed as if the Trumps spent precious little time at home. Donald turned their marriage into a whirlwind of socializing and politicking. He was always wheeling and dealing or, to use the more descriptive phrase Ivana coined, "scheming and beaming." As in the prenuptial agreement negotiations, Roy Cohn remained his main mentor on both the social and business fronts.

"Roy provided the Trumps with connections in Manhattan," recalled author Bob Colacello, a former Andy Warhol aide who partied in Cohn's circle. "Roy used to have big birthday parties at his home out in Greenwich, Connecticut, and lots of dinner parties at his town house in New York. It was always a very eclectic high-powered group. There were Republican types like Ned Regan and Alfonse D'Amato, and Democratic types like Carmine De Sapio, Meade Esposito, and Stanley Friedman in the same room with Andy Warhol. You'd also see people like [publishing magnate] Si Newhouse, [blue blood socialite] C. Z. Guest, [cosmetics queen] Estée Lauder, Cindy Adams and Joey Adams, [Studio 54 nightclub owners] Steve Rubell and Ian Schrager, and Claudia Cohen, who was writing 'Page Six' for the *New York Post* at the time. Suddenly there were Donald and Ivana."

At Donald's direction, Ivana gained entrée to New York café society by the traditional practice of serving an apprenticeship on the board of a charity gala affiliated with the so-called disease ball circuit. Her choice of diseases, cerebral palsy, was dictated by her husband's contacts—namely, ABC's president, Leonard Goldenson and his wife, Isabell, and textile magnate Jack Haussman and his wife, Ethel, who were on the board of United Cerebral Palsy. But Ivana made some of her first prestigious social contacts at Roy Cohn's parties. Two of the most important were Estée Lauder and C. Z. Guest, who started inviting Ivana to ladies' luncheons and to the peculiar kind of New York party at which rich and famous celebrities who hardly know each other mingle with other celebrities simply because they, too, are rich and famous. But as a Czech-born outsider Ivana initially basked in her husband's reflected glory.

Meanwhile, Donald had to act nimbly to protect his financial future. On September 8, 1977, Ed Koch and Mario Cuomo finished first and second in the Democratic mayoral primary. Incumbent Abe Beame, the Trumps' longtime ally, came in third. On November 8 Koch won the general election with 50 percent of the vote. Donald's option on the Commodore Hotel was due to expire on January 20, 1978, and he still did not have his financing in place. Since the Trumps had not supported Ed Koch, there was no way of knowing whether the new administration would renew the city's stamp of approval or attempt to block the project before he could even break ground.

Donald decided to get some one-of-a-kind political insurance with a little help from his lame-duck friends at City Hall. His chief inside operative was Beame's outgoing deputy, Stanley Friedman. In late December 1977, less than three weeks before the change in administrations, Friedman orchestrated an unprecedented "escrow closing" on the Commodore Hotel deal. No one around City Hall had ever heard of an escrow closing before, mainly because it was such a transparently gratuitous type of transaction that no one had dared suggest before. But the legal effect of the fine print in the escrow closing documents was to bind the city and the state Urban Development Corporation to their agreed-upon roles in the pending transaction almost regardless of what happened to Donald Trump in the coming months.

On December 29, 1977, Friedman delivered another political plum. He rushed through a franchise agreement for Donald that allowed him to build a glass-enclosed "Garden Room" restaurant extending from the second level of the Grand Hyatt eighteen feet over the side-walk on Forty-second Street. Two days later Friedman's boss, Abe Beame, punctuated his long history of Trump cronyism by announcing his support for the Thirty-fourth Street convention center site. Upon leaving city government at the end of the year, Friedman went to work at Saxe, Bacon, & Bolan, better known as the law firm of Donald's attorney, Roy M. Cohn.

When New Year's Eve of 1977 rolled around, Donald J. Trump found plenty of reasons to celebrate. In addition to being the day of Mayor Beame's final political favor, it was the first anniversary of his marriage proposal to Ivana. It was also the day his first son was born, The child arrived exactly eight months and twenty-two days after the Trump wedding. The couple decided to name him Donald John Trump, Jr.

In May 1978, more than three months after the official expiration date of his option with Penn Central, Donald finally closed the Commodore Grand Hyatt deal. A few weeks later, having obtained a construction loan from Manufacturers Hanover Trust jointly guaranteed by Hyatt and Fred Trump, Sr., he triumphantly hosted ground-breaking ceremonies. Then he opened an office around the corner from the project at 466 Lexington Avenue and set about making his dreams come true.

Donald's aggressively intrusive, shoot-from-the-hip management style, which set the pattern for years to come, was not always appreciated by the professionals charged with building the hotel. He would show up unannounced at all times of the day and embark on an impromptu tour of the construction site, soliciting comments and opinions from everyone, from the lowliest laborer to the highest-paid consultant, at every turn. This kind of helter-skelter information gathering alarmed and disconcerted the architectural project manager Ralph Steinglass of Gruzen Partners.

"Hey, let me know if you're going to be coming in, because I don't want you to talk to these people and get the wrong impression," Steinglass would plead, warning, "The kind of advice you get in discussions like that is haphazard at best. It could come back and bite you."

Further complicating matters was the fact that Donald kept revising his overall scheme for the Grand Hyatt. He had started out with plans for a mid-priced hotel. Then he realized that the only way to accommodate the increasingly ambitious designs he envisioned was to turn it into a first-class hotel. Donald pestered Irving Fischer, the president of HRH Construction, to give him a fixed figure for the construction costs to satisfy his lenders. But he kept making so many design changes that the Grand Hyatt became a "cost-plus" project. The original construction budget called for a total expenditure of $40 million. According to Fischer, the actual cost of construction turned out to be $70 million.

Not all the astonishing cost overruns on the Grand Hyatt were Donald's fault. As Fischer and his crew discovered, the Commodore Hotel had much more serious structural flaws than any of the engineers had anticipated. Donald wanted to strip the old facade and affix a curtain wall of mirrored glass to the existing steel frame of the hotel. But much of the steel had rotted and had to be replaced with expensive new girders. Similarly, the process of actually tying the glass to the steel proved to be more difficult—and thus more time- and money-consuming—than anyone expected. Yet throughout the Grand Hyatt project Donald exuded an aura of confidence, a charm and charisma, that won over even those he antagonized.

"His reputation would lead you to believe that he's awful to work for," Steinglass allowed in a later interview, "But curiously enough, most of those I've talked to enjoyed working for him. I think people appreciate working with somebody with a lot of energy and a lot of involvement. He turned things upside down a few times. The project took a little longer to build. But in the end he got exactly what he wanted. Which wasn't exactly what other people wanted. But they got to live with it. And they learned to like it."

Much the same thing could have been—and was—said about Ivana. Shortly after Donny was born, the Trumps moved out of Olympic Towers into an eight-room apartment at 800 Fifth Avenue. Ivana designed a skylighted solarium between the dining room and the living room and an entertainment area she called "the galleria," which resembled a fanciful disco parlor. She installed dark marble floors, trimmed the mirrors with tiny lights to create the effect of a waterfall, and furnished the room with an Italian coffee table made of bone. She covered the dining room tables with goatskin, covered the living room floor with beige pile carpeting that matched the upholstery, and strung a hammock across a picture window overlooking Central Park.

Ivana then redid The Donald's wardrobe. At her insistence he discarded the plum-colored suits and loafers of his swinging singles period. Twice a year, when he was "in a good mood," she took him down to Barney's and helped him pick out ten or fifteen new outfits, mostly dark blue suits by designers such as Pierre Cardin and Bill Blass. She also tried, with considerably less success, to redo The Donald's diet. As she recalls, "In the first two years of the marriage I fixed him meals with all sorts of fancy sauces, but he just didn't like them. Donald is a meat and potatoes man."

In addition to looking after Donny and his dad, Ivana maintained a rigorous schedule of business appointments and glamour treatments. Whereas her husband usually awoke at six o'clock in the morning, she arose around eight, breakfasted on grapefruit, then attended exercise classes three times a week. She got her hair done twice a week and returned home in the afternoon for massages. "I have to look pretty and fresh," she explained to an interviewer, "because we have to entertain people so much."

But Ivana was hardly just a fluttering social butterfly. During the construction of the Grand Hyatt she visited the job site almost every day. Like her husband, she volunteered instructions to carpenters, electricians, steelworkers, and plumbers, but her chosen area of interest was the interior design of the hotel. She exercised her taste by selecting pink paradiso marble for the main lobby, which she accented with gleaming gold handrails, bronze column covers, and jagged metal hanging sculptures.

Ivana's input was not always well received by the Grand Hyatt construction crew. "I thought it was inappropriate because her training wasn't for that kind of work," grumbled project manager Ralph Steinglass. "I thought that undercut the people who had been delegated to work on the job. She brought some good things to the project, but I've worked with more sympathetic people that are smoother in their relationships and have a way of convincing people rather than just bullying them."

Ivana made no apologies for her iron maiden image on the job site. "I have to put on this tough act," she confided one day, "because

if you say please, please to these guys, the job will never get done the
way we want it done."

By the summer of 1978 Donald was already "scheming and beaming" over another even more ambitious development destined to bear
the family name, a glittering, skyscraping edifice to be called Trump
Tower. He knew exactly where he wanted to build it, too. "If you go
to Paris, if you go to Duluth, the best location is called the Tiffany
location," he noted years later. "I set out to get the true Tiffany location—the location right next door to Tiffany's. The location is probably the most prestigious address in New York."

The so-called Tiffany location that Donald coveted happened to
be at the corner of Fifth Avenue and Fifty-sixth Street. It was occupied by Bonwit Teller, one of the city's most chic retail stores. Bonwit's, in turn, was owned by a conglomerate named Genesco that was
in the throes of a financial crisis and a top management change. Donald enlisted the aid of the ubiquitous Louise Sunshine, who happened to be close to friends of newly installed Genesco chief John
Hanigan. In August 1978 Hanigan signed a letter of intent agreeing
to sell the Bonwit building and the land lease for $25 million.

Donald put together the remaining pieces of the puzzle mainly
with bluff, bluster, and shrewdly calculated misdirection. His bankers
refused to fund the Trump Tower project until he bought the land
underlying the Genesco lease. The land happened to belong to the
Equitable Life Assurance Society, which was providing long-term
financing for the Grand Hyatt project. Donald told Equitable chief
George Peacock that he could simply renovate the Bonwit site if the
company declined to join him in constructing a new building, leaving
Equitable with low-priced long-term lease payments. The verbal ruse
worked. In September 1978 Equitable agreed to become a fifty-fifty
partner in developing the Bonwit site.

Donald's next important coup was obtaining the air rights over the
Tiffany Building next door to Bonwit Teller's, which enabled him to
construct a much larger building than otherwise permissible under
existing zoning regulations. Before commencing negotiations with
Tiffany's president, Walter Hoving, Donald had architect Der Scutt

prepare two scale models of his proposed high rise. One model showed how the building would look if he weren't able to get Tiffany's air rights; it was an intentionally horrid boxlike structure rising fifty stories straight up. The other model showed a far more attractive glass tower with "beautiful picture windows on the side of the building overlooking Tiffany." The Tiffany chief was duly horrified by the first model and duly impressed by the second. When Donald offered him $5 million for the air rights to the building, garnished with a promise to "preserve Tiffany's" in perpetuity, Hoving agreed.

The last major hurdle standing between Donald and his dream for Trump Tower was the city. The scale of the building's design was circumscribed by the floor area ratio (FAR). Put simply, the square footage of the building had to be based on a ratio determined by the size of the lot. That was why having the Tiffany air rights, which effectively increased the size of the lot, was so crucial. The maximum FAR for any building in the city was 21.6. Without the Tiffany air rights, the permissible FAR for the Trump Tower site was only 8.5.

Fortunately for Donald, there were several ways to obtain so-called FAR bonuses. One way was to devote more floors of the building to residential rather than office usage, which would presumably limit congestion. Another way was to set aside public areas for pedestrians in the form of a through-block arcade. A third means of increasing the FAR was to provide more than minimal retail space in the building. All three considerations strongly influenced the design of Trump Tower. The most visible repercussion was the creation of the soon-to-be-famous six-story retail atrium at the base of the building, which, as Donald later bragged, was destined to become "a hit on its own terms."

Just as in his negotiations with Walter Hoving over the air rights, Donald used alternative architectural renderings as leverage to win approvals form the city. Der Scutt produced no fewer than three dozen different drawings of the proposed high rise. The design Donald preferred was a seventy-story glass tower, with the lower floors terraced to the height of the adjacent Tiffany building and the upper floors "sawtoothed" in cubed columns that gave the structure twenty-eight different sides. But Der Scutt also designed a so-called as-of-right building that could be erected without winning additional variances or bonuses. The renderings showed a horrific-looking four-sided boxlike structure rising eighty stories and cantilevered over the Tiffany Building. Essentially Donald told the city, "If you don't let me build the seventy-story sawtoothed tower, I'll put up this as-of-right monstrosity."

That kind of talk naturally inflamed Trump Tower's opponents. One of the most vocal critics was City Councilman Henry Stern, who had been one of the few public servants even to question Donald's very good deal with the city on the Commodore Hotel property. Stern objected that the seventy-story glass tower design proposed for the skyscraper would perpetrate an architectural rape of the neighborhood. He lobbied for a limestone facade more compatible with surrounding buildings. He further insisted on limiting Trump Tower's height to fifty-eight stories. Ironically, Fred Trump, Sr., also objected to his son's design. The fact that Donald allowed his architect to draw in all those fancy (and costly) corners confirmed the old man's opinion that he just could not do anything right.

"We've been putting up buildings with four sides all over Queens and Brooklyn," Fred fumed, "and here you're planning to build one with twenty-eight sides in Manhattan."

"It's important," Donald shot back. "These are luxury condominiums and the building is designed so that every apartment has two different views over the city."

In early June 1979 Donald invited the influential *New York Times* architecture critic Ada Louise Huxtable, who harbored a well-documented distaste for skyscrapers, to inspect his design for Trump Tower. The gambit worked. The following month, Huxtable headlined her Sunday Arts and Leisure section column A NEW YORK BLOCKBUSTER OF SUPERIOR DESIGN. Though Huxtable launched into a predictable diatribe about zoning law loopholes that allowed developers to erect such monolithic structures, she praised Trump Tower on its own merits. "A great deal of care has been lavished on its design," she noted. "It is undeniably a handsome structure."

Donald later claimed that Huxtable's praise "probably did more for my zoning than any single thing I ever said or did." In October 1979 the City Planning Commission approved the zoning for Trump Tower. The commission later granted the project a FAR of 21, just a smidgen below the maximum of 21.6. Donald later maintained that the city "gave me the equivalent of a sixty-eight story building." But according to official documents filed with city, Trump Tower was only fifty-eight, not sixty-eight, stories high. To lend credence to his statements, Donald simply renumbered the floors. There was another motive at play in Donald's renumbering scheme besides simple machismo. The higher the building, the more he could charge for the upper floors.

But even at fifty-eight stories Trump Tower was Donald's biggest building to date. Some would say it was also his best ever. With an estimated budget of almost $200 million, it cost nearly three times what the Commodore / Grand Hyatt project cost, and it would take over two years to build. Donald got the money for Trump Tower from the Chase Manhattan Bank in October 1979 following his zoning victory. He hired HRH Construction, the company with the contract on the Commodore / Grand Hyatt deal, to build the building. Donald expected Ivana to contribute to the success of Trump Tower just as she was doing with the Grand Hyatt project. And as in the past, Ivana was more than willing to comply with her husband's wishes. But by now she had her own expectations about what he should do for her.

"Galanos—I just ordered eight pieces from him," Ivana told an interviewer in the spring of 1979. "Then I like Valentino and Chloé for evening, and, for after ski, Kamali. But I don't like Saint Laurent. For shoes, Charles Jourdan. They make a fortune off me."

Ivana still spoke in a Czech accent thickened with too many *v*'s and *z*'s, but she came off sounding like a cross between shoe-hoarding Filipino first lady Imelda Marcos and New York hotel maven Leona Helmsley, later dubbed the Queen of Mean for her pettiness and tax evasion schemes. In the otherwise auspicious summer following their second wedding anniversary, as The Donald's ambitious bid to take Manhattan bore its first financial fruit, Ivana insisted on getting a fair share of her husband's highly publicized success.

On July 24, 1979, the Trumps signed a contract that voided and replaced their 1977 prenuptial contract. Once again Donald was represented by Roy Cohn, and Ivana was represented by Cohn-recommended attorney Larry Levner. The second nuptial contract improved Ivana's financial security, but it did not come close to giving her an equal or even fairly proportionate share in her "partnership" with Donald. Donald's alimony payments in the event of separation or divorce were increased from the $20,000 to $30,000 range to $75,000 for the first ten years and to $100,000 a year thereafter. He also agreed to pay an additional $30,000 a year in child support for each of their offspring. In return, Ivana made several key concessions. She agreed to waive her claims to all other property owned by her husband and her legal right to take advantage of any future changes in the New York divorce and marital property statutes.

The Trumps' second nuptial contract happened to coincide with a far more disquieting event in Donald's thirty-three-year-old life: the return of his alcoholic older brother, Fred Trump, Jr. After a few dispiriting years as a pilot for TWA, Freddy had divorced wife Linda and had tried to cool out by running charter boats off the Florida coast. But he started drinking heavily again. Family friends finally stepped in and sobered him up. In the spring of 1979 Freddy, then age forty, moved back into the Trump mansion in Jamaica Estates, and went to work for his father as a lowly maintenance crew supervisor. He soon resumed his drinking. One day Fred, Sr., came home and found a closet stuffed with upwards of forty empty vodka bottles; the old man flew into a terrible rage, lambasting his namesake son for disgracing the family by wasting his life.

By this time the Trumps had already concocted an authorized mythology of Freddy's tragic deterioration. They blamed his drinking problems on a "bad marriage." But privately the other men in the family blamed Freddy's allegedly innate weakness of character for his failure to achieve what they unquestioningly accepted as the measure of success in life, making big money and a big splash in the real estate business. Yet beneath his swashbuckling public persona, Donald harbored a gnawing shame about his contribution to Freddy's problems and a nagging doubt about his own self-worth.

About the same time that Freddy returned to the family home, Donald decided to embark on a bold new venture in the Atlantic City gaming industry. Donald had first become keen on the profit potential of casino gambling back in 1975 after reading that Hilton's 2 hotels in Las Vegas accounted for nearly 40 percent of the net generated by all 150 hotels in the Hilton chain. In 1976 New Jersey had passed a law authorizing casino gambling in Atlantic City. When promoter James Crosby opened Atlantic City's first casino under the banner of Resorts International, customers stood in around-the-block lines for hours just to play the slot machines. But Crosby's initial success attracted a wave of speculators, who promptly drove local real estate prices through the roof. Donald, preoccupied with promoting the Penn Central properties in New York, decided to remain on the sidelines until the speculators further thinned themselves out.

Then, in the winter of 1980, he took a second look at Atlantic City. It was prompted by a call from a local architect named Alan Lapidus who had promised to scout potential casino sites for him. Lapidus said that a prime two-and-a-half-acre site on the Boardwalk next door to the Atlantic City Convention Center might become available. Not too surprisingly, the Atlantic City site Donald coveted was also mired in difficulties. The stampede of local speculators had fragmented the ownership of the location into a broken mirror of separate parcels, and many of these were entangled in legal disputes over purchase options, liens, and titles.

By the early summer of 1980, however, a newly formed real estate partnership operating as SSG Enterprises assembled and acquired what became one of the three largest contiguous portions of the site. SSG was named after its three principals, two of whom had rather suspicious backgrounds. One was Daniel J. Sullivan, a burly and broad-shouldered labor consultant who had been a dissident labor union organizer and later an informant for the FBI on alleged mob influences in the teamsters' union. Sullivan had been arrested for offenses ranging from impersonating a police officer to passing bad checks and attempted gun possession. According to Sullivan, he and Donald had first met back in 1979, when Sullivan was called in to settle a labor dispute on the Grand Hyatt job site.

One of Sullivan's partners in the SSG syndicate had a far more nefarious reputation. His name was Kenneth Shapiro, and he was the son of a former teamsters' union official. Shapiro controlled a company called Cleveland Wrecking, which had done the demolition work on the Commodore Hotel / Grand Hyatt site in New York. According to organized crime investigators, Shapiro was acting as the secret banker for investments by Philadelphia mob boss Nicky Scarfo. Shapiro was later named as an unindicted co-conspirator in bribery charges leveled against Atlantic City Mayor Michael Matthews, who was accused of accepted cash donations in return for favors to the mob; those contributions were allegedly funneled through Shapiro. Matthews was eventually convicted, ousted from office through a recall, and sent to prison.

In July 1980 Donald gained his first foothold in Atlantic City through a complicated deal to acquire the SSG leases. Here again his father played a key role behind the scenes. The deal with SSG required Donald to make an initial payment of about $1.5 million. At the time, however, he had yet to complete his first big real estate deal in New York. He got the money from the same line of credit at the Chase Manhattan Bank that his father had set up to fund his Grand Hyatt cost overruns. Fred, Sr., showed up in Atlantic City to cosign the documents attendant to the SSG deal. Though the old man had warned that casino gambling was a business in which the Trump family had no expertise, Donald would not listen.

"You've got to do something to keep life interesting," he told a friend, "while you're waiting to die."

Meanwhile, back in New York City Donald was in a hurry to tear down Bonwit's building to make way for Trump Tower. He intended to ask the city to grant a Section 421-A abatement, which provided a generous tax exemption for developers of residential projects on "underutilized land." The exemption started at 100 percent and decreased by 20 percent every two years over a ten-year period. If the Bonwit site for Trump Tower were declared "underutilized," Donald would enjoy a $40 million tax savings.

The covert phase of the Bonwit demolition got under way in December 1979, four months before the city issued an official demolition permit. The work was supervised by a small-time contractor named William Kaszycki, who recruited a brigade of illegal nonunion laborers from Poland with the promise of free transportation to the United States, free housing, and a wage of $4 to $6 an hour. Kaszycki later testified that Donald offered to pay him $750,000 for demolishing the Bonwit site with a $25,000 bonus for finishing the job ahead of schedule. Kaszycki ordered the Poles to sneak into Bonwit's at night and go directly to the top floors. At the time the stores on the lower floors were still open, and the electricity and water were still on, making the job both extremely difficult and extremely dangerous.

Even so, Bonwit's demolition proceeded surreptitiously for more than two months. Then, in March 1980, some forty members of Housewreckers Local 95 joined the work force. The housewreckers' local threatened to stop work unless Kaszycki came up with his required contributions to the union pension fund. According to a legal complaint filed by the union, Donald gave Kaszycki the money for his pension fund contribution on behalf of the union workers but did not supply a pension fund contribution to cover the Polish brigade. To make matters worse, Kaszycki had yet to pay the Poles their promised wages. A large faction of the brigade decided to mutiny.

According to labor consultant Dan Sullivan on July 27, 1980, Donald telephoned Sullivan, the co-owner of the future casino site he was leasing in Atlantic City. Donald explained that he was facing a September 1 "tax deadline" and needed to have the Bonwit demolition work completed as soon as possible. "I told him he was nuts," Sullivan testified in court a decade later. "I warned Trump that employing illegal aliens would jeopardize his attempts to win a casino license in New Jersey." Despite the warning, Sullivan agreed to see what he could do. From late July through late August 1980 he and Donald were allegedly "in constant contact" about the labor disputes at the Bonwit site. The demolition work was completed prior to the September 1 deadline. But most of the Polish workers were laid off, and many of them were never paid, a fact that came back to haunt their employer.

With the demolition of the Bonwit site completed, Donald immediately focused on securing a $40 million tax abatement for Trump Tower. To his dismay, he found that the Koch administration was not nearly as obliging as the old Beame regime. According to Koch's interpretation, the 421-A program was designed to boost flagging real estate development in "marginal neighborhoods"; it required that the developer replace a "functionally obsolete" building with a new structure. Thanks to the demolition job performed by the nonunion Polish workers and their union co-workers, the Bonwit Teller Building was now a shambles. But as Koch archly observed, the location at Fifth Avenue and Fifty-sixth Street in the heart of the city's luxury retail section was hardly a "marginal neighborhood."

Donald resorted to the clubhouse pressure politics that had worked so well in the past. He called his pal Andrew Stein, who was then the Manhattan borough president. Stein arranged a meeting with Anthony Gliedman, the commissioner of the city's Housing Preservation and

Development agency. But Gliedman did not succumb to the behind-the-scenes lobbying effort. On March 20, 1981, he denied Donald's application for a 421-A tax abatement. That evening, according to Gliedman, Donald called to deliver a thinly veiled threat: "Tony, I don't know if it's still possible for you to change your decision or not, but I want you to know that I am a very rich and powerful person in this town and there is a reason I got that way. I will never forget what you did."

After unsuccessfully attempting to pressure Koch directly, Donald decided to sue for the tax abatement. He also sued the city and Gliedman personally for $10 million in damages. Over the next three years the tax abatement case was heard by progressively higher appellate courts. Donald won round after round, only to be told by the appellate courts that he had to resue the city to get his tax break. Finally, on July 5, 1984, the Court of Appeals, the state's highest court, ruled in his favor. Donald later dropped his damage suit against Gliedman and offered him a job in the Trump Organization, which Gliedman gladly accepted. But the fight over Trump Tower's tax abatement proved to be the beginning of a long, simmering feud between Donald and Mayor Koch. The animosity between the two men eventually escalated into a tragicomic war, whose fallout proved disastrous for both protagonists.

In the interim Donald suffered his first major public relations fiasco because of his haste in demolishing the Bonwit site. The entrance to the building was framed by grillwork made of Benedict nickel in interlocking geometric designs measuring twenty feet high and thirty feet long. Between the eighth and ninth floors of the building, there were two fifteen-foot-high art deco limestone sculptures of partially nude female figures. Donald had promised to donate the grillwork and the friezes, whose value was estimated by art dealers at hundreds of thousands of dollars, to the Metropolitan Museum of Art. But he found out it would take up to two weeks to dismantle the art. On his orders, the demolition workers cut up the grillwork with acetylene torches. Then they jackhammered the friezes, dislodged them with crowbars, and pushed the remains inside the building, where they fell to the floor and shattered in a million pieces.

The destruction of the Bonwit artwork sparked a furor in the New York art world. Donald's critics charged that preserving the pieces would have cost only $32,000, far less than their estimated worth. At first Donald responded to media inquiries through a mysterious spokesman named "John Baron." He later admitted that "John Baron" was a "pen name" frequently used by him and other Trump Organization executives when trying to maintain anonymity. According to Donald / "John Baron," the additional time spent on removing the pieces intact would have cost him an extra $150,000 in real estate taxes, $250,000 in extra interest charges, and up to $200,000 in lost revenues because of a delayed building opening. An editorial in the *New York Times* branded Donald's action as the "aesthetic vandalism" of an "unenlightened developer."

But once again Donald got the last laugh. The destruction of the Bonwit artwork may have generated plenty of adverse publicity, but he claimed that it also generated advance apartment sales while Trump Tower was still a rendering on the drawing boards. He boasted that King Khalid of Saudi Arabia wanted to buy an entire floor for $11 million and that actress Sophia Loren was interested in buying a single apartment for $1.8 million. According to Donald, his future tenants would be paying "the highest prices ever paid by man.

"Trump Tower will be the greatest building in New York," he proclaimed. "There will never be another skyscraper built like it. Because of me, they've changed the midtown zoning. And it's kind of sad because there is nothing I can do that will be greater after this."

Or so it briefly seemed.

On September 5, 1980, Donald J. Trump celebrated the opening of the Grand Hyatt. It was, at least so far, his finest hour. The decaying old facade of the Commodore Hotel had been transformed into a dazzling icon of the brave new world to come, a shimmering mountain of gray mirror glass rising thirty four stories. On the formerly seedy Forty-second Street level, silver chrome-covered columns framed a chrome-corniced main entrance of revolving doors. Inside, there was a breathtaking pink marble-floored lobby trimmed with gold railings, brass pillars, an enormous brass suspension sculpture echoing the gurgling of a four-tiered interior waterfall, and a restaurant called Trumpet's.

All the major players in Donald's life came out to cheer his triumph. His old man was there, his mother, his brothers and sisters, Ivana, Roy Cohn, Governor Hugh Carey, Mayor Ed Koch, former Mayor

Abe Beame, former Deputy Mayor Stanley Friedman, Victor Palmieri, Bunny and Sandy Lindenbaum, Louise Sunshine, and, of course,
the architect Der Scutt. But it was Donald, the true artist of the deal,
who stole the show. "I really started a renaissance here with the Grand
Hyatt," Donald crowed. "People weren't working. They all left New
York City. Now they're coming back, they're all coming back."

Timing, of course, is everything, especially in the real estate business. During the twenty-six months it took to construct the Grand
Hyatt, New York City's economy commenced a dramatic comeback
that more than compensated for Trump's egregious cost overruns.
Conventions came to town in record numbers. Between 1978 and
1980 hotel occupancy soared to 85 percent, a full ten points above
the standard break-even occupancy level. Donald had originally
expected to charge $47 a night for lodging at the Grand Hyatt. Now
he could charge more than $100 a night. Three more new hotels
were nearing completion, including the soon-to-be-more-illustrious
Helmsley Palace on Fifty-first Street. But Donald had a singular
opportunity to exploit the city's resurgence as the first of the new
kids on the block.

During the opening months of 1981 Donald launched a campaign
to expand his Manhattan real estate empire. On February 10 he
formed a partnership with his brother Robert and longtime aide Louise
Sunshine to develop the corner of Third Avenue and Sixty-first Street
into a thirty-nine-story luxury residential cooperative to be called
Trump Plaza. In the spring Sunshine learned that the thirty-nine-
story Barbizon Plaza Hotel, on Central Park South and an adjacent
fourteen-story rent-controlled apartment building were up for sale.
Donald bought both properties from a syndicate of wealthy investors
for a bargain-basement price reportedly in the range of $13 million.

He soon discovered that he had bought himself a landlord's nightmare on Central Park South. Donald had planned to convert the
apartment building next door to the Barbizon Plaza into a luxury
condominium. But before he could proceed with the plan, the tenants had to move out. Some of them, such as designer Arnold Scaasi,
who created fashions that Ivana favored, were millionaires. Most of
the tenants, however, were middle-income people and retirees, living
on $900 a month Social Security payments. Led by resident stock-
broker John C. Moore III, the tenants commenced a five-year legal

battle to keep their apartments. Donald retaliated with a vengeance, intent on showing he was a "killer" in his old man's image.

"Basically Trump planned to let the services deteriorate," Moore recalled. "The water was off. The steam pipes were about to burst. The elevator was out for extended periods of time. Indeed, he said to me at lunch one day that if didn't get his way, he would leave this building a rotten, blackened hulk to mar the landscape of New York to show how he felt about rent stabilization."

On September 18, 1981, just as Donald seemed bound to win every battle on every front, he suffered a grievous loss. That night his older brother, Fred C. Trump, Jr., died of a massive heart attack. Freddy was survived by his ex-wife, Linda, who still lived in a Trump-owned apartment building near Jamaica Estates, his daughter, Maxey, and his son, Fred C. Trump III. Freddy left his heirs an estate valued at slightly more than $2 million; it consisted mostly of interests in his father's apartment projects.

"Our family environment, the competitiveness, was a negative for Fred," Donald told an interviewer from *Playboy* magazine years later. "I was very close to him and it was very sad when he died . . . toughest situation I've had . . . . But his death affected everything that has come after it. . . . I think that I never really gave him thanks for it. He was the first Trump boy out there, and I subconsciously watched his moves."

Donald claimed that Freddy's tragic life and death had taught him an important lesson. "I saw people taking advantage of Fred," he told *Playboy*, "and the lesson I learned was always to keep my guard up 100 percent, whereas he didn't. He didn't feel that there was really a reason for that, which is a fatal mistake in life." At another point Donald stated the lesson he had learned from his older brother more simply and in terms that echoed their old man's dictums: "Freddy just wasn't a killer."

chapter five
TRUMP TOWERS

■ IVANA TRUMP MARCHED into her husband's second-floor office in the Crown Building directly across Fifth Avenue from the Trump Tower construction site to deliver an ultimatum. It was the early spring of 1982, and she was pregnant with the couple's second child, a girl who was to be named Ivanka after her mother. Ivana had recently gone to see the Broadway play *Evita*. According to The Donald, the story of the power-hungry Argentinian leader Evita Perón had inflamed her own ambitions. True or not, Ivana had come to the Trump Organization's executive headquarters to make a very specific demand.

"I do wish to be promoted to vice-president," she declared.

The Donald assured her that would be no problem. Conferring vice-presidential "promotions," which cost him nothing in monetary terms, had become one of his favorite motivational ploys. In the past couple of years his younger brother, Robert Trump, who had quit his real estate finance job at Shearson Loeb Rhodes to join the Trump Organization just as Donald was expanding into Atlantic City, and several other key employees had been given vice-presidential titles.

Ivana felt she deserved to be recognized as an equal of any and all top-ranking Trump Organization executives. She was not about to settle for anything less than they had received. Nor was she satisfied with The Donald's lip service to her demand. She insisted that he circulate a memo to the staff officially announcing her "promotion."

"It is important that everybody knows I am a vice-president," she informed her husband.

In fact, Ivana was playing an even more active role on the Trump Tower project than she had played on the Grand Hyatt. She designed uniforms for the doormen complete with beehive-shaped Beefeaters' hats. She helped set up the model units used to sell apartments. She even flew to Italy to select the dramatic (and expensive) pink-hued breccia pernice marble to be used in the building's six-story public atrium. Ivana later boasted of excavating over half a mountain until she got the slabs she wanted. When critics suggested that the breccia pernice marble might be too flashy for sophisticated Fifth Avenue, she dismissed them with a self-righteous screech: "What do they prefer—the cheap white travertine [marble] that is used in banks? It is too cold, too common. Donald and I are more daring than that."

But Ivana's dual role as boss woman and boss's wife put her in constant conflict with her supposed peers within the Trump Organization hierarchy. As at the Grand Hyatt, she conducted painstakingly detailed inspections of the Trump Tower job site and forcefully advocated changes whenever she saw fit. Many of the full-time paid professionals on the project, especially the women, Louise Sunshine and construction manager Barbara Res, resented Ivana's alleged interference. On the surface, everyone maintained a cordial decorum. But inside, jealousies simmered. And much, if not all, of the internal conflict was deliberately provoked by The Donald. He appeared to take perverse delight in the complaints and criticisms his female subordinates lodged against Ivana behind closed office doors, as if such talk helped him keep his wife in her place.

In fact, as Ivana's precarious position in the pecking order indicated, the Trump Organization bore a striking resemblance to the archetypal social organization of the decade, the dysfunctional family. While Fred Trump, Sr., played a key behind-the-scenes role as patriarch of the family purse, Robert Trump became Donald's corporate alter ego and designated whipping boy. The Trump brothers made a most unlikely pair. As more than one insider observed, were it not for their striking physical resemblance (six feet tall, bushy eyebrows, blondish hair), one would never have thought they were related. Where Donald was obsessive and irascible, Robert was easygoing and affable. A graduate of Boston University, he drove an old car owned by one of his father's companies and lived in Donald's old bachelor apartment until he married a socially ambitious divorcée named Blaine

Beard; the couple subsequently moved into an apartment Donald let them use in a Trump apartment building on Third Avenue.

Nothing Robert did ever seemed to be good enough for Donald. Time and again Donald would burst into an ongoing business meeting, take Robert to task on some point about which he himself was ill informed, then cuss out his younger brother in front of other Trump Organization executives and visiting outsiders. Many of these internecine attacks would occur at the regular Friday morning meetings Robert attended to discuss the development of the West Side yards. One bone of contention concerned a long-studied proposal to move the West Side Highway inland to provide pedestrians with better access to the Hudson River. "Robert, you're a fucking moron," Donald screamed. "That's the stupidest fucking idea I've ever heard." He did not give Robert a chance to share the news that the proposal had already gained wide support from community groups and the city as well as from the Trump Organization staff.

While disdaining his brother, Donald looked to a trio of nonfamily males for business counsel. His chief financial adviser was Harvey Freeman, a teddy-bearish attorney who had once advised embattled real estate developer Arthur Cohen. Donald's "personal stock-broker" was Alan C. ("Ace") Greenberg, a fast-talking Oklahoma-born investment banker who was chairman of Bear Stearns. But his most trusted adviser, with the exception of the now mysteriously ailing Roy Cohn, was attorney Gerald Schrager of Dreyer & Traub. An unusually soft-spoken but somewhat eccentric health enthusiast whose office at various times sported an exercise bike and a basketball hoop, Schrager was as much a businessman as a lawyer. His greatest services to Donald included talking him out of such potentially disastrous deals as a plan to build a luxury apartment building surrounded by a medieval-style moat.

"Any success Donald enjoyed was because of Jerry Schrager," one insider later claimed. "Any mistakes he made were made because he ignored Jerry's advice."

No one in the Trump Organization, family or nonfamily, was immune from Donald's mood swings and vituperative personal assaults. It was as if he were constantly testing all his associates to see how they could handle the pressure. While Trump Tower was still on the drawing boards, for example, he gave prospective tenants permission to make extensive changes in the design of their apartment units, then ordered Barbara Res or real estate marketing executive Blanche Sprague to execute the changes without causing delays. The experience left Res with an ulcer and eventually prompted at least one female staffer to seek psychiatric counseling concerning her relationship with the boss. "You were either the greatest person who ever lived or the worst piece of shit on earth," one Trump Organization executive observed. "With Donald there was no middle ground."

Meanwhile, the dubious legacy of Donald's father haunted the erection of Trump Tower from bottom to top. Trump Tower was a so-called fast-track building, which meant the structure was still being designed even as it was being built. The architects were on the job site every day. As in the demolition of the Bonwit Teller building, the pace was intense, nerve-racking, debilitating, and dangerous. At any one time the work force on the job site numbered more than two hundred strong. Two people were killed in the course of construction; a third narrowly escaped losing his life in a flash fire.

The key material in the construction of Trump Tower was concrete, which was especially suited to the construction of a fast-track building. Besides being more rigid than steel, concrete was far less expensive to redesign on the job site since it did not have to be sent to a steel mill for recasting. Back in the 1960s Fred Trump, Sr., had pioneered the use of reinforced concrete in building the flooring for Trump Village. Donald went a giant step farther. In addition to using reinforced concrete for the floors of Trump Tower, he used reinforced concrete for the superstructure instead of the conventional steel beams used in most skyscrapers. Trump Tower was, in fact, the tallest reinforced concrete structure ever built up to that time.

As in Fred Sr.'s heyday, working with concrete in New York City entailed working with the mob. Various federal investigations and voluminous testimony in the 1992 murder trial of Gambino crime family boss John Gotti confirmed that mob-connected unions and contractors maintained a monopoly over the $500-million-a-year local concrete industry. The mob-controlled cartel or "club" allegedly demanded payoffs equal to 2 percent of the gross value of all concrete contracts in the city. Among the cartel's biggest jobs besides Trump Tower were the Starrett City housing project in which the

Trump family had a partnership interest, the Helmsley Palace Hotel, the Harley Hotel, 101 Park Avenue, and the IBM Building.

But working with the mob presented no more of a problem for Donald than promoting Ivana to the post of vice-president in the Trump Organization. While some developers, such as Sam LeFrak, publicly decried mob influence over the industry, Donald seemed more than content to cooperate. The structural work on Trump Tower was done by the Dic-Underhill joint venture, which had subcontracted work on Trump Village back in the early sixties; the concrete itself was supplied by Transit Mix, a firm controlled by hotel magnate Bif Halloran that also allegedly belonged to the cartel. Donald's principal go-betweens were his attorney, Roy Cohn, who represented members of several organized crime families, and his father, Fred Trump, Sr., who reportedly reviewed construction plans with one mob-related contractor on the Trump Tower job.

Hardly content to defer to his elders, Donald could not resist doing some of the dirty work himself, for as one top-ranking employee attested, he seemed to have a "fatal attraction to sleaze." Donald established a particularly close working relationship with John Cody, president of Teamsters Local 282. Cody, a bald and barrel-chested hustler in his early sixties, was subsequently convicted and sent to prison on federal racketeering charges. Drivers belonging to Cody's union were responsible for delivering to the Trump Tower job site virtually all the construction materials, including the concrete. Since the concrete had to arrive at precisely timed intervals or it would spoil, delays or work stoppages could be devastatingly costly.

Cody allegedly promised Donald that Trump Tower would not suffer any form of labor unrest during the construction process. Indeed, he even ensured that the building's top floors were completed without disruption or delays amid a citywide strike during the summer of 1982. In return, Donald allegedly promised Cody an apartment in Trump Tower. He wound up with much more than that. Cody called on Donald to arrange for a mysterious and mercurial lady friend named Verina Hixon, who had no visible means of financial support, to purchase a suite of Trump Tower apartments worth an estimated $10 million with Trump-arranged bank mortgages.

The Trump-Cody-Hixon triangle became even more curious when Trump Tower opened for occupancy. During the ill-fated appeal of his racketeering convictions, Cody claimed he was unable to pay some $70,000 in fines levied against him. But he somehow managed to lend Hixon $500,000 drawn from a Swiss bank account for interior alterations on her apartments. The work included construction of the only swimming pool in Trump Tower. In 1984, following the exhaustion of Cody's appeals and his incarceration in a federal penitentiary, Donald sued Hixon for allegedly failing to reimburse him for $250,000 worth of work on her apartments. In 1985 Donald agreed to settle his lawsuit with Hixon. Instead of collecting the money she allegedly owed him, Donald paid Hixon $500,000. Six years later, in the wake of Donald's own highly publicized financial demise, Hixon's apartments were repossessed by the banks.

While his construction crew raced to top off the upper floors of Trump Tower, Donald redirected his own energies toward the creation of a gaming empire in Atlantic City. On March 15, 1982, he appeared in a jam-packed Trenton, New Jersey, hearing room where the state Casino Control Commission had convened to rule on Donald and Robert Trump's applications for gaming licenses. Donald knew that all his chips were on the line. But he also knew that Atlantic City needed Donald Trump even more than he needed the challenge of a bold new deal.

"I am trying to give an honest statement of Atlantic City, and I don't want to talk out of turn," Donald told the commissioners. "People do not think of Atlantic City as being the kind of place I think it can be. Atlantic City needs some quality. It needs some pizzazz. It needs something that's going to bring people, and right now it really has certain elements, but it doesn't have the right combination of elements. We feel our facility will be the finest in Atlantic City."

Any suspense about how the commission would rule on Donald and Robert's license application was merely imaginary. The deal had already been done behind the scenes over a year before the formal public hearing. Back in February 1981 Donald, Robert, and attorney Nick Ribis had met with the New Jersey attorney general and the director of the state's Division of Gaming Enforcement. When the

DGE director allowed that the licensing investigation might take up to a year, Donald had laid down an ultimatum: "Well, if it takes a year, I'm out of here."

The watchdogs of New Jersey's gaming industry went overboard to meet the Trump timetable. On October 16, 1981, barely five and a half months after Donald formally filed his application for a casino license, the DGE issued a telephone book-thick report that pronounced him qualified for licenses. The DGE report included the transcript of an unintentionally revealing interview with the applicant. Among the few tough questions were those concerning the character of the SSG partners from whom Donald had leased the site for his first casino. At one point he was shown a newspaper article from the summer of 1980 in which labor consultant Dan Sullivan claimed that Donald was an "old friend" he knew from Manhattan, an oblique reference to their contacts during the Polish workers' dispute at the Bonwit demolition site.

"I absolutely do not know him from Manhattan," Donald insisted, claiming he had met Sullivan in Atlantic City. Asked if he had discussed any labor disputes with Sullivan during the SSG negotiations, Donald replied, "I don't believe so." Asked if he had any knowledge of Sullivan's labor background, Donald said, "None whatsoever really."

Donald's disingenuous statements about Sullivan appeared to be part of a pattern of deception designed to sanitize the unsavoriness of his past business associations. The New Jersey gaming license application form asked applicants if they had ever been the subject of a criminal investigation. Although the applicants' answers remained confidential, there were indications that Donald did not respond with the whole truth. Back in 1979 he had been the subject of a criminal investigation by the U.S. attorney in Brooklyn regarding his relationship with the Penn Central shareholders' attorney David Berger. That fact evidently did not become known to state gaming authorities until they were apprised of the criminal probe by an investigative reporter in 1992, nearly a decade after Donald had submitted his application.

The Casino Control Commission was proud of its reputation for strict by-the-book adherence to all gaming laws. Judged by its treatment of Donald J. Trump, however, the commission merely confirmed the charges of critics who contended that it was interested only in creating the appearance of strict regulation. If a common blackjack dealer or cocktail waitress lied or omitted substantive infor-mation on an application form, he or she would be barred from Atlantic City. Donald was accepted with open arms. The Casino Con-trol Commission approved the Trumps' application in record time. The entire hearing on March 15, 1982, took less than two hours. Donald was on the witness stand for only seventeen minutes.

The only cloud that hung over the Trumps' application and the site of the casino Donald intended to call Trump Plaza was the SSG matter. Several months later after the hearing, the commissioners ordered the Trumps to buy out their SSG landlords, as they subse-quently did for a reported $8 million.

In May 1982, just six weeks after winning his casino license, Don-ald showed he had more nifty tricks up his sleeve. That month he broke ground for the construction of Trump Plaza, a project he esti-mated would cost $220 million. When he testified at the hearing in Trenton, Donald had claimed that he his financing was in place. But according to former construction manager Tom Pippett, every bank Donald had approached summarily refused to lend him money to build his casino. And according to the DGE's reports, his personal checking account showed an average monthly balance of $384,000, while his personal savings account showed an average balance of only $5,000.

Donald's chief source of ready cash appeared to be a $35 million unsecured line of credit from the Chase Manhattan Bank. In the fall of 1981 the outstanding balance was about $15 million. Donald had drawn on the Chase credit line to provide $28.5 million in funding for the Grand Hyatt and, later, $8.9 million for his Atlantic City proj-ect. He had subsequently repaid Chase with loans from his father and his father's companies totaling over $8.5 million. The DGE report exposed the dirty little secret behind Donald's seemingly phenome-nal success: He was still heavily dependent on the old man's money—and the well was starting to run dry.

Then, just as Donald appeared to be on the verge of crapping out in Atlantic City, he got a call from Michael Rose, the president of Holiday Inns. Harrah's, the hotel chain's casino-owning subsidiary, had recently built a gambling hall in the relatively remote marina district of Atlantic City. Donald proposed that Holiday Inns enter a fifty-fifty partnership to develop the Trump Plaza site on the Board-

walk. Rose tentatively agreed to contribute $50 million toward con-
struction and reimburse the Trumps for $22 million in expenses.
Donald would supervise construction, but Harrah's would manage
and operate the casino hotel facility, an area of expertise that Donald
lacked. The only major hurdle that remained was winning approval
of the Holiday Inns' board of directors. Rose said that he would
schedule a meeting of the board in Atlantic City in June so the directors could inspect the project site firsthand.

Donald put on a show for the Holiday Inns directors the likes of
which none had ever seen. On the day the directors arrived to inspect
their proposed investment, the Trump Plaza site hummed with frenetic activity. Crews of construction workers plowed about the partially excavated pit with earth movers and lifting cranes. Only one of
the obviously impressed Holiday Inns directors happened to notice
that there was no apparent method to this madness. "How come,"
the befuddled board member asked Donald, "that guy over there is
filling up that hole which he just dug?" Donald somehow managed
to double-talk the Holiday Inns director long enough to dispel his
skepticism. About 2:15 P.M. the Holiday Inns board called to inform
Donald it had voted to come in as his partner. It was another triumph
of the art of the spiel, one of the most important for Donald to date.
As construction manager Tom Pippett noted afterward, "Trump Plaza
was Donald's flagship in Atlantic City, much as Trump Tower was
the flagship in New York. It gave him the momentum to go forward
in Atlantic City."

But as Donald divided his time and attention between New York
and Atlantic City, he seemed to suffer a concomitant split in personality. "I liked Donald Trump very much when we first met," former
Harrah's executive John Allen remembered. "I was impressed by his
humility. We would go to a local greasy spoon to have lunch, and
everybody knew him. And regardless of their stature in life, Donald
would smile and be pleasant, shake hands, just be a great guy, ordinary and down-to-earth. And then, lo and behold, I just watched him
change right before my eyes."

Donald's change of character was not for the better. According to
Allen and other former insiders, his ever-increasing obsession with
matters involving the Trump name soon led to nasty quarrels with
his new Atlantic City partners. First, he insisted that Harrah's incor-

porate his name, which he claimed had intrinsic public relations value, into the logo of the casino hotel. The project officially became known as Harrah's at Trump Plaza. But that was not enough for Donald. He spent countless hours arguing in expletive-spiced language over the relative sizes of his name and Harrah's name as they appeared on everything from doorways down to stationery and complimentary matchbooks on which type sizes differed by a only a hundredth of an inch.

When not feuding with his partners, Donald seemed hell-bent on impressing them by detailing his patently duplicitous approach to the art of deal making. "Here's how I work," he informed John Allen one day while recounting his success in selling apartments in Trump Tower. "I call the society editor [of one of the New York tabloids] and tell them that Princess Di and Prince Charles are going to purchase an apartment in Trump Tower. And they, in turn, investigate the source, call Buckingham Palace. And the comment is 'No comment.' Which means that it appears to the public that Princess Di and Prince Charles are going to purchase an apartment in Trump Tower."

While the impetus for Donald's mood swings appeared to trace directly back to the oedipal battles of his youth, there was also another probable cause for his fits of distemper: drugs. On April 19, 1982, during the period between his license hearing before the Casino Control Commission and the groundbreaking on the Trump Plaza site in Atlantic City, Donald paid a visit to the midtown Manhattan office of Dr. Joseph Greenberg. According to the doctor's records, Donald had been recommended by his friend Charles Goldstein, an attorney involved in the Penn Central deals. The ostensible purpose of Donald's visit was to seek assistance in losing weight. He had gone to the right place. Dr. Greenberg was an endocrinologist who specialized in providing patients with drugs to control obesity.

Dr. Greenberg determined that Donald had a "metabolic imbalance," a kind of catchall diagnosis that opened the door to writing a prescription. But he was careful not to break the law. Having previously been investigated by the CBS television program "Sixty Minutes," he knew better than to dole out schedule II controlled substances such as amphetamines, whose illegal usage could subject both doctor and patient to severe penalties. Instead Dr. Greenberg prescribed a schedule IV controlled substance called Tenuate Dospan, which was described by the *Physicians' Desk Reference* as pharmacologically "similar to . . . amphetamines."

Donald was so delighted with the results that he started recommending Dr. Greenberg's treatments to his brother Robert, various friends, and celebrity acquaintances such as Diana Ross. The diet drugs, which he took in pill form, not only curbed his appetite but gave him a feeling of euphoria and unlimited energy. The medical literature warned that some potentially dangerous side effects could result from long-term usage; they included anxiety, insomnia, and delusions of grandeur. According to several Trump Organization insiders, Donald exhibited all these ominous symptoms of diet drug usage, and then some.

"The first thing I would do when I got to the office in the morning," recalled one former vice-president, "was to go see Norma Foerderer and ask her, 'Is this a Dr. Greenberg day?' If she said yes, I would do everything I could to stay out of Donald's way."

But staying out of Donald's way was more easily said than done. He was all over the place. On Valentine's Day 1983 he opened Trump Tower's atrium to the public for the first time. It was truly a monument to Mammon. The breccia pernice marble walls rose one hundred feet high from the breccia pernice marble floors, past an eighty-foot-high frond-garnished waterfall (which Trump claimed cost "almost" $2 million) and five decks of escalators covered with reflective glass. Forty-four luxury stores, including Asprey, Cartier, Buccellati, Harry Winston, and Charles Jourdan, occupied the six floors of retail space around the sides of the atrium. They sold such items as $75-a-pair baby shoes and $230,000 replicas of American bald eagles.

Trump Tower's atrium suddenly became a sociocultural happening. *New York Times* architecture critic Paul Goldberger praised the atrium as far superior to public spaces in such buildings as Olympic Tower, the Galleria, and Citicorp Center, allowing that it "may well be the most pleasant interior public space to be completed in New York in some years." Donald naturally waxed even more enthusiastic than anyone else. "*Vogue* is planning to do a cover, Merv Griffin is going to do a show from here," he boasted. "It's sort of what happened to Studio 54 except I hope it will last a little longer. The whole world is talking about this place."

Donald claimed that sales of Trump Tower apartments grossed $240 million. After subtracting construction costs of $190 million, that yielded a $50 million profit. Donald boasted that he personally pocketed $10 million in commissions on the condo sales. He also held 12 of the 263 units off the market as long-term investments. Though Donald's account of virtually every one of the deals that followed was to be exposed as self-servingly false, even his staunch critics had to admit that Trump Tower was his second—and greatest—home run.

"The enormous success of Trump Tower enabled Trump to introduce a brand name to a class of products that previously had no brand names, a textbook marketing strategy," *Fortune* magazine observed a few short years later, adding, "That name indisputably adds value." And just why was that so? The answer, according to *Fortune,* was that "There is undeniably a Trump mystique. Some people love him, others despise him, but everybody talks about him. He has become a cult hero for many people around the world who seem to regard this flamboyant billionaire as the most heartening example of the American dream come true since [Texas computer king] Ross Perot."

Donald's old man appeared to be almost equally impressed. Back when Trump Tower was being designed, Fred, Sr., had fumed about the extravagance of the twenty-eight-sided saw-toothed architecture, reminding his son that he'd done quite well building four-sided box structures in the outer boroughs. Now, at least when talking to the media, Fred spouted the same line he had used following the signing of the Grand Hyatt deal: "Donald is the smartest person I know. Everything he touches turns to gold."

That pronouncement, as it turned out, marked the beginning of Donald's fall from financial grace. On September 23, 1983, he called a press conference in the atrium of his brand-new building and, with the waterfall gurgling in the background, announced that he was buying himself a professional football team. He could not get, and probably couldn't have afforded, a $70 million franchise in the well-established National Football League (NFL). Instead Donald spent an estimated $9 million to purchase the New Jersey Generals, a franchise in the struggling new United States Football League (USFL), whose teams played in the spring rather than in the traditional fall season.

Donald later described his plunge into pro football as "a lark I could afford to take." That may have been one of the most unintentionally ironic understatements he ever made. The deal for the New Jersey Generals marked several firsts in Donald's career. It turned out to be his first big money-losing venture, as well as one of the first big blows to his credibility in business circles. Yet at the same time it provided a boost to his public image and name recognition beyond his wildest expectations.

In their spring 1983 debut season, the USFL team owners had collectively lost $30 million. Donald realized that what the USFL lacked—like Atlantic City—was pizzazz. He proceeded to give it some. Shortly after announcing his purchase of the New Jersey Generals, he gave a deliberately inflammatory interview to the *New York Times*. TRUMP WOULD LIKE TO TAKE ON NFL, blared the headline. Donald, who advocated moving the USFL schedule from the spring to the fall, cavalierly put the USFL's established competition on notice that he was one new owner who did not intend to remain in second place among professional football leagues for long. "In my opinion, some USFL teams could beat NFL teams," he boasted.

The New Jersey Generals already boasted one of the USFL's few truly outstanding players, former Heisman Trophy-winning runner Herschel Walker. In the fall of 1983 Donald launched a series of recruiting raids on the NFL that provided his team with six veterans from the USFL's rival league. On New Year's Eve he signed New York Giants all-pro linebacker Lawrence Taylor to a $3.2 million "futures contract." The Giants were ultimately forced to pay him $750,000 to buy back their rights to Taylor.

Donald's raids on the NFL touched off a blizzard of national publicity for the USFL and for him. He later observed that announcing a $70 million real estate deal might get four inches of play in the *New York Times;* his exploits in the USFL made headlines in the *Times* and in newspapers all over the nation. Much to the NFL's further chagrin, Donald started appearing during NFL network telecasts as a featured guest on half time shows. The handsome and outspoken

New York real estate developer was becoming the new media darling. And as his high-priced football players and anyone else could
see, he loved it.

Ivana Trump was not just along for the ride. On January 6, 1984,
Ivana gave birth to the couple's third child, a boy whom they christened Eric. But she was not content simply to play the role of socialite
hausfrau and mother. As if to attest to that fact, she resumed her
responsibilities at the Trump Plaza project in Atlantic City in record
time. "She delivered the baby on a Friday," recalled construction
manager Tom Pippett, "and returned to work the next Tuesday."

Ivana tackled Trump Plaza in Atlantic City in much the same way
she had tackled the Grand Hyatt and Trump Tower projects. Because
of the distance from the Trump Tower home at 800 Fifth Avenue in
Manhattan, she did not visit the job site quite as often as she visited
Trump Tower. But she definitely made her presence felt by assuming responsibility for the interior design of the facility. Determined
to create an aura of eye-catching elegance appropriate for a casino
hotel, she selected an orange and black color scheme of carpets, wall
coverings, and furnishings highlighted by expensive crystal chandeliers.

"I know what I like," Ivana later informed an interviewer. "There
is no wallpaper, no fabric, no lacquer, no carpet, no marble in any of
our buildings that didn't get my approval. Then, of course, I bring it
to my husband for his approval."

Predictably Ivana became embroiled in a series of internecine rival-
ries in Atlantic City that mirrored her conflicts with the Trump
Organization's female vice-presidents. The bosses of the construction
crews often bridled at her input, disdained her alleged poor taste,
and accused her of baiting them into shouting matches. Back in New
York, Ivana tried to give Trump Plaza on Third Avenue a look
remarkably similar to her husband's casino in Atlantic City. She decorated a sample hallway with gold and orange Ultrasuede wallpaper
and installed a carpet patterned with gold, red, and black geometric
squares. The effect made many of the apartment building's prospective tenants feel cross-eyed. "You couldn't tell where you were putting your foot," complained one of the salespeople. Donald felt the

repercussions right on the bottom line. According to one insider, he was unable to sell a single apartment in Trump Plaza for nearly four months. Finally he directed sales manager Blanche Sprague to contact designer Angelo Donghia and order new wallpaper.

Donald now tried to use his paid employees to give his wife a termination notice. "You call up Ivana and fire her," he ordered Blanche Sprague one day. When Sprague refused, he demanded that she call Ivana and "tell her she's no longer involved in design" at Trump Plaza. Ivana apparently never got the message, but after her decorative touches were removed, the apartments started selling. The condominium buyers included such luminaries as top-ranked tennis player Martina Navratilova, entertainment mogul Dick Clark, and celebrity TV broadcaster Phyllis George, the former Miss America who had wed Kentucky Governor John Y. Brown.

After her ill-fated experience at Trump Plaza, Ivana focused her attention on the New Jersey Generals. She designed new red, white, and blue uniforms for the cheerleaders and held a selection contest at which artist Andy Warhol and *Penthouse* publisher Bob Guccione presided as judges. She also laid down a strict policy of no dating between players and cheerleaders, a controversial dictate that did not enhance her popularity with either group. When a reporter suggested that if her husband were so interested in owning "quality" properties, he would have been better off buying the Dallas Cowboys, who were enjoying a media-made interregnum as "America's Team," Ivana rejected the notion as patently preposterous.

"Cowboys?" she exclaimed in naïve disbelief. "We don't want cowboys. Where can we go with cowboys?"

Ivana's efforts to participate in her husband's latest enterprise were tinged with a secretly lovelorn desperation. Donald later admitted that their marriage was already in the process of sad, gradual deterioration. According to several of her friends, Donald and Ivana did not have much of a sexual relationship after the very early part of their marriage. Donald was apparently the one who lost interest first. Ivana confided to female friends that Donald had difficulty achieving and maintaining an erection. "He's only interested in the oral sex," Ivana complained. By her account, Donald was not very adept at giving sexual pleasure to his spouse. One day Ivana arrived late for lunch at Le Cirque carrying a copy of a sexual manual entitled *The G*

Spot and Other Recent Discoveries about Human Sexuality by Alice K. Ladas, which describes how to massage a female clitoris to achieve orgasm. "I have to give this to The Donald," she told her luncheon companion. "He can never find the spots."

The Trumps inevitably expressed their sexual frustrations in financial terms. Shortly after Eric was born, Ivana asked Donald to revise their nuptial agreement, last updated in 1979. Another battle royal ensued. As in the past, Donald was represented by Roy Cohn; Ivana was represented by Cohn crony Larry Levner. The Trumps had recently purchased a weekend estate near Cohn's suburban retreat in Greenwich, Connecticut. Whenever Donald balked at her demands, Ivana would refuse to speak to him, pack up the kids, and go off to Connecticut. "I am in Greenwich," she would inform him by telephone, "and will stay here until this is resolved."

The major sticking point, not surprisingly, was the amount of money Donald would pay Ivana in the event of separation or divorce. Under the 1979 agreement she was guaranteed a relatively paltry $75,000 a year for ten years and $100,000 a year thereafter so long as she remained unmarried. Ivana thought that she deserved much more, and understandably so. Before the year was out, *Forbes* magazine calculated her husband's net worth to be $400 million. Like most of the other Trump myths later propagated by and through the national media, that unaudited estimate proved to be extremely generous. But in documents prepared during the couple's third round of nuptial contract negotiations, The Donald himself claimed to have assets worth "in excess of $300 million."

"I've done it all so fast," Donald exclaimed. "I wonder if I wouldn't have been better off spreading it out over a lifetime."

Twenty-twenty hindsight was to prove him right. According to most veteran real estate analysts, the Manhattan market tended to rise and fall in seven-year cycles. As his own most favored architect, Der Scutt, observed at the time, that meant that the city's astronomically high property values were due for a major fall by late 1985 or early 1986. But Donald failed to read the writing on the walls of the Manhattan real estate market. He tried to cash in on his newfound national name recognition in the wake of his pro football venture by announcing plans to build a state-of-the-art residential community called Trump Castle. It would consist of six towers, the largest of which would be sixty stories tall, topped with medieval turrets and surrounded by a moat with a high tech drawbridge.

The Trump Castle apartment project never got off the drawing board. Thanks in part to such recently completed buildings as Trump Tower, the demand for luxury high rises in Manhattan was almost satiated. Donald decided that the risks associated with Trump Castle outweighed the potential reward. "I've never been associated with anything that's a loser," he declared.

On May 14, 1984, Harrah's at Trump Plaza celebrated its grand opening. The new casino hotel was the fanciest gaming hall Atlantic City had ever seen. Auspiciously situated at the very center of the Boardwalk adjacent to the Atlantic City Convention Center, the thirty-story facility was a sparkling monolith of white concrete and dark mirrored glass tailor-made to accommodate high rollers. The Trump name was prominently displayed throughout. It appeared on decals marking the revolving doors, on banners draped above the gaming tables, and in his and her variations marking interior spaces that recalled the fiefdoms of a feudal manor. There was a gourmet restaurant called Ivana's that featured French nouvelle cuisine. The main cocktail lounge on the ground floor was named Trump's.

An estimated nine thousand people invaded Harrah's at Trump Plaza during the first day of operation. But both they and co-owner Donald Trump were in for a shock. Harrah's vice-president for finance Walter Haybert, who later joined the executive ranks at the Trump Taj Mahal, had attempted to introduce a new slot machine accounting system. That was a fatal mistake. The new accounting system failed amid what one gaming industry wag described as "a congress of oddities." All 734 slot machines had to be closed down under orders from the DGE. By early June, as Atlantic City's busiest season got under way, only 72 percent of the slot machines were back in operation. The revenue lost during this unanticipated downtime amounted to at least $5 million, but the public relations losses caused by the inconvenience to slot players were even more costly.

Less than two weeks after the badly bungled opening of Harrah's at Trump Plaza, Donald reached a compromise on the home front. On May 25, 1984, he and Ivana signed their third nuptial agreement. The new deal promised increased financial security for her and a new measure of protection for him. In the event of divorce or Donald's death, Ivana was to get $2.5 million in cash (compared with roughly $750,000 under the 1979 agreement) plus the couple's country estate in Greenwich. But the contract also stipulated that if Ivana walked out on Donald "without just cause or provocation," she would get only $250,000 a year and rent-free use of the Greenwich estate until she remarried or moved in with another man. As in the previous agreements, Ivana again promised not to take advantage of revisions in the New York family laws providing for equitable distribution of a couple's assets in the event of divorce.

The way Donald financed the legal work on nuptial agreement number three foreshadowed his next major business gambit. As in the past, Ivana paid her attorney, Larry Levner, whose fees amounted to roughly $13,000, out of her personal bank account. Donald gave Roy Cohn a diamond-studded Tiffany watch worth roughly the same amount in lieu of legal fees. But Donald sweetened the barter by promising his attorney a shot at far more lucrative legal work in the future: representing the USFL in a multibillion-dollar antitrust suit against the NFL.

Donald didn't let on that he was acting out of desperation. But his underlying motivations quickly became clear when the USFL concluded its second full season in June 1984. Fourteen of the USFL's eighteen teams reported combined losses of $76 million; the New Jersey Generals lost $5 million of the total, bringing the deficit on Donald's football venture to $14 million. When *Sports Illustrated* published a detailed accounting of the USFL's financial woes, Commissioner Chet Simmons candidly admitted that he did not see how the league could continue to withstand such staggering losses.

Donald knew that the situation was even worse than it appeared. Unbeknownst to the public and his fellow owners, he had attended a secret meeting with NFL Commissioner Pete Rozelle at the Pierre Hotel in New York City in March 1984. According to both men's accounts, Rozelle had suggested that the NFL might be willing to make a place for Donald and the New Jersey Generals if mutually acceptable terms could be negotiated. Donald listened but did not accept or reject Rozelle's offer. He later claimed that he was merely keeping all his options open. But in the weeks that followed, he failed to persuade either NBC or CBS to televise USFL games if the league moved to the fall. Donald kept the bad news to himself and proceeded to manipulate the media in accordance with his own newly formed secret agenda: an all-out legal war against the NFL.

On October 17, 1984, the USFL filed a $1.32 billion antitrust suit against the NFL in the U.S. District Court for the Southern District of New York. The next day Donald and newly appointed USFL attorney Roy Cohn, whose hiring he railroaded to approval, held a press conference to discuss the bill of particulars. Cohn accused the NFL of illegal monopolistic practice, charging that the USFL's rival had formed a "secret" committee to destroy the competition. Donald claimed that the NFL was "petrified" at the prospect of defending itself in court. He did not mention that at this point his only hope for recovering the millions he had lost on his football venture was by winning the lawsuit.

To the typical American consumer, the winter of 1985 might have seemed like a very bad time to go on a buying spree. Not to Donald J. Trump. The fact that the New York real estate market happened to be on the cusp of another recession only kindled his acquisitiveness. As he saw it, there were major bargains ripe for the taking. It was a perfect opportunity to employ the same formula that had helped make the Grand Hyatt such a smashing success: Buy low now, and hold on until the market improved.

But Donald was motivated by something other than classic economics. Emboldened by the wave of national publicity he had generated with his USFL venture, he was now even more convinced that attaching his name to a project instantly added value to it. But he himself knew the fleeting nature of such fame-driven enterprises. Part of the challenge for Donald, beyond seeing his name in lights again and again, was seeing what he could get away with, how long he could keep fooling all the people all the time.

As he and only a handful of top subordinates well knew, the myth of the Trump wealth was just that, a myth. *Forbes* might calculate that he had a net worth of $400 million. He might concede in his nuptial contract negotiations with Ivana that he had a net worth of at least $300 million. But those figures were based on extremely optimistic estimates of the prices his real estate assets might bring on the open market. In order to come anywhere close to realizing his claimed net worth, he would have to sell everything, a prospect he abhorred.

Even at this early stage of his empire building, Donald J. Trump was already in the throes of what proved to be a perpetual cash-flow crunch. Whatever income he generated was being consumed by the carrying costs of previously acquired real estate properties and by the hemorrhaging of his investment in the New Jersey Generals. The only way he could finance a buying spree was with "OPM"—other people's money—borrowed from banks and junk bond investors.

"It was all a shell game," recalled a former high-ranking Trump Organization executive. "We never had any unencumbered cash. We were always creating new partnerships and corporate entities to shift the money around. We were always robbing Peter to pay Paul."

Donald's lenders at major banks, such as Citicorp, Manufacturers Hanover, and Chase Manhattan, were, in effect, his partners and co-conspirators. So, too, were his friends at the investment firms of Bear Stearns and Merrill Lynch, who underwrote the billions in junk bond offerings he used to pay for his expansion into Atlantic City. These otherwise sober-minded institutional financiers were more than happy to fund Donald's buying spree. After all, the way banks made money was by "renting" money—i.e., using their deposits to make interest-paying loans. It was actually much easier, and more profitable, to deploy a bank's portfolio by renting money in large amounts than it was to rent money in small amounts; the same amount of paper work was required for a small transaction as for a big one, and a big loan could be syndicated to other banks for lucrative fees.

Besides wanting to borrow money in large amounts, Donald offered another incentive to the banks he approached for loans: a high public profile. The banks themselves would not have to indulge in what some considered the unbankerly practice of touting their deals in public and in the media. Donald would do that for them. Thanks to his talent for media manipulation, lending to him almost automatically guaranteed free publicity for the bank, which, in turn, served to attract new customers. And if the banks had any doubts about Donald's financial strength, all they had to do was consult the media to be reminded that, as Fred Trump, Sr., had pointed out, everything Donald touched turned to gold.

If Donald qualified as a premier borrower, he met his lending alter ego in the Chase Manhattan Bank's regional real estate chief, Conrad Stephenson. Six feet two inches tall with gray hair and sagging jowls, Stephenson, who was in his early fifties, even looked like an older version of Donald. Stephenson prided himself on being a "relation-ship" banker. Instead of evaluating loan requests from anyone who walked in off the street, he tried to develop long-term close working relationships with selected blue-chip clients. In most cases he offered to fund their projects at lower interest rates and on much more gen-erous terms than those offered to ordinary bank customers. In some cases he also worked behind the scenes to advance his blue-chip clients' projects and endeavored to thwart their competitors.

The Trumps were some of the bluest of Stephenson's blue-chip clients. Back in the seventies he had helped work out the refinancing of some of Fred Trump Sr.'s outer borough properties to provide capital for Donald's assault on Manhattan. It was Stephenson who had arranged the $35 million unsecured line of credit that Donald drew upon to fund his Grand Hyatt project and his initial foray into Atlantic City. Stephenson later provided a $30 million second mort-gage on the Grand Hyatt, a $130 million financing package for Trump Tower, and a $50 million loan to purchase the properties at 100 and 106 Central Park South. He also performed some truly extraordi-nary services for Donald in connection with his biggest Manhattan real estate deal of the mid-eighties, the reacquisition of the West Side yards.

Back in 1979 Donald had let his option on the West Side yards expire as he devoted his energies to the Grand Hyatt and Trump Tower projects. An Argentinian real estate mogul named Francesco Macri had then purchased a 65 percent interest in the property, which was also partially owned by a Trump crony named Abe Hirschfeld. But by late 1982 Donald had his sights set on getting the West Side yards back in his grasp. Stephenson spent many months quibbling about the concessions Macri had promised the city, which included the installation of a new subway line through the property. In early 1984, after insisting on protracted renegotiations of the terms on which he would lend construction money to Macri, Stephenson finally refused to finance the project at all unless the Argentinian allied with a "real estate developer acceptable to Chase."

The real estate developer Stephenson had in mind was his most favored client, Donald J. Trump. The Chase banker allegedly leaked confidential information to Donald about his renegotiations with Macri virtually from start to finish. When Donald started offering to buy Macri's interest in the West Side yards, he seemed to possess inside information that enabled him to lower his initial offer by $30 million at just the time when Macri was being squeezed by their mutual banker, Conrad Stephenson. Then Donald slyly recruited the media to abet his plan to recapture the West Side yards. In April 1984 the *New York Times Magazine* ran a profile of Donald which suggested that he had already convinced Macri to sell him the property.

Donald's big lie became reality, thanks in no small part to Stephenson. On July 18, 1984, Chase started foreclosure proceedings against Macri. Exactly ninety days later he agreed to sell his interest in the West Side yards to Donald. In his first book Donald claimed that he paid $90 million. The actual purchase price was $115 million. Donald closed the deal in January 1985 with an $85 million loan from Chase. Over the next few years Chase increased the amount of the mortgage to $215 million. As in many past deals, Donald later hired several key players formerly on the opposition side, including Macri's lawyer, planner, and two environmental consultants.

Before the year was out, Donald added two other midtown Manhattan trophy properties to his portfolio. In late July 1985 he paid Harry Helmsley and his partner $74 million for the St. Moritz, a dilapidated and often half-vacant hotel just across Sixth Avenue from the properties Donald owned at 100 and 106 Central Park South. Then he persuaded Bankers Trust to provide an $80 million mortgage loan on the St. Moritz and pocketed the $6 million cash difference between the loan and the purchase price. That fall he paid $40 million for a corner on Third Avenue occupied by the New York Foundling Hospital. As if to prove that Trump Tower was no fluke, he announced plans to build another luxury high rise on the old hospital site to be called Trump Palace. He then convinced Citibank to mortgage the property for $60 million, a full $20 million above the purchase price.

Donald's next big acquisition of 1985 was inspired in no small part by Ivana and the Trump family's ongoing disputes with their Atlantic City partners from Holiday Inns. One afternoon that winter Ivana came storming into the lobby of Harrah's at Trump Plaza, muttering expletives in Czech and English. She had just come from a meeting with Harrah's executive David Hanlon, the casino hotel's chief operating officer. Ivana had been complaining to Hanlon about the alleged lack of cleanliness and decorum afflicting their property. Hanlon had impolitely told her not to interfere with his management until such time as she applied for and received a gaming license from the Casino Control Commission.

Ivana was greeted in the lobby of Harrah's at Trump Plaza by Trump casino consultant Al Glasgow. A short, sharp-tongued, hard-drinking Jewish gaming industry gadfly in his late fifties, Glasgow, whose birth name was Jerry Segal, came from a moderately wealthy family whose money he had invested in a variety of ill-fated ventures in the concrete industry. In 1971 he had been the target of a Mafia hit contract prompted by a "misunderstanding" in the concrete business. Shortly after New Jersey voters approved a measure to legalize gambling in the state, he began publishing a newsletter called *Atlantic City Action.*

"How many casinos can one family own?" Ivana demanded to know before Glasgow even had a chance to ask her what had happened upstairs.

"Three," he replied.

"Then we will own three casinos," Ivana declared, adding, "And this will be one of them."

Glasgow knew that Ivana's complaints about Harrah's at Trump Plaza were well founded. In his view the joint's financial performance could be summed up in one word: "shitty." At the end of its first year of operations Harrah's at Trump Plaza was to rank seventh out of the ten Atlantic City gaming halls in gross revenues even though it boasted one of the largest casino floors in town. Management had projected first-year gross operating profit at $48 million; the actual figure turned out to be $23 million.

Glasgow blamed the problems in large part on Harrah's condescending approach to the Atlantic City market and on a crew of managers he disdained as "a bunch of brown suits from Reno." The brown suits evidently believed that Nevada gamblers far outclassed their counterparts in the mid-Atlantic. Likewise, the brown suits did not seem to trust their own customers or the house's proved mathematical advantage in the odds. "Whenever some guy would get on a roll and start winning big money at one of the crap tables, he would suddenly get surrounded by house security men with walkie-talkies," Glasgow complained. "I remember one high roller turned to me and said, 'This is like shooting craps in a police station.' The next thing I know, the guy is out the door headed for another casino across the street."

Glasgow also knew that Ivana was not the only Trump who rankled over Harrah's alleged mismanagement of the casino hotel. Her brother-in-law, Robert Trump, had voiced similar complaints about the brown suits' lack of hospitality and attention to detail. Hanlon was already drafting letters to both Ivana and Robert ordering them to keep off the property. Donald did not take kindly to the rebuffs of his wife and brother. But there wasn't much he could do. Under his agreement with Holiday Inns, he was merely the builder; it was up to Harrah's to operate the facility as it saw fit.

On February 14, 1985, as Harrah's at Trump Plaza stumbled through its third full quarter of operations, Donald learned that New Jersey officials had denied hotel scion Barron Hilton a casino license. That was a true shocker. The Hilton chain's annual report had described the company's move into Atlantic City as "the largest undertaking in our history." Phase one, which was already well under way, called for construction of a 615-room hotel with a sixty-thousand-square-foot casino and a three-thousand-car parking garage overlooking the marina. Hilton had already invested more than $300 million in his Atlantic City project prior to going through the licensing process. But the Casino Control Commission objected to his relationship with a controversial Chicago lawyer named Stanley Korshak, who allegedly represented mobsters. Acting on Al Glasgow's advice, Donald informed Hilton that he might be willing to buy him out. Hilton remained noncommittal.

Then Steve Wynn entered the fray. A tall, handsome charmer with a penchant for $2,000 silk suits and an eye for a well-turned ankle, Wynn was Donald's archrival. Like Donald, he had attended the Wharton School at the University of Pennsylvania. And like Donald, he had learned his trade at his father's knee. In Wynn's case, however, the family business was gambling, not real estate. In December

1980, having parlayed a minor stake in the Nevada-based Golden Nugget into the position of board chairman, he had opened a Golden Nugget casino on the Boardwalk in Atlantic City. Appearing in TV commercials with pals such as singer Frank Sinatra, Wynn later got credit for bringing Las Vegas-style glamour and flair to the rather unglamorous New Jersey gaming capital.

Like Donald Trump, Steve Wynn believed that Hilton's failure to get licensed signaled a great business opportunity. He was already planning to expand his operations on a fourteen-acre site next door to Hilton's property in the marina district. But unlike Donald, he had grander visions than merely buying Hilton's unlicensed casino hotel by the Atlantic City marina. On April 14, 1985, Wynn launched an uninvited bid for control of the entire Hilton Corporation. At the time the market value of Hilton stock was about $67 a share. Wynn informed Barron Hilton he was willing to pay $72 a share for a 27 percent block of the company's stock and a like amount for the remaining 73 percent if his initial offer was accepted.

As he later confided in his first book, Donald believed that Steve Wynn's hostile bid for control of Hilton Corporation was "the best thing that could have happened to me." In retrospect, nothing could have been further from the truth. In addition to confirming Donald's paranoid suspicions that his archrival was bent on dominating the Atlantic City gaming industry, Wynn's takeover attempt incited Donald's competitive instincts to a fever pitch. That, in turn, clouded his judgment, impaired his fabled negotiating skills, and led him to make one of the greatest business blunders of his career.

A few days after Wynn's tender Donald offered to buy Hilton's casino hotel in Atlantic City for $250 million. Barron Hilton was hardly in a position to dictate price. He needed Donald to buy him out much more than Donald needed another casino. But Hilton rejected Donald's initial offer as too low. He noted that the hotel chain had invested close to $320 million in its Atlantic City project and insisted that he could not tell his shareholders that he had to sell the property for a loss. Incredibly, Donald agreed to meet Hilton's price. He would pay the full $320 million subject to only one relatively minor deal point. Perhaps even more incredibly, Donald made his offer to Hilton and closed the deal without ever walking through the property in person.

"It was a deal based almost entirely on my gut . . ." Donald later admitted in his first book. "If I'd told my father the story, he would have said I'd lost my mind."

What Donald failed to mention in his autobiographical account of the Hilton deal was that he wound up borrowing more than the $320 million purchase price—substantially more. Manufacturers Hanover lent him $280 million secured by a first mortgage on the casino hotel. Manny Hanny also provided him with a personally guaranteed loan for $70 million. That brought his total indebtedness to $350 million, or $30 million more than he paid Hilton to buy the property. According to documents filed with the New Jersey Casino Control Commission, he used $25 million of that money as working capital for the casino. The other $5 million went directly into the pocket of Donald J. Trump.

After christening his new casino hotel Trump's Castle, Donald determined to reduce his personal liability by turning to the hot new financing scheme of the 1980s, the high-risk, high-yield securities popularly known as junk bonds. In return for a percentage fee, an investment bank would sell paper securities to other financial institutions and to the general public with a specified face value, or par, representing shares of the total bond offering. Like stock prices, the price of the bonds could fluctuate up or down as the securities began trading on the open market. The bonds offered the attraction of paying interest at an annual rate usually just under 14 percent. This interest, or yield, was substantially higher than that paid on bank deposits or money market funds. But junk bonds also carried substantially higher risks. While they were secured by the assets of the companies that issued them, the companies in question were typically untested firms involved in ventures with a high probability of failure.

Although Donald had no performance record as a casino operator, several major firms presented Donald with bids for the right to float Trump Castle's bonds. The differences in the bids usually involved the total amount of money an investment bank estimated could be raised through the sale of the bonds and the size of the fee demanded for that service. One of the bidders on the Trump's Castle deal was Drexel Burnham, the firm that had pioneered junk bond offerings under the aegis of the soon-to-be-notorious Michael Milken. The bidder that got the deal, however, was Bear Stearns, the firm led by Donald's "personal stockbroker," Ace Greenberg.

Ominously, Bear Stearns ran into some unanticipated problems in trying to sell Trump's Castle bonds. The face value amount of the offering was $350 million, the same amount Donald had borrowed from Manufacturers Hanover. But where investment bankers had vied to sell the bonds, the market resisted the offering because of Donald's inexperience as a casino operator. Bear Stearns wound up selling some of the bonds at a discount. In the end Donald received about $300 million from the offering. He used $280 million of the proceeds to pay off the first mortgage loan from Manufacturers Hanover. He disbursed the other $20 million to Donald J. Trump.

Before Trump's Castle even completed its first full quarter of operations, Donald had enjoyed a personal cash surplus on the deal of $25 million. The catch was that he and his new property were also more deeply in hock. He was still responsible for the $70 million loan from Manufacturers Hanover guaranteed by his signature. And the casino hotel was now mortgaged to junk bond holders for $300 million. That raised the total indebtedness on the deal from an original $350 million to $370 million. But then all that was other people's money, borrowed funds that he confidently believed would be repaid by the profits from the casino.

Donald now had to find someone to run Trump's Castle. The slot machine and accounting fiasco attendant to the opening of Harrah's at Trump Plaza had soured his taste for outside management. In hopes of avoiding another such debacle, he gave the job of running Trump's Castle to Ivana. Ever reluctant to praise his wife's accomplishments, he would judge her initial success in the casino industry to be confirmation of his own genius. "I'd studied Atlantic City long enough to be convinced that when it comes to running a casino, good management skills are as important as specific gaming experience," he wrote later. "She proved me right."

Although Ivana was the titular chief, Hilton's people were still in charge during the transition. Led by John Fitzgerald, who later became president of the Las Vegas Hilton, the Hilton executives hired a full complement of employees to staff the casino hotel and supervised the construction crews putting the finishing touches on the hotel building overlooking the marina. But it was Donald who demon-strated that motivational skills were as important as management skills. In early June he joined Ivana and Fitzgerald at a preopening pep rally for the casino hotel's staff. Both Ivana and Fitzgerald received polite rounds of applause from the assembled employees, but when Donald took the podium, the crowd cheered wildly.

"I've been having a problem with a casino over there with my name on it," he declared, refering to Harrah's at Trump Plaza. "Harrah's doesn't know what they're doing. That's why I hired all you people. We're going to show them how to run the best casino in the world. Hilton didn't plan on opening until August sixth. I wanted to open in June. Casino experts told me I couldn't do it. But when you hire the best people, you can do anything."

On June 15, 1985, Trump's Castle opened on schedule with a stampede to the gaming tables. In sharp contrast with the opening of Harrah's at Trump Plaza, there were no embarrassing slot machine breakdowns. In its first full month of operations, the casino grossed $20,159,800, the highest opening month total in Atlantic City his-tory. When Ivana actually took over later that summer, Trump's Cas-tle did even better. The queen of Trump's Castle set a very ambitious goal for her casino hotel. It was to be number one, not just among Trump casinos but in all Atlantic City, on both the top line (gross revenues) and the bottom line (net profits). For the six months end-ing in December 1985 Trump's Castle reported gross revenues of $131 million, putting it in fourth place citywide; Harrah's at Trump Plaza reported a gross of $123 million for that same period.

"Ivana was a quick study," reports one former Trump's Castle vice-president. "She became Donald's match." With the help of casino consultant Al Glasgow, Ivana assembled a management team distin-guished by a mix of youth, experience, and a rare, at least for the gaming industry, degree of feminine influence at the top. One of Ivana's new vice-presidents was Nancy Bauer, a petite and perky spe-cialist in bus program marketing who came over from Resorts Inter-national. Ivana also kept several members of the Hilton team, including financial vice-president Bob Fiore and Willard G. ("Bucky") Howard, a backslapping good old boy who specialized in catering to high roll-ers. But unlike The Donald, Ivana did not simply leave the day-to-day details to her minions. She flew from New York to Atlantic City three to four times per week aboard a chartered helicopter, arriving at 9:45 A.M., then flying back at 5:00 P.M. to be with her children.

Ivana's helicopter commuting put her in contact with a shadowy figure on the fringes of the Trump empire. His name was Joe Weichselbaum, and he was a balding, long-sideburned vice-president and pilot for Damin Aviation, which provided charter service for many of the big Atlantic City casinos. A two-time loser previously convicted of grand larceny (1965) and embezzlement (1979), Weichselbaum was also part of a ring that had smuggled cocaine and marijuana from Florida to Ohio and Kentucky in 1981. Even as Ivana took over Trump's Castle, a federal grand jury was preparing to indict Weichselbaum on drug charges. And yet Weichselbaum maintained a suspiciously friendly relationship with Ivana's husband.

In addition to paying up to $180,000 a month for Damin's helicopter services, Donald provided Weichselbaum with an apartment in Trump Plaza in New York City. The rent on the apartment was paid half in cash and half in helicopter services. The FBI and other law enforcement agencies were already formulating a theory about the Trump-Weichselbaum connection. According to reports from undercover agents, they had reason to believe that Weichselbaum might be part of a scheme to supply cocaine to high rollers at the Trump casinos. Although Weichselbaum eventually pleaded guilty to the Florida drug charges, he later denied being involved in an Atlantic City drug-smuggling scheme.

In any event Ivana's success at Trump's Castle was not a panacea for festering problems on the home front. She and Donald became like two choppers passing in the night, seeing and speaking to each other less and less frequently. While she spent most of the workweek in Atlantic City and weekends in Greenwich, he spent most of the workweek in New York and weekends in Atlantic City. Just as his Ivana yearned to prove herself, Donald vowed to do her—and everyone else—one better. Indeed, as the summer of 1985 wore on, he hatched ever more grandiose schemes for bannering the Trump name across the national skyline.

On November 18, 1985, Donald called a press conference to announce plans for a multibillion-dollar development of the West

Side yards to be called TV City. The centerpiece of the project would be a 150-story skyscraper touted as "the world's tallest building." TV City would also include eight thousand apartments, forty acres of parks, and specially designed spaces for television and film production studios. Donald claimed he had been conducting talks with NBC, whose executives had already made it known that they were considering moving out of the company's Rockefeller Center headquarters to a less congested and less costly location in New Jersey.

Donald had carefully feathered his political nest in preparation for the TV City announcement. He had given a whopping $270,000 to the reelection campaign of Manhattan Borough President Andrew Stein and another $30,000 to Comptroller Harrison J. ("Jay") Goldin, whom he perceived to be supportive of his plans for the West Side yards. He and his father had also contributed $25,000 to Mayor Ed Koch's 1985 reelection campaign. At the same time Donald hired Koch's campaign manager Jim Capalino as a paid Trump Organization consultant on the West Side yards project.

But Donald did not count on NBC's reaction or the reaction of local residents. Network officials promptly informed the media that they had made no firm commitments to Trump or anyone else. Then a coalition of community activists led by a group called Westpride announced its opposition to TV City. Savvy, well organized, and well financed by a long list of resident celebrity authors, actors, and artists, Westpride complained that TV City would dramatically increase traffic congestion on the West Side Highway, block existing buildings' view of the Hudson River, and effectively destroy the area's quiet residential neighborhoods. And despite Donald's lavish political contributions, Westpride's objections found plenty of sympathetic people in city government who pledged to block the project.

Undaunted by the controversy swirling about TV City, Donald wasted no time in acquiring the next and most illustrious of his new crown jewels; Mar-a-Lago, the Spanish Mediterranean style estate of the late Marjorie Merriweather Post nestled between Lake Worth and the Atlantic Ocean in Palm Beach, Florida. Mar-a-Lago's amenities included a 118-room main house with 58 bedrooms, 33 bathrooms, 3 bomb shelters, a movie theater, a dining room large enough to seat fifty, and an inventory of art, antique furnishings, china, and silverware that were major assets in their own right. Outside, there was a nine-hole golf course, a gaggle of guest and superintendent's cottages, and an adjoining strip of beachfront; after the Trumps moved in, they added a swimming pool and tennis courts.

If Ivana saw Mar-a-Lago as a tremendous potential boost to her social ambitions, Donald saw it as another trophy property he was able to snatch at a bargain price. In 1973 Mrs. Post had donated the estate to the Department of the Interior in hopes that the government would use it as a kind of local embassy. But in 1981 the U.S. government had returned it to the Post Foundation after Congressman Paul Rogers of Florida introduced a bill blocking further appropriations for upkeep. According to local myth, it cost upwards of $1 million a year to maintain the estate. In fact, the government had spent less than $50,000 during the entire period it held the property. Prior to the fall of 1985 several announced bids, including a $14 million offer from a Houston developer, failed to go through. Donald bid $8 million for Mar-a-Lago and offered another $2 million for a strip of beachfront that had previously been sold off from the estate. Like the other bidders before him, he made it clear that his long-term plans called for subdividing the property.

The deal for Mar-a-Lago bore striking similarities to the deal for West Side yards, especially in terms of bravura and underhandedness. Donald bought the estate with special assistance from Chase banker Conrad Stephenson and some local lawyers and real estate brokers with close ties to Congressman Rogers. Prior to leaving Chase in the fall of 1985, Stephenson arranged for Donald to get a highly unusual unrecorded mortgage of $10 million, the equivalent of an unsecured personal loan. As Trump biographer Wayne Barrett later revealed, this secret transaction enabled Donald to buy Mar-a-Lago with less than $3,000 paid out of his own pocket, even as he gave the public impression that he was making an extravagant cash purchase.

Although Stephenson appeared to be richly rewarded for his services, his deals with Donald may have tainted his career and his marriage. His reputation as a great banker from the borrower's point of view reportedly figured in the decision by his superiors at Chase to pass him up for a promotion to national real estate chief. He subsequently left Chase to take a short-lived position at another New York bank, then wound up working for a local mortgage broker. In 1987 he bought an apartment in Trump Parc for $190,000, some $50,000 below the market price. He put the apartment in the name of a trust and did not tell his wife about it.

As Stephenson struggled with his personal problems, the Trumps' dreams for Mar-a-Lago turned nightmarish. Rather than welcome Donald and Ivana into the fold, the snobbish dowagers of Palm Beach society sniped at them both in public and behind their backs. Although the Trumps' new estate was only a nine-iron shot from the prestigious Bath and Tennis Club, local wags sneered that the only way the couple could get through the club doors was with a bazooka. To make matters worse, Donald started bitching about the fact that Mar-a-Lago lay directly beneath the flight paths into and out of West Palm Beach International Airport. He soon commenced a highly vocal but unsuccessful campaign to have the airport moved, which only made him more of a laughingstock in the salons of the Palm Beach aristocracy.

A few months after closing on Mar-a-Lago, Donald made another dubious Palm Beach deal, this time in partnership with the Chrysler Corporation chairman Lee Iacocca. The two men knew each other socially through their mutual friend William Fugazy, a New York limousine tycoon and Trump golfing partner Donald nicknamed Willie the Fug. In the summer of 1986 Donald and Iacocca bought a twin-towered West Palm Beach condominium project that had been foreclosed on by Marine Midland Bank. They renamed the project Trump Plaza of the Palm Beaches and cosigned a $41 million note to finance the purchase, thereby cementing a partnership whose promotional flair far exceeded its business judgment.

Trump attorney Jerry Schrager tried in vain to talk Donald out of making the deal the first time they walked through the building. "I know construction," Donald proclaimed as he banged his fist against one of the Sheetrock walls, "and this is good construction." But as anyone who really knew construction could attest, about the only thing that could be discerned by banging a fist against a section of Sheetrock was whether or not there was a concrete wall behind it. In fact, Trump Plaza of the Palm Beaches was plagued by shoddy construction. One of the towers lacked sufficient plumbing for air-conditioning units, which were essential in the Florida heat, and there were no risers to accommodate steam and water flow.

Trump Plaza of the Palm Beaches was also on the wrong side of the tracks or, more precisely, the wrong side of Lake Worth from Palm Beach proper. "The neighborhoods across the street were populated mostly by black people, and there was a lot of drug dealing going on," recalled a former Trump executive. "When the cops would make a raid, the drug dealers would run across the street toward the Trump Plaza parking garage and get in shoot-outs." To make matters worse, Trump Plaza of the Palm Beaches was located even closer than Mar-a-Lago to the airport that Donald wanted to get moved.

Both Donald and Iacocca evidently believed that their mutual celebrity and wealth of business contacts would be enough to turn the project around. At one point Iacocca offered to send letters to Chrysler suppliers and distributors soliciting prospective apartment buyers. But when an Iacocca associate asked for ten thousand sheets of Trump Organization stationary to use for the mailing, real estate executive Blanche Sprague balked. She questioned the ethics of Iacocca's soliciting Chrysler distributors and suppliers, and she worried about the legality of his associate's making representations about the project when he was not an official sponsor of the condominium. Donald refused to cooperate with Iacocca's associate but put the blame on Sprague.

Over the first eighteen months of the Trump-Iacocca partnership, Trump Plaza of the Palm Beaches sold only 93 of 221 apartment units. The bank called for the partnership to make a cash payment of about $5 million. According to one insider, "Iacocca screamed like a stuck pig. He thought all he had to do was sign some papers and Donald would make millions for him." Ironically, Donald had by now become disenchanted with Iacocca for failing to write solicitation letters to prospective apartment buyers even though Donald himself had nixed the idea. "Don't you think this is a good time to get rid of him?" he asked one of his real estate executives when Iacocca objected to the bank's call for funds. Donald answered his own question by taking over Iacocca's half interest in the project, though he did so in secret without any of the public relations fanfare that had accompanied the formation of their partnership.

Back in New York, Donald suddenly found himself under a renewed counterattack from the tenants at 100 Central Park South. In November 1985 he erroneously claimed that the state Division of Housing and Community Renewal had rejected the tenants' harassment complaint. Tenant leader John Moore responded by calling him "a deceitfully, vicious liar . . . who can't distinguish between fact and fiction." Donald branded Moore "an unsuccessful man who nobody ever heard of except that he's a tenant fighting Donald Trump." But plenty of people did begin hearing about Moore and his fellow tenants, for *New York* magazine and other local media picked up the story of the David versus Goliath battle and made it a cause célèbre.

Ultimately Donald settled for a Pyrrhic victory. In late 1985 the appellate division of the state supreme court dismissed the harassment charges against him. By that time Donald claimed that a trend toward postmodernist architectural tastes by high-income tenants and a reexamination of zoning restrictions on the site had inspired him to change his plans about demolishing the building. The tenants agreed to drop further harassment proceedings against him, and he agreed to drop eviction proceedings against them. He then renamed the Barbizon-Plaza next door Trump Parc and went ahead with plans to renovate the building as a luxury condominium.

Donald reacted to his unaccustomed wave of bad press by lashing out. Opposing tenants' groups and community activists were not his only or even his primary targets. Instead he took out his frustrations on those closest to him, including family members, trusted employees, and business partners. First, he came to blows with the Equitable Life Assurance Society over the management of Trump Tower. According to his side of the story, the dispute reached a crisis point when Equitable executives began complaining about the fact that he was spending nearly $1 million a year on maintenance of the building. Among the expenditures in question was Donald's insistence on having every piece of brass in the building polished twice per month. According to a former Trump insider, there were also disputed charges for Donald's personal security guards. Barely able to control his boiling rage, Donald arranged to buy out Equitable's half interest in Trump Tower.

Down in Atlantic City, Donald's ongoing dispute with the management of Harrah's at Trump Plaza quickly evolved into a rerun of the Trump Tower episode. After more than a year of operation, the casino hotel still lagged in eighth place among the eleven gaming halls in town. Holiday Inns, the managing partner, complained that one of the reasons for the property's poor performance was the fact that Donald had not yet completed construction of a major parking facility next door. But Donald attributed the depressed revenues to incompetence. "I gave them a Lamborghini," he complained, "and they don't even know how to turn on the key."

Donald determined to resolve the dispute by cutting another fee-shaving deal that would put cash in his pocket and pile debt on the backs of the investing public. Using $250 million worth of junk bonds, he bought out Holiday Inns' half interest in the casino hotel. As in the purchase of Trump's Castle, the bonds were issued by his friends at Bear Stearns, who collected a $7.6 million fee on the transaction. According to documents submitted to the New Jersey Casino Control Commission, a little more than $152 million of the junk bond proceeds went to Midlantic Bank to pay off the existing mortgage on the property. Holiday Inns received $59.1 million as payment for its half interest. Another $9.7 million was reserved for renovations and locally mandated casino reinvestment obligations. A hefty $20.7 million was disbursed to Donald J. Trump.

In the closing months of 1985, just before the buyout of Holiday Inns, Donald became embroiled in an even more unfortunate dispute with longtime real estate and political aide Louise Sunshine. The genesis of the dispute may actually have traced to Sunshine's rivalry with Ivana Trump, whom she viewed as a high-handed interloper in Trump Organization projects. Sunshine had had enough and was determined to start her own independent real estate consulting business. Before she left, Donald presented her with a $1 million tax bill related to her 5 percent interest in Trump Plaza on Third Avenue. When Sunshine objected, Donald suggested that she could avoid paying the tax bill by selling her 5 percent share of the project back to him.

Not one to be railroaded, Sunshine turned to her friend Leonard Stern for advice. Stern, who was the chief executive of Hartz Mountain Corporation and a grudge-carrying critic of Donald Trump, immediately wrote out a $1 million check so Sunshine could pay her assigned share of the property taxes on Trump Plaza. "You tell Trump that unless he treats you fairly, you will litigate," Stern instructed

Sunshine, "and as a result, the details of his duplicitous treatment will come not only to the attention of the public but also to the Casino Control Commission."

Sunshine proceeded to hire Arthur Liman, a politically connected New York attorney who later represented such clients as the Getty Oil Company and financier Michael Milken. Liman eventually negotiated a settlement of the Trump-Sunshine dispute. Donald agreed to buy out her 5 percent interest in Trump Plaza for $2.7 million. Sunshine, in turn, used $1 million of the settlement money to repay Leonard Stern. Sunshine saw the episode as confirmation of a dangerous change in Donald's modus operandi.

"When I first went to work with him in 1974, Donald was very hands-on, in total control, and on top of everything, leaving no stone unturned," she recalled in an interview years later. "But as his figure began to loom larger and larger in the press, he became distracted by the idea of becoming a celebrity, a presidential candidate, and a movie star." According to Sunshine, Donald was now starting to lose his greatest intangible asset, his focus.

Donald's focus became even fuzzier when publishing magnate S. I. Newhouse, owner of Random House, proposed that the developer, who had yet to reach his fortieth birthday, write an autobiography. While pondering Newhouse's idea, Donald agreed to do an interview for *Playboy* with journalist Tony Schwartz, who had recently published a highly critical article in *New York* magazine about Donald's battle with the tenants of 100 Central Park South. Donald evidently hoped to use the *Playboy* interview to convince Schwartz to revise his view of the tenant dispute. But as the interview progressed, Schwartz complained that he was not getting good material. Donald then admitted he was saving his best stories for the autobiography Newhouse had proposed.

"You're too young to write an autobiography," Schwartz declared. "I think you ought to write a book about the art of the deal."

Donald took Schwartz's suggestion to heart. In January 1986 he signed a contract to write a book for Random House with Schwartz as the designated coauthor. According to Random House editor Peter Osnos, the advance was half a million dollars. The working title was *Trump: The Art of the Deal.*

chapter six
HOUSE OF CARDS

■ MARLA MAPLES GLARED at the tall, dark, and handsome man across the living room.

"I can't believe your colossal ego!" she huffed, thrusting both hands to her hips.

"Either convince me you're innocent," the man replied coolly, "or say good-bye."

Marla parted her lips revealing a bloodred cosmetic smudge across her front teeth. She was wearing a white silk blouse, collar buttons open and tails tied at the waist, and a strand of snowy white costume pearls. Her thick blond hair was swept back in the layered coiffure popularized by actress Farrah Fawcett.

"Where do I begin?" she asked.

"At the beginning," instructed the man across the room.

"At the beginning of where I first met Zona, found out about her, or that night?"

"All right, I'll start you off," offered Marla's male antagonist. "How long have you and Link been having an affair?"

"What Link and I have is not an affair," Marla shot back.

"One person's married, the other isn't," the man pointed out. "What do you call it?"

"When I started seeing Link, I didn't know he was married," Marla insisted. "When I found out he was, I broke it off."

A few minutes later the director yelled, "Cut!"

Marla Maples walked off the set with no idea that her life was about to imitate that scene in haunting detail. It was the spring of 1986.

The twenty-two-year-old former beauty queen from Dalton, Georgia (population twenty-five thousand), had finally gotten where she had always wanted to be: in New York City, where she was auditioning for a role in a daytime TV soap opera entitled "Loving." Marla did not get the role, but she was able to take the rejection in stride. She had just met the man who would prove to be a real-life counterpart of her illicit paramour in "Loving." And anyone who had ever visited the Little Sodom in the South from whence she came could understand why Marla had a feeling that meeting had been predestined.

Marla's hometown of Dalton lay snuggled against the rolling green foothills of the Blue Ridge Mountains eighty-eight miles north of Atlanta and thirty miles south of Chattanooga, Tennessee. In bygone days the town marked the embarkation point for the forced migration of Cherokee Indians on the "Trail of Tears." During the Civil War it was one of the first Confederate strongholds ravaged by Union soldiers on General William Tecumseh Sherman's march to the sea. In the late 1950s a man named Gene Barwick invented a cotton tufting machine that transformed Dalton into the "Carpet Capital of the World" with more than 200 manufacturers and 150 factory outlets.

By the time Marla Maples came along, Dalton claimed to have more millionaires per capita than any place in the United States. As one local wag observed, "Folks who made clips that held carpet samples onto display racks became rich overnight." So did modern-day carpetbaggers from New York who came down to capitalize on the carpet boom. But the town still had the look and feel of a suburbanized backwater. The main drag off Interstate 75 was chockablock with beauty parlors, gas stations, and fast-food franchises of every conceivable deep-fried flavor. A mobile poster sign on the outskirts of town advertised Sunday worship services on the top lines and water beds on the bottom lines. The most popular night spot was Sensations, the bar at the local Holiday Inn.

The *Washington Post* would one day dub Dalton the capital of the "Killer Blondes," for the town also claimed leadership in two other inextricably related fields: homegrown beauty queens and divorce. The abundance of local beauties, who included former NBC "Today" anchor Deborah Norville and a host of Miss Georgia and Junior Miss finalists, was often attributed to environmental and nutritional factors. "Our girls eat the peaches and the North Georgia apples," observed Whitfield County Commissioner Walter Mitchell. "And the water coming out the mountains here is pure. That's how we like our women." Ambition was an equally important factor. Just as sports could provide northeastern urban youths the only means to get out of the ghetto, beauty pageants offered the quickest route out of town next to I-75.

Along with the carpet boom, the beauty queens were blamed for the high rate of divorce. A county courthouse clerk researching records at the request of a local preacher found three times as many divorces as marriages. It had become fairly common practice for newly rich mill town moguls to trade in their first wives for younger and more streamlined second, third, and even fourth wives as one might trade in a used Cadillac for a brand-new Ferrari. Such marital transactions, however, could be far more costly. One local divorce case was reportedly settled for a cool $30 million. "We're the Peyton Place of the South," boasted a local café owner.

Marla Ann Maples was both a beneficiary and a victim of her hometown's preoccupations. She was actually born about ten miles north of Dalton in even tinier Cohutta, Georgia, on October 27, 1963. Her father, Stan Maples, was a kind of small-town counterpart of Donald Trump. A tall, broad-shouldered man with enormous blue eyes, he came from a family that owned a concrete block factory. Like Fred Trump, Sr., his father was a strict, strong-willed patriarch nicknamed the Chief. Though Stan eventually entered the real estate business, he was gifted with a mellifluous voice. He sang in the Baptist choir and in a high school rock band, developed a wicked Elvis Presley impersonation, and later auditioned for the "Ted Mack Amateur Hour."

Marla's mother, Ann Locklear Maples, a distant cousin of the actress Heather Locklear, was a full-breasted beauty in her own right with raven hair and high cheekbones that hinted at a drop of Indian blood. When Marla reached her late teens, she and her mother were asked to pose together for *Playboy,* an offer they refused. Whereas Marla's father harbored a not-so-secret longing to become a professional crooner, Ann yearned to be a professional dancer. But unlike Stan, her former high school sweetheart, she was mysteriously unable to indulge her show business fantasies on even an amateur level. "Ann always seemed to regret not doing anything with her life," recalled a family friend. "She had a hard time leaving the house. She was always late for everything, like two hours late. I remember times she couldn't even get it together to go to church."

As an only child Marla did not want for creature comforts or emotional support. She spent her early years in a modest single-story brick house in Cohutta, then moved into a split-level ranch-style house her father had built in a nearby subdivision. One of the few little girls in a clan full of males, she was especially adored by her maternal grandparents, the Locklears. Her grandfather, a retired insurance executive, was a lovable old coot who still fumed over the fact that the South had "given up" the Civil War. The family nicknamed him Ding Daddy because he had gotten so dingy that he often failed to finish his sentences. Marla's grandmother, nicknamed Meemaw, was a fawning matriarch who cooked enough at every meal to feed an army. Marla loved spending summer days at Ding Daddy and Meemaw's lake house up near Gainesville, Georgia.

Marla starred on the girls' basketball team at North Whitfield High School and earned As in the classroom. She also learned the tricks of the beauty queen trade. Her tutor was Margaret Culberson, a bubbly blond housewife and mother who had coached future TV star Deborah Norville. Though Culberson later claimed that "Marla wasn't the most beautiful girl in town," she nevertheless put her in fashion shows almost from the time she was a toddler. "Her mother and I pushed her," Culberson recalled, adding that she also offered moral teachings. "I used to tell all my girls—Marla, too—'Save it for the right one. Keep your pants on.' "

But by the time Marla turned sixteen, there was trouble in peach paradise. Stan Maples suffered a series of reversals in the real estate business that threatened him with bankruptcy. A workaholic, he spent longer and longer hours away from home trying to stave off the collapse of his home building company. He and his wife began to quarrel. ("Ann was a clean freak, like Felix Ungar in *The Odd Couple*," recalled a friend. "She drove Stan crazy.") The stress prompted the first major crisis in Marla's life: her parents' divorce. Stan offered to try to keep the marriage together, but Marla told him, "If you're really so unhappy, don't stay for my sake." Both of Marla's parents later remarried. It took Ann Maples over half a dozen years to wed a locally prominent carpet designer named David Ogletree. Stan

Maples moved much faster. Following his split with Ann, he remarried three times; his third wife was a woman a year younger than Marla.

"Marla was devastated when her parents split up," one of her close friends recalled years afterward. "She had been a very secure child. Now it seemed like her whole world was falling apart." As if hoping that romance could help her pull herself together, she pursued a tempestuous relationship with boyfriend Jeff Sandlin, an athletic blond heartthrob she met as a high school sophomore in Dalton. Years later, in the wake of revelations of Marla's affair with Donald Trump, Sandlin sold the inside story of his love affair with Marla to the *National Enquirer*. Though he told his tawdry tale from a clearly one-sided point of view, the basic details were later confirmed by friendlier sources.

Sandlin claimed that Marla was a virgin when the two started dating. But by her junior year in high school, just as her parents were splitting up, they had sex for the first time. "It wasn't something we rushed into—we talked about it first," Sandlin remembered. "Marla was very eager. And she was a wonderful lover right from the beginning." The couple split up in 1981, after Marla graduated from high school and enrolled at the University of Georgia in Athens. But after only two years of college, Marla dropped out of school to pursue a career as a model and actress. Rather than move to New York or Hollywood, however, she returned to Dalton and resumed her romance with high school sweetheart Jeff Sandlin. In the summer of 1984, at the age of twenty, she got pregnant. According to Sandlin, the couple was at her mother's house when Marla broke the news. Both of them burst into tears.

"I held her gently in my arms and told her I was willing to marry her—but I really didn't want to," Sandlin recalled. "Over the next few days we tried to consider the options: marriage, abortion, adoption. It was against Marla's religious beliefs to think about an abortion. But she wanted to be a movie star—not pregnant in some backwater Georgia town. We decided on an abortion."

Sandlin and Marla drove up to the Northside Family Planning Clinic in Atlanta for the procedure. He later claimed that there was no place in Dalton to have it done and that the couple was anxious to avoid the small-town gossip that would inevitably result. He added that Marla went into the back room of the Atlanta clinic alone. "Oh, Jeff, I'm so scared," she sobbed as she went in. "Say a prayer for me." When Marla emerged from the clinic a little more than an hour later, she whispered, "I know we did the right thing." But she and Sandlin continued to feel the emotional pain of the experience. "We drove back in silence," Sandlin reported. "It was the worst day of my life. Marla told me it was the worst day of hers too. After that, whenever we'd see a mother with a baby carriage, we'd look at each other, and there was a deep sadness between us. We knew that baby could be ours."

Over the next few months Sandlin's romance with Marla disintegrated into a series of shouting matches. He complained that she was always trying to change him. Marla still dreamed of becoming a movie star like her idol, Marilyn Monroe. She told Sandlin he could also be a model and actor, but he refused to go along with the scheme. "We would have horrible fights," Sandlin recalled. "She slapped me, socked me—and threatened to kill herself. She talked about suicide often. She told me, 'If you ever leave me I'll just kill myself. I don't want to live without you."

In November 1984 Sandlin moved to Atlanta "to get away from Marla," but she tracked him down and convinced him they could work out their problems if they lived somewhere besides Dalton. The couple moved into an apartment together for what Sandlin later described as a "trial marriage." But less than six months later, in March 1985, Sandlin moved out, ending the relationship. "Marla was always attracted to the bright lights, to important people," he remembered. "She needed someone who was rich and famous—and that wasn't me." Sandlin went on to confide that after one of their fights Marla had written him a poem attempting to explain the root problem of their romance. According to Sandlin, she opined: "We love too much . . . to allow each other to find our individual desires."

Marla determined to find her individual desires without further delay. After modeling for billboard advertisements and getting a few small movie parts, she decided that making it in the big time meant leaving Atlanta for New York. She got her big chance thanks to Jerry Argovitz, the president of the Trump-owned New Jersey Generals football team. They met in Florida, where Argovitz was judging a beauty contest sponsored by the Hawaiian Tropic suntan lotion company. Marla placed third in the contest, but she won Argovitz's heart. According to her confidants, he would stand in the parking lot outside her motel room playing romantic rock music on a portable tape player.

Argovitz offered to take Marla to New York and introduce her around. Through Argovitz, she met a number of good-looking young professional athletes including Gamblers quarterback Jim Kelly and New York Giants punter Sean Landetta, both of whom she subsequently dated. Being introduced to Donald Trump proved to be an unexpected part of the package. Their first encounter occurred in early 1986 just a few months before Marla's audition for the television soap opera "Loving." Donald was hosting a meeting of USFL team owners at Trump's Castle in Atlantic City. Argovitz arrived with Marla in tow. Donald later claimed that he did not really remember being introduced to her. Marla did not place any special importance on the introduction either. She had already met New York billionaire Ted Forstmann, head of the investment banking firm Forstmann Little & Company. Forstmann had generously squired her around the city without actually commencing an affair and even lent her $5,000, which she eventually repaid in full.

"Teddy Forstmann was the richest guy Marla knew in New York," recalled a friend, noting that Donald's name identification among the nonbusiness general public was still far from its future peak. "At the time Trump wasn't Trump yet."

Shortly after Marla returned to New York to study acting, she met Tom Fitzsimmons, the handsome ex-cop turned model-actor-screenwriter. They began an affair almost as tempestuous as her affair with Jeff Sandlin, though without the complication of an unwanted pregnancy. Marla lived in Tom's two-bedroom apartment on Third Avenue and Ninety-first Street for the better part of a year. During that time he invited her to act in a self-produced video teaser of his script *Blue Gemini* suitable for pitching to Hollywood studios. But the couple soon began locking horns. One of their most heated arguments occurred during a visit to Marla's father's home in Dalton. Tom discovered that Marla had a habit of walking around the house without a stitch of clothing.

"Please don't walk around like that in front of your father and me," he requested, adding, "It is not respectful."

"What do you know?" Marla shot back, and further shocked her Yankee boyfriend by throwing a very unladylike temper tantrum— all the while adamantly remaining completely nude.

Ironically, Tom never lusted for Marla the way he had for other models and actresses. He could see that she had a shapely figure and a comely face, but she just didn't excite him much. They had few interests in common besides a desire to make it in show business. Although Marla was no teetotaler, she did not share Tom's love of barhopping on the Upper East Side night after night. While he stepped out to have a few beers with the boys, she often stayed home alone, greeting him upon his return with a pointed diatribe about his alleged lack of heterosexual libido.

"What's the matter with you, Tom?" Marla would screech. "Are you queer?"

Fortunately for all concerned, Marla's spats with Tom never escalated into the kind of violent conflicts that had sabotaged her "trial marriage" with Jeff Sandlin. As the months passed, their initial infatuation evolved into an asexual, platonic relationship. By the time Marla moved out in the summer of 1987, the former lovers could truthfully say they had formed a lasting friendship. But unbeknownst to either one of them, Tom Fitzsimmons was destined to play a more important role in Marla's life than any previous lover, thanks to his friendship with Donald J. Trump.

On March 1, 1986, shortly after Donald met Marla Maples for the first time, he and Ivana hosted a special party at Mar-a-Lago for his mentor Roy Cohn. Two years earlier Cohn had been diagnosed with AIDS. He had tried to keep the terrible news confidential, but by this point he could no longer hide the fact that his health was failing. The guest list for the party included the mix of business and social connections in which Cohn delighted: Manhattan Borough President Andrew Stein, Stein's father, Jerry Finkelstein, and his wife, Chrysler Corporation Chairman Lee A. Iacocca, and Cohn's male companion, Jay Taylor.

"The place settings were astronomical," Taylor later told one of Cohn's biographers. "The candelabra was [sic] more than I was going to make in the next six months. . . . It was fun, like we all gave tribute.

'I'd like to thank Roy.' They all knew. It was obvious at that time that he was going and let's hurry up and give him a dinner and thank him."

Donald quickly realized how much he himself would miss Roy Cohn. A few weeks after the dinner at Mar-a-Lago a federal grand jury indicted Cohn's law partner Stanley Friedman, the former Beame deputy who had rushed through the tax abatement deal for Donald on the Grand Hyatt Hotel. He was charged with conspiracy, racketeering, and mail fraud in connection with the city's parking violations bureau. The incapacitated Cohn could not save him. Friedman was convicted of the charges that fall. The following spring he was sentenced to twelve years in a federal penitentiary.

Donald longed for Cohn's counsel even more when the USFL's antitrust suit against the NFL went to trial in May 1986. The USFL owners' hopes for the future and for recovery of past losses on the order of two hundred million dollars rested with winning a major damage award. Cigar-chomping attorney Harvey Myerson attempted to cast the NFL owners as "predators" seeking to destroy his clients' "itty bitty league." He made a fairly convincing case until Donald took the stand. As USFL historian Jim Byrne later observed, "There is nothing about Donald Trump that conveys an 'itty bitty' image. . . . The jurors might have been a bit more sympathetic if they had been exposed to a couple of owners who could convince them that they had shed real blood."

On July 9, 1986, the jury found the NFL guilty of "willfully acquiring or maintaining a monopoly." But it awarded the USFL only $1 in damages. The USFL owners met to lick their wounds on August 4, 1986, the same day Roy Cohn was buried. They voted to appeal the jury's damage award verdict. Donald then persuaded them to suspend play temporarily. As Byrne observed, "When Donald Trump pulled the plug, it was all over."

According to his own estimate, Donald lost $22 million on the USFL between 1983 and 1986. He could easily have lost much more. When the USFL folded, Donald was still responsible for the $13 million worth of contracts the New Jersey Generals had signed with running back Herschel Walker and quarterback Doug Flutie, some $9 million of which was personally guaranteed. But Donald wisely assigned team president Jerry Argovitz to use his skills as a former players' agent to effect damage control. "You just bang their heads and make sure they don't get it," Donald ordered. "That's what you're here for."

Argovitz proved to be an even more artful deal breaker than his boss. He seized upon an innocent remark Flutie made to the press about the possibility of retiring to invoke an obscure cancellation clause in the quarterback's contract. Then he told Walker's agent, who was in the process of negotiating an NFL contract with the Dallas Cowboys, that he would force the star running back to stand outside Trump Tower wearing a "funny hat" unless he released the Generals from their financial obligations before attempting to sign on with the Cowboys. At the time Donald still owed Oklahoma oilman J. Walter Duncan a final payment on his original contract to purchase the New Jersey Generals. But following the USFL owners' decision to suspend play, he rushed to the courthouse to block Duncan's efforts to collect. Then he turned his attention back to New York City.

In the summer of 1986, just as the USFL was collapsing, the local media revealed that Donald had secretly retained the services of the law firm Weiss, Blutrich, Falcone, & Miller. What made the revelation particularly newsworthy was that one of the partners in the firm was Lucille Falcone, a former aide to New York Governor Mario Cuomo. One of the firm's associates was Cuomo's son, Andrew, who was also Falcone's boyfriend. Donald, who had so far contributed more than $18,000 to Cuomo's gubernatorial campaigns, claimed that the firm was currently representing the Trump Organization in "a very significant transaction."

Although Donald never disclosed the specific nature of this transaction, he knew that Cuomo's influence—or at least the perception of such influence—could be particularly helpful to the development of the West Side yards. In the spring of 1986 he hired attorney Susan Heilbron, former counsel to the Urban Development Corporation in the Cuomo administration. Over the next eighteen months Trump interests assiduously lobbied the state Department of Transportation to get various key concessions on the West Side yards project, including items related to the relocation of the West Side Highway and the location of access ramps serving the proposed development. Internal Department of Transportation memos noted that the agency's cooperation was being given "as discreetly as possible."

Fortunately for Donald, reports of his curiously close links to the governor through Andrew Cuomo's law firm were buried beneath a barrage of media coverage of his most celebrated undertaking to date, the renovation of Wollman Rink in Central Park. Built in 1950, the rink encompassed nearly three-quarters of an acre, making it one of the largest outdoor ice skating facilities in the world. The city had closed the rink in 1980 and had spent close to $13 million on renovation work. But the rink was nowhere near completion. There had been endless debates over such what kind of coolant system to install and what kind of sidewalk to build around the rink. In the interim some twenty-two miles of copper pipes had been damaged by snow and rain and sliced up by vandals.

The city blamed its slow progress on statutes requiring competitive bids on all municipal projects and the related Wickes Law, which mandated that any construction job over $50,000 be divided among at least four contractors. In May 1986 the city announced that it had decided to start all over and now expected it would take another two years to finish the rink. Donald blamed the Wollman debacle on Mayor Koch. In 1984 he had offered to build the rink for the city with his own money if he could lease it back and operate the facility for a profit. On May 28, 1986, he wrote the mayor a letter reiterating his previous offer. "The incompetence displayed on this simple project," Donald gibed, "must be considered one of the greatest embarrassments of your administration."

Koch replied that the city would not allow Donald to operate a public facility for private profit but would gladly accept a $3 million donation to use for completing the rink. "With bated breath I await your response," the mayor wrote. Then Koch made a fatal strategic error: He released copies of his correspondence with Donald to the public.

The news media descended on the Wollman Rink controversy like a pack of hungry wolves. They portrayed Koch as an obstructionist boob and Donald as a civic-minded hero. Three of New York's major dailies published editorials calling for the city to accept Donald's offer at once. "The Koch administration," declared the *Daily News*, "is hemming and hawing over Donald Trump's offer to rebuild and operate Wollman Rink in Central Park. . . . Maybe the problem [is that] Koch & Co. are embarrassed that they've squandered $12 million on Wollman."

In the early summer of 1986 Koch finally agreed to let Donald take over the renovation. Donald pledged to complete it in less than six months. Well aware that his assiduously cultivated public credibility was on the line, he called in favors from his most important business partners. He convinced Chase Manhattan Bank, to provide $3 million in financing at no interest and put the arm on HRH Construction to supervise the project.

Donald later claimed that HRH "generously offered to do the work at cost." But a well-placed source at the firm that had built both the Grand Hyatt and Trump Tower insisted that the firm was offered an under-the-table incentive. "Trump said if we built the Wollman Rink at no profit, he'd give us the contract to build the West Side yards." Whatever the motivating factor, the project literally skated to completion. With the prospect of getting a multibillion-dollar job in the future, HRH made sure the unions and subcontractors would not even think of causing costly delays in supply deliveries or concrete pouring.

On November 13, 1986, Donald presided over a gala opening ceremony. It was staged by Ivana's pal Aja Zanova-Steindler, the former Czech skating champion, and featured such well-known American skating stars as Dick Button and former Olympian Peggy Fleming. Donald's delighted in noting that he had completed the renovation in a month ahead of schedule and $750,000 under budget. "I hope I haven't embarrassed anyone," he gloated disingenuously.

The Wollman Rink project proved to be a major milestone in Donald's career, for both good and ill. The battle with Mayor Koch created an irreconcilable rift that was to have dire consequences for both antagonists. At the same time Donald's triumphant success inflated his celebrity to gargantuan proportions. Suddenly the developer known for his alleged tax abatement windfalls and tenant eviction battles became the toast of the town. It seemed there was nothing that Donald could not do if he set his mind on it.

"Wollman Rink was a turning point," recalled one of Donald's publicists at Howard Rubenstein & Associates. "After that Donald started referring to himself in the third person. He'd call me and say, 'What did you think of that story about Trump in the newspaper today? What did you think of the story about Trump on TV?' I'd say to him, 'Hey, Donald, you are Trump.' "

Donald followed the Wollman Rink opening with a far more unusual ceremony—a mortgage burning in the atrium of Trump Tower on December 23, 1986. The mortgage was on a 715-acre farm in Burke County, Georgia, owned by Annabel Hill, a sixty-six-year-old widow. In February 1986 Hill's husband had committed suicide in order to prevent a bank from foreclosing on the farm. He had hoped that the proceeds from his life insurance policy would be enough to pay off the mortgage. That was not the case. But by September 1986, as the bank started a second foreclosure proceeding, the national news media picked up the story.

Donald later claimed that he first heard about Annabel Hill's plight in a report by Tom Brokaw on "NBC Nightly News." In fact, it was Ivana who called the story to his attention. "Come in here and look at this," she urged. "This lady really needs some help. Why don't you help the lady out?"

At first Donald believed he could solve Hill's problem simply by sending her a check for $18,000. Then he discovered that a total of $185,000 would be required to save the farm. Though he was unwilling to part with so large a sum personally, he joined forces with radio talk show host Don Imus, then on WFAN in New York, to raise money for the Annabel Hill farm rescue fund. He also flew Hill to New York for a press conference in Trump Tower to increase public awareness of her tragic situation. When the fund-raising effort came up short, Donald agreed to contribute the final $40,000 needed to pay off her mortgage.

"The only way I can explain it was God touched his heart," Hill said later. Strange as it seemed, she may have been right. Donald generated at least two great rounds of self-promoting publicity through his efforts to help save Hill's farm, the first at the Trump Tower press conference and the second at the mortgage-burning ceremony. But he also showed a rare glimpse of genuine human sympathy and concern.

"I saw a side of him that was very caring, very sincere," recalled Hill's friend Frank Argenbright, who started the fund-raising effort for her in Georgia. "He would call her up and check on her [even after the publicity died out]. There was no feeling of 'Well, Frank, okay, you've done the deal. Annabel's gone. The publicity is over with. There's no benefit to Donald Trump now.' Not any of that ever."

While Donald continued to gloat about showing up Mayor Koch on the Wollman Rink project, he took more perverse delight in embarrassing Ivana. Following the opening of the rink, rumors circulated that he was having an affair with Peggy Fleming, the shapely brunette champion ice skater who also happened to be married. Fleming later denied the stories, but Donald did nothing to stop the tongue wagging. In December 1986 he asked Ivana to consider the idea of an "open marriage." Ivana would not hear of such a thing. "If I ever catch you being unfaithful," she informed him, "I'll kill you."

Donald knew that she did not mean that literally. But he began to realize that his wife wasn't to be trifled with. After all, she had modeled herself after him. That was nowhere more apparent than in Atlantic City. Rather than work together as a team, husband and wife now found their marital strife ritualized in an increasingly bitter business rivalry between "his" casino and "hers." If Ivana was queen of Trump's Castle, Donald was out to prove that he still ruled the roost—and the family gaming division.

In the spring of 1986, following the dissolution of his partnership with Holiday Inns, Donald recruited a high-priced new management team for Trump Plaza led by Golden Nugget veteran Steve Hyde and his protégé Mark Etess. A third former Golden Nugget executive, John R. ("Jack") O'Donnell, joined the Trump Plaza crew in early 1987. O'Donnell later turned on Donald Trump and published a vengeful memoir entitled *Trumped!: The Inside Story of the Real Donald Trump—His Cunning Rise and Spectacular Fall* In fact, O'Donnell's account told only one side of the story, but it provided an accurate account of Donald's marching orders for the new team at Trump Plaza. "Trump had sized up the competition and envied Steve Wynn's success at the Nugget," O'Donnell observed. "Steve Hyde was to be his weapon to raid the high end of the gambling market."

Hyde faced several competitive disadvantages. Trump Plaza's luxury suites did not come close to matching the size or elegance of the high-roller suites at Caesar's and other nearby facilities. And even though it was centrally located on the Boardwalk at the end of the Atlantic City Expressway, Trump Plaza did not have sufficient parking to handle middle- and low-end drive-in gamblers. In March 1986 Trump Plaza began construction of a $60 million parking garage ten stories high with 2,650 car spaces and 13 bus slots, but the facility would take nearly eighteen months to complete.

Trump Plaza's most serious problem, however, was that it was locked into direct competition with the boss's wife. Hyde and company blamed Ivana for the allegedly tasteless design of Trump Plaza's luxury suites. In an effort to lure high rollers away from Caesar's Palace and other competitors, Donald soon redesigned Trump Plaza's interior, marbling the lobby and upgrading the luxury suites at a cost one insider estimated to be the neighborhood of $40 million. But Trump's Castle was going after all three major segments of the gambling market, high, middle, and low, and doing so with considerable vigor. "I think Ivana was even more competitive than Donald," recalled Trump casino consultant Al Glasgow. "She'd call me up in the middle of one of her feuds with Hyde and the boys at Trump Plaza and start screaming into the phone, 'Zose mutha-fuckas!' "

Ivana also proved herself more adept at coddling customers than did her mercurial husband. Every month Trump's Castle gave a lavish reception for the casino hotel's favored high rollers. "The casino hosts hated those parties because the high rollers were typically a pretty boring and boorish group," recalled a former top executive. "But Ivana was so good at entertaining that everybody had a good time." Once she even led a band of twenty high rollers in a bunny hop dance from the reception room right through the lobby and onto the casino floor.

She was equally adept at motivating her staff. Ivana made sure to attend every employee of the month award ceremony and made a point of dancing with even the lowliest hirelings at staff parties. Likewise, she went out of her way to see that the Castle fulfilled state-mandated guidelines calling for casinos to let 5 percent of their gross purchasing contracts to minorities. Trump Plaza had little trouble meeting the quotas since payments to boxers such as Mike Tyson qualified as minority contracts. One of the more substantive ways in which Ivana met her minority quotas was by threatening not to do business with Hormel and Oscar Meyer unless they used a company owned by former major-league baseball star Bobby Brown as their local food distributor.

Ivana's efforts paid off on the balance sheet. At the end of 1986 Trump's Castle reported gross revenues of slightly over $226 million,

or about $2 million more than Trump Plaza, the second-highest fig-
ure ever posted for an Atlantic City casino's first year of operation.
She did even better on the bottom line. Trump's Castle reported net
profits of $65.9 million, a full $10 million higher than Trump Plaza's
net for the year. "Steve Hyde was pissed," Glasgow recalled, "because
Ivana was kicking their asses." Donald played both sides against each
other. He would threaten to fire Hyde and replace him with "another
blond model" like Ivana. But he also threatened to dismiss Ivana if
the Castle ever slumped.

"He hated it when Ivana grabbed the spotlight," recalls a former
Trump's Castle executive. "He tried to mold her in his own image,
and she tried to please him. When he saw what she was becoming—
a real rival to him—he didn't like it."

Donald had other reasons to fret over his Atlantic City empire that
had nothing to do with Ivana. In July 1986 the Division of Gaming
Enforcement forced recently indicted drug smuggler Joe Weichselbaum to resign his position at Damin Aviation. Weichselbaum's attorney succeeded in having his case transferred from federal court in
Ohio to federal court in New Jersey, where it was assigned to Donald's sister, Judge Maryanne Trump Barry. Three weeks later Judge
Barry recused herself and handed the file to another judge. Weichselbaum pleaded guilty to two counts of the drug-smuggling
indictment and started serving time at the Manhattan Correctional
Center in January 1988. One year later Weichselbaum's girl friend,
Ronnee Lake Teitler, paid over $2.35 million for apartments 49A
and 49B in Trump Tower with what she claimed was her own money.
Following his release from prison, Weichselbaum moved into the
Trump Tower duplex with Teitler. He told the parole board he
intended to become a helicopter consultant to Donald Trump.

In the summer of 1986 Donald started playing another dangerous
game—corporate greenmailing. His initial targets were two rival casino-
owning companies: Holiday Inns, his former partner in Atlantic City,
and the Bally Corporation. Although these were the halcyon days of
Drexel Burnham Lambert's controversial financial wizard Michael
Milken, he and Donald never formally joined forces in a casino junk
bond offering or a stock acquisition. But Drexel executive Daniel Lee
did play an active behind-the-scenes role in the Holiday and Bally
deals. In both cases it was Lee who encouraged Donald's interest in

buying the stocks. And in both cases Lee wound up representing the target companies, earning large fees for Drexel.

Donald later boasted that he made a total of $56 million on the two casino stock gambits. That was a typically gross exaggeration. But according to documents filed with the New Jersey Casino Control Commission, he did make a pretty fair killing, thanks in part to the introduction of some new Trump ploys. In both the Holiday Inns and Bally deals, Donald utilized a highly controversial put-call stock-trading arrangement with Bear Stearns. Under ordinary circumstances, a put is an option to sell a stock at a certain price; a call is the corresponding option to buy the stock at a certain price. But this particular put-call service was unusual and highly mysterious. All trades were conducted by means of confidential numbered accounts. Donald's personal account number was 049-50544-2-1. The corresponding Bear Stearns account was number 049-50549-2-6. The numbered accounts served to disguise the identity of the buyer or seller of a stock from the general public. In many instances the actual buyer of the stock was not Donald Trump but Bear Stearns.

The acquisition of Holiday Inns stock demonstrated the uniquely lucrative nature of this put-call arrangement. In August 1986 Donald bought 245,800 shares of Holiday stock via account 50544. The following month Bear Stearns acquired 854,200 shares of stock via account 50549. That brought the amount of stock held on Donald's behalf to 1.1 million shares, about 4.9 percent of the total shares outstanding. The market price was a little over $69 million. On September 12, 1986, Donald notified the Nevada State Gaming Control Board of his Holiday stock acquisition and applied for a nonrestrictive gaming license in the state. That move naturally prompted speculation that he would be launching a takeover attempt.

Donald later claimed in documents submitted to the Casino Control Commission that he put up $34.5 million "to pay the 50% margin requirement" on the Holiday stock purchases. But that may have been another ploy to disguise the fact that his put-call arrangement with Bear Stearns was really just a call arrangement. With takeover rumors boosting the price of Holiday stock, there was little chance that Bear Stearns would have to put, or sell its shares to Donald for less than the original purchase price. In effect, he appears to have been able to control the 854,200 shares Bear Stearns bought for account 50549 without putting up any of his own money. *Spy* magazine writer John Connolly later alleged that Donald's arrangement with Bear Stearns may have come perilously close to stock parking, or broker-client profit sharing, a practice strictly prohibited under stock exchange rules.

Both Donald and Bear Stearns benefited handsomely from the deals. His profit on the shares held in account 50544 was $4.3 million; his profit on the shares in account 50549 was about $12 million. That was far less than the $35 million he bragged about making on the Holiday Inns deal, but it still amounted to an impressive gain of over $16 million. On a normal transaction of this size, the brokerage fees would have been less than $200,000. But in this case Bear Stearns's fee was $6 million. Despite protestations that everything was on the up and up, the Justice Department later charged that Donald Trump had violated reporting requirements of the Hart-Scott-Rodino Act. On April 5, 1988, Donald paid a $750,000 fine to settle the case.

Donald's purchases of Bally Corporation stock followed the Holiday Inns gambit. In late November 1986 he used most of his profits from the Holiday trades to buy $14.9 million worth of Bally stock, which was held in account 50544. Bear Stearns bought $47.6 million worth of Bally stock for account 50549. The combined holdings of the two accounts put Trump's stake in Bally at 9.9 percent of the total shares outstanding. That same month Donald and his brother Robert complemented his latest casino stock plays with the acquisition of $43 million worth of stock in the Alexander's department store chain. Although he had little interest in retailing, Donald envied Alexander's portfolio of prime location real estate properties in Manhattan and the outer boroughs, which he appraised as far greater than the market value of the stock reflected.

Then things started popping down in Atlantic City. In December 1986 Bally sued Donald to block his alleged takeover attempt. At the same time Bally also announced that it was making an offer to buy Steve Wynn's Golden Nugget casino in Atlantic City for $440 million. Donald promptly countersued to block Bally's acquisition of the Nugget. When the smoke cleared, he emerged with another sack of greenmail. In February 1988 he agreed to sell his 9.9 percent stake back to Bally's and to drop attempts to block Bally's acquisition of the Golden Nugget. Donald claimed that he made a $21 million profit on the Bally deal, but records filed with the Casino Control Commission indicate that his actual gain on the stock was closer to $15 million.

In any case, Donald achieved three very desirable goals in the Bally deal. First, he came away with a tidy cash profit. Second, and perhaps even more important in his mind, he indirectly ensured that his archrival Steve Wynn would be leaving Atlantic City for good. Third, he built up a war chest for future acquisition attempts. But ominous changes were already blowing in the wind. In late December last-minute revisions to the Tax Reform Act of 1986 virtually destroyed incentives for speculative investments in real estate partnerships. And seven years after the advent of legalized casino gambling in Atlantic City, there were signs that the boom was turning into a bust.

But Donald could not stop now. Contrary to widespread misconception, he did not really believe his own hyperbole and braggadocio. He knew even better than his bankers and junk-bond holders that his empire was leveraged to the hilt. But with his first autobiography due out in the fall of 1987, he was on the verge of enjoying the kind of mythic fame and popular acclaim that made his quest for fortune worthwhile. Rather than prudently pull in his horns, he determined to keep making bigger and bigger deals at almost all cost. "He was like the alcoholic," recalled a former high-ranking Trump Organization executive, "and we were like the enablers."

Donald began the new year by amassing a private air force. On January 28, 1987, he bought a 1984 Aérospatiale AS322L Super Puma helicopter from an affiliate of Warner Communications for $2 million. An executive version of a chopper originally designed to transport crews to and from offshore oil wells, the Super Puma came with eighteen seats and twin Turbo-Meca Makila 1A engines that provided it with a four-hour flying range. Aircraft broker Hugh Redditt strongly advised Donald against the purchase, pointing out that the Super Puma was inordinately expensive to operate and that Warner had removed its capacity to float by filling the sponsons with air-conditioning equipment. "Donald is making a big mistake," Redditt warned a Trump attorney. "He's going to kill himself."

Donald ignored the warning. At the time he wanted Warner Communications to sign a major lease for his proposed TV City project. Buying the Super Puma was his way of sweetening the deal. But there was a second and even stronger motivation for the purchase: Donald's rivalry with Steve Wynn. A few years back Wynn had bought the only other similarly equipped Super Puma in the United States. After customizing the chopper and painting the fuselage black, Wynn had experienced numerous mechanical problems. He wound up sending the helicopter back to Aérospatiale and successfully sued the company for a refund. Donald seemed to believe that he could one-up Wynn by buying himself a properly performing Super Puma instead of a lemon.

Donald christened his whirlybird *Ivana* and customized it in accordance with Trump tastes. The new interior featured ten seats, including four reclining swivel club chairs and two couches, covered in beige leather, and was accented by gold-plated seat belt, ashtray, and doorknob fixtures. The extensively soundproofed cabin, which measured five feet wide and twenty-two feet long, was paneled in light-colored wood and carpeted with dark brown shag. There were telephones at each end of the cabin and a microwave oven in the galley. He had the fuselage painted black with red pinstripes and plastered the name Trump in white block letters on the tail.

About six weeks after purchasing the Super Puma, Donald bought a Boeing 727-100 jet aircraft from a subsidiary of the Diamond Shamrock Corporation. The price was $8.3 million, roughly 40 percent above market value. Just as lavishly customized as the helicopter, the 727 featured twenty passenger seats and specially designed work and conference areas with burgundy velvet couches, pecan-colored wood tables, and a sleeping compartment with a bathroom and shower. Like the Super Puma, the tail of the 727 was emblazoned with the name Trump. Once again, aircraft broker Redditt argued against the purchase, noting that Boeing had sent out numerous safety bulletins advising owners of the 1960s vintage plane to check for corrosion, cracks, and faulty rivets. But according to casino consultant Al Glasgow, there were other overriding considerations. Steve Wynn owned a stretched-out DC-9, and as in the case of the Super Puma, "Donald had to outdo Steve Wynn."

Following Wynn's return to Las Vegas, Donald attempted to assume undisputed leadership in Atlantic City. In March 1987 he made his biggest stock play to date, a bid for control of Resorts International. A financially embattled multinational conglomerate whose principal assets included most of the prime real estate on Paradise Island in the Bahamas, Resorts owned the first casino to open in Atlantic City and a still-uncompleted gargantuan gaming hall called the Taj Mahal. By the time Donald Trump began eyeing the company as a potential takeover target, company founder James Crosby had died of heart failure. Effective control of the corporation had passed to the late visionary's surviving family members.

The Resorts bid marked a fateful turning point in Donald's meteoric career, for it proved to be yet another giant step down the primrose path to deeper and deeper indebtedness. Prior to Crosby's death, the company claimed to have $300 million in cash and virtually no long-term debt. By the spring of 1987 Resorts had virtually no cash and was $740 million in debt. This extraordinary reversal of fortunes was partly attributable to Crosby's eccentric—and ultimately disastrous—investments in the commodities market, a $30 million shrimp farm, and a $50 million seaplane-manufacturing venture. But the greatest drain on the corporate financial coffers was the ongoing Taj Mahal debacle, on which Resorts had spent an estimated $500 million.

Donald later claimed that the daunting challenge of rescuing Resorts—and the Taj Mahal—was what inspired his takeover bid. But his lust for Resorts was actually intensified by the fact that the company had been targeted by two more experienced and financially powerful takeover artists, Jack Pratt, the chief of the Dallas-based chain called The Pratt Hotel Corporation, and Marvin Davis, a billionaire oilman turned Hollywood movie mogul. The Crosby clan had summarily rejected Davis's offer in fear of his announced aim to dismember the corporation's unprofitable branches. The family had also turned down Pratt's initial offer and coyly stalled his subsequent attempts to negotiate a compromise deal.

Almost all of Donald's top-ranking executives and advisers urged him to reconsider. The only one to voice enthusiasm for taking over Resorts was the newly installed Trump Plaza president, Steve Hyde, who allegedly aspired to rule over an ever-expanding gaming division. Robert Trump opposed the idea. So did attorney Jerry Schrager, attorney Nick Ribis, financial chief Harvey Freeman, and casino consultant Al Glasgow. The Trump minions expressed alarm about the untold and potentially crippling costs of completing the Taj. Reminding the boss that New Jersey law prohibited him from owning

more than three casinos in Atlantic City, they pointed out that he
would wind up with a four-casino empire (Trump Plaza, Trump Castle, the Taj, and the original Resorts casino on the Boardwalk) if and
when the Taj finally opened for business. As a result, he might be
forced to divest at least one of his prize gaming properties at a fire
sale price.

At the end of a marathon debate one evening, Donald told his
inner circle that he had decided to drop his proposed takeover attempt.
The following morning he issued a public announcement that he
intended to bid for control of Resorts after all. The news stunned the
Trump Organization along with the rest of the unwitting outside world.
But when Al Glasgow, who had participated in the previous night's
debate, called to ask what had prompted such a sudden change of
heart, he was even more shocked by the boss man's simplistic explanation. "If I don't buy Resorts," Donald declared, "somebody else
will."

Donald's leverage in the Resorts deal rested on the fulcrum of the
company's A-B stock structure. The Class A common stock, which
was held by nonfamily investors, accounted for over 90 percent of
the company's financial equity. It traded at prices ranging $10 to $20
a share. The Class B preferred stock, held by the Crosby family,
accounted for less than 10 percent of the total equity and sold for a
premium price of $135 a share. But under the provisions of the cor-
porate charter, each share of Class B stock could outvote each share
of Class A stock by a ratio of 100 to 1. Rather than risk upward of
half a billion dollars to buy 50 percent of the common stock, Donald
could effectively gain control of Resorts with an investment of less
than $100 million in the purchase of the Crosby family's preferred
stock.

As if to assure Trump Organization doomsayers that he had not
lost all his marbles, Donald found a way to pay for the Resorts stock
without spending a penny of his own cash. He borrowed the entire
amount of the purchase price, which worked out to be $96.2 million,
from a miniconsortium led by Citibank. Then he made sure to cover
his downside regardless of what happened to the market value of his
Resorts stock. In July 1987, upon officially assuming the position of
chairman of the board, he began lobbying the company's directors to
approve an extraordinary "management contract" that would pro-

vide him with a personalized "golden parachute" worth over $60 million in cash. When the directors balked, Donald threatened not to complete the facility at all unless he got his management contract. In the fall of 1987 the Resorts board finally acquiesced to his demands.

Donald's "scheming and beaming" in Atlantic City paralleled another nasty battle on the home front. In the summer of 1987, just as he was completing his bid for control of Resorts, he and Ivana flew to Moscow along with their personal assistants, Norma Foerderer and Lisa Calandra, to discuss a possible hotel venture in the Soviet Union. That project never panned out, but by the time the Trumps returned to New York, Ivana was intent on renegotiating their marital joint venture agreement. Displaying the same sort of chutzpah The Donald had shown to the board of Resorts International, she simply marched into his office and announced, "I want a better deal."

After advising Ivana to consult attorney Larry Levner, the Roy Cohn crony who had represented her in previous nuptial contract negotiations, The Donald attempted to frustrate his wife's demands at every turn. In fact, he negotiated with her just as he negotiated with a rival businessman. There was no question that Ivana deserved "a better deal." Allowing her one was in The Donald's interest, as well as hers, especially when it came to ensuring some modicum of domestic tranquillity. But he was not about to give in easily.

No one, including his wife, really knew exactly how much The Donald was worth. He publicly professed to be a billionaire and bitterly complained about a recent *Forbes* magazine estimate that he was worth only half a billion. But there had never been a comprehensive independent audit of his assets and liabilities. The closest reliable estimate of her husband's wealth came in sworn statements he had submitted to the Casino Control Commission in the spring of 1987, and even those numbers were flawed. On a summary sheet The Donald claimed to have assets of $1.8 billion and a personal net worth of nearly $820 million. A closer look at the line items, however, revealed that his arithmetic was incorrect. His assets actually added up to $1.7 billion. Subtracting liabilities of $979.4 million left him with a net worth of $702.3 million.

In any case, Ivana would wind up with a relative pittance if their marriage were terminated by her husband's death or a divorce. Her own net worth was far easier to calculate than The Donald's. It consisted of $800,000 worth of jewelry, furnishings, and personal property and about $400,000 in cash, representing the accumulated interest and principal of the $100,000 certificate of deposit her husband had given her upon their marriage. Under the terms of their 1984 agreement she would get just $2.5 million in cash, the Trump Tower triplex, the estate in Greenwich, Connecticut, and annual support payments of $30,000 per child.

As the Trumps' negotiations dragged on through the fall of 1987, it became clear to both parties that one subtext of the dispute involved Ivana's performance as chief executive of Trump's Castle. In the first quarter of the year Ivana had come within a whisker of achieving her overall goal of being number one in Atlantic City as well as number one among the Trump properties. After starting the year in fourth place, the Castle climbed to the number two spot with gross revenues of over $20 million in both February and March. Though more centrally located on the Boardwalk, Trump Plaza languished in the middle of the pack. In March the Plaza reported gross revenues of only $19 million, which put it five notches below and $1.6 million behind the Castle.

Ivana's successes and excesses at the Castle continued to infuriate her male counterparts at Trump Plaza. Besides being embarrassed by Ivana's month-to-month leadership in gross revenues, Plaza President Steve Hyde viewed her as a threat to his own career ambitions. He secretly feared that Ivana was conspiring to become chief executive in charge of all the properties in the Trump gaming division, an as-yet-nonexistent post The Donald had supposedly promised to create for Hyde in the future. Hyde constantly complained about Ivana's allegedly extravagant perquisites, such as her insistence on keeping her old office at the Plaza even though she spent almost all her time at the marina facility. At Hyde's urging, The Donald had recently ordered her to relinquish the space to newly hired Plaza Vice-President Mark Etess. But the wounds inflicted during this seemingly minor turf battle made it impossible for either side to bury the hatchet.

If anything, Ivana's symbolic retreat from the Plaza's executive office suite only increased her competitors' paranoia. Trump Plaza executive O'Donnell later claimed that he and Etess believed that the Castle "had somehow tapped into our phone lines or had planted an operative in our data processing branch" to steal the casino's preferred customer lists. Trump casino consultant Glasgow delighted in feeding this paranoia. When the boys at Trump Plaza let him in on their telecomputer conspiracy theory, he let them in on a startling piece of intelligence. Glasgow claimed that on a recent visit to the Trump estate in Greenwich, he had spied a gaggle of men in white coats muttering to one another in Czech. His story was a complete fiction, but it had the intended effect of upsetting Ivana's competitors no end.

The rivalry between Ivana and the boys at the Plaza took a new turn in June 1987 with the opening of Central Park, the 2,650-car garage adjacent to the Boardwalk casino. Glasgow predicted that the new parking facility's contribution to increasing the volume of gambling in Atlantic City would have "as much impact on the market as the opening of a new casino." He was right. Trump Plaza suddenly shot up from number eight in monthly revenues to number three, with a June 1987 gross of $21.1 million. The Castle fell from its previous number two position down to seventh place, with a gross $2 million below the Plaza's.

The dramatic reversal of positions between the Castle and the Plaza was not just a short-term aberration. After faltering slightly in July, the Plaza climbed up to second place in August, setting a monthly gross revenue record for the property of $27.7 million, up 21 percent from the previous year. The Castle remained mired in seventh place with a disappointing August gross of $22.9 million, down 2.1 percent from 1986. The Donald blamed the Castle's slump on Ivana. He now began castigating her in front of the casino's vice-presidents and managers as if she were one of the lowliest of the hired help.

"Without me, you're nothing!" The Donald ranted. "You're doing a shitty job down here. If you don't get your act together, you're gone!"

The confrontations in Atlantic City mirrored the conflicts in the Trumps' marriage. On the rare occasions when they both were back home in New York at the same time, Ivana liked to go to plays or to the ballet. The Donald had no interest in such time-consuming cultural events and adamantly refused to accompany her. Ivana usually wound up being escorted by such "walkers" as jewelry designer Kenneth Lane and socialite Jerry Zipkin. She became a rising star in the gossip columns and on the society pages as she twinkled about town in five-, ten-, and twenty-five-thousand-dollar dresses by such designers as Arnold Scaasi, Chanel, Dior, Givenchy, and Christian Lacroix, matching pumps by Charles Jourdan, bedazzling baubles borrowed from Kenny Lane, and hang-to-the-shoulders hairstyles by Jennifer Lawrence at the Louis Licari salon.

The Donald complained often and out loud about his wife's allegedly spendthrift life-style. "Norma!" he would scream at his executive assistant, Norma Foerderer. "How much money can one person spend on shoes!" At her boss's behest, Norma would verify Ivana's charge records and attempt to justify them. The moment she completed that task, The Donald would complain about his wife's household expenses. "Norma! What is somebody spending eight hundred dollars for a vacuum cleaner for?" The Donald wailed one day. "How could vacuum cleaners cost eight hundred dollars? Call and find out what vacuum cleaners cost."

And yet, as if to confuse and confound his much-maligned spouse further, The Donald called Ivana at least once every day and told her, "I love you."

"I love you, too," she always replied.

Ivana started to believe that the key to saving her marriage and saving face was to get the Castle back on top of the competition. In the fall of 1987 she launched an aggressive busing campaign aimed directly at low-end customers who might otherwise flock to Trump Plaza. The program appeared to pay off. Trump Plaza climbed to the number one position in November with gross revenues of over $22 million, but by December the Castle had taken over the number two spot, while the Plaza slipped back to third place. But the expenses entailed in raising the Castle's gross revenues ate away at the casino hotel's net profits.

While The Donald ostensibly had an equal stake in the success of both his Atlantic City casinos, he clearly intended to make the Plaza his flagship operation. On October 16, 1987, Trump Plaza hosted its first major heavyweight championship fight featuring Mike Tyson and Tyrell Biggs. The audience included a heart-stopping blonde named Marla Maples, who came with her ex-boyfriend Tom Fitzsimmons. The bout itself lasted only seven rounds, with Tyson winning by a technical knockout. But the crowds attracted to Atlantic City for the event increased citywide revenues for the month by 20 percent and boosted the Plaza's gross by nearly 30 percent.

Unfortunately for Donald, that Friday the stock market fell by a record 108.36 points. The Friday plunge turned out to be an ominous prelude to the 500-point crash that occurred three days later on "Black Monday." Donald gave the media the impression that he had seen the crash coming and got out in the nick of time. That was another big lie. In fact, he suffered losses in the value of his stock in Resorts International and the Alexander's department store chain that reportedly totaled, at least on paper, more than $100 million.

Not to be outdone by the Plaza's new flash, Ivana determined to go after the high-end gambling market, too. She had far classier things in mind for the Castle than common fisticuffs. The casino hotel she had taken over from Hilton had been designed as a middle-market facility. Because there were no truly luxurious high-roller suites and no grand ballroom, New Year's Eve was a nightmare. But Hilton's original blueprint had also contemplated a future expansion that included a second hotel tower. In the fall of 1987 Ivana convinced The Donald to follow through on Hilton's plans. He allocated $78 million to upgrade the Castle's high-roller suites and build a fourteen-story hotel addition known as the Crystal Tower. She hoped this ambitious expansion program would put the Castle on top to stay. She had no idea it would set the stage for her departure from Atlantic City once and for all.

Of far more immediate concern to Ivana were her efforts to negotiate a new nuptial agreement. As the summer leaves turned to autumn red, The Donald remained intransigent. He offered to increase the amount of her cash payment in the event of his death or a divorce from $2.5 million to $3 million but adamantly refused to raise the ante any further. Ivana's attorney, Larry Levner, seemed unwilling or incapable of putting on the proper pressure. Ivana saw no alternative but to "go on strike," as she had done back in 1984. She climbed into her red 1979 Mercedes, drove up to Greenwich with her mother, and announced that she would stay there until The Donald gave in.

Back in New York City, Donald began to devote more and more of his personal attention to a new project: promoting his forthcoming autobiography, *Trump: The Art of the Deal.* He saw the book as a perfect panacea for the festering problems in his empire. If it made *The New York Times* best seller list, he could potentially increase both his fame and his fortune to new heights. But Donald's ego did not blind him to the fact that he was still relatively unknown outside the New York and Atlantic City metropolitan areas. Unless he could gain some instant nationwide publicity, sales of the book would probably be confined to his home turf.

Donald's desperate search for a way to promote his book onto the best seller list inspired one of the most cynical schemes of his career: the Trump for President campaign. He launched his "campaign" in cahoots with his publicist, Dan Klores. It was, from beginning to end, a fraud. Back in the summer a few casual acquaintances and cocktail party admirers had broached the notion of Donald's running for president. He never took them more than half-seriously. ("What do you think?" he would ask Klores in his patented third-person style of self-referencing. "Can Trump run for president?") Even now he had no intention of actually entering the primary races. He simply wanted to fuel rumors of his political aspirations for commercial gain.

Donald and Klores proceeded to enlist the services of veteran Washington lobbyist Roger Stone, a partner in a predominantly Republican firm that included Bush campaign aide and future party chairman Lee Atwater. Stone came up with the idea of running "open letter" newspaper ads as the crucial initial step in Donald's fictitious presidential bid. On September 2, 1987, the first of these open letter ads, an unsolicited diatribe about U.S. defense policy, appeared in the *New York Times, Washington Post,* and *Boston Globe.*

"There's nothing wrong with America's Foreign Defense Policy that a little backbone can't cure," Donald's letter declared. "For decades, Japan and other nations have been taking advantage of the United States. . . . Make Japan, Saudi Arabia, and others pay for the protection we extend as allies. Let's help our farmers, our sick, our homeless, by taking from some of the greatest profit machines ever created. . . . Let's not let our great country be laughed at anymore."

On October 22, 1987, Donald flew to Portsmouth, New Hampshire, on his brand-new Super Puma helicopter to keep a speaking engagement arranged by Stone at a local Rotary Club luncheon. He found himself greeted by larger crowds than those that had turned out for legitimate presidential candidates Alexander Haig and George

Bush. Donald delighted the Rotary Club members by delivering a fiery speech with the same basic theme as his open letter newspaper ads.

"I'm not here today because I'm running for the presidency," he declared. "I'm here because I'm personally tired of seeing this great country of ours being ripped off. . . . We should have these countries that are ripping us off pay off the two-hundred-billion-dollar deficit." Shamelessly playing to the jingoistic sentiments in the room, Donald went on to propose that the swiftest and surest way for the United States to rectify economic injustice was by attacking Iran and taking over the oil fields. The crowd erupted into an orgy of cheering and clapping as *New York Times* reporter Fox Butterfield dutifully took notes on the crazed scene.

The next day, the *Times* ran a story on Donald's campaign-style appearance at the Rotary Club under the headline NEW HAMPSHIRE SPEECH EARNS PRAISE FOR TRUMP. One member of the audience noted that the turnout for Donald was greater than the that for declared Republican candidates Bob Dole, Jack Kemp, Pat Robertson, and Alexander Haig. The wife of a former Rotary Club president had a ready explanation. "He's very exciting," she said of Donald, adding, "Money is power, and power is the ultimate aphrodisiac."

ABC News interviewer Barbara Walters fell head over heels for the Trump aphrodisiac. On December 11 she anchored a segment about him for the program "20/20" that was entitled "The Man Who Has Everything." The dual theme was "Donald Trump, businessman" and "Donald Trump, possible presidential candidate." Walters lavished both Donald Trumps with praise.

"Look, up in the sky! It's a bird! It's a plane. No, it's superbuilder Donald Trump's ten-million-dollar French Aérospatiale helicopter heading for the Sixtieth Street Heliport to pick up the brash forty-one-year-old billionaire businessman and whisk us off to check up on part of his ever-expanding empire," Walters gushed at the outset of the segment.

"What do you feel like when you look at that wonderful skyline?" she asked Donald. "Do you say, 'I own that and that and that and that'?"

"Well, I look at that skyline, Barbara, and I really say it's the greatest in the world, the greatest city in the world," Donald declared, "and everybody knows it, everybody acknowledges it, and I'm very proud to be part of it."

Walters took her viewers on a guided tour of the Trump trophy properties in New York and Atlantic City, where she observed that "the Trumps are treated like American royalty." Then she turned to the matter of Donald's presidential ambitions. After Donald had coyly denied having any plans to make a bid for the White House in the foreseeable future, Walters posed her most trenchant question of the segment.

"If you could be appointed president and didn't have to run, would you like to be president?" she asked.

"I don't know, interestingly," Donald replied. "You know part of the enjoyment of something and part of the whole thing is the battle. If you could be appointed, I'm not sure that would be the same ball game."

"It wouldn't be any fun for you?" Walters pressed.

"The seeking, it's the quest that really, I believe—it's the hunt that I believe I love," Donald insisted.

Walters closed her segment by sharing an exclusive anecdote with co-anchor Hugh Downs. She recalled having attended a luncheon with Donald earlier in the week that the State Department hosted for Soviet Secretary-General Mikhail Gorbachev. Rather than go through the receiving line with his back turned to the surrounding gaggle of news photographers, Donald told her, he "maneuvered Gorbachev around so that we were standing side by side, and the result is this UPI picture which was on the front page of some of the newspapers. And there is Donald Trump telling Gorbachev what to do and you see his face."

Walters's fawning segment on "20/20" attested to the promotional success of the "Trump for President" charade. It was a perfectly timed national network advertisement for his newly released autobiography.

"I don't do it for the money," Donald declared on page 1 of *Trump: The Art of the Deal,* which was published by Random House in November 1987. "I've got enough, much more than I'll ever need. I do it to do it. Deals are my art form. Other people paint beautifully on canvas or write wonderful poetry. I like making deals, preferably big deals. That's how I get my kicks."

If Donald's book claimed any distinction in the field of American business literature, it was as a classic in self-serving myth creation. While the reading public naturally expected any autobiographer to write with an unexpurgable measure of personal bias, it also expected him or her to tell his or her side of the story as fully and truthfully as possible. No one expected Donald to give away trade secrets or make public his tax returns. But no one was prepared for the shameless lies, half-truths, omissions, distortions, exaggerations, image burnishings, and lily gildings of *Trump: The Art of the Deal.*

Donald's fatuous statements ranged from the sublime to the ridiculous. He said that he had met Ivana "during the summer Olympics in Montreal" when he actually met her at a New York City singles spot, and he claimed that she had skied on the Czech Olympic team when she had not. He devoted a whole chapter, entitled "The Cincinnati Kid," to describing what he claimed was his first big real estate deal, the purchase of an apartment complex in Ohio called Swifton Village. Donald maintained that he made the deal for Swifton Village while still a student in college; in fact, as published newspaper reports confirmed, Fred Trump, Sr., actually made the deal while Donald was still in military school.

In recounting the Grand Hyatt deal, Donald openly admitted that when the city asked to see his option agreement to acquire the property from Penn Central, he provided a copy signed by only one party, Donald J. Trump. He failed, however, to mention the unprecedented role his political crony Stanley Friedman played in rushing the deal through City Hall in the closing hours of the Beame administration. Likewise, when describing the demolition of the site of Trump Tower, he made no mention of employing illegal Polish workers to do the job. He boasted about his adroit use of junk bonds in refinancing his Atlantic City casinos but omitted the fact that he had shaved off more than $20 million in personal fees on the deals. He vastly inflated the profits he supposedly made from his stock and real estate deals without revealing that whatever success he did enjoy was due to his very unusual put-call arrangement with Bear Stearns.

Although he scorned casino hotel chain heir Barron Hilton as a member of the Lucky Sperm Club, Donald disingenuously failed to acknowledge that he, too, had benefited from the accident of birth. He tried to come across as an outsider, a streetwise kid from Queens, when he was heir to a centimillion-dollar family real estate fortune. He hinted at his early struggles to stand up to his father, whom he described as "my best friend," but made no mention of his continuing oedipal battles with the old man. And in a book that ran nearly 246 pages long, he devoted less than two pages to his late older brother, Fred, Jr.

Although otherwise loyal Trump Organization insiders archly dubbed Donald's book "The Art of the Spiel," it was greeted with the kind of critical reception usually accorded a noteworthy work of non-fiction. This was still the heyday of the Reagan era. The damaging revelations of the Iran-contra scandal were months away, and so were the indictments of Michael Milken and his junk bond wizards at Drexel Burnham. Donald's book articulated the materialistic ethic of a decade that had elevated avarice to the status of a respectable, if not indispensable, national value. And as if to prove their patriotic fervor, the so-called liberal media fell over themselves in acclaiming the author and his exploits.

"He makes one believe in the American Dream again," gushed veteran *New York Times* book reviewer Christopher Lehmann-Haupt. "The how-to memoirs of a modern day Midas," cheered the *Boston Globe*. "This is the entrepreneurial mind at work if there ever was one," chimed *People* magazine. "If your goal in life is to make a million, read this book," advised the *New Orleans Times-Picayune*.

The public reception for *Trump: The Art of the Deal* surpassed even the author's wildest dreams. Donald put an enlargement of the book's cover in the atrium of Trump Tower and made a practice of popping down from his office suite to sign autographs. Whenever he showed up, crowds of up to eight hundred people seemed to materialize out of thin air to buy his book. When he arrived for a scheduled book signing at a West Palm Beach, Florida, shopping mall, the turnout was so large and enthusiastic that the local police briefly feared they might have a riot on their hands.

Not surprisingly, Donald's literary venture proved enormously profitable. *Trump: The Art of the Deal* sold over 950,000 hardback copies. For Donald and co-writer Tony Schwartz, those sales figures translated into author's royalties of over $3 million, including paperback and foreign rights. Schwartz used his share of the royalties, which was estimated to be $1.5 million, to escape the grind of writing for monthly magazines so he could concentrate on independent book projects. Donald had promised to donate his $1.5 million royalty share to charity. But according to former Trump Organization insiders, the artist of the deal evidently decided to contribute only a few thousand dollars to charity and kept the lion's share of his book royalties for himself.

One day shortly after *Trump: The Art of the Deal* hit the bookstores, Donald was walking down Fifth Avenue toward his office when a buxom blonde standing in front of the Pierre Hotel caught his eye. He could not remember if he had met her before, but she remembered meeting him.

"Hello," she said. "My name is Marla Maples. I'm a friend of Jerry Argovitz."

Slowly it dawned on Donald that Marla was the beauty queen the former New Jersey Generals president Jerry Argovitz had brought to the USFL meeting in Atlantic City more than a year before. This time he would not forget her face or her name.

Later that afternoon Marla telephoned Tom Fitzsimmons to ask about Donald Trump. Her ex-boyfriend filled her in on the real estate mogul, noting a very salient fact. "Marla," he told her, "Donald's a married man."

Then Fitzsimmons's call waiting signal beeped. He put Marla on hold and picked up the second call. It was Donald Trump.

"Who is this Marla Maples broad?" Donald wanted to know. "She is one incredibly beautiful girl. You've got to bring her around, so I can get to know her."

"Donald," Fitzsimmons reminded him, "you're married."

"You've got to bring her to my book party," Donald insisted.

Fitzsimmons was speechless—and suspicious. Although his pal had made similar requests before, the present object of Donald's desire was different from all the females he had pursued in the past. Fitzsimmons did not regard Marla Maples as just another bimbo to be used, abused, and abandoned: she was both a former lover and a faithful friend. Something told him to hang up the phone before he got caught in the crossfire of an adulterous love triangle. But Fitzsimmons also knew that his even older friend and former fellow skirt chaser would not take no for an answer.

"Okay," he promised, "Marla and I will be there—with bells on."

On the night of his New York book party Donald John Trump showed why he had grown up to be a self-made American myth. Even the infamously snobby New York literary glitterati decked out in black tie and evening dresses drew audible breaths as they filed past the klieg-lit security stanchions on the red-carpeted sidewalk in front of Trump Tower. Upon entering the atrium, they were greeted by an army of white-jacketed waiters serving champagne and serenaded by red-sashed violinists. All six floors of the atrium were ablaze with Christmas lights and red poinsettias and filled with cornucopian buffet tables. Disco music blared from the bistro level, inspiring some of the estimated two thousand guests to dance on the ledges of the waterfall.

Donald stood in a serpentine receiving line with Ivana on one side and Random House owner Si Newhouse on the other. Donald's parents, Fred and Mary Trump, hovered nearby with the rest of the family as the likes of movie star Michael Douglas, model Cheryl Tiegs, recently separated socialite Anne Bass, boxing promoter Don King, New Jersey Governor Thomas Kean, and former Kentucky Governor John Y. Brown and TV celebrity wife Phyllis George marched by to offer their congratulations to the host-honoree. Then Tom Fitzsimmons arrived with Marla in tow.

"You could see the fireworks go off the second Donald and Marla set eyes on each other," Fitzsimmons later told a mutual friend. "I'll never forget the way he kept winking and staring at her even though Ivana was so close to them she couldn't help seeing the whole thing."

When the receiving line finally broke up, Donald went from one part of the atrium to another until he tracked down Marla and her escort. The encounter turned out to be surprisingly anticlimactic. Donald seemed so love-struck he was, for perhaps the first time in his life, at a loss for words. He finally regained enough bravura to ask for her phone number and promised to call her to arrange a lunch date.

Donald then began one of the most curious courtships in the history of postmodern philandering. Instead of sending Marla flowers and candies, he sent her press clippings about his business exploits and the latest rave reviews of his best-selling book. Their first lunch led to a second and a third. Then the lunch dates turned into dinner dates, followed by late-night talks about life, love, and the pursuit of happiness. Marla's friends warned her about the dangers of getting intimately involved with a married man, especially a high-profile rake like Donald J. Trump. But she insisted that their relationship was merely platonic.

"When Donald's around me, he doesn't act like a big bad business-man," Marla informed one worried confidant, adding that she had seen another side of his larger-than-life persona in private. "He's always so sweet and so kind. And he wants to help my career."

chapter seven
THE DEALS THAT MADE NO SENSE

■ ON CHRISTMAS EVE 1987 Mr. and Mrs. Donald J. Trump raised their glasses for a champagne toast. It was shortly before suppertime, and though The Donald virtually never partook of spirits, this was a very special occasion. After six months of bitter negotiations, he and Ivana had just signed their fourth nuptial agreement. Both parties felt genuinely relieved. The gossip columns were full of the news that Anne Bass, wife of Texas oil billionaire Sid Bass, had just filed a divorce action to claim her half of the community property because of her husband's affair with socialite Mercedes Kellogg.

"Mercedes Kellogg is a grease dog," The Donald told Ivana. "Sid Bass is going to find out she was the most expensive fuck of his life."

The Donald had covered his own divorce risk much better than Sid Bass. If he and Ivana got divorced, he would have to pay her an initial lump sum of $10 million in cash, up from $2.5 million in the 1984 nuptial contract, and annual support payments of $350,000 until she married or moved in with another man. As in the previous agreement, Ivana would also get the house in Greenwich, the use of Mar-a-Lago for the month of March, and occupancy of the Trump Tower triplex until it was sold, at which time she would collect another $4 million.

Significantly enough, the Trumps' new nuptial contract omitted a clause that had distinguished their past deals. The clause, which had appeared on the first page of the 1984 version, had nothing to do with money. It simply stated that the parties had reached agreement "because of the great love and affection each has for each other and because of the close relationship both marital and business between IVANA and DONALD. . . ." There was no "great love and affection" phraseology in the 1987 contract.

Ivana nevertheless looked lovingly at The Donald and gave him a quick kiss. Then she gulped down her champagne and rushed off to midnight mass at St. Patrick's Cathedral with her mother, who had flown in from Czechoslovakia for the holidays.

Donald slept with Marla Maples for the first time within days of signing his 1987 nuptial agreement. He later claimed that he could not remember the exact date of this initial assignation. But the timing had potential critical legal significance. If he and Marla had had sex prior to Christmas Eve 1987, a case could be made that he had entered into his nuptial agreement with Ivana with patently fraudulent intent. In any event Donald boasted to friends that sex with Marla was the best sex he had ever had. Despite her subsequent public denials of having said the same thing about sex with Donald, Marla seemed to enjoy their lovemaking as well. "He's an animal in bed," she informed one confidant with a satisfied smile.

Donald's dalliance with Marla quickly became an open secret in the Trump Organization. In New York she occupied a fourth-floor room in the St. Moritz, just three blocks from Trump Tower. Most afternoons Donald would try to slip away from the office for a couple of hours and rendezvous with Marla at the hotel. In Atlantic City, where Ivana ruled Trump's Castle, Marla typically stayed at Trump Plaza, registering under the name Fitzsimmons.

The secretarial staff in Manhattan and the casino executives in Atlantic City had orders to accommodate Marla's wishes as discreetly as possible. "Norma Foerderer would always try to keep it hush-hush," recalled a former Trump secretary. "Marla would call just about every day, but she never came up to the office or went to society parties. . . . Everyone [on the secretarial staff] liked Marla. She was always very nice. She'd always say, 'How are you? How are things going?' " Accommodating Donald's wishes with regard to Marla was not so easy. He drove the accounting staff crazy by demanding that it find ways to send her ever-increasing amounts of off-the-books cash spending money.

The word around the office was that Donald had arranged to keep Ivana preoccupied with her duties in Atlantic City so that she would seldom have time to drop by the Trump Organization headquarters in New York. That was just fine as far as many members of the staff were concerned. "Ivana was a bitch to work for," a former secretary remembered. "She tried to adopt the same savvy as Donald. Whenever she was in town, people were always trying to placate her. She talked down to her employees. She called people assholes and shot them the finger. She'd scream just like Donald, 'You're a fucking moron!' "

By this time Ivana was embroiled in yet another rivalry with Robert Trump's new wife, Blaine Beard Trump. Five feet nine inches tall with mousy blond hair and a preppie perkiness, Blaine was born in the South and grew up in Japan, where her father worked for IBM. She had attended finishing schools in Switzerland and France, where she acquired the bearing and manners of a pedigreed socialite. A divorcée with one school-age son, Blaine had married Robert in 1984. They lived in a thirty-sixth-floor apartment in Trump Plaza on Third Avenue. Blaine still held a paying job at Christie's auction house, but she devoted increasing amounts of time to high-profile charities and social events such as benefits for the Lenox Hill Hospital and a salute to designer Christian Lacroix by Bergdorf Goodman.

Much to the chagrin of both Donald and Ivana, Blaine seemed to get nothing but fawningly favorable press. *Women's Wear Daily* had dubbed her "Nouvelle Society's Ingenue." *New York* gossip columnist William Norwich referred to Blaine as "Her Blondness," while rival columnist Suzy (Aileen Mehle) called her "Darling Blaine." Family friends claimed that the supposed ill will between Blaine and Ivana was orchestrated by Donald and vastly exaggerated by uninformed gossips. Indeed, the two often sat side by side at fashion shows, laughing with conspiratorial glee. But some Trump Organization insiders found Blaine almost as dislikable as the allegedly overbearing Ivana.

Donald treated his children in much the same way he treated his wife. He made sure a separate limousine was on call at all times to shuttle them back and forth to classes and other appointments. But he was apparently so uninterested in and ill informed about their activities that he could not remember which schools each attended. The Trump Organization staff had to remind him of the dates of his children's birthdays and buy presents for them. Norma Foerderer made a practice of getting reports from the nannies and giving them to her boss. "Donald, your son was in a play today," she would remind him. "Don't forget to ask him about the play."

As far as the Trump children could tell, the most serious new rival for their father's attention was world heavyweight boxing champion Mike Tyson. On January 22, 1988, Trump Plaza in Atlantic City hosted the overhyped "Heavyweight History" title bout between the twenty-one-year-old Tyson and thirty-eight-year-old former champ Larry Holmes. Donald promoted the match with the same flashy style he used to promote his book. His personal guest list featured a constellation of movie stars and celebrities including Barbra Streisand, Don Johnson, Cheryl Tiegs, Bruce Willis, and Jack Nicholson, whom Donald paraded through the Atlantic City Convention Center arena like a captive army before and after the fight. At one point Nicholson, who received the noisiest accolades from the fight fans, allowed that he just might open his own casino across the street and call it "Jack's No Trump."

Donald did not appreciate the humor. Trump Plaza had paid $2 million to outbid Caesar's Palace in Las Vegas for the Tyson-Holmes fight. The casino recouped $2.6 million at the gate and another $2.4 million of a record $8.4 million gambled at the tables and slot machines that night. The total take for the weekend minus fight promotional fees worked out to over $4 million. But even before Tyson knocked Holmes to the canvas in the fourth round to win the fight, Donald saw still-bigger dollar signs flashing from Iron Mike's gloved fists.

Following the death of his mentor, Cus D'Amato, Tyson had signed a management contract with D'Amato's heir apparents, Jim Jacobs and Bill Cayton. Days later Jacobs died of leukemia. Among those who envied Cayton's contract with Tyson and wanted to break it was controversial fight promoter Don King, a bushy-haired convicted felon with a deal-making spiel that sounded like an African-American version of Donald Trump's. Donald himself hoped to get a piece of the action by continuing to stage Tyson fights at his casinos and by becoming Tyson's financial adviser. But suddenly a new player entered the picture: svelte and ambitious twenty-three-year-old television actress Robin Givens.

On February 9, 1988, less than three weeks after the Holmes fight, Tyson and Givens were married in a civil ceremony in Chicago. A few days before, Givens had told Tyson that she was pregnant with his child, a claim that was later doubted by almost everyone in the champ's inner circle. Shortly after the marriage Don King started showing up at the Trump offices with Tyson, Givens, and her mother, Ruth Roper, in tow. After Donald's secretaries had fed and watered the heavyweight champion, Iron Mike and Robin would go into Ivana's empty office and watch television while King and Roper discussed business with Donald.

"Donald was by far the dominator in the Trump-Tyson relationship," recalled a former Trump Organization insider who watched the interaction. "It was perfect for Donald. He loved it when people looked up to him, and Mike Tyson really looked up to him."

On June 27, 1988, Trump Plaza hosted "Once and for All," a bout between Tyson and Michael Spinks for the undisputed world heavyweight championship. The casino paid $11 million to outbid Steve Wynn's Golden Nugget for the rights to the fight, making it the most expensive heavyweight championship in history. Although Tyson knocked Spinks to the canvas in one minute and thirty-one seconds of the first round, Trump Plaza grossed more than $18 million and won over $2 million from its gambling customers that weekend. The combined weekend gross for all twelve Atlantic City casinos exceeded $40 million, prompting Donald's grateful competitors to run a full-page ad in the local newspaper saying, "Thank you, Mr. Trump." But the stage was set for a nasty confrontation between the members of the champ's inner circle. Just before the bell for round one, Tyson's attorney served papers on manager Bill Cayton; the legal intent of the papers was to abrogate Cayton's contract by alleging fraud.

Behind the scenes Donald was already playing the champ for a chump. Although several associates claimed that he had often made racial slurs against blacks in the past, he seemed to be more than a little enamored with Tyson's beautiful young wife. Donald and Givens had appeared together on ABC's "Good Morning America" television program the morning of the Tyson-Spinks fight; according to Tyson biographer Montieth Illingworth, they had been seen together in Trump Plaza late the night before after Tyson went to bed. According to at least one Trump insider, Donald knew full well that he was playing with fire, which was exactly what excited him about hanging around with Givens: "Robin was his biggest risk."

Two weeks after his victory over Spinks, Tyson held a press conference at Trump Plaza in Atlantic City to announce the formation
of Mike Tyson Enterprises. The members of the company's "board
of advisers" were Tyson's attorney, Michael Winston, his mother-in-
law, Ruth Roper, and Donald Trump. The champ told the assembled
media that henceforth he, not Bill Cayton, would be "calling the shots"
and that he would "manage my own self."

But Donald had his own heavyweight championship agenda. He
wanted Tyson to stick to the schedule Cayton had arranged, which
included a bout against Frank Bruno in London, so that the champ
could return to Atlantic City later in the year to fight Evander Holyfield at Trump Plaza. He quickly negotiated a settlement between
Tyson and Cayton. Under the terms of the compromise it was agreed
that Cayton would continue as Tyson's manager, but his share of the
purse would be reduced from one-third to 20 percent.

Then Don King made his move. On October 2, 1988, Tyson received
a private detective's report reportedly compiled at King's behest. It
described an afternoon and evening Robin Givens and Donald Trump
had spent together on the newly purchased *Trump Princess* yacht the
previous summer and a photograph of Givens wrapped in a bath
towel. That night Tyson and his wife had a terrible fight. Givens and
Roper called a psychiatrist, Dr. Henry McCurtis, who reportedly
advised that Tyson was manic-depressive and should be committed
to a mental hospital. Then they fled for Los Angeles.

Tyson briefly retreated to the arms of Bill Cayton, who phoned
another psychiatrist for a second opinion. Dr. Abraham Halpern
concluded that Dr. McCurtis, who had prescribed lithium and Thor-
azine to control Tyson's "mood regulatory problem," had based his
diagnosis on biased information from "Mrs. Tyson and her mother."
On October 6 Don King took Tyson around to each of his bank and
brokerage accounts, which contained close to $15 million, and ordered
them not to honor any checks issued by or to Givens and Roper. By
so doing, they were able to stop payment on a check for over $580,000
Givens had written to Robin Givens Productions for "reimbursement
of expenses."

About this same time the November issue of *Vanity Fair* came out
with an article on the supposedly blissful Tyson-Givens marriage. It
was accompanied by a photograph of Donald and Givens on the *Trump*

Princess that appeared remarkably similar to the one in the private detective's report given to Tyson. Donald had a fairly sound alibi for being photographed with Givens. After all, she had suggested the *Princess* as the venue for the photo shoot, and at the time he was still acting as Tyson's financial adviser.

Donald publicly denied any sexual involvement with Givens. "I'd have to be crazy to sleep with the wife of the world heavyweight champion," he declared. But according to Montieth Illingworth, associates of Don King told Tyson that they had overheard Donald complaining that Givens was inept at oral sex. "She's got the sharpest teeth in the world," Donald reportedly remarked. According to Trump Organization insiders, he later advised Givens to establish a legal residence in California so she could take advantage of the state's community property laws in lodging a claim to Tyson's millions.

Amid his double-dealing with Tyson, Donald embarked on his biggest, boldest gambit in Atlantic City. In early March 1988 he offered to buy all the outstanding stock in Resorts International that he did not already own with the intention of taking the company private. It was a cheeky move, and a desperate one. Following the October 1987 market crash, Donald had suffered a paper loss of more than $75 million on his Resorts stock. He now planned to use additional bank borrowings to purchase the Class A stock while it was selling at a postcrash discount. Then, after going deeper in debt to salvage what seemed to be a bad investment, he hoped to refinance his stock purchase and pay off Resorts' $650 million in corporate debt via a junk bond offering underwritten by Ace Greenberg and his friends at Bear Stearns.

But things did not go according to plan. Donald offered to buy Resorts' Class A stock for $22 a share, almost twice the market value of the stock. Then, just as the board appeared to be on the verge of accepting his increased bid, Merv Griffin appeared on the scene. Known to most of the public as a portly former TV talk show host and big band singer, Griffin had recently sold a package of game shows he had produced, including "Jeopardy" and "Wheel of Fortune," to Coca-Cola for a reported $250 million. Now he had his sights set on acquiring a casino hotel chain. Shortly after Donald made his offer for Resorts, Griffin's lawyers filed a lawsuit challenging the company's two-tiered stock structure. On March 17, 1988, Griffin announced he was making his own offer for Resorts at $35 a share, an astonishing $13 a share above the Trump bid.

Donald later dubbed Griffin's tender "The Deal That Made No Sense." It was that, but not just for such obvious reasons as Griffin's excessive offering price. As it turned out, there was quite a lot of alleged mob-related activity taking place behind the scenes. Sometime prior to March 17 a former used-car dealer from Rochester, New York, named Fedele ("Dale") Scutti acquired 5 percent of Resorts' Class A common stock. Unlike the Resorts board, Scutti thought Donald's offer of $22 a share was too low. Hoping to find a white knight who might pay a much higher price for Resorts, he hit on a roundabout way to get Merv Griffin involved.

Through the offices of a New York lawyer friend, Scutti met a controversial stock speculator named Ernest Barbella. Part owner of an investment firm called Equities International, Barbella was later accused of being a member of the Gambino crime family, a charge he vehemently denied. Barbella shared an office at 900 Third Avenue in Manhattan with his former college roommate Michael Nigris, who happened to be president of the Griffin company. Barbella introduced Scutti to his friend Nigris, who agreed to a deal that would get Scutti a much higher price for his Resorts stock than Donald had offered. Scutti gave Griffin Enterprises an option to buy a little over half his Class A stock in Resorts at $22 a share. Nigris, in turn, promised that Griffin Enterprises would launch a $35-a-share offer for all the outstanding stock in Resorts, including the Class B shares for which Donald had paid $135 a share.

But a few hours prior to the announcement of Griffin's bid for Resorts, another Barbella associate named Peter Aiello allegedly bought a large block of Resorts stock for just under $23 a share. When Griffin's bid became public, the price of Resorts stock shot up, and Aiello allegedly made a quick $70,000 profit. Aiello was later indicted on insider trading charges in connection with the transaction. Barbella pleaded guilty to related charges and agreed to cooperate with the government. Months after Griffin had discovered Nigris's connections to Barbella, he fired Nigris from his company. Nigris retaliated with a wrongful termination suit against Griffin.

In the meantime, Donald had no intention of selling his Class B stock in Resorts at a loss of $100 per share. On March 18 he filed a lawsuit against Merv Griffin, Griffin Enterprises, and Dale Scutti. It charged that Scutti had "failed to disclose the existence of the individuals with whom he had agreed to act in concert, their backgrounds and identities." In order to defend themselves against the lawsuit, Scutti, Nigris, and Orens would have to allow Trump attorneys to question them about their dealings with Barbella; the attendant revelations might prompt the Casino Control Commission to block the deal.

Rather than risk such an embarrassing scenario, Griffin agreed to meet Donald in his Trump Tower office to negotiate a compromise. On May 27, 1988, they unveiled the basic outlines of a deal to split Resort into two pieces. Griffin agreed to pay $36 a share for all outstanding Class A shares in Resorts and $135 a share for Donald's Class B stock. He also agreed to pay Donald another $63 million in cash to buy out the management contract he had signed with Resorts the previous year. As compensation for their roles as intermediaries, Scutti and Orens would collect fees of $6 million and $1.9 million respectively.

Ironically, "The Deal That Made No Sense" would have made millions of dollars for Donald if he had stopped there. With his initial stock investment in the Class B stock fully recouped, Donald would also walk away with a $63 million cash windfall from the buyout of his management contract. But he did not intend to quit until he had a shot at finishing the Taj Mahal. Under the announced accord with Griffin, he agreed to buy the uncompleted casino hotel from Resorts for $273 million. Then he announced that he would rename the facility the Trump Taj Mahal and cavalierly compared it with "a large-scale Wollman Rink."

During the seven months the Casino Control Commission devoted to examining the proposed Resorts deal, Donald's top executives urged him to reconsider. "It was probably the largest construction disaster I had ever seen," former Trump construction manager Tom Pippett concluded after he and Donald had walked through the Taj in the summer of 1988. "The building was open to the ocean right through to the back. Everything had been sitting there for years open to and exposed to the weather and the salt air. There were birds nesting in the sheet metal ducts."

The Trump Plaza president, Steve Hyde, who had been one of the few to endorse Donald's original decision to buy stock in Resorts, worried about the unprecedented management problems the Taj would pose if the construction work were ever completed. Hyde's protégé Mark Etess, the Plaza's executive vice-president, pointed out the potentially huge hidden costs of the time and labor required to run a facility the size of the Taj. "It just can't be operated efficiently," Etess protested.

Donald obstinately refused to change his mind. Two years later, when recounting his version of the deal, he wondered aloud at Merv Griffin's apparent lack of foresight in "saddling himself" with $925 million in debt and interest payments that would exceed anticipated income by $109,000 per day, a financial burden that would eventually force Resorts into bankruptcy. "Ego," Donald concluded scornfully. "That's probably the only way to explain The Deal That Made No Sense. Certainly something was preventing Merv, a sharp guy, from truly seeing the numbers that people kept placing in his path."

Donald missed the irony in his disparaging words about Merv. As numerous present and former employees observed, he was not infatuated with the Taj merely because of its profit-making potential. He regarded it as a chance to create a commercial monument to himself. "The Taj was the last casino Donald could own in Atlantic City [under the three-casino legal limit], so it had to be the most magnificent," observed Tom Pippett. "It had to be the fulfillment of a dream."

While awaiting the Casino Control Commission's formal approval of the Merv Griffin deal, Donald made some of his other unfulfilled dreams come true. In January 1988 he bought the 282-foot-long yacht *Nabila*, which he promptly renamed *Trump Princess,* from the creditors of embattled Saudi financier Adnan Khashoggi. The purchase price was $29 million, but he spent six months and another $8 million on renovating the pleasure craft, only to discover that the boat was too large to dock next to Mar-a-Lago and would have to tie up in front of the Best Western hotel in Palm Beach.

Then in the spring of 1988 Donald made yet another deal that made no sense, the purchase of the landmark Plaza Hotel in New

York City. Once owned and operated by the Westin Hotel chain unit of United Air Lines, the Plaza had recently been acquired by Texas oil heir Robert Bass, the younger brother of Sid Bass, and his partner John Aoki, a Tokyo construction tycoon. In early 1988 a Bass emissary offered Donald a chance to buy the hotel for $450 million. Donald countered with a bid of $350 million. The parties eventually settled on the still-astronomical compromise price of $407 million.

Donald's purchase of the Plaza was greeted with howls of ridicule by his rivals in the Manhattan real estate industry. The hotel reportedly generated a cash flow of about $20 million a year. According to the accepted purchase price multiple of fifteen times cash flow, that meant that the Plaza's market value was about $300 million. By that measure, Donald had overpaid to the tune of $107 million. The only way the Plaza could possibly make the interest payments on its bank debt out of cash flow was by filling up all 814 rooms 365 nights per year at a going rate of $500 per room.

If the Plaza Hotel deal seemed to evince a fundamental financial insanity on Donald's part, his lunacy was indulged and abetted by an enthusiastic co-conspirator, the Citibank unit of Citicorp, which lent him the entire amount of the purchase price plus tens of millions of dollars more for renovations. Although Citicorp was the nation's largest banking institution, the firm was remarkably cavalier and inept at what most laypeople would believe to be any big bank's principal area of expertise—i.e., lending money. This curious situation had resulted partly from the policies of Citicorp's recently retired chairman, the legendary Walter Wriston, and partly from the policies of Wriston's successor, John S. Reed.

In hope of leading Citicorp to the top of the international banking world, Wriston had approved tens of billions of dollars in loans to third world countries. When Reed took over in 1984, many of those countries were in the process of defaulting on their loans. After shocking Citicorp stockholders by writing off $3 billion of the third world debt in one fell swoop, Reed determined to make up for the bank's losses, and save his own neck, by engineering a dramatic comeback. As one insider recalled, "Everyone knew that we were under tremendous pressure to increase earnings as quickly as possible."

Reed hoped to increase earnings by lending large amounts of money to supposedly secure and well-collateralized U.S. and Canadian real estate projects. Along with generating interest for Citicorp, those loans could generate additional income by being syndicated to foreign banks, which would not only share the risk but pay generous fees for the privilege of participating in the loans. Citicorp critics later accused the bank of not doing enough syndication. But in the case of the Trump portfolio, one of the few things the bank did right was syndicate his loans.

Unfortunately for Citicorp, its chairman had no experience in real estate lending. Reed's claim to fame, and the reason for his rapid ascendancy, had been running the firm's increasingly profitable consumer banking operations, which boasted the most extensive and efficient automatic teller machine systems in the industry. Upon taking over the post of chairman, however, Reed reportedly became loath to venture outside his executive suite. On a rare visit to one of the building's lower floors, he shocked a subordinate by asking about the purpose of a plastic card dangling from the man's belt. "That's an access card, John," the subordinate replied. "You need it to enter the doors on every floor but yours."

Vice-Chairman Lawrence Small, the man assigned to supervise Citicorp's loan-driven comeback, was also inexperienced in real estate lending. A creature of the bank's highly competitive and highly politicized internal culture, he had ambitions of filling the vacuum created by the departure of former Reed rival Thomas Theobáld, who had left to run Continental Illinois Bank, and possibly even rising to the chairmanship if Reed stumbled. But in an effort to cut costs, Small had inadvertently sown the seeds of his own downfall. According to insiders, he refused to keep the salaries of Citicorp's middle managers commensurate with those of executives at investment banks. As a result, the bank lost many experienced executives to competing Wall Street firms.

Small's fatal mistake, however, was to direct his real estate loan officers to lend money primarily to big-name customers such as the flamboyant Canadian developer Robert Campeau. Although Campeau's high-profile empire was ultimately doomed to a spectacular collapse, Citicorp sources later claimed that his highly leveraged balance sheet was subjected only to the most rudimentary "due diligence" scrutiny by bank officers. The reason for the lapse, these sources maintained, was that Campeau had become a particularly close personal friend of Lawrence Small. "Larry was known around the bank as Bob Campeau's man," one disillusioned insider recalled.

Another high-profile and highly leveraged Citibank customer who benefited from Small's lending policies was Donald J. Trump. Like Campeau, Donald was apparently regarded as the kind of developer who could generate plenty of favorable free publicity for the bank. Donald could also help improve the bank's earnings by paying interest on large loan amounts, provided, of course, that his projects produced sufficient cash flow. Small later claimed that he and Donald had met only once in a social situation and that he had left supervision of the Trump loans to subordinates. But Small set the tone from the top. Even so, Citicorp's own legal counsel was aghast at the economics of the Plaza Hotel purchase. "All this due diligence doesn't mean shit," complained a lawyer assigned to review the financial documents submitted along with the loan application. "We're just lending to Donald Trump."

Donald tried to defend the deal, and his honor, by taking out a full-page advertisement in the *New York Times* entitled "Why I Bought the Plaza." His ad copy stated: "I haven't purchased a building, I have purchased a masterpiece—the Mona Lisa. For the first time in my life, I have knowingly made a deal which was not economic—for I can never justify the price no matter how successful the Plaza becomes. What I have done, however, is to give to New York City the opportunity to have a hotel which transcends all others! I am committed to making the Plaza New York's single greatest hotel, perhaps the greatest hotel in the world."

But Donald had ulterior motives for purchasing the Plaza apart from and in addition to his purported civic-mindedness. He announced that he was putting his wife, Ivana, in charge of the hotel's operations and its renovation program, promising to pay her "one dollar a year and all the dresses she can buy." That apparently came as news to Ivana. The next day she put out a press release from Atlantic City stating: "Mrs. Trump remains fully in charge as chief executive officer of Trump's Castle." But her statement turned out to be a futile exercise in wishful thinking.

Over the past several months the simmering rivalry between Ivana and the Trump Plaza president, Steve Hyde, had come to a boil. Hyde continued to fear that his boss's wife was intent on taking con-

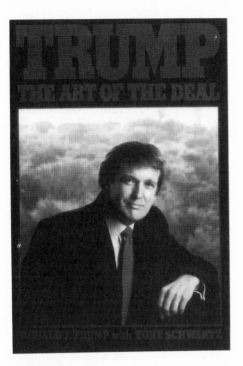

Michele Singer / Outline Press; Design: © 1987 Random House, Inc.

Michael O'Brien; Design: © 1990 Random House, Inc.

Donald J. Trump's spectacular rise and fall were chronicled on the covers of *Time* and *Newsweek* and in two best-selling autobiographies.

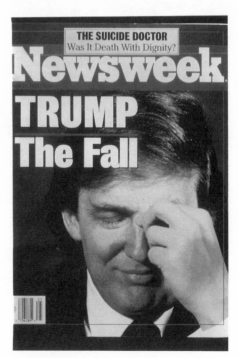

Donald Trump's rise to fame and fortune was made possible by the influence of his attorney, Roy Cohn *(top left)*, who showed him how to handle politicians such as New York Mayor Ed Koch and New York Governor Hugh Carey *(bottom left)* and New York City Council President Andrew Stein *(right)*.

© by Marina Garnier

Ivana Trump was a model before she met The Donald. *Weco-Presse / Gamma Liaison*

Ivana Trump's first true love, George Staidl, was killed in a car crash in Czechoslovakia in 1972.

Ivana Trump with hus-
band, Donald, in happier
times before her plastic
surgery. © *by Marina Garnier*

Ivana Trump after her
plastic surgery with her
mother, Maria Zelnicek. ©
by Marina Garnier

Trump Tower, at the corner of Fifth
Avenue and Fifty-sixth Street in New
York City, is the headquarters of the
Trump Organization. *Randy Bauer / Ron
Galella, Ltd.* © *1990*

Donald Trump's bankers forced him to give up
a 49 percent ownership in the landmark Plaza
Hotel. *Randy Bauer / Ron Galella, Ltd.*

Donald Trump's renovation of Wollman Rink in Central Park was his greatest public relations
coup. *Ted Thai /* Time *magazine*

The name Trump dominates the skyline of Atlantic City. *From left,* Trump Plaza, Trump Regency, and Trump Taj Mahal. *Florence Garrett Photo Source*

Trump's Castle was ruled by Ivana Trump until Marla Maples entered the picture. *Florence Garrett Photo Source*

Mar-a-Lago, the Palm Beach estate Donald Trump purchased from the heirs of Marjorie Merri-weather Post. © *1992 by Ray Fairall / Photoreporters, Inc.*

Donald Trump seldom sailed on his 282-foot yacht, *Trump Princess,* before the banks foreclosed. *Anthony Savignano / Ron Galella, Ltd. © 1988*

The tragic helicopter crash that killed Trump gaming division executives Steve Hyde, Mark Etess, and Jon Benenav proved to be an omen of things to come. *The* Press *of Atlantic City* © *1992*

Marla Maples was Donald Trump's secret mistress for more than two years. © *by Marina Garnier*

The confrontation between Donald, Ivana, and Marla on the slopes of Aspen was captured by the paparazzi. © *1990 by William Davila*

Marla Maples's longtime publicist, Chuck Jones, was accused of stealing more than thirty pairs of shoes. © *1991 by Harry Benson*

Marla Maples made her Broadway debut in *The Will Rogers Follies.* © *1992 by Martha Swope*

Donald's parents, Fred and Mary Trump, were upset by the scandalous publicity surrounding his split with Ivana. *Anthony Savignano / Ron Galella, Ltd. © 1989*

Donald Trump lorded it over his younger brother, Robert; Ivana was jealous of her publicity-seeking sister-in-law, Blaine. *© by Marina Garnier*

Donald Trump proposed that former heavyweight champion Mike Tyson pay his way out of a prison sentence for rape. *Anthony Savignano / Ron Galella, Ltd. © 1989*

Merv Griffin sold Donald Trump the Taj Mahal after Trump sold him Resorts International. *Smeal / Ron Galella, Ltd. © 1990*

Donald Trump tried to feed off Michael Jackson's celebrity. *Randy Bauer / Ron Galella, Ltd. © 1990*

Ivana's avenger: attorney Michael Kennedy, and his wife, Eleanore. *Kelly Jordan / Ron Galella, Ltd. © 1991*

Ivana Trump with her boyfriend, Riccardo Mazzucchelli, and aide Lisa Calandra. *© by Marina Garnier*

Donald Trump loved being linked to women such as model Rowanne Brewer *(top left)*, actress Robin Givens *(top right)*, actress Catherine Oxenberg *(bottom left)*, and model Carla Bruni-Tedeschi *(bottom right, shown with Eric Clapton)*.

In the fall of 1992 Donald Trump accounced that he was making a comeback and celebrated by giving himself a surreal party at the Trump Taj Mahal. *Photo by Tom Mihalek © 1992*

trol over both Trump casinos in Atlantic City. He bad-mouthed Ivana behind her back and in front of Donald at every opportunity. She, in turn, referred to Hyde as "nothing but a big fat fucking piece of shit." But the queen of Trump's Castle appeared to be losing the battle against Hyde and the boys at the Plaza on both the top and bottom lines.

In February 1988 Trump Plaza had again become the number one ranking casino in Atlantic City with gross revenues of over $22 million. The Castle had slipped to fifth place with revenues of $18.3 million, down nearly 10 percent from the year before. In an effort to turn things around, Ivana launched yet another aggressive marketing campaign. The Castle began busing in almost three times as many middle- and lower-market customers as Harrah's, its marina side neighbor. Harrah's monthly gross revenues nevertheless continued to exceed those of the Castle by almost two to one. By April 1988 the Castle had slipped to sixth place in monthly revenues, while the Plaza recovered from a temporary slump to regain the first-place spot.

The Donald never let his beleaguered wife hear the end of it. His tactic, as the former Plaza vice-president Jack O'Donnell noted, "was to shove the Plaza's performance in Ivana's face, like a mirror, holding it up for her to see the reflection of a less than successful manager." He also bitched about the exorbitant costs of enlarging and upgrading the Castle's hotel facilities. Determined to make the new fourteen-story Crystal Tower's complement of ninety-seven luxury suites the finest in town, Ivana had selected twenty-three different types of marble, wool carpeting priced at $100 per yard, and gold-plated bathroom fixtures that ran $1,800 apiece. But Donald could not foist all the blame on his wife, for he sat with her on the project committee, which included a team of design, construction, and casino hotel professionals.

According to O'Donnell and other former insiders, the blunder that may have broken Ivana's back came in the early spring of 1988, when she tried to convince her husband to hire as a vice-president at Trump Plaza an executive she had recruited from a competing casino. Steve Hyde believed his worst fears were coming true and demanded that Donald nix the new hire. "Ivana was attempting nothing less than a coup d'etat," O'Donnell charged. "If successful, Steve's authority would have been permanently undermined. It probably would have forced his resignation." In fact, Hyde did give Donald an ultimatum. The cutthroat competition between the Plaza and the Castle threatened to destroy both properties, he declared. He simply refused to put up with any more of Ivana's alleged schemes to steal the show. "Either she goes," he told the boss, "or I go."

Like it or not, Ivana felt she had no choice but to do her husband's bidding. A few days after announcing the Plaza Hotel purchase, The Donald gave his wife and Hyde their marching orders. Ivana would return to New York and devote full-time to running the Plaza. Hyde would assume responsibility for running both casinos in the Trump gaming division.

On May 18, 1988, Donald hosted a dinner in Ivana's honor at one of the ballrooms at Trump's Castle. At the conclusion of her formal remarks to the 130 invited guests, she made the mistake of shedding a few tears of regret. Donald proceeded to embarrass her further by taking the podium and declaring, "Look at this, I had to buy a three-hundred-and-fifty-million-dollar [*sic*] hotel just to get her out of here and look at how she's crying. Now that's why I'm sending her back to New York. I don't need this, some woman crying. I need someone strong in here to take care of this place." He evidently intended his comments to be taken as a joke. But Ivana's female friends in the audience did not see the humor and started booing. Donald quickly excused himself from the podium and left. Ivana and her friends stayed and partied until 5:00 A.M.

The following afternoon more than fifteen hundred employees jammed into the lobby of Trump's Castle to bid farewell to their departing boss. As Ivana made her way down the escalators and out the front door, she passed by cheering throngs of well-wishers, who lavished her with bouquets of roses as if she were a real queen. Many female employees were crying. By the time Ivana climbed into her waiting limousine, she was sobbing, too. As she drove off, her arch-nemesis, Steve Hyde, turned to Trump casino consultant Al Glasgow and opined, "Well, I guess that's the end of an era."

Donald wasted no time in returning to his most dangerous game. As soon as Ivana was reassigned to New York, Marla Maples moved into Trump Plaza in Atlantic City. Although his extramarital affair was by now common knowledge among his top gaming executives, Donald vacillated between flaunting his girl friend in public and virtually sequestering her in the casino hotel. He increasingly called on the services of his two primary Atlantic City bodyguards, a pair of tall, broad-shouldered, and brown-mustached men named Lynwood Smith and Jim Farr. Smith and Farr became captains of the "Corvette squad," so named because they shuttled Marla about town in Corvettes whose slanted, dark-tinted windshields helped conceal the identities of both driver and passenger.

Much like his late personal hero, Howard R. Hughes, Donald seemed to grow more reclusive and eccentric. During his trysts with Marla in Atlantic City, he often holed up with her in one of Trump Plaza's high-roller suites for days at a time, refusing to come out even for meals or business receptions. Room service sent up trays full of seafood and champagne for Marla and pasta or steak for Donald, who alternated between gorging himself and "fasting" on popcorn and candy. On other occasions Donald consorted with Marla behind Ivana's back but in full view of anyone else who cared to notice. That summer he took Marla along on his trip to the 1988 Republican National Convention in New Orleans.

He also continued to fuel rumors about his adulterous exploits with other women besides Marla. One day in the summer of 1988 Donald telephoned his publicist Dan Klores with a brazenly nonsensical request concerning gossip about his alleged interest in actress Catherine Oxenberg, one of the stars of the TV series "Dynasty." "I want you to leak to the gossip columns that Catherine Oxenberg is chasing me," he instructed Klores.

"Donald, you're a married man with three children," Klores reminded. "Why do you want me to do something like that?"

"Just do it," Donald ordered.

Although Klores later claimed that he refused to accede to Donald's request, rumors about the Trump-Oxenberg romance quickly circulated in both New York and Atlantic City. Several of Donald's friends later claimed to have bumped into Oxenberg while she was shopping with his credit cards. But some of those same Trump Organization insiders also claimed that as far as they could determine, the rumored romance was never consummated. Oxenberg herself later denied the rumors.

Donald celebrated the Fourth of July 1988 by sailing the maritime version of a trophy property—the 282-foot-long *Trump Princess*—into New York Harbor. Operated by a crew of thirty-one, the yacht featured a helipad, a swimming pool, a discotheque, a screening room, a minihospital, a sixteen-seat main dining room with a gurgling waterfall, three elevators, and 250 telephone lines. Each of its eleven double guest berths was named after some type of precious metal or jewel. Like its sibling suites, the master bedroom "Diamond Suite" was equipped with a television, a videocassette recorder, a compact disk player, a chamois ceiling, an onyx shower stall, and gold-plated bathroom fixtures.

No fewer than eleven film crews documented the yacht's arrival. President Ronald Reagan sent a special telegram of congratulations. Splashy life-style stories appeared in *Newsweek* and other national media organs. The same Hollywood movie stars and professional celebrities who flocked to Trump-sponsored boxing matches now vied for invitations to parties aboard his fabulous new boat. Donald himself sailed on the boat only once. He spent his first and last night on board when the *Princess* completed the final leg of its maiden voyage from the Azores via New York to Atlantic City. He was so unnerved by the horrific sound of weighing the anchor, which hoisted to a niche directly below the master bedroom, that he stayed wide-awake all night.

Meanwhile, Trump casino executives in Atlantic City complained that the value of the *Trump Princess* as a marketing tool was in no way commensurate with its cost. Donald really did not care what they thought. He arranged for Trump's Castle to lease the *Princess* for $400,000 a month plus operating costs and to pay $1 million more for the dredging of Absecon Channel off Atlantic City required to prevent it from scraping bottom. The money did not come directly out of his own pocket. By charging all these expenses to Trump's Castle, he effectively stuck the casino hotel's bondholders with the tab. The Castle was to end 1988 with a net loss of $3.1 million. Were it not for the costs associated with the *Princess,* the casino hotel would have shown a net profit for the year.

"It's inconceivable that this kind of quality can be done on a boat," Donald boasted to a *Newsweek* reporter. "You look at great homes and they don't have this kind of quality. Quality means everything."

It was during the year of the *Trump Princess*'s maiden voyage that

Donald allegedly perpetrated a series of financial and media manip-
ulations that amounted to the ultimate scam. Many of these deals
involved a controversial Atlantic City gambling customer known,
appropriately, as the ultimate high roller. His name was Robert LiButti,
and he was a bald, plump, and profane horse breeder from New
Jersey. Back in the early seventies LiButti had participated in schemes
to conceal the identities of owners of champion racehorses for various commercial and tax-related considerations. Although horserac-
ing authorities in New York, New Jersey, and Kentucky subsequently
banned him from the sport, LiButti continued to run his equine
interests through his daughter, Edie, an attractive blonde in her early
thirties whom Donald had tried, unsuccessfully, to seduce.

Bob LiButti happened to be by far the biggest customer at Trump
Plaza in Atlantic City. Between 1986 and 1989 he wagered no less
than $20 million at the casino's crap tables. A self-confessed "gam-
bling addict," he wound up losing a staggering $8 million during that
period. According to Casino Control Commission records, Trump
Plaza partially offset LiButti's losses by providing him with $3.5 mil-
lion worth of comps, including free hotel rooms, meals, event tickets,
trips, limousine services, automobiles, and other noncash gifts. All
this was perfectly legal under New Jersey gaming statutes. But
according to LiButti, Trump Plaza and its owner, Donald Trump,
also covered his losses in a variety of illegal ways.

"We had an elaborate marketing scheme," LiButti claimed later,
"so Trump Plaza could knock off Caesar's Palace and be number one
[in citywide gross revenues]."

The elaborate marketing scheme, as LiButti described it, violated
the spirit and letter of New Jersey gaming laws. His role was to help
Trump Plaza inflate the table drop, or total volume of chips wagered,
by $6 million to $8 million a year. While increasing the table drop
would not necessarily increase net profits (since the house might or
might not win a percentage of the money wagered), it would increase
the casino's gross revenues, which were measured according to the
amount of chips purchased from the cage. Increasing the gross revenues would supposedly make Trump Plaza appear to be a more
attractive property in the eyes of potential buyers should Donald be
inclined to sell.

All LiButti had to do was what he did on every trip to Atlantic City:

gamble. He could keep whatever money he won. If he lost, Trump Plaza allegedly promised to reimburse him. The important thing was that LiButti keep going back to the cage and purchasing more chips. On one occasion, LiButti claimed, the Trump Plaza president, Steve Hyde, encouraged him to withdraw $100,000 worth of chips in the morning, return them to the cage when he stopped for lunch, then withdraw the chips again that same afternoon. Although LiButti gambled only a total of $100,000 that day, the casino's books would have reflected a table drop of $200,000 because of his two trips back and forth to the cage.

Trump Plaza allegedly rewarded LiButti through at least two other indirect means. One involved his daughter, Edith LiButti, and his brother-in-law Jimmy Roselli, a nightclub singer whose popularity once rivaled that of Frank Sinatra until he reportedly ran afoul of Sinatra and the mob years before. Edie LiButti received $20,000 per show for booking Roselli at the casino; her elementary school-age daughter received $1,500 a show for carrying a bouquet of roses up to the stage. Trump Plaza also treated Edie to a gala party celebrating her thirty-fifth birthday on August 21, 1989. The party, which lasted three days, was held mostly on the *Trump Princess*. The engraved invitations cost $250 a piece. Jimmy Roselli received $25,000 simply for singing "Happy Birthday." Bob LiButti charged that Trump Plaza also bent the comp rules by giving him expensive cars, a perfectly legal act, so that he could sell them for cash and gamble the proceeds, an illegal act in terms of the alleged overall intent.

When LiButti lost $350,000 at the crap tables in February 1988, the owner of Trump Plaza allegedly broke the law against comping a casino gambler in cash, a violation that could subject him to license revocation. LiButti claimed that after he informed Steve Hyde of his losses, Hyde called Donald Trump. A short time later Donald supposedly appeared in the lobby, where LiButti was cooling his heels, and handed over a check for $250,000. "I want to present this to you myself," Donald allegedly told his casino's most valuable customer. Donald later denied LiButti's allegations and even went so far as to claim in an interview with *Philadelphia Inquirer* gaming expert David Johnston that he would not be able to recognize LiButti in person.

The "elaborate marketing scheme" that LiButti allegedly helped execute nevertheless appeared to work according to plan. In December 1989 Trump Plaza reported annual gross revenues of slightly more than $305 million, enough to take over first place in Atlantic City from Caesar's Palace, which reported revenues of $303 million.

But LiButti's relationship with Donald and Trump Plaza proved extremely double-edged. In the summer of 1988 LiButti offered to sell a Kentucky colt named Alibi to Steve Hyde. LiButti claimed that Alibi, which had been sired by former champion Raise a Native, had the potential to be another Secretariat, the fabled Triple Crown winner. Hyde realized that such a colt could provide his boss with a perfect pretext for hobnobbing with the high-rolling casino customers who frequented the tracks. Donald agreed to buy Alibi for the asking price of $500,000. Then he insisted on changing the colt's name to DJ Trump, proclaiming that he had automatically increased the animal's value by $250,000 and should therefore have to pay only half the originally agreed-on price.

Worse, Donald demanded that DJ Trump be shipped up from Florida to start racing right away. At the time the barn where the colt was stabled happened to be housing an equine virus known as sniffles. After running a full-speed time trial against the advice of the trainer, DJ Trump caught the bug, which blocked the circulation of blood in his forelegs. The only way to save the animal was to amputate its hooves. The operation did not affect DJ Trump's future capacity as a stud, but it ended his racing career.

When Hyde told LiButti that Donald no longer wanted to buy the crippled horse, the ultimate high roller vowed never to gamble at Trump Plaza again. "The great Donald Trump, ritz and glitz son of a bitch," LiButti fumed. "Because of him, we ruined a $20 million animal." In hope of placating his best customer, Hyde arranged for his wife, Donna, to buy DJ Trump for $150,000. That turned out to be the first of several horse deals involving LiButti, the Hydes, and later, the Trump Plaza vice-president Jack O'Donnell and his wife. Mark Etess was the only one of the casino's top executives who expressed concern about the obvious potential for conflicts of interest and declined to participate in the horse trading.

Several months after the DJ Trump episode, LiButti allegedly caused a new round of problems for the boys at Trump Plaza. In February 1989 the Division of Gaming Enforcement charged the casino with discriminating against blacks, Asians, and females. The complaint was based on testimony from several Trump Plaza employees who charged that higher-ups had them removed from the crap tables at LiButti's behest because he did not like to gamble in the presence of women and minorities. The Casino Control Commission subsequently fined Trump Plaza $200,000 in connection with the complaint. The following year the gaming authorities filed an administrative action against Trump Plaza for providing LiButti with expensive automobiles in an alleged scheme to circumvent limits on comps. The casino was later fined $450,000 for the alleged violations.

But for all its nefarious elegance, the "elaborate marketing scheme" Donald allegedly executed in cahoots with Bob LiButti paled in comparison with another scheme he perpetrated on the mass media and the banks. During the 1980s great wealth had ceased to be measured in millions; it was now measured in billions. In 1980 there were an estimated 574,000 millionaires in the United States. By 1988 the number had soared to 1.5 million, making millionaires commonplace in almost every community of any size. According to surveys by *Fortune* and *Forbes* magazines, the increase in American billionaires was equally dramatic. In 1982 there were just 13 billionaires in the United States. By 1988 the number was reportedly over 50.

Donald was determined to be recognized as the most glamorous and acquisitive of the new American billionaires, despite the fact that he did not rightfully qualify as one. In the summer of 1988 the Trump Organization public relations machine produced a one-page financial statement labeled "Confidential" but expressly intended for public consumption. The document estimated Donald's total net worth at a staggering $3.734 billion. Unlike a conventional financial statement, however, it did not list liabilities (such as bank and bond debt) in a separate column from the assets. Instead it noted in capital letters that the figures provided next to the list of assets were "NET OF MORTGAGES OR DEBT."

The values assigned to Donald's trophy properties were hyperinflated by several orders of magnitude. The net worth of Trump Plaza in Atlantic City was estimated at $300 million even though it carried a junk bond debt of $250 million. That meant the estimated market value for the property was $550 million, or more than $100 million higher than the top price ever paid for an Atlantic City casino. The estimated net worth of the still-unzoned and undeveloped West Side yards, for which Donald paid $95 million, was pegged at a whopping $750 million.

Donald's surrogates circulated his "Confidential" financial statement to a variety of mass media, including *Fortune* and *Forbes*. Almost any other wealthy man in America would have considered such an act insane or suicidal or both. Publicizing one's net worth was tantamount to inviting scrutiny by the Internal Revenue Service and harassment by would-be blackmailers, extortionists, and kidnappers of all description. But Donald wanted to make the media believe he was a billionaire even though he really was not one. Why? So he could use his Midas-like media image to impress bankers and bondholders into lending him more and more money for bigger and bigger deals.

The ruse worked. *Fortune* certified Donald as a billionaire for the first time in a cover story entitled "The Billionaires" that appeared in the issue of September 12, 1988. The magazine displayed his photograph in a dominant position on the cover montage and estimated his net worth at $1.3 billion, which put him in the number eighty-seven spot worldwide. (The sultan of Brunei ranked number one with an estimated net worth of $25 billion.) In November 1988 *Fortune* ran yet another article about the world's "most acquisitive" billionaire entitled "Will Donald Trump Own the World?"

"Despite all the publicity, the breast-beating, and even the best-selling book, the story of how Trump makes all that money has until now never been told," *Fortune* declared. "Looking into it reveals not only a no-fooling billionaire, but also an investor with a keen eye for cash flow and asset values, a smart marketer, and a cunning wheeler-dealer given to tough-guy tactics."

Regrettably, *Fortune* also failed to tell the real story of Donald's money-making magic. If *Fortune*'s editors had done more than superficial "looking into it," they would have found that Trump was not a billionaire at all, much less "a no-fooling" one. Prior to his most recent round of acquisitions, his net worth might have been in excess of $500 million if he had been able to sell all his properties at record prices, a highly speculative scenario. In fact, if all his bank loans had been called immediately, he might actually have had a net worth of zero, if not a negative net worth. That was discreetly evidenced by the fact that he had his inner circle constantly scrambling to help him make new highly leveraged deals that he hoped would generate fresh income streams to buttress his debt-laden empire.

In October 1988, shortly after *Fortune* had named him to its list of billionaires, Donald announced the sale of the St. Moritz, the aging hotel overlooking Central Park where Marla briefly encamped, to Australian beer baron Alan Bond for $180 million. That price, if legitimate and payable, would be more than twice the $80 million mortgage Donald had on the property. If the deal went through as stated (and there was some doubt at the time due to the precarious-ness of Bond's own finances), he would walk away with a cool $100 million profit. But instead of sitting back and waiting for the deal to close so he could pocket some profits free and clear of any mortgages or bank loans, he promptly contrived another even bigger deal that made no sense.

On October 12 Donald announced that he was going to buy the Eastern Shuttle commuter airline from the Texas Air chairman Frank Lorenzo for $365 million. The Eastern Shuttle's assets included an aging fleet of seventeen Boeing 727s and exclusive access to airport gates in New York, Boston, and Washington. But the Eastern Shuttle did not have exclusive routes; it still had to share the northeast com-muter corridor with the Pan Am Shuttle, which continued to claim about 60 percent of the market. Airline industry wags scoffed that Donald was overpaying by $100 million to $150 million.

Upon closing the deal for the Eastern Shuttle, Donald planned to rechristen it the Trump Shuttle and let the added value supplied by his fabled name fly the airline to new heights of profitability. But a former shuttle executive later claimed that no one in the Trump Organization bothered to seek an independent appraisal of the air-line's assets, much less run through a detailed cash-flow analysis. "Donald and his brother Robert just assumed that the shuttle was a cash cow," the executive recalled.

Donald's scheme for applying his brand name to the Eastern Shut-tle was temporarily delayed by another anti-Lorenzo backlash. A few days after the infamously abrasive Texas Air chairman announced the sale of the Eastern Shuttle, three of the airline's labor unions filed suit to block the deal. The proposed sale became hamstrung by a protracted legal battle that lasted through the following spring. In the end Donald forced Lorenzo to sweeten the deal by throwing in four more 727s. He then borrowed over $405 million from a Citibank-led consortium to buy the airline and capitalize a renovation program.

In November 1988, the month after announcing his purchase of the Eastern Shuttle, Donald closed his deal with Merv Griffin to sell Resorts International and buy the Taj Mahal. He wanted Ace Greenberg and his friends at Bear Stearns to underwrite a junk bond sale of $675 million, more than twice the offerings floated on the other two Atlantic City properties, but they refused. Several Wall Street insiders suggested that rumors about the impending indictments of Michael Milken and Drexel Burnham on securities fraud charges may have made Bear Stearns wary of expanding its junk bond exposure. Greenberg later cited fundamental financial misgivings. "We felt the Taj Mahal could only support a bond offering of three hundred seventy-five million dollars," the Bear Stearns chairman claimed.

Merrill Lynch, the nation's largest brokerage firm, blithely assured Donald it could raise the full amount of money by marketing the bonds through its nationwide retail network. On November 22, 1988, Merrill made good on its promise by selling all $675 million worth of Taj Mahal bonds to the public. According to Casino Control Commission documents, the firm collected a fee of $24 million. Donald used about $267 million of the proceeds to pay off the bank loan he had obtained as interim financing to buy the Taj from Griffin and allocated $266 million to pay for the actual construction of the Taj. He reserved the remaining $118 million to cover the first three interest payments due to bondholders. That meant that the Taj bondholders were effectively lending themselves the money that Donald would use to pay them back.

During the weeks that followed, a mass media controversy erupted over who had got the better of whom in the Trump-Griffin trade fest. The *Los Angeles Times* contended that it was Merv Griffin who taught Donald Trump the true art of the deal. *Business Week* took a diametrically opposite pro-Trump view of the deal. CBS correspondent Mike Wallace persuaded the two protagonists to appear together on "60 Minutes," the nation's top-ranking newsmagazine show, but the Trump-Griffin confrontation turned out to be a simpering, slaphappy sparring match. "The fact is that the two of you, both of you, each of you looked like the cat that swallowed the canary," Wallace remarked as Donald and Merv shook hands and posed arm in arm for the TV camera.

As time soon made apparent, both Donald and Merv had consummated deals that made no sense. Bear Stearns's refusal to handle the Taj Mahal junk bond offering proved to be a prescient warning of what was in store for Atlantic City's largest casino hotel. The Resorts junk bond offering was handled by the ubiquitous Daniel Lee of Drexel Burnham, who had advised Donald on his Holiday and Bally stock plays. The new junk bonds Griffin floated to finance his acquisition of Resorts brought the company's total junk bond exposure to $930 million. But the interest on the bonds exceeded Resorts' anticipated income by more than $100,000 per day, an early signal that the company was headed toward bankruptcy.

Despite predictions that a similar fate awaited the Taj Mahal, Donald insisted on rubbing Griffin's nose in the dirt. With the boss's blessing, Trump casino consultant Al Glasgow led the media offensive. When a reporter asked Glasgow to assess Griffin's chances of success in the gaming industry, he responded with a pointed allusion to rumors that the Hollywood celebrity, who often appeared in public with actress "girl friend" Eva Gabor, was a closet homosexual. "I think he's got a better shot at getting Eva Gabor pregnant," Glasgow opined with a sneer, "than he has of making money with Resorts." By contrast, Glasgow declared the Taj's chances of making money was "like spitting on the floor. It can't miss."

While Donald allowed Glasgow to do the cheerleading in public, he was not about to forgo the pleasure of bashing Griffin in private. On New Year's Eve he attended a lavish party in Aspen at the home of TV personality Barbara Walters and her movie mogul husband, Merv Adelson. Asked to make a wish for his fortunes in the year ahead, he declared, "I wish I had another Merv Griffin to bat around." Lacking another Merv, he settled for the next best thing: batting his wife around.

On May 25, 1988, six months before The Donald closed his purchase of the Taj Mahal, Ivana Trump shuffled into Manhattan federal court with 141 other anxious aliens. Distinguished from the unwashed masses by her designer-label clothes and elegant blond coiffure, she was dressed in an off-white Chanel suit cut above the knees, a pair of Charles Jourdan pumps, and a blue-and-white-striped blouse. But like the rest of her fellow immigrants, she realized that this was one of the most important days of her entire life. At the age of thirty-nine, some sixteen years after fleeing her native Czechoslovakia, she was about to become a naturalized citizen of the United States of America.

Ivana choked back tears of joy as Judge Charles S. Haight, Jr., ordered everyone to raise his or her right hand. In unison with the multilingual accents of the assembled co-petitioners, she recited the same oath taken by thousands of immigrants before her. "I welcome all of you as United States citizens with the freedom to follow your dreams," Judge Haight declared. "By your presence, America is vastly enriched."

The Donald made his own presence felt during Ivana's day in court. Because of the limited seating capacity, the relatives of almost all the other newly naturalized citizens had to wait outside. The Donald, however, arranged to stand inside the courtroom with Ivana's friend Jackie Miner, the wife of his pal U.S. District Court Judge Roger Miner. Judge Miner sat down on the bench next to Judge Haight and delivered a ten-minute oration on the duties of citizenship in which he alluded to a "special friend" taking the oath that morning.

When Ivana emerged from the courthouse following the ceremony, she heard an all-too-familiar sound: click, click, click. It was the sound of the high-speed camera shutters of the photographers assembled on the courthouse steps. Seizing the opportunity to turn his wife's citizenship ceremony into a publicity event, The Donald was holding an impromptu press conference starring the husband of the country's newest citizen. "I'm very proud of my wife," he told the media. "I'm very proud of my country. It's a great country, and that's where a great woman should be. Now they're both matched up perfectly."

Ivana seemed bent on making the Plaza Hotel her answer to the Taj Mahal. Restoring the Plaza's physical condition was merely the first step in her master plan. The second step was restoring the Plaza to its former position at the pinnacle of New York City social and cultural life. Drawing on her experience as a runway model, she aimed to recapture the lion's share of the lucrative biannual fashion show business that nearby competing hotels such as the Pierre had long since stolen away. She promised to give each prospective exhibitors two full days of shows in the Grand Ballroom and the Terrace Room at discount rates. In addition to forgoing charges for set-up and break-down time, she offered free use of adjoining rooms for wardrobe and changing areas.

Ivana's incentives produced impressive results. Nine of New York's most prestigious designers chose to premiere their spring 1989 lines at the Plaza. That was more than twice the number of shows the hotel hosted the previous spring before The Donald bought it. Among the famous fashion names were Arnold Scaasi, Oscar de la Renta, Caro-lyne Roehm, Carolina Herrera, Albert Nipon, and Mary Ann Res-tivo. For several years prior to 1989 Ivana had flown to Paris for the couture shows, claiming that such trips saved time because she could buy all her dresses for the upcoming season in a single shopping expedition. ("Then I only have to shop for shoes and handbags dur-ing the year," she said, adding, "And I buy them at the shops in Trump Tower.") But in another self-consciously patriotic gesture, she announced that she would henceforth bypass the Paris shows in order to patronize American designers.

Ivana's patriotism did not extend to the Plaza's staff. She gave most of the holdovers from the Westin regime six months to decide whether to stay or leave. Staying meant working according to the dictates of the new first lady and her husband. One of the first to go was former manager Jeff Flowers, who had been occupying the hotel's pricey presidential suite. ("Son, we've got a problem," Donald reportedly informed him. "You're living better than I am.") Flowers was replaced by Richard Wilhelm, who came from Trump's Castle. At least a quarter of the upper-echelon executives followed Flowers out the door.

"There was a movement to get people with Trump loyalty," recalled another former Trump's Castle staffer who joined Ivana's new man-agement team at the Plaza.

Despite Ivana's professed loyalty to American clothes designers, there was also a movement to create a European style image for the hotel. Some front desk and concierge desk staffers did not fit that image by virtue of their racial origins. "Asians were not a problem," recalled a former staffer. "Ivana felt that they presented a good image and could be helpful to the hotel's important Asian clientele. But neither Ivana nor Donald wanted blacks out there." Ivana was similarly discriminating on the matter of age. "She wanted older people at the concierge desk," one insider reported, "not young kids."

Ivana's obsession with image included the hotel's paying guests. Like the staff, they were expected to conform to strict dress code requirements, banning such apparel as tattered jeans and shorts. One former executive claimed that despite the dress code, no paying guests were ever turned away. But whenever Ivana spotted any nonpaying tourists wandering through the lobby dressed in what she deemed inappropriate attire, she ordered the staff to escort them out.

In the late summer of 1988, barely three months after taking charge of the foundering hotel, Ivana announced, "We have turned the Plaza around. It is well on its way to its former glory." As proof of her claim, she boasted: "In my second month here we had revenues of $5.9 million, compared to $2.5 million for the same month last year. Donald and I thought it would take at least well into 1989 to turn a profit here. We are amazed that the turnaround has come so fast."

Ivana's glowing progress report contained no more than a grain of truth. The Plaza's revenues were up primarily because she had raised room rates from an average of $190 a night to $260 immediately upon taking over from Westin. But no one short of Atlas himself could have "turned the Plaza around." Given the purchase price of nearly $400 million, the hotel had to make interest payments in excess of $40 million a year. Although Donald had borrowed another $25 million for renovations, that was not enough to complete the Trumps' ambitious designs for the Plaza. According to former top executives, the actual cost of the renovation project eventually amounted to at least $60 million, a large portion of which came out of the hotel's cash flow. Even if the Plaza could generate as much as $35 million in gross operating profits, as some insiders claimed, the idea of "turning" a real net profit in the face of such high debt service and renovation expenses was ludicrous.

Nevertheless, Ivana was showered with the same kind of fawning publicity her husband had enjoyed following the opening of the Grand Hyatt and Trump Tower. In one typically misinformed profile, *Newsweek* reported that she had "obtained a decorator's license," even though the American Society of Interior Decorators, the industry's only official licensing body, had never issued her one. *Vanity Fair* dismissed allegations about her mismanagement of the Plaza with a single fatuous quote. "I don't fire people on the spot and I don't shout at the people who work for me," Ivana proclaimed. "I run my business with dignity and I'm a lady."

No one did more to perpetuate the Lady Trump's self-made myth than *New York Daily News* columnist Liz Smith. "Kudos . . . for the tasteful beauty of their refurbishing [of the *Trump Princess*]," Smith wrote in the summer of 1988, adding that the yacht was "not a garish boat" but rather "almost understated." Smith went on to praise the Trumps as the 1980s version of such celebrity couples as Richard Burton and Elizabeth Taylor, and Aristotle and Jacqueline Kennedy Onassis. Ivana, in turn, praised Smith as "a great writer and a super lady."

The Donald reacted to Ivana's headline making with bitterly mixed emotions. On the one hand, he saw dollar signs in her celebrity. In January 1989, the same month in which he appeared on the cover of *Time* magazine, he helped her file an application to trademark the name Ivana as the brand for a new perfume. But even when praising his wife in public, Donald reminded the media that he was paying her only "a dollar a year and all the dresses she can buy," snidely adding without any documentation that Ivana's clothing bills proved she was getting the better end of the bargain. Behind closed doors, he repeatedly belittled his wife with the same old litany of complaints that he had commenced after signing their last nuptial agreement:

"You're too skinny. . . ."

"Your tits are too small. . . ."

"You're doing a shitty job. . . ."

"Without me, you're nothing. . . ."

The Donald wreaked further revenge with icy indifference in the bedroom. In June 1988 he accompanied Ivana on a trip to London, where he treated her to a rare burst of sexual passion. In retrospect, that appeared to be his perverse way of rewarding her for accepting the assignment of managing the Plaza. It was also the last time the couple would have sex for almost a year and a half. Upon returning to New York, The Donald allowed that Ivana deserved a special Christmas present: a $1 million diamond ring from Harry Winston jewelers. "This is for all the shit you've had to put up with," he blurted as he presented her with the unexpected gift.

Ivana still appeared to be blissfully unaware of the other women in The Donald's secret life. Her girl friends could not believe she was so blind. Like everyone else plugged into the New York social grapevine, they kept hearing rumors about The Donald's alleged affairs with movie stars and wives of close friends. The most frequently repeated names were those of actresses Catherine Oxenberg, Robin Givens, and Carol Alt; designer Carolyne Roehm, who was married to takeover czar Henry Kravis; and Georgette Mosbacher, wife of Secretary of Commerce Robert Mosbacher and chairman of her own cosmetics firm.

Several times Ivana confronted The Donald with what she had heard. Though he always denied that he was having an affair with these alleged paramours or anyone else, she kept stumbling across evidence to the contrary. One night when he was supposedly off at a hockey game in Madison Square Garden with male friends, Ivana happened to turn on the television sports channels just as the camera zoomed in on the front-row seats. The Donald was there all right—sitting beside Carol Alt.

Ivana still refused to believe the worst. A few days after the *New York Post* had run a cryptic story suggesting a romantic link between The Donald and Marla Maples, one of Ivana's closest friends took her to lunch at Le Cirque and screwed up the courage to warn her that the stories about The Donald's infidelity were more than idle rumors. Vowing never to speak to the woman again, Ivana stormed out of the restaurant. But neither blinding rage nor naïve denial could quell the scandalous talk. One night at yet another fancy party Ivana had a particularly unsettling conversation with *New York Post* gossip columnist Cindy Adams.

"I understand that you and Donald are having problems," Adams said.

"Absolutely not!" Ivana screeched. "Donald and I are happily married. Where did you hear such a thing?" Then, without waiting for a reply, she turned and marched away, vowing to herself never to talk to Adams again.

Incredibly The Donald also planted false rumors of extramarital romantic interests to antagonize his business rivals as well as his wife. During a February 1989 interview with *New York Daily News* writer Glenn Plaskin he leaked a not-for-attribution "report" that Allison Stern, the ex-model and television producer wife of Hartz Mountain chief Leonard Stern, had "continually phoned Trump's office asking for a date." Allison Stern later called the story "absurd" and "the product of a juvenile mind." Her husband privately debated plans to sue both Donald and the *Daily News*. But Donald stuck by his story about Allison. "She called," he insisted. "I wasn't interested."

The "report" of Allison Stern's purported phone calls came amid a rapidly escalating running battle between Donald and Leonard Stern. Back in December 1985 Stern had helped former Trump aide Louise Sunshine settle a partnership dispute with Donald. The following year the two men butted heads over their competing bids to entice NBC to relocate from Rockefeller Center. Donald wanted NBC to move to his proposed TV City development on the West Side yards. Stern hoped NBC would move to his property in the Meadowlands of New Jersey.

Though NBC eventually decided not to relocate, Donald and Stern continued to trade verbal blows in the media and through their attorneys over other issues. In May 1988 a short-lived Stern-owned weekly called *7 Days* published a story questioning the quality of construction in Trump Tower. Donald won a "reinvestigation" after threatening a lawsuit. A follow-up story by *7 Days* nevertheless concluded that Trump Tower apartments were a risky buy.

By the time Donald leaked his "report" about Allison Stern calling him for a date he had got word that Stern was backing a television documentary titled "Trump—What's the Deal?" The documentary was being produced by six-time Emmy winner Ned Schnurman. Stern put up a total of $600,000 to finance the project. Donald charged that the documentary "intended to get Trump." He also claimed that the documentary makers had misrepresented themselves to secure an interview with Ivana. Trump lawyer L. Peter Parcher accused Stern of "abusing and utilizing the First Amendment as a device to further . . . personal antagonisms" and intimated that Donald was going to produce a sixty-second commercial countering the Schnurman documentary.

Stern's attorney, Victor Kovner, replied that Donald's "threats of libel action" and "his ludicrous defamatory statements about Mr. and Mrs. Stern" would not intimidate the documentary makers. But Schnurman soon encountered unexpected troubles behind the scenes. The project ran over budget and missed a projected June 1989 air date. Then the syndicator, LBS Communications, informed Schnurman that none of the independent television stations in the New York area wanted to purchase the piece. James Grau, the husband of Donald's sister Elizabeth, later confirmed that he had expressed concern over rumors about the negative tone of the documentary to LBS president's, Henry Siegel, a fellow Friars Club member.

In September 1989 the documentary makers missed another projected air date. Stern refused to provide any more money to support the project. Although Schnurman finished his documentary the following year without further financing from Stern and began screening it for private audiences, the piece never aired on network or independent television stations. Donald took credit for winning a great victory over both Stern and Schnurman. But once again the list of losers included Ivana, who had suffered the indignity of witnessing her husband publicly confirm the "report" about Allison Stern's romantic interest in him.

If the rumors about The Donald's illicit affairs battered Ivana's self-esteem, so did a vicious exposé in the May 1989 issue of *Spy* magazine. *Spy* writer Jonathan Van Meter compared Donald's infatuation with Ivana to that of Shakespeare's Titania in *A Midsummer Night's Dream* who "believed the donkey-headed Bottom to be the very vision of love." The Donald raged at the magazine for defaming the Trump name. He also castigated Ivana for causing him public embarrassment. Some of the couple's friends later claimed that the *Spy* article caused the breakup of the Trumps' marriage. That was giving it more blame or credit than it rightfully deserved. The Trumps' marriage had been heading on a collision course with disaster long before *Spy* sank its teeth into Ivana.

About the time *Spy* rolled off the presses in mid-April of 1989, Ivana disappeared from New York City for more than two weeks. She returned just in time for the Police Athletic League SuperStar dinner on May 12 with a totally transformed physical appearance. Some of Ivana's closest friends and most constant media admirers did not recognize her. Several socialites at first mistook her for Catherine Oxenberg, one of The Donald's reputed paramours. Ivana played coy about her new look. She had one of her secretaries tell the media that she had "completely, completely changed her makeup." In truth Ivana had spent her time away from New York in the care of Los Angeles plastic surgeon Steven Hoefflin. But The Donald was not sufficiently smitten by Ivana's new look to resume having sex with her.

At seven on the morning of June 8, 1989, a 727 bearing the name Trump in bright red letters took off from La Guardia Airport on its inaugural flight from New York to Washington. Only minutes before, a make-over crew had completed the task of covering the old Eastern Shuttle logo with the new Trump Shuttle logo. Inside the cabin a string quartet serenaded the VIP passengers as flight attendants wearing shiny new pearl necklaces poured champagne. The owner of the airline talked to the media about the importance of the commuter carrier's fleetwide name change, which had been accomplished overnight.

"If I'd called the Trump Shuttle something else," said Donald J. Trump, "it wouldn't be nearly as successful."

That statement was soon open to debate. On the first day of operation Trump Shuttle's market share leaped from 15 percent to 40 percent. Male commuters seemed to enjoy the elegant new attendants' uniforms and, as Donald had predicted, the still-untarnished glamour of the Trump name. Pan Am fought to retain its market share by offering corporate discount fares. By December 1989 Trump Shuttle's market share had risen to only 48 percent, far short of its original goal of a 60 to 65 percent share. The airline needed to generate roughly $190 million per year to cover operating expenses ($150 million) and interest expenses ($40 million). Assuming total commuter traffic continued to hover at the level of four million passengers a year, the airline could generate only $170 million a year with a 48 percent share.

To make matters worse, an economic recession was battering the Northeast, and the size of the pie Trump Shuttle and Pan Am were fighting over was shrinking. With commuter traffic slumping to about

3.5 million passengers a year, Trump Shuttle could not hope to survive unless a planned $28 million capital expenditure program was delayed. Donald would not hear of such a thing. He informed the airline president, Bruce Nobles, Harvey Freeman, and his brother Robert, who formed the Trump Shuttle board of directors, that he had $600 million cash in his bank accounts. He assured them he would have no trouble providing the airline with additional capital from his own pocket, if need be, in early 1990.

Undaunted by the dark cloud looming over his financial horizon, Donald kept expanding in both New York and Atlantic City. At the start of 1989 he convinced Citibank to lend him an initial $51.5 million of a $220 million financing package to start construction of a fifty-five-story high rise at Third Avenue and Sixty-ninth Street in Manhattan to be called Trump Palace. According to a former high-ranking Trump Organization executive, the convincing process was tantamount to bank fraud. When his chief real estate saleswoman Blanche Sprague prepared an estimate of the prices he could realistically expect to get for apartments in Trump Palace, she came up with a total sellout figure of $179.2 million; in other words, if he sold every unit in the building, he would take in some $40 million less than the money he wanted to borrow from Citibank. That, according to Donald, would never do. He ordered Sprague to go back to her calculator and arrive at a number much higher than the loan amount.

"You told me to up the number to '$260 million plus,' " Sprague wrote in an internal memo to Donald, "even though I told you it would be impossible to realize this number." Sprague eventually came up with a list "showing a sell-out of $265,008,000 per Donald's instructions." But she refused to sign off on the revised list and forwarded a copy of the list to Trump attorney Jerry Schrager with a letter disavowing the figures. Citibank, which never saw Sprague's disclaimer, eventually gave Donald the $220 million loan.

"Donald had this death wish. He wanted to get caught," recalled a former Trump Organization insider. "It was like he wanted to keep taking risks he knew he shouldn't take and leave it to the rest of us to fix it for him. He'd start one project and then go off and start something else. He'd say, 'Look at all the people who want to give me money. Look at Citibank.' But he knew we'd fooled Citibank. He knew and we knew that it was all a lie. We had all these assets, but we never had any money in hand. That's why we had to keep doing more deals."

Later that summer Donald announced plans to buy and renovate the Atlantis Hotel, which was located next door to the Atlantic City Convention Center, with an $85 million line of credit. Since he already owned three casinos in town, New Jersey law prohibited him from operating the Atlantis, soon to be renamed Trump Regency, as a casino. But Donald believed owning the Regency was a way to prevent competitors such as Steve Wynn from gaining another toehold on the Boardwalk. He envisioned the noncasino hotel as a holding tank for guests who could not be accommodated at Trump Plaza during such big-draw affairs as world heavyweight boxing matches. As it turned out, the Trump Regency continued to lose so much money that Donald was forced to subsidize its operations with "lease payments" made by the profit-making Trump Plaza.

Undaunted by the cash hemorrhaging of the Trump Regency, Donald borrowed another $56 million to buy an unfinished hotel and a parking garage site on the Boardwalk owned by *Penthouse* publisher Bob Guccione. The purchase came in the wake of a Byzantine series of sexual innuendos and legal maneuverings involving *Penthouse* and the Pratt Hotel Corporation, which had also tried to acquire the properties. Back in the summer of 1988 Donald had moved to block the proposed sale of the *Penthouse* properties to Pratt by raising environmental impact concerns. Then a *Penthouse* lawyer allegedly implied to Trump casino consultant Al Glasgow that the magazine was prepared to publish an exposé of Donald's still-secret affair with Marla Maples. When Donald finally bought the *Penthouse* properties, Pratt retaliated with an as-yet-unsettled lawsuit that has so far consumed more than $4 million in legal fees; at last report, those legal fees were being carried on the books of Trump Plaza.

Even as Donald continued to expand his Atlantic City empire, the Trump Taj Mahal, the original "Deal That Made No Sense," kept draining money out of the pockets of Trump bondholders. According to construction manager Tom Pippett, the budget for finishing the Taj drawn up in late 1988 was about $322 million. In the course of more than thirteen months, however, there were an estimated $23 million worth of "operational changes" (a euphemism for cost overruns caused by mid-course revisions) that brought the actual expenditures up to $345 million. Steve Hyde, the chief of Trump's gaming division, had to answer to the boss each time something went awry at the Taj even if the problem was not his fault. In keeping with his informal absentee management style, Donald flew down from New York to Atlantic City on weekends, rounded up Hyde and an entourage of executives and bodyguards, and struck out on an expletive-spewing tour of the project.

"Sometimes Donald's mere presence would intimidate," Pippett recalled. "He would talk to maybe fifty people, from the guy running the vacuum cleaners to the top manager, and just harass them all. He'd tell them how bad the place looked, what he thought they were doing wrong. He would call them all stupid and dumb. Because he terrorized and intimidated, people would go the other way when Donald Trump was on the property."

To the further consternation of Trump gaming division executives and their boss, Marla Maples was getting impatient playing hide-and-seek. She particularly objected to having to register in Atlantic City under "Fitzsimmons," the name of the obliging ex-boyfriend who sometimes served as her escort when she and Donald appeared together in public. According to Trump Plaza executive Jack O'Donnell, she kept "putting a greater strain on the luxury accommodations" usually reserved for high-roller gambling customers by demanding VIP services and hotel rooms for herself and a growing contingent of family and friends, whom she took to beauty parlors, restaurants, shows, and the like.

Though Tom Fitzsimmons and other male friends could see that Donald still seemed hopelessly enamored of Marla, he had a hard time expressing affection for her. When she arrived in Atlantic City to celebrate her twenty-fifth birthday in October 1988, he had O'Donnell buy her presents and a happy birthday card. In February 1989 Donald brought Marla and her father to Trump Plaza for a closed-circuit screening of a Mike Tyson boxing match being held that evening out in Las Vegas. When he saw a scantily clad showgirl parading around the ring with a card indicating the number of the next round in the match, Donald turned to Marla and declared sarcastically, "We finally found something you can handle. . . . You can be a round card girl at Trump Plaza."

In private, Donald was often far more generous. In the hope of boosting his girl friend's show business career, he telephoned TV star Larry Hagman, who owned a $2 million apartment in Trump Parc, and arranged for Marla to make a guest appearance on an episode of the prime-time series "Dallas." He also started sending checks to Marla's mother on a periodic basis and agreed to help bail out Marla's father, Stan Maples, whose Dalton area residential developments had foundered amid the local real estate slump. Likewise, he gave Marla's stepfather, David Ogletree, known around Dalton, Georgia, as a top carpet designer, a chance to bid on the contracts for carpeting the massive hallways of the Trump Taj Mahal.

But Donald's mean side kept surfacing. In return for his largess to Marla and her family, he made her sign a management contract paying him 30 percent of all she earned from her acting and modeling jobs. When Ogletree arrived in New York to discuss the Taj carpeting bids, the other contractors disparaged him as a country bumpkin who did not know what he was talking about. Donald refused to give Ogletree the contract, ignoring the possibility that Ogletree's critics might have simply been embarrassed by the fact he was underbidding them. "I don't want anything to do with the guy," Donald told Tom Fitzsimmons. "He's a real loser."

Marla found herself continually whiplashed by the ambivalence of Donald's affections. In the summer of 1989 Donald ordered his staff to start preparing a permanent residence for her at the Trump Regency, the newly renamed noncasino hotel he had purchased on the Boardwalk near Trump Plaza. Before his orders could be carried out, he decided to nix the plan. "I'm finished with her," he informed a top casino executive. But less than a week later he reappeared in Atlantic City with Marla by his side.

Donald's mental state became even more unbalanced following the helicopter crash that killed Trump gaming division executives Steve Hyde, Mark Etess, and Jon Benenav in October 1989. His highly publicized $7.5 billion bid to take over American Airlines collapsed, and his search for a way to alleviate his worsening cash-flow crisis grew desperate. His attempt to streamline his flabby physique and arrest his baldness through plastic surgery only caused him more frustration and pain. His violent sexual assault on Ivana all but destroyed any hope for a marital reconciliation. Marla had finally recovered from her foot-fracturing temper tantrum earlier that fall. But Donald seemed to sense, at least on a subconscious level, that by following through on his plans to take her to Aspen over the New Year holidays, he risked the exposure of his illicit affair and possibly the exposure of all the big lies he had been telling for years.

Back in June, Donald had turned forty-three years old. He was now the same age as his late older brother, Fred, had been when he died of alcoholism. But Donald was not about to go down without a fight. Increasingly isolated and alone, he determined to show his pal Tom Fitzsimmons that he had not lost everything and everyone. At least not yet. To prove it, he took Fitzsimmons on a limousine cruise through Manhattan and beckoned to his longtime bodyguard and sometimes chauffeur Matthew Calamari for a show of moral support.

"You'd do anything for me, wouldn't you, Matty?" Donald called out from the rear of the limousine.

"Yes, sir, Mr. Trump," Calamari assured him.

"Anything at all?"

"Yes, sir, Mr. Trump."

"Would you kill for me, Matty?" Donald pressed.

"Yes, sir."

"Would you kill for me, Matty?" Donald repeated, as if he were a cheerleader inciting a crowd to riot.

"Yes, sir, Mr. Trump!"

"Would you kill for me, Matty?" Donald said again in an even louder voice.

"Yes, sir, Mr. Trump!"

"See." Donald grinned, turning back toward Fitzsimmons. "Matty would kill for me."

Part three

Best Sex Ever Had

chapter eight
THE ASPEN
INCIDENT

■ SHORTLY BEFORE SUNSET on December 27, 1989, the Trump jet starts its descent toward Aspen, Colorado. It is a very tight approach. The postage-stamp airport is nestled against a bowl of white-capped peaks that whip the winds as if with an invisible eggbeater. The pilots are glad to be coming in ahead of the postsunset landing curfew for private aircraft. On their previous trip with Ivana and the children, they arrived in the Aspen area thirty minutes after nightfall, only to have the tower divert them about ninety miles downvalley to Grand Junction.

When the Trump jet taxis to a stop on the tarmac, Donald and Marla exit the aircraft together and walk right through the terminal as if they were just another rich married couple. There is no need to be surreptitious. Donald knows that his wife, Ivana, who loves to socialize with the après-ski set, will not be coming out to the airport. But Marla's friend Kim Knapp, who arrived a few minutes earlier on a commercial flight, is there to greet them.

Outside, Donald, Marla, and Kim climb into a waiting limousine, a citified anomaly among the four-wheel-drive Jeeps and Jimmys idling by the curb. Then, as a sub-freezing starlit darkness starts falling all around, they drive into town on a treacherous two-lane highway flanked by majestic mountains. The slopes are studded with an incongruous array of multimillion-dollar vacation homes, exclusive ski resorts, barrackslike employee housing, and not so artfully dilap-idated former gold-mining shacks.

As in holiday seasons past, Aspen twinkles with the sinful cheer of

Sodom while savage class conflicts between haves and have-nots, pro-growthers and no-growthers, simmer below the snow-covered surface. A pair of pending voter referendums, one calling for a ban on sales of animal furs and the other demanding the construction of more "affordable housing" for year-round residents, has split the citizenry. But even though the town's economic problems are compounded by a continuing ski industry slump, gaggles of fur-wearing socialites and free-spending young impresarios can be seen filing into the fashionable bar at the Hotel Jerome on Main Street.

Donald is already pondering ways to profit from Aspen's identity crisis. As the limousine circumnavigates the Hotel Jerome, he can see construction cranes towering above a gaping hole on a prime parcel at the base of Ajax Mountain. The hole is supposed to be the site of a 257-room Ritz-Carlton Hotel planned by a Washington-based developer named Mohammed Hadid. In an effort to limit the size of the hotel, the city council recently yanked Hadid's construction permits and put the issue up for yet another referendum. Donald hopes the local electorate will vote to block the project so he can breeze in and build his own hotel.

For the next few days, however, Donald will be preoccupied with more pressing business than real estate. He and Ivana are staying a few short blocks from the Ritz-Carlton site at Little Nell's, a newly opened luxury hotel with an emerald green oval roof and a gourmet restaurant that is owned by billionaire Marvin Davis. But the limousine drives right past Little Nell's and turns down a side street. It stops in front of a discreetly nondescript two-bedroom condominium. Marla and Kim make plans to meet Donald on the slopes the following morning. Then they pile out of the limousine and disappear inside the condominium.

Donald orders the limousine driver to take him back to Little Nell's, where Ivana is waiting.

At half past six on the evening of December 28 the telephone rings in the Trumps' suite at Little Nell's. Donald picks up the phone in the living room. Ivana picks up a separate extension in the bedroom. The caller is Charles Weaver, a well-connected Aspen realtor who helped find the condominium where Marla and Kim are staying.

"That Marla sure is a piece of ass!" Weaver exclaims, obviously believing that he is speaking only to Donald. Then he makes a similar remark about Marla's friend Kim.

Donald cringes. He already realizes that Ivana is listening in. He knows his wife will put him through an inquisition the moment Weaver hangs up. But Ivana misunderstands Weaver's pronunciation of the name Marla. She thinks he is talking about someone called Moolah.

"Who is this Moolah?" Ivana demands when her husband replaces the receiver.

"She's someone who's been chasing me for about two years," Donald replies half-truthfully. Then he lies outright. He tells his wife there is nothing going on between him and the other woman.

Ivana is understandably annoyed—and suspicious. For the next two days she scurries about Aspen asking questions. Who is this "Moolah" woman her husband is supposed to be interested in? Who is her friend Kim? What do they look like? Where are they staying? Whom do they know? The Aspen grapevine provides only partial answers to her questions. Ivana does not like what she hears.

On the morning of December 31 Donald and Ivana board a high-speed gondola outside Little Nell's and ride up the ski slope of Ajax Mountain. Donald is dressed in black from wind pants and parka to woolen cap. Ivana is wearing a peach-colored designer racing suit and a white doughnut-shaped ear muffler. She is not in a happy mood. The day before, she saw her husband get off one of the ski lifts with a blonde whom she will later recognize as Kim Knapp. Ivana still has no idea what her rival, "Moolah," actually looks like. But she is about to find out.

At 1:00 P.M. the Trumps stop for lunch at Bonnie's Beach Club restaurant, a rambling blue clapboard shack tucked beside a rocky ledge about halfway down Ajax Mountain, Bonnie's is known for such specialties as chili dogs and hot chocolate spiked with peppermint schnapps, and for its sun deck, which is adorned with the flags of thirteen nations. The sun deck is the place to see and be seen. The trick is to get through the interminable cafeteria-style food line before the sun deck tables fill up. Donald and Ivana arrive in the middle of the midday rush and have to settle for a table inside.

As the Trumps finish eating lunch, Marla Maples is just getting in the cafeteria line. Like Donald, she is wearing a black ski outfit with a white doughnut-shaped ear muffler identical to Ivana's. Marla has sent Kim to find a place to sit. Kim sees Donald and Ivana get up from their table. Then she sees Ivana zero in on her. Kim tries to get lost in the cafeteria line next to Marla, but Ivana follows her.

"Are you Kim?" Ivana asks with a shaky voice.

Kim nods and shakes Ivana's outstretched hand.

"I'm Ivana Trump. I hear you have a best friend, Moolah, who's been chasing my husband for two years."

"I'm sorry," Kim replies disingenuously. "I don't know anyone named Moolah."

Donald looks at Kim with a baleful frown. Then he and Ivana walk back outside to put on their skis, arguing all the while. Kim disappears into the rest room downstairs. But Marla sees the Trumps quarreling and decides to go outside.

Donald spots Marla coming off the sun deck and keeps glancing in her direction. Ivana follows his eyes until she focuses on the blonde who has captured her husband's attention. She strides right over to her.

"Are you Moolah?" Ivana asks.

Marla does not answer.

"Why don't you leave my husband alone?" Ivana demands, reaching for Marla's arm.

"Are you happy?" Marla asks.

"Stay away from my husband," Ivana rejoins, and gives Marla a quick shove.

By this point almost all the skiers lunching on the sun deck notice the apparent confrontation between Donald, Ivana, and Marla. So do the paparazzi, who routinely show up at Bonnie's during the holidays. The cameras start shooting just as Kim Knapp reappears on the sun deck looking for Marla.

"I think I'd better go," Marla purrs, and rushes over to join Kim.

Donald beats a hasty retreat down the mountain. Ivana, who is a far better skier, catches up with him halfway to the lift below Bonnie's. She whirls around and starts skiing backward, shaking her finger as if she were scolding a naughty child. Finally Donald pulls over.

"Ivana," he wheezes, "you're overreacting."

That night is New Year's Eve. It is also Donny's birthday. The Trumps have been invited to a party at billionaire David Koch's house, as were Marla and Kim, and to a party hosted by Little Nell's owner, Marvin Davis, and his wife, Barbara. But they decide not to go out. Instead they celebrate the birthday of their firstborn son at Little Nell's. Then they repair to their suite and argue.

"Are you in love with her?" Ivana wants to know.

"No, I'm not," Donald insists.

"Will you call her and tell her that it's over—if there was anything." Donald says he will make the call.

"If you don't love her, if you can finish the relationship," Ivana says, "I'll give you anything, including my Christmas present."

"Well, let's just say it's over," Donald assures her.

But Donald does not act like a faithful husband. On New Year's Day they go to dinner with veteran New York publicist Eleanor Lambert at Little Nell's. When the Trumps escort Lambert back to her room, Donald keeps asking about an attractive young woman who joined them at the table along with her date for the evening.

"Is her figure as good as it looks?" he wonders aloud.

Lambert blushes in embarrassment. She does not understand how Donald could dare to talk that way in front of Ivana.

Donald keeps on giving Ivana mixed signals. That night he makes love to her for the first time since "the rape" back in early November. When he is finished, he turns to her and says, "Now you can't say that we didn't have sex."

The next morning Donald is driven to the airport. Ivana, who planned to stay in Aspen with her mother and the children for a few more days, comes along for the ride. She looks tense and distraught. But Donald is laughing and unusually glib. He bids his wife good-bye, then climbs into the Trump plane and takes off for New York.

On January 8, 1990, shortly after returning to New York from Aspen, Ivana slips into a coffee shop next to the Louis Licari Color Group salon on Madison Avenue. She is greeted by Michael Kennedy, the ruddy-faced attorney with gold wire-rimmed glasses and an Irish temper who once rented his Long Island guest cottage to

Ivana and Donald. He and his wife, Eleanore, a vivacious jury selection expert and socialite, are two of the Trumps' closest friends.

Kennedy is an accomplished criminal defense lawyer, not a divorce lawyer. He has represented such infamous clients as drug guru Timothy Leary, murderess Jean Harris, Irish Republican Army activist Bernadine Dohrn, and *High Times* magazine. But Ivana is not ready to file for divorce. She wants to attempt a reconciliation. She believes the Kennedys might be able to talk some sense into Donald and make him agree to reconcile.

Over the next few weeks the Kennedys and the Trumps meet separately and in tandem. Michael talks to Donald man to man. Then Eleanore tries to make Donald see the wifely point of view. Then Michael, Eleanore, and Ivana triple-team Donald. They keep repeating a key question: "Donald, are you in love with Marla Maples?"

Donald keeps hedging. He will not admit that he has fallen head over heels for Marla. Nor will he come out and say he wants a divorce. Instead he tells Ivana, not for the first time, that he would like to have an "open marriage." Ivana will not even consider such a thing.

"You want it both ways," she fumes.

As the arguments escalate, Donald grows depressed and ever more fatalistic. He starts talking crazily, alluding to both suicide and murder. "Why don't you just shoot me?" he asks his wife at one point.

Ivana is unnerved. She calls Donald's executive assistant, Norma Foerderer, and has her come up to the Trump Tower triplex to retrieve a pistol that is kept in a metal strongbox in the couple's bedroom. Given the volatile situation, Ivana does not want any guns within reach. Her concerns are twofold. She is afraid The Donald might lose his temper and turn on her. She is also afraid he might claim that she wants to use the gun on him, as he suggested she do.

Ivana decides that the couple ought to go see a psychiatrist. The Donald flies into a rage, screaming that there is nothing wrong with him and that he considers the very idea an insult. When Ivana persists, he changes tack. "Okay, I'll go," he says, "but only if you think it will fix what's wrong with you." The Trumps eventually arrange to visit a psychiatrist. But after attending only one session, The Donald refuses to continue the therapy.

Meanwhile, the Trumps try to keep up appearances in public. On

January 13 they fly to Los Angeles together on the Trump plane.
Ivana has promised to attend an elaborate ladies' dinner hosted by
Marvin Davis's wife, Barbara. Donald has business to take care of.
That morning Ivana accompanies him to a press conference in the
old Ambassador Hotel on Wilshire Boulevard, where Donald
announces that he has joined the Power Company, owners of the
Ambassador, in a new partnership called Trump Wilshire Associates.
With a flair reminiscent of his West Side yards project in Manhattan,
he declares that he is going to build on the hotel site a 125-story
skyscraper that will be "the world's tallest building."

Upon returning to the East Coast, Donald finds that his own words
are coming back to bite him. The March 1990 issue of *Playboy* magazine has just come out. The cover photograph shows Donald standing beside a voluptuous model who is attired only in the coat of his
tuxedo. "Nice magazine," reads Donald's quote line. "Want to sell it?"
That month's *Playboy* interview by Glenn Plaskin is far more provocative. Among other immemorable passages, it includes Plaskin's
question "What is marriage to you? Is it monogamous?" and Donald's
reply: "I don't have to answer that."

Although Ivana is understandably outraged by her husband's *Playboy* interview, Donald tries to convince her to accept his proposal of
an open marriage. One night they fly down to Atlantic City together
and attend a Jimmy Roselli concert at Trump Plaza. Bob LiButti, the
"ultimate" high roller, happens to be sitting next to them on the front
row.

"Hey, Bob, do you play around on your wife?" Donald asks.

LiButti cannot believe Donald would ask him such a question in
front of Ivana. "I'm not married anymore," the portly, bald-pated
horse breeder and gambler advises. "If I was, I probably wouldn't
play around. Look at me. Any young girl that would go after me
would just be after my money."

"But how about when you were married?" Donald persists. "Did
you play around."

"Sure," LiButti admits. "I guess I did some."

Donald turns to Ivana with a triumphant grin. "You see, every
married man plays around on his wife."

Ivana glares at him stone-faced.

The next time LiButti sees Donald is on Monday, February 5. The two men run into each other in front of Trump Tower in New York. Donald is hurrying to the airport where the Trump jet is waiting to fly him to Tokyo. He asks LiButti if he wants to come along. LiButti politely declines. He has business in the city. As Donald climbs into a waiting limousine, LiButti asks how things are going with Ivana.

Donald gives LiButti an exclusive scoop. He says that he and Ivana have decided to separate.

"Bob, it's over," he chirps.

Then Donald commands his chauffeur to drive him to the airport.

On Wednesday, February 7, Ivana calls *New York Daily News* gossip columnist Liz Smith, her most sympathetic friend in the media, to give a not-for-attribution interview about the Trumps' decision to separate. Ivana still does not intend to file for divorce. But talking to Donald has not worked. She and her attorney, Michael Kennedy, are hoping that the shock of seeing the news in print will prompt Donald to reconcile. In an effort to counteract Donald's well-oiled publicity machine, they have hired prominent Manhattan public relations consultant John Scanlon, who helped defend the image of CBS News in the Westmoreland libel case.

Smith wants to hold the item until the following Monday, when the most well-heeled members of her reading public will have returned from their weekend jaunts. But her editors at the *Daily News* believe the story is simply too hot to hold. They schedule it to run that Sunday on the tabloid's front page. That is perfect timing as far as Ivana's advisers are concerned. Scanlon knows that Donald is expected to be in Tokyo or flying back on Sunday; he will be incommunicado as far as the U.S. media are concerned. For once Ivana will get the jump in the public relations war between the Trumps.

Donald looks distraught and sickly when the Trump jet lands in Alaska to refuel for the final leg of the flight to Tokyo. The trip takes twenty-two hours in each direction. He and his party, which includes executive assistant Norma Foerderer, top legal adviser Jerry Schrager, chief financial adviser Harvey Freeman, and real estate vice-president Blanche Sprague, plan to spend at least three days in Japan. But Donald has brought only the one suit he is wearing and no lug-

gage. He is miffed about the fact that he will be out of telephone
contact with New York once the plane leaves Alaska.

He is also in something of a quandary about what to do when he
finally arrives in Japan. Although the banks and the media still have
no idea of the grave nature of his financial situation, he knows he has
to make some big deals in short order or his house of cards will come
tumbling down. But his agenda is just a list of maybes. Maybe he will
try to sell some more apartments in Trump Palace to the Japanese.
Maybe he will broach the idea of selling stock in the Plaza Hotel to
the Japanese. Maybe he will find a buyer for his yacht, the *Trump
Princess*. Maybe he will try to drum up business for his casinos by
meeting with a Japanese high roller named Akio Kashiwagi who likes
to gamble millions of dollars on baccarat.

But there is a fundamental problem underlying every potential item
on Donald's agenda: his publicly proclaimed hostility toward the Japanese. In the advertisements he ran in connection with his faux presidential campaign in the fall of 1987 and in subsequent statements to
the media, he expressed his contempt for the failure of American
politicians to make the Japanese pay a larger share of their defense
costs. Likewise, he has accused the Japanese of taking unfair advantage of the United States through trade barriers and the like. Ironically, the Japanese have so far been among the biggest buyers of
Trump apartments. At the same time, however, they are acutely aware
of Donald's anti-Japanese remarks, which they consider both offensive and uninformed.

The only fixed appointment on Donald's schedule other than a
couple of formal dinners with Japanese bankers and financiers is a
Mike Tyson boxing match. The heavyweight champion, who recently
divorced Robin Givens and patched up his relationship with Donald,
is scheduled to fight an unimpressive contender named Buster Douglas on Sunday morning. The bout promises to be a laugher. Douglas
has a record of twenty wins and four losses, all against virtual
unknowns. Tyson, on the other hand, is undefeated as a professional, with thirty-seven wins, thirty-six by knockout. For Donald and
the rest of the boxing world, the main interest in the Tyson-Douglas
bout is seeing Iron Mike take another step in his quest to surpass the
late Rocky Marciano's record of forty-one knockouts.

As if to confirm the theory that he is haunted by a death wish,

Donald has already set himself up for a fall. Prior to leaving New York, he told real estate vice-president Blanche Sprague that singer Michael Jackson would be accompanying them to Tokyo. Unaware that the boss's claim was just another big lie, Sprague leaked word to the media that Jackson would be coming along. The rumor subsequently traveled around the globe to Japan. Upon arriving in Tokyo, Donald and his party find a horde of Japanese reporters and camera crews waiting in the airport concourse.

"Stop!" Donald commands his minions, forging ahead of them at a quickened pace. "I'll go out by myself. They're here to see me."

But when Donald reaches the end of the concourse, the media horde does not react or even seem to know who he is. By the time the rest of his traveling entourage catches up with him, the Japanese are staring dumbfounded.

"Where is Michael Jackson?" a Japanese media spokesman asks in English.

One of Donald's party informs them that Jackson could not make the trip, then hastens to add, "Mr. Trump is here and will give you a brief photo and question opportunity about his reasons for coming to Japan."

The media spokesman looks baffled. He turns to the assembled horde of reporters and camera crews and says something to them in Japanese. The entire group turns and drifts off without bothering to ask a single question of their American visitor. Donald is visibly shaken. Fearing that the Japanese media's snub might put him into a dangerous depression, Norma Foerderer and Blanche Sprague grab Donald by the arm and escort him through the airport.

The Tokyo airport reception proves to be an omen of things to come. When Donald and his party arrive at their hotel, they see a throng of six thousand people milling about the entrance. The Trump entourage brightens, thinking that the crowd might be waiting for Donald. Then they all realize the crowd is populated almost entirely by teenagers. At first they fear the crowd has turned out for Michael Jackson and that they will again face the embarrassment of explaining why Jackson did not accompany Donald to Tokyo. But the truth is even worse than the Trump people imagine. The crowd has come out to greet the Rolling Stones, who are staying at the hotel. Donald is being upstaged by the same rock and roll band that insulted him at their December 1989 preconcert press conference in Atlantic City.

For the next two days Donald suffers from an extreme case of jet lag. Dressed in the same rumpled suit every waking moment, he takes on a gray pallor, his eyes swell, and he refuses to ingest Japanese food. ("I'm not going to eat any fucking raw fish," he rails.) The first night in Tokyo he and his traveling party attend a formal dinner with a group of Japanese bankers. Before the meal is served, Donald gets up and walks out, leaving his underlings to deal with the their insulted hosts.

The first real meal Donald eats in Tokyo is a hamburger for lunch the next day at a Japanese McDonald's. Feeling better, he decides to take a walk through the Imperial Gardens. The walk inspires a new idea. "Call the emperor," Donald orders his entourage. "Tell him I want to see him." But like the Japanese media at the airport, the emperor's spokesman does not seem to know who Donald is. He informs Donald's intermediary that an appointment might be arranged one year from the following Thursday, provided that the emperor is supplied with a written request stating the purpose of the visit.

On Saturday Donald decides that being in Tokyo is a waste of time. He instructs his entourage to prepare to leave after the boxing match the following morning. Later that evening he takes a group of Japanese high rollers to Mike Tyson's hotel suite to introduce them to the world heavyweight champion. Tyson is infamous for being moody, but on this particular evening he seems unusually cheerful and gracious. Donald is also in an upbeat mood, for he expects Tyson to rack up another easy victory.

"You know, I drive all the way to New Jersey and I see you murder some guy in sixty seconds," teases a female member of the Trump group. "I've just flown twenty-two hours. I hope it's worth it."

"You won't be disappointed," Tyson assures. "I know how to take care of business, baby."

On Sunday morning a different Mike Tyson shows up to defend his world heavyweight championship. In sharp contrast with the night before, he looks listless and distracted, prompting at least one member of the Trump entourage to wonder if he is on some kind of drug. Tyson's handlers are also worried. Besides being in a protracted emotional funk, the champ was recently knocked down in a sparring match by former Olympian Greg Page. On the other hand, Buster Douglas seems extremely fit and totally unintimidated, despite the fact that his mother has just died. At 260 pounds, he appears to be a giant compared with the 220-pound Tyson.

The two boxers fight just the way they look. Douglas is the aggressor throughout the first six rounds. Tyson is flat-footed and ineffectual. In round seven Tyson rallies briefly, and knocks Douglas to the canvas with a right uppercut. But Douglas bounces back up just before the bell. The bone-weary Tyson opens the tenth round with a hard right to Douglas's jaw. But that is the champ's last solid blow. Douglas lands an uppercut that makes Tyson reel backward. As Tyson falls, Douglas connects with a hard left. Tyson hits the canvas so hard his mouthpiece pops out. Ten seconds later the referee signals that the fight has ended. Buster Douglas is the new heavyweight champion of the world.

"It's over for him," Donald observes ominously as Tyson's handlers guide the fallen former champ from the ring. "He'll never come back from this."

The Trump group expects to go back to Tyson's dressing room to commiserate, but the boss has other ideas. "I'm going to Buster Douglas's dressing room," Donald announces. "He's the champ."

"What about Tyson?" asks a member of the Trump entourage.

"I'm not going to Tyson's dressing room," Donald declares. "I can't go near him. It might rub off. The same thing could happen to me."

Minutes later Donald and his entourage drive out to the airport and board the Trump plane for the twenty-two-hour flight back to New York. The boss's mood is now darker than ever. Throughout the first leg of the return trip he keeps repeating his postfight postmortem of Tyson's career: "It's over for him. . . . He'll never come back from this. . . . He's finished. . . . I can't go near him. . . . It might rub off. . . . The same thing could happen to me. . . ."

When the Trump plane finally arrives in Alaska to refuel, Donald's mood suddenly brightens. He is now back in telephone contact with New York. It is time to start "scheming and beaming" anew. But without warning he gets a call from a Trump Organization staffer in New York, who hits him with a metaphorical knockout punch. The front page of the Sunday edition of the *New York Daily News* carries a banner-headlined photograph of Mike Tyson going down for the count in Tokyo. But the front page also features a mug shot of gossip columnist Liz Smith and a double deck of bold-faced type that says:

LOVE ON THE ROCKS
Ivana Trump devastated "that Donald was betraying her"

"The marriage of Ivana and Donald Trump seems to be on the rocks, and inside sources say lawyers are already at work trying to divide the complex Trump holdings," Liz Smith reports in the lead piece of a four-page inside spread. She adds that "intimate friends say the couple's impending split is shaking the dynamic, magnetic and highly publicized Trump empire to its foundations."

Liz Smith is not only the first outsider to break the news of the Trumps' split but also the first to take sides. Her sympathies are clearly with Ivana. In the body of her column Smith portrays Ivana as a faithful wife and devoted mother who has been an "active partner" in building the family fortune. "According to sources," Smith declares, "Mrs. Trump was so involved with taking care of 'The Donald,' rearing their three young children and being her husband's full-time business partner, that she had absolutely no idea the marriage was in trouble."

While Smith does not reveal that her "informed sources" are all from Ivana's camp, she hints as much by going overboard in documenting Ivana's purported business contributions. According to Smith, Donald's recent trip to Tokyo is "the first time in the 12-year partnership that Ivana did not accompany him on a business trip." That statement, of course, is dead wrong.But Smith is right about the fact that America's most glamorous new rich couple is breaking up, and she cannot resist the temptation to boast about her exclusive story.

"Over four months ago, I talked to Donald Trump, personally, telling him that I was not the only one who was aware of rumors that his marriage was in trouble and asking him to comment," Smith claims. "He seemed not to take me seriously and said he would advise me if there was any development. After Christmas, I wrote him a letter asking if he would talk to me about rumors concerning a blowup with Ivana in Aspen. He did not respond."

Donald does not remain unresponsive for long. He calls Liz Smith from the Trump plane en route to New York and gives her a piece of his mind.

"Congratulations on your story," he says sarcastically. Then he snarls: "I've had it with Ivana. She's gotten to be like Leona Helmsley."

"Shame on you, Donald," Smith scolds. "How can you say that about the mother of your children?"

"Just write that someone from Howard Rubenstein's office said it," he rejoins, referring to his New York publicist.

Liz Smith then copies down Donald's side of the story as she hears it from him and an anonymous "spokesman" (most likely Trump himself) riding with him in the plane. "Donald Trump is NOT negotiating," Smith is told at the outset of their conversation. She is reminded that he and Ivana have a nuptial agreement, which is, in Smith's paraphrase, "signed in gold" and cannot be broken. Then Donald's unnamed mouthpiece hastens to minimize his wife's contribution to their storied success.

"Ivana Trump did not help build the Trump empire," Smith's anonymous source maintains. "She doesn't know that much about business. Donald just let her run the Plaza Hotel to keep her busy. He could have easily found the best Swiss hotel manager in the world to run the Plaza and he can still do so. And there is no possibility that if Ivana had gone to Japan with Donald, she'd have sat in on his business negotiations there."

Donald then goes back on the record and gives Smith a statement implying that he is the one who initiated the breakup: "It is better for Ivana and me to separate at this time. But I am leaving because I want to leave. Ivana is a wonderful woman and a very good woman and I like her. We might even get back together. I can't say we won't. Who knows what could happen. And as for those other women I've been linked with, well, I want to say that we are all just friends, and that's as far as it goes."

That same evening Donald contacts the New York Post, the tabloid rival of the Daily News, and attempts to discredit Liz Smith's story. "While Mr. Trump thinks Ivana is a wonderful woman," his anonymous spokesman tells the Post, "unfortunately the marriage is no longer working out. A few hours before his trip to Tokyo, he told her he wanted to leave her. . . . The Liz Smith article was clearly planted by sources close to Ivana, most likely her attorneys, because of the gross inaccuracies," the unidentified Trump spokesman contends. "Ivana hardly ever accompanied Mr. Trump on business trips. She had absolutely nothing to do with the business of the Trump Organization. She was just a figurehead in Atlantic City."

When Donald's limousine pulls up in front of Trump Tower later that evening, he finds himself in the middle of a three-ring circus complete with floodlights and popcorn vendors. Every entrance to the building is surrounded by concentric cordons of television cameras, flashbulb-popping paparazzi, note-jotting journalists, and question-shouting curiosity seekers. Stunned speechless, Donald leaps out of his limousine and rushes up to the Trumps' triplex apartment on the sixty-seventh floor.

Ivana is nowhere in sight. As Donald later learns to his chagrin, she was tipped off to his arrival at the airport and has beaten a hasty retreat with the children to the Kennedys' apartment a few blocks up Fifth Avenue. Still seething over the Liz Smith story, Donald packs some clothes and moves downstairs to apartment 63J, the unit usually reserved for his father, Fred C. Trump, Sr.; it is right across the hall from the unit in which Marla Maples briefly stayed just before the confrontation in Aspen.

Donald does not know that he is playing right into the hands of Ivana's attorney. The minute he moves out, Michael Kennedy has a locksmith come into Trump Tower and change the locks on the doors to the triplex. The lockout is designed to be the ultimate humiliation. Donald J. Trump, the man who built Trump Tower, is unable to enter his own home.

On Monday morning, February 12, the front page of the *New York Post* is dominated by the banner headline SPLIT plastered across a fractured photograph of The Donald and Ivana. The news of the Trumps' marital problems takes precedence over news that South African authorities have just freed black activist Nelson Mandela after twenty-five years in prison. The Mandela item is reported in a one-inch box at the bottom of page one alongside a notice declaring, TODAY'S THE DAY FOR SECOND CHANCE LOTTO.

The *Post*'s curious sense of front-page news priorities is not the only thing that distinguishes the day's edition. The *Post* is also the first publication to identify Marla Maples as a participant in the Trump marital scandal. The newspaper's four-page-plus inside spread on the Trump story features a black-and-white photograph of Marla evidently cropped from her modeling portfolio. Next to Marla's mug shot are photographs of two other beauties who have been romantically linked to Donald: actress Catherine Oxenberg and ice skater Peggy Fleming. But unlike Marla, both Oxenberg and Fleming will adamantly deny having any sexual involvement with Donald.

The *Post*'s sensationalistic coverage of the Trump-Maples love triangle sets the pattern for the media frenzy to come. Over the next few months the story will garner cover, front page, or feature play in such diverse publications as *Newsweek, Time, People, Forbes, Vanity Fair, Vogue*, the *Globe*, the *Star*, the *National Enquirer*, the *New York Times*, the *Los Angeles Times*, the *Washington Post*, all the major television networks, and newspapers and magazines all across Europe, the Middle East, and Australia. The 1988 presidential campaign generated a greater number of news stories, but not even winning candidate George Bush was celebrated with such a wide variety of coverage.

The *New York Post* story throws a scare into Marla Maples. She is suddenly the most sought-after news figure in the country, if not the entire world. Ironically, she is hiding out right in the center of the world's media capital, the New York Hilton on Seventh Avenue. But Marla knows that her risk of being cornered by the scoop-hungry packs of reporters combing the streets increases with each passing hour. So does her still-protective ex-boyfriend Tom Fitzsimmons, who telephones Donald in alarm the morning the *Post* story carrying her photograph hits the newsstands.

"Donald, we've got to keep her out of sight," Tom urges, "or the press is gonna kill her."

"Yeah, yeah, yeah," Donald replies with striking ambivalence as if he realized such a move might deprive him of continuing publicity. As usual he leaves it to Tom to come up with a solution.

Tom telephones Larry Russo, a realtor friend in his early thirties. Russo, who grew up in the Bronx, where he used to work at the zoo, is presently employed by Donald's friend Marty Raynes, the son-in-law of billionaire Marvin Davis. But he has met Donald during past business deals, and he is anxious to do a valuable favor. Tom knows that Russo owns a house on Narrow Lane in Southampton that he occupies only in the summer months. Russo readily agrees that his Southampton house would be a perfect hideaway. That afternoon Marla and Kim Knapp pack their clothes and drive out to Long Island in Russo's white Land Rover.

While his mistress hightails it out of the city, Donald retaliates for being locked out of Trump Tower. When Ivana shows up for work at the Plaza Hotel that morning, she finds a pair of Trump security guards blocking the door to her office. Her lockout does not last long. By early afternoon the security guards retreat to Trump Tower on the boss's orders. Michael Kennedy later claims that Donald realized he made a mistake by forgetting that Ivana is the one who provides the Plaza with its social cachet. Donald, for his part, disingenuously denies that he was serious about barring his wife from the hotel in the first place. He claims through a spokesman that he has "not yet made up his mind about what role Mrs. Trump will assume at the Plaza."

But Donald quickly adds insult to Ivana's injury by planting a barb in the *New York Post* through the public relations firm of Howard Rubenstein and Associates. According to Rubenstein publicist Dan Klores, Donald supposedly confided to a friend, "I don't want to create another Leona Helmsley." The reference to Helmsley, who was recently found guilty of income tax evasion, is a repeat of the remark Donald made on the phone to Liz Smith the previous night. But unlike Smith, who scolded Donald for saying such a thing and did not print it, the *Post* runs the secondhand comment in full.

The Ivana/Leona comparison ignites what both sides call "the war of the faxes." Michael Kennedy faxes off a missive to Howard Rubenstein threatening to sue him for libel. "[P]ublicity agents from your agency purportedly speaking for Donald Trump have been slandering Mrs. Trump," Kennedy writes. "Specifically attributed to your agency are statements that attack Mrs. Trump's professional competence, allege a disrespect and dislike of her by her co-employees within the Trump Organization and liken her to Leona Helmsley, a convicted criminal."

Kennedy nevertheless spends the better part of the afternoon locked in one-on-one negotiations with Donald. His avowed aims are twofold: to save the Trumps' marriage and to ensure financial security for Ivana. Kennedy gets Donald to admit, at least tacitly, that the

Trumps' nuptial contract is in need of revision. In fact, Donald later offers to pay Ivana $2.5 million per year for twenty years, a $50 million package that is more than double the amount specified in their current agreement. But by the end of the day Donald is already planting stories in the local media that Ivana is making exorbitant demands. He later blames the leaks on Michael Kennedy.

The hot-tempered Kennedy keeps his cool. Most of the media and the general public assume that the Trumps' separation has to lead to formal legal action: Either Donald or Ivana will inevitably sue for divorce. But Kennedy says nothing publicly about filing for divorce. Unbeknownst to Donald's attorneys, their client's adulterous relationship with Marla Maples is also of secondary importance to Kennedy, though he prefers to let his adversaries believe otherwise. The Trumps' controversial nuptial agreement, which affects any potential property settlement between husband and wife, remains his primary concern.

"This is an extremely difficult time for Mrs. Trump and her children," Kennedy says in a formal statement issued to the media. "She is a family woman. Her marriage and her family have always been the most important things in her life. Mr. Trump has now left her and the children. While one hopes for a reconciliation, my mandate is to document . . . the years of marriage and partnership in the Trump holdings."

It is not an easy task. Kennedy knows that the tentacles of Donald's influence reach to virtually every corner of the local law enforcement and private investigation worlds. So in addition to hiring divorce specialists of the law firm of White & Case and private detectives from Investigative Group Inc., he secretly contacts Houston-based private investigator Clyde Wilson, the former chief of security for Tenneco Inc. and a seasoned divorce case sleuth. Wilson and his cohorts, whom Kennedy dubs "the cowboys," fly up to Atlantic City and start compiling a thick dossier on Ivana's contributions to the Trumps' financial success.

The war of the faxes is immediately followed by the battle of the tabloids. The principal combatants are Liz Smith of the *New York Daily News*, who sides with Ivana, and Cindy Adams of the *New York*

Post, who gets her scoops directly from The Donald. On Tuesday, February 13, Smith writes a front-page story headlined IVANA BETTER DEAL. Adams counters with a front-page story headlined GIMME THE PLAZA . . . THE JET AND $150 MILLION, TOO. Smith portrays Ivana as the woman wronged, financially and every other way. Adams depicts Ivana as a "smart . . . savvy . . . well-educated" gold digger out for "big bucks." According to Adams, "Donald knows he is going to get hit."

Remarkably Donald seems to relish the fire storm of faxes and tabloid publicity. He spends Tuesday morning down in Wilmington, Delaware, at a press conference promoting the next Tour de Trump bicycle race scheduled for May 1990. He shows some signs of stress in the narrowing of his eyes and the bloat of his cheeks. In a departure from his usual feigned candor, he says he will not answer any "personal questions." But his manner and mood remain blithely ebullient. When the photographers ask him to pose beside a comely Tour de Trump race queen, he jokes, "Better get some guys in the picture."

Ivana, on the other hand, is riding an emotional roller coaster. The tabloid stories and the lockout maneuvers over the past forty-eight hours have left her shaking with fear, anxiety, and humiliation. Ivana realizes that she is more vulnerable than ever. She owns virtually nothing except personal items in her own name. She is not protected by love or marriage. And as she learned the previous morning, the one thing she does have, her job at the Plaza, is subject to her husband's goodwill.

Worse, Ivana is a hostage in her own Trump Tower home. While Donald cannot get into the triplex, she is understandably afraid to go out. The sidewalks around the building have become the scene of a constant vigil by camera crews, reporters, and scandal-mongering passersby. Besides the children, her only companions are Michael and Eleanore Kennedy, her mother, Maria Zelnicek, and her executive assistant, Lisa Calandra. She spends most of her time drinking brandy and staring out the oversize plate glass windows. She also finds herself wrestling with an unexpected social quandary.

On February 18, five days hence, Ivana will turn forty-one. But Wednesday, February 14 is Valentine's Day, and Eleanore Kennedy is scheduled to host a ladies' luncheon in Ivana's honor at La Grenouille, a pricey and socially prestigious French restaurant on Fifty-second Street. Though the party has been planned for months, Ivana shudders at the thought of showing her face in public after all the embarrassing media coverage. She considers the idea of having the party catered in Trump Tower. Then Eleanore Kennedy convinces her that would only feed the vicious gossip. They vow to go ahead with the luncheon as planned.

"I am afraid," Ivana tells her gossip columnist friend Liz Smith that evening. "I know the children and I will be Donald's next project. I know how he is. He will simply zero in on us."

Just as Ivana might have predicted, The Donald arrives unannounced at the Trump Tower triplex. The ostensible purpose of his visit is to show her a civic award he has received that week. As he walks back out the door, he turns to her and smiles. "I love you," he says.

Ivana feels her heart skip a beat. The Donald knows just how to get to her. And he obviously intends to use his hypnotic power for all it is worth.

"Ivana doesn't want the money," Donald tells *New York Daily News* columnist Mike McAlary in an interview that same evening. "She wants Donald. She loves me totally."

Incredibly enough, that isn't just another Trump brag; it is fact.

By half past high noon on Valentine's Day, there is a near riot at 3 East Fifty-second Street in front of La Grenouille. Overcoat-clad crowds of celebrity worshipers and newshounds have flocked to the restaurant, hoping to catch a glimpse of the leading lady in *l'affaire de Trump*. The clamoring hordes bring both pedestrian and vehicular traffic to a halt, forcing police officials to block off the street. As a force of eight Trump bodyguards attempt to clear the way for Ivana's arrival, their leader is accidentally punched in the gut by one of his own men.

"This is worse than Bernie Goetz, Bess Myerson, and Robert Chambers," complains a local television reporter, referring, respectively, to the notorious cases of the New York subway rider indicted for shooting an alleged mugger, the former Miss America charged with bribing a judge, and the perpetrator of the so-called preppie sex murder in Central Park.

Ivana's pal Liz Smith has tipped off the party crashers by mentioning the La Grenouille luncheon in her column that morning. She gushes that the tumult on the sidewalk is of historic proportions. According to Smith, New Yorkers have not seen anything like it in the twenty-five years since the tempestuous affair of actress Elizabeth Taylor and actor Richard Burton. She is not far wrong.

At 1:00 P.M., as Ivana's Mercedes pulls up in front of La Grenouille, the crowd erupts in cheers and applause.

"Yea, Ivana!" shrieks a gaggle of female fans.

"Twenty-five million is not enough!" shouts one of the many male sympathizers on the scene.

"Take him for all he's worth!" urges another diehard Donald hater.

Ivana bursts out of the limousine in a blinding flash of freshly coiffed blond hair. In observance of Valentine's Day, she is wearing a cherry-colored Chanel suit, a white silk blouse, and a gold choker with a blaze red ruby amulet. Startled, intimidated, but sincerely touched by the spontaneous outpouring of support from the people on the street, she wedges herself between a pair of broad-shouldered bodyguards and bolts toward the front door of the restaurant, smiling through her tears.

Inside the exclusive confines of La Grenouille, Eleanore Kennedy ushers Ivana up to a private dining room on the second floor, where she is greeted by thirty of her closest confidantes and kinfolk. Among the more prominent figures on the guest list are the ubiquitous Liz Smith, television journalist Barbara Walters, fashion designer Carolyne Roehm, fellow Czechoslovakian Aja Zanova-Steindler, celebrated socialites Anne Bass, Georgette Mosbacher, Carroll Petrie, Eva O'Neill, and Nina Griscom; Ivana's mother-in-law, Mary Trump; and her sisters-in-law, Maryanne Trump Barry, Elizabeth Trump, and Blaine Beard Trump. Each has come, as per invitational instructions, bearing a heart-shaped gift.

"Bless us, O Lord, for these thy gifts, and for thy bounty which we are about to receive," Eleanore Kennedy intones as she says grace over a champagne feast of lamb chops, asparagus en croûte, and chocolate cake. "On this day we pray that people all over the world can find the strength to be more loving toward one another."

Ivana does not know whether to laugh or cry. Over the next two hours she does a lot of both. The Donald's unseen presence looms over the luncheon like a ghostly specter torturing the psyche of the honoree. But each time Ivana is moved to tears, her table mates rally to her side with champagne and sympathy.

"Now pull yourself together, Ivana," chimes Nina Griscom, a twice-divorced and soon-to-be-remarried celebrity model who will be the only one of Ivana's rich and famous friends to offer financial help in her time of crisis.

Donald's octogenarian mother tries to bridge the troubled waters when she rises to toast her beleaguered daughter-in-law. "I feel like the villain on the premises," Mary Trump admits. "But I consider you one of my daughters. I hate the expression 'in-law.'"

Blaine Beard Trump, the wife of Donald's brother, Robert, belies the widely rumored rivalry between her and Ivana by offering a diplomatically worded toast. "We are always going to be as close as we are now," Blaine assures her sister-in-law.

Just as Ivana's friends, who know better, begin exchanging disapproving looks, Barbara Walters breaks the tension by interjecting a bit of double-edged levity. Walters has brought along a "telegram" purportedly sent by black activist Nelson Mandela. She rises from her seat and reads it aloud.

"Please give me a break," Mandela's faux wire message says, "and get off the front pages."

Everyone in the room, Ivana included, bubbles with laughter. "I think you ought to run for mayor," socialite Carroll Petrie suggests half-seriously.

After the waiters serve dessert, Ivana is treated to another surprise: a second chocolate cake. It arrives with a note from bankrupt former Saudi Arabian billionaire Adnan Khashoggi, who is lunching downstairs in the main dining room. Khashoggi, the original owner of the *Trump Princess*, recently became the butt of mocking tabloid headlines because he tried to impress his bankruptcy judge by taking the subway to court.

"He is an old friend." Ivana blushes. "But now I will be the second one on the subway." Once again the room rolls with laughter.

The lighthearted mood lasts until it is time to leave La Grenouille for the reality of the outside world. Ivana rightly fears that her exit will spark a repeat of the riotous reception that greeted her arrival. In an effort to insulate her, Eleanore Kennedy instructs the guests to form a circle around the guest of honor; then a contingent of Trump bodyguards encircles the entire party and escorts them out of the restaurant.

Thanks to her hastily devised human shield, Ivana manages to slip into her waiting Mercedes before the teeming crowds on the street realize what is happening. As she makes her chauffeur-driven escape down Fifty-second Street, Barbara Walters stands beside the police barricades and graciously feeds a few morsels of inside poop on the luncheon to the avaricious media.

"Nobody even mentioned Donald's name," Walters reports. "It was just friends."

Donald does not suffer his wife's Valentine's Day blues. He spends part of the morning preparing for a February 15 press conference at the Plaza Hotel to announce a boxing match between Thomas ("Hit Man") Hearns and Michael ("The Silk") Olajide scheduled for April. He also keeps up his personal public relations offensive by having a "heart-to-heart" talk with *New York Post* columnist Cindy Adams.

"I'm really stunned at the media attention," Donald tells Adams. "I figured it would last one day, but this is beyond anyone's imagination. It just doesn't stop."

In sharp contrast with Ivana, however, Donald is reveling in the furor over his marital problems. He believes that the incessant hype is good for his business interests. "The last three days my casinos in Atlantic City are leading the whole town," he brags. "Whatever the media says now is irrelevant. The negative publicity has absolutely no effect on my life at all."

Donald soon finds out different. His cozy chat with Cindy Adams is followed by a telephone call from his father. Fred Trump, Sr., is incensed about the scandalous stories he keeps seeing about Donald and his extramarital affairs.

"If you don't stop what you're doing," the Trump family patriarch tells his errant son, "it's going to give me a stroke."

Donald is in no mood to listen. He gloats every time a news story links him to some beautiful woman, especially if it is someone other than Marla. Rather than dispel the innuendos, he directly and indirectly encourages them by issuing coy no comments or by asking pals to plant still more stories of his alleged sexual exploits in the local tabloids.

"Do you believe all these women love me?" he exclaims to Tom Fitzsimmons.

Soon rumors begin to emanate from the Trump Organization that Donald is sowing new wild oats. His alleged co-conspirator is realtor Larry Russo, a close friend of John Casablancas, the head of the Elite modeling agency. According to the inside gossip, Russo is hosting parties at his apartment to introduce Donald to various New York models. When Donald sees a picture of Marla plastered across the pages of the newspapers or flashing across the television screen, he laughs aloud.

"What am I going to do about Marla?" he asks one of their mutual friends with obvious delight. "She's going to commit suicide if she finds out about all the beautiful women that are after me."

Marla Maples is starting to feel almost as miserable and abandoned as Ivana, and far more paranoid. She has spent the last forty-eight hours hiding out with Kim Knapp at Russo's summer home in Southampton. Every morning she disguises herself in a pair of sunglasses that belong to Russo's girl friend and stuffs her blond locks into a blue baseball cap embroidered with the logo of a local eatery named C. J. Thorne's. Then she and Kim climb into Russo's white Land Rover and drive into town.

But the charade quickly becomes tiresome. As during previous off-season months, Southampton is virtually deserted, at least by socially conscious New Yorkers. If there is little chance Marla will be noticed by someone who knows Donald or Ivana, there is also little to do except eat, drink, and check out the latest stories about the Trump love triangle that are being bandied about by the tabloids. And as her time in temporary exile wears on, Marla does not like what she reads or what she hears from some of Donald's confidants.

On Valentine's Day morning Marla sees one of her full-length modeling photographs splashed across the front page of the *New York Post* beside the headline DON JUAN! In the lower left corner of the page there is an inset photo of Donald next to a subhead that says tantalizingly, "Secret visits to model Marla at Hotel St. Moritz hideaway." Although Donald is quoted as saying that Marla is just a "friend," the *Post* reveals that she stayed in the St. Moritz for about two months and that Donald had paid "frequent visits" to her room at the hotel. In the same story Tom Fitzsimmons tries in vain to defend her honor and Donald's. "I never saw them carry on in any way," Tom fibs. "The whole thing has been blown out of proportion."

But the *Post* reports that Donald confided to an intimate that Marla is "so much better than a 10 you can't believe it." As if to attest to that remark, the tabloid runs a tongue-in-cheek statistical comparison between Marla and Ivana, noting their respective height, weight, hair color, eye color, dress sizes, hobbies, and "Proudest Recent Accomplishment." In Ivana's case, the latter category includes finding "enough shades of enough colors to decorate each of the 614 rooms in an Atlantic City hotel a different color." In Marla's case, it is playing "the oh-so-crucial part of the 'Second Woman' in a Stephen King horror film about runaway trucks."

The next day the *Post* runs an even more salacious front-page photograph of Marla clad in a bathing suit with the headline THEY MET IN CHURCH. The tabloid claims that "Donald and Marla used to share the same pew" at Marble Collegiate on Fifth Avenue. That, of course, is not quite accurate. Donald and Marla actually met in Atlantic City. And as Tom Fitzsimmons, who accompanied Marla to church dozens of times, later attested, Donald was not a regular churchgoer or, for that matter, even a church member. But the *Post* accurately reports that back in December 1988 Donald sought counseling from the church minister, Dr. Arthur Caliandro, about his disintegrating marriage and his adulterous affair with Marla, who is a church member in good standing.

By now Marla is convulsing with embarrassment. She spends hours on the telephone with her mother, Ann Ogletree, her ex-boy friend Tom Fitzsimmons, and Chuck Jones, her loyal New York agent and publicist, in an effort to counter the torrent of tacky publicity. Jones, who has been frantically fending off reporters anxious to discover Marla's current whereabouts, decides that their only viable option is to lie, lie, and lie again. In an interview with the *New York Daily News*, Jones flatly denies that Marla has had "anything to do with Donald Trump."

Marla still trusts in Donald and his love for her, but her faith is being sorely tested. She can tell by the tone and tenor of Donald's phone calls that he is up to something. Although she refuses to believe that Donald is being as unfaithful to her as he has been to Ivana, she is tormented by unconfirmed suspicions. She decides to call Fitzsimmons.

"Please, Tom," she begs, "you've got to find out what's going on."

Back in New York Tom clicks off his cordless phone, and peers out the plate glass window of the twenty-fifth-floor Upper East Side apartment he once shared with Marla. He is in a no-win situation. He dares not share the gossip he has heard about Donald's philandering for fear that Marla will shoot the messenger. At the same time, however, he hates to see Donald play her for a fool. The *National Enquirer* will soon offer $250,000 for Tom's inside story. He could surely use the money, but he is too much of a gentleman to sell out his friends.

Thirsting for insight, inspiration, and his customary late-afternoon beer, Tom decides to ponder his dilemma at Mumbles, his favorite corner bar. As soon as he opens the door of his apartment, he sees he is walking right into a trap. A cadre of reporters and photographers is loitering about the hall in front of the elevator bank. He does an about-face and slams the door. Then the phone rings. It is Hal Bundy, the bartender at Mumbles.

"Tom, don't come over here," Hal advises. "There are reporters waiting for you all over the place."

Tom thanks Hal for the warning and clicks off the cordless. He suddenly realizes that he and Marla are in the same predicament. Both are effectively under involuntary house arrest, he in his apartment and she in Russo's place in Southampton. The only participant in the Trump love triangle who feels free to show his face in public is Donald, the man who got them in this mess.

The phone rings again. This time it is Marla's agent-publicist, Chuck Jones. "Tom, I hope you're sitting down."

Jones says that he has just gotten wind of a potentially devastating story about Marla and Donald that the *New York Post* plans to run in the next day's edition. The story is based on an interview with an unnamed woman who attended acting school with Marla. Besides portraying Marla as a bimbo, the woman claims that Marla told her

Donald is the greatest lover she ever had. She also claims Marla told her that Donald had promised to divorce Ivana so he could marry Marla.

"Holy shit," Tom exclaims, "I better call Donald."

When the phone rings in Donald's office on the twenty-sixth floor of Trump Tower, he already knows all about the *New York Post* story in progress. He is consulting with his divorce attorney, Jay Goldberg, a tall and bald Harvard Law School graduate who could pass as Donald's alter ego. Goldberg wants to block the story by threatening a lawsuit. But Donald obviously feels flattered by the idea of being depicted as a great lover.

"What's the downside?" Donald asks when he takes Tom's call.

Tom points out that the story will surely hurt Marla's feelings and muddle Donald's legal battle with Ivana. "We've got to sue," Tom insists.

"No, no, we're not suing anybody," Donald rejoins. "I don't want people to think I'm a killer."

Then he turns to Goldberg and says, "Don't block it."

On Friday, February 16, the *New York Post* runs the most sensational front-page headline of the entire Trump affair:

MARLA BOASTS TO PALS ABOUT DONALD:
"BEST SEX I'VE EVER HAD."

"The sex is really great because Donald is a wonderful, wonderful lover," Marla's ex-classmate quotes her as saying. "We have the best time together, and I love him very much."

"All the guys loved [Marla] because she always wore sheer, clingy outfits that showed off her big chest and her amazing figure," the ex-classmate recalls. "She had an incredible body, and she was really sweet, but she had no acting talent, not too much upstairs. Nobody could see her making it—especially in New York."

Just as Fitzsimmons warned, Marla reacts to the *Post* headline with a mixture of outrage, incredulity, and pain. For the first time she begins to wonder if Donald has had a hand in planting or failing to prevent publication of the story. Tom knows the truth, of course, but he is afraid to share it with her for fear it will cause her even more hurt. The same goes for Chuck Jones. "It's a blatant lie," she complains when her agent-publicist phones her on Friday morning.

While Marla remains in hiding, Jones mounts a media counterattack. He tells the *Post* that the anonymous former acting school classmate "came on to her . . . and Marla's so innocent she didn't realize it." He adds that Marla "feels terrible about this. She had feelings." According to Jones, Marla's decision to keep her mouth shut attests to her high moral character. He claims that the *National Enquirer* offered her $250,000 for the rights to her "exclusive story." Marla rejected the offer, he says, and would likewise decline any and all future requests to discuss the Trump affair with the media.

Even so, Jones knows better than to protest too much. Thanks to the *New York Post,* Marla Ann Maples, a struggling actress-model from small-town Georgia, has become a major American sex symbol overnight. *Playboy, Penthouse,* and virtually all the other mass-circulation men's magazines are prepared to pay six-figure sums to photograph her in the nude. A number of prominent corporations, including a clothing manufacturer known for exploiting previous national sex scandals, want her to be their marketing representative. And her mysterious absence from public view only makes her more sought after.

Out in Southampton, Marla is chagrined at her present predicament. So long as she remains faithfully protective of Donald, she does not see anything wrong with capitalizing on the new commercial opportunities that might come her way. Donald, after all, is the master of such self-promotion. She longs to break her vow of silence even though she knows she cannot—at least not yet.

"One day when this is all over, I want to come forward," she tells family and friends who phone her hideaway, "so I can tell everybody the truth."

Ivana Trump sits by the window in the master bedroom on the top floor of her Trump Tower triplex and slugs back a shot of cognac. She has more in common with Marla Maples than either of them could ever know. Like her rival, Ivana is reeling from the aftershocks of reading the front-page headline in the *New York Post*. She, too, feels humiliated, helpless, betrayed, and abandoned. But even though Ivana spends most of the afternoon in solitary seclusion, she realizes that she does not suffer alone.

The real victims of the Trumps' tabloid sex scandal are their children, especially the older two. Unlike her youngest son, Eric, who has just celebrated his sixth birthday, their twelve-year-old son, Donny, and their seven-year-old daughter, Ivanka, are able to read the newspapers and grasp what is going on. All day long their schoolmates at Buckley and Chapin taunted them with snide remarks and cruel jokes. Donny retaliated with his fists; little Ivanka came running home in tears.

Ivana pours another cognac. Her friends have been calling all morning long to offer sympathy and support. But there is nothing they can do to soften the blow of the "BEST SEX" story.

"Things can't get any worse than they are now," she sobs to one intimate.

Shortly before the winter afternoon sun begins to set, Ivana hears the doorbell ring. The butler comes around to announce that her parents are ready to depart for the airport. The Zelniceks are going to fly down to Palm Beach to celebrate Ivana's birthday at the Mar-a-Lago estate. Donald's parents, Fred and Mary Trump, are also scheduled to appear. The only question mark is The Donald: Will he join them or will he stay away?

Ivana picks up her traveling bag. Then she remembers there is a secret stop on her itinerary between Trump Tower and the airport. Hoping to fortify herself on the way, she returns to the window where she has been sitting, grabs the cognac bottle, and sticks it in her purse.

Outside on the street, two limousines are waiting to take Ivana's children, her parents, and their luggage to the airport. The convoy is intended to be a decoy. Ivana slips into a third car sent over by Michael Kennedy and drives around the corner to St. Patrick's Cathedral for a private meeting with John Cardinal O'Connor.

Ivana hopes Cardinal O'Connor might be able to save her marriage. O'Connor says he will be glad to meet with the Trumps to discuss their marital problems whenever they like. But there is not much he can do unless The Donald is willing to cooperate. In the meantime, O'Connor can offer only the same one-word advice he gives to all troubled couples: "Pray."

Donald prowls about his twenty-sixth-floor Trump Tower office while Norma Foerderer frantically screens an avalanche of incoming calls. In diametric contrast with his emotionally distraught wife and mistress, he seems to take a perverse pride and pleasure from the repercussions of the *New York Post*'s sensational "BEST SEX" headline. He believes it will boost his business and his image as a sex symbol.

"Did you see it?" he chortles when Fitzsimmons telephones that morning. "Wow! Is that terrific?"

Beneath his braggadocio, however, Donald is still not sure what net effect the weeklong blizzard of Trump stories will have on his image versus Ivana's and Ivana's image versus Marla's. Pro-Ivana columnists such as Liz Smith have cast his wife as the classic "woman wronged," while otherwise nonpartisan colleagues in the press have castigated Marla as a "home wrecker." Donald is caught in the middle, hated by housewives and envied by henpecked husbands. He decides to hedge his position by playing killer and Cupid at the same time.

Even as the *New York Post* story hits the stands, Donald launches a covert attack on Liz Smith. Earlier the same week the *New York Times* ran a haughty article about the other media's gossip-mongering coverage of the Trump scandal, charging that Liz Smith was being "manipulated" by Ivana's publicist, John Scanlon. Smith's rival, Cindy Adams of the *New York Post,* whose sympathies appear to lie with Donald, follows with an item claiming that news of the Trumps' split was "leaked" to Smith, insinuating that such a common journalistic occurrence amounts to some sort of crime. The following week Donald himself will demand that the *Daily News* fire Smith for allegedly fabricating a quote about his delight over the "BEST SEX" headline.

On Saturday, February 17, Donald unveils the second phase of his media counteroffensive. TRUMP BLINKS: THE DONALD WOULD RECONCILE, declares a front-page headline in the *New York Post.* The story inside quotes "a source close to Trump" as saying that over the last few days Donald has been able to "test the waters of public opinion and the results seem quite clear"—i.e., he is coming out on the losing end of the image battle. That same morning a reporter for the *New*

York Daily News is surprised to find Donald at work in his Trump Tower office.

"There's always a chance for reconciliation," Donald tells the *Daily News,* adding that Marla Maples is "merely a good friend." He then complains that the media is treating him "unfairly" and singles out his alleged enemy at the *News*. "Liz Smith is being used, she was played like a fiddle," he charges. "What she's doing is hurting them, Ivana and the children."

Donald is then asked if in the spirit of potential reconciliation, he plans to fly down to Palm Beach for his wife's birthday party. "I was asked whether I would go," he notes elliptically, "and it's possible that I might, but I'm here."

That afternoon, however, Donald speeds out to Southampton, where he sees Marla in person for the first time since she fled from the media onslaught. The two of them spend the night together in the master bedroom of Larry Russo's vacation home on Narrow Lane.

When Donald awakes the next morning, he finds that the *New York Daily News* contains an independent test of the "waters of public opinion." The results are not in his favor. According to a call-in telephone poll conducted by the *News*, Ivana has won the public's sympathy by a landslide margin of 82 percent versus only 18 percent for Donald. Likewise, a whopping 70 percent of the callers say that a rumored divorce settlement of $100 million for Ivana is not enough.

That afternoon Donald boards the Trump plane and flies down to Palm Beach. The move is an obvious attempt to regain the moral high ground. According to his publicist, Dan Klores, Donald is "going to Florida to be with his children, whom he loves."

chapter nine
KING OF CRASS

■ ON SUNDAY, FEBRUARY 18, a troupe of violinists drives through the imposing Mediterranean-tiled gates of Mar-a-Lago. They are followed by a truck full of flowers and a sleek black limousine carrying the master of the house, Donald J. Trump. He is arriving just in time to celebrate Ivana's forty-first birthday with their children, both sets of grandparents, and a handful of invited guests. According to a family confidant, "The violins were Fred Trump's idea. He wanted to make things romantic for Ivana and for Donald."

Fred Trump, Sr., also wants to repair the emotional damage Donald has done to the entire family. On Saturday afternoon he and Mary Trump took their three grandchildren on a shopping spree at the local Toys 'R' Us store. Then they ate lunch at the predominantly Jewish Palm Beach Country Club with their longtime friends from the Queens real estate business Ruth and Bert Mack. When the elder Trumps returned to Mar-a-Lago, the place was surrounded by an army of reporters; the old man had to get out of his Rolls-Royce and pound on the gates before the security guard would let him back in.

"Mary and Fred are very disturbed," Ruth Mack admits to the media following the lunch. "They like Ivana a great deal, and they are concerned about the kids. They are hoping for a reconciliation, and perhaps there will be one."

Donald, however, keeps sending out mixed signals. When a *New York Daily News* reporter telephones Mar-a-Lago on Sunday afternoon to get the latest on the Trumps' attempts at reconciliation, Donald takes the call but refuses to provide a progress report. "You'll have to call back next weekend," he instructs. Then eschewing his customary business suit, he puts on a blue blazer, slacks, and an open-collar shirt, and marches downstairs to join the rest of the family in the living room for cocktails.

"Hello, Vaska, happy birthday." Donald grins, obviously hoping to endear himself by using his wife's pet name. "You look incredible."

Ivana forces a nervous smile.

"Happy birthday, Vaska," Donald repeats as he bends over and kisses her on the cheek.

Suddenly the entire room is hushed. Fred and Mary Trump exchange quizzical glances. So do Milos and Maria Zelnicek. No one knows what to say. It is impossible to make polite conversation or simpleminded small talk in light of what has transpired over the past week.

After several agonizing minutes the butler sounds the dinner bell. He leads the way outside the main house to the cloister overlooking the estate's lushly landscaped gardens, where three round tables have been set up for the festivities. Little Ivanka waits until all the adults are seated, then rises to her feet and serenades her mother with their favorite song, "Edelweiss." Ivanka's song temporarily breaks the awkward silence, but it does not save the birthday party from disaster.

"The tension was so thick you could have cut it with a knife," one of the guests recalls afterward.

Donald tries to pretend that he is having fun. But Ivana can tell that he is enjoying the affair about as much as previous seated dinners at Mar-a-Lago, which he considered the equivalent of psychosocial torture. Afterward someone asks Donald if he liked the violinists his father brought in for the party.

"Yeah," he replies unenthusiastically, "they were nice."

On Monday, February 19, the *New York Post* reports in another front-page headline that the Trumps had slept in "SEPARATE BEDS" during the weekend in Palm Beach. In the same edition Donald's attorney, Jay Goldberg, lays to rest any lingering rumors that the "Divorce of the Decade" might be headed toward a reconciliation.

"I'm a killer," Goldberg declares. "I can rip the skin off a body." Asked if there might be some upward adjustment in Ivana's nuptial agreement, Goldberg vows, "Not a penny, not a dollar, not a dime will be added, It's like 'High Noon.' Somebody has to stare somebody down. Ivana's lawyer figures what's to lose. He's willing to go to court."

Goldberg's remarks reignite the war of the faxes between Donald's advisers and Ivana's. "He sounds like a street mugger, not an officer of the court," snorts Ivana's publicist, John Scanlon. "This is a contract dispute, not the Spanish Inquisition." Scanlon adds: "Mrs. Trump immigrated to America from a repressive police state where violence was commonplace. She did not expect that she and her children would ever again be threatened, certainly not by her husband's lawyer."

Ivana's attorney, Michael Kennedy, fires off a missive to Goldberg informing him: "Mrs. Trump views these statements of yours as threats against her and her children's lives and mental well being." Kennedy says he will henceforth refuse to engage in any further settlement talks with Donald's attorney, a remark Goldberg promptly dismisses as mere saber rattling.

Donald returns to New York late on Monday afternoon aboard the Trump jet. Perturbed patriarch Fred Trump, Sr., accompanies him, but Ivana and the children remain in Palm Beach, awaiting a later flight. "It was a wonderful trip," Donald fibs to the *New York Post* when he touches down. "It was a loving time for me, Ivana, and the entire family. She stayed with the kids to stay away from the circus atmosphere in New York." Donald also insists that he has "never" cheated on his wife and claims that Marla Maples is simply "an unfortunate victim" of the Trumps' marital scandal.

"I still love Ivana," he adds. "Marriage is an incredible institution. Nothing is better than a good marriage. Nothing."

To judge by the tongue wagging back in Florida, the Trumps' public relations war is still an old-fashioned standoff. Palm Beach socialite Mary Lou Whitney, the wife of old-money scion Cornelius Vanderbilt Whitney, clearly sides with Ivana. "Donald is crazy," she proclaims. "I figure every man's going to have a flirtation or two—but Donald made the fatal mistake of flaunting his and that's embarrassing. It should be done with discretion and not flaunted." But Gregg Dodge, the widow of automotive heir Horace Dodge, believes that Ivana is wrong for making a public fuss over Donald's semipublic dalliance with Marla. "I'm sure if she kept the lid on the whole thing, she would have won him back."

On Tuesday, February 20, the *New York Daily News* registers one of the few truly notable firsts in the media frenzy over the Trumps' split. It is the first major publication to raise questions about the impact of a divorce on the Trump business empire. According to the *News*, at least a few Wall Streeters are starting to hedge their bets on the future of Donald J. Trump. "If he were to finance something new," says former Drexel Burnham Lambert executive Daniel Lee, "his situation would have to be clarified."

The *News* suggests that Donald's "situation" might be more illiquid than most outsiders suspect. The New York real estate market is in a slump, and he is carrying a total of $1.3 billion in junk bond debt on his Atlantic City casinos, most of it on the still-unfinished Taj Mahal. Trump casino bonds are selling at depressed prices ranging from 75 cents to 84 cents on the dollar. Veteran analyst Marvin Roffman of Janney Montgomery Scott observes that if Donald is forced to sell one or more of his casinos, the situation in Atlantic City is such that "no one else may want the properties."

In fact, Donald's fortunes in Atlantic City are coming under siege from a foreigner. During the week the Trump marital scandal dominates the front pages, Japanese high roller Akio Kashiwagi arrives at Trump Plaza. At first Kashiwagi's arrival appears to be one of the few positive repercussions of Donald's ill-fated trip to Tokyo. Although his Tokyo company officially lists sales of only $15 million a year, Kashiwagi lives in a lavish palace near the foot of Mount Fuji and boasts an income of over $100 million a year. Casino industry executives familiar with his background and gambling history speculate that Kashiwagi, whom Donald presented with an autographed copy of *Trump: The Art of the Deal,* is a *sarakim,* a loan shark, with connections to the *yakuza,* the Japanese mob.

More important, the chain-smoking fifty-three-year-old Kashiwagi is one of the rare breed of high rollers who are known as whales because they love to gamble millions of dollars per hour. While Kashiwagi's penchant for such high-stakes play means that he can lose enormous sums to the house in a very short time, he can also win big. In December he had won the Australian equivalent of $19 million in Darwin, bankrupting the casino. When Kashiwagi sits down at Trump Plaza's baccarat tables, he wagers $100,000 a hand, the house limit. In two days Kashiwagi wins $6 million, twice the amount of the largest previous win by a gambler in Atlantic City. The house's winnings from other players do not offset Kashiwagi's take. That week Trump Plaza reports a net loss at its gaming tables of $3.6 million.

For most supposedly savvy financial analysts, however, the shimmering myth of Donald's wealth still overshadows the rapidly tarnishing reality. "The possibility that Mr. Trump could be forced into a divorce settlement that could affect his business empire is very remote," assures David Leibowitz of American Securities. "If a child has 22 Nintendo [computer game] cartridges and someone takes one away, that certainly doesn't stop him from playing Nintendo."

Marla Maples awakes early on Wednesday, February 21, with a terrifying feeling that things are about to go from bad to worse. For the past ten days she has been playing a real-life Nintendo game against the media. The name of the game is hide-and-go-seek, and she is "it," ready or not. The media are determined to find her despite being blindfolded by officially disseminated lies and misdirection. As she watches the sun rise over the suburbanized meadows of Southampton, her instincts warn that her pursuers are finally getting hot.

It is a minor miracle that Marla has managed to remain undiscovered so far. She owes most of the credit to her publicist, Chuck Jones, and Tom Fitzsimmons, who keep concocting new schemes to hold the media at bay. They have just pulled off one of their craftiest ploys thanks to the inspiration and cooperation of Tom's twin brother, Bobby, who is now a private investigator based in a suburb of Miami.

On Monday, February 19, just as Donald was departing from Palm Beach, Bobby Fitzsimmons planted a false lead in the local press. He told reporters that Marla had spent the weekend of Ivana's birthday party relaxing with his wife and him at the Fitzsimmonses' home in Coconut Grove, Florida, over seventy miles south of Mar-a-Lago. Although Bobby refused to divulge Marla's current whereabouts, he left the impression that his guest might not have traveled far by fabricating a most timely departure date. "She left here Sunday," he fibbed with a straight face, adding that she had asked him to pass along a message to the media.

"I'm upset by all of this," Marla reportedly said. "Donald and I are just friends. Why can't everybody understand that? Why can't people understand that I'm being made out to be something I'm not?"

Back in New York, Chuck Jones tried to stoke sympathy for Marla by touting her untapped talent and detailing the deadening paralysis of her present plight. "She is the Marilyn Monroe of the '90s," Jones proclaimed to the *New York Daily News.* "When I walk down the street with Marla, people literally walk right into me. She's that beautiful." He further claimed that his client's current celebrity clearly out-stripped that of her rival in the Trump love triangle. "Look what the press did at Mrs. Trump's lunch," he observed in a self-explanatory reference to the mob scene at La Grenouille. "If I called a press conference for Marla, they would shut down the city."

According to Jones, Marla had just missed the chance to try out for "an important movie." He added that she still had a standing offer to pose for No Excuses jeans in the tradition of former presidential candidate Gary Hart's femme fatale, Donna Rice. But Jones insisted that was the kind of thing she absolutely refused to do. As a result, she was feeling lonely, forlorn, and blue. "She is never going to be the same," Jones predicted.

Jones then announced that Marla was hiring an attorney, named R. Emmett Heaphy, to "stop the character assassination" by the media. Though Heaphy was best known for handling gun possession cases, Jones assured that like Donald's attorney, Jay Goldberg, he was "a killer also," and added: "There is retribution to be paid [by Marla's media slanderers]. They're making Marla feel pain. Well, now they're going to feel pain—in their pocketbooks."

In the meantime, Marla has to cope with the pain of alleged betrayal by people she thought she could trust. On the night of Tuesday, February 20, she received a series of anxious phone calls from Jones and other confidants in New York warning that the *New York Daily News* might have been tipped off to the location of her Southampton hideaway. According to Jones, the tipster was Larry Russo, the owner of the house and alleged enabler of Donald's most recent skirt-chasing activities. Jones advised her to move to another location at once. Shortly after sunup on Wednesday morning, Marla's suspicions are confirmed when she gets a telephone call from Larry Russo himself.

"Don't go now," Russo pleads. "No one can find you out there."

Minutes later Marla and Kim Knapp climb into Russo's white Land Rover and head westbound on the Long Island Expressway. Upon reaching the outer boroughs of New York, they detour south to the Garden State Turnpike and drive directly to a new hideaway in Atlantic City. Rather than return to their former quarters in Trump Castle, where they would risk almost certain exposure, they esconce themselves in a suburban mansion owned by the former Resorts International president Jack Davis and his wife, Caroline.

Marla's escape from Southampton turns out to be almost too well timed. Less than two hours after her departure a pack of reporters and photographers from the *New York Daily News* descends on Larry Russo's house. The next day Marla's name is back on the front page of the *New York Daily News* next to photographs of her, Larry Russo, and Russo's house in Southampton. The *News* also provides a thumbnail profile of Russo and a résumé of his biggest real estate deals.

"Ivanamania is sweeping the city," declares *Advertising Age* magazine shortly after Marla makes good her escape from Southampton. According to celebrity booker Marty Ingels, "marketers already see Ivana as the hero in the foofaraw and believe it's Donald who's been besmirched." Ingels claims that Ivana is being "held up as a champion of women's rights. In today's marketplace, she'd be a natural spokesperson for Visa, MasterCard, a computer company, a line of clothing, even an automobile. She'd show some strength, and those products tend to fall into a man's world. . . . Beauty is not her personal calling . . . it's more strength and fortitude."

Ingels does not know that Ivana, like Marla, has already been approached by No Excuses jeans, which she has summarily turned down. But Ingels's remarks come as something of a surprise to feminist leaders who remember The Donald's statement that Ivana works at the Plaza Hotel for "a dollar a year and all the dresses she can buy." "It goes to show you how poorly women's work is valued," says Françoise Jacobsohn, director of the New York chapter of the National Organization for Women (NOW). Women's rights activist Muriel Siebert observes that the consensus of her female peers is that "no one relates to Ivana."

By the end of the week Ivana is in tears. Her distress does not stem from the remarks of feminists but from some sensationally inaccurate reporting by the *New York Post* about her "dark past." On Friday, February 23, the *Post* runs a front-page story revealing that she was married to Alfred Winklmayr prior to marrying Donald. While that is factually correct, the *Post* falsely claims that she was raised in a "filth-ridden" apartment in Czechoslovakia, that her father was an "office clerk," and that ex-husband Winklmayr is dead.

Ivana breaks the news of her former marriage to her own children for the first time, then flees New York for Mar-a-Lago, leaving attorney Michael Kennedy to defend her honor against the latest media attacks. Accusing the *Post* of "false and malicious" reporting, Kennedy holds a press conference at which he reports that Ivana was actually raised in a clean middle-class apartment, that her father was an electrical engineer, and that Winklmayr, an Austrian-born former ski instructor whom she divorced in 1973, is alive and well. Kennedy adds that Ivana's marriage of convenience was never sexually consummated and that The Donald has known about the entire episode for years.

A few weeks later ex-husband Winklmayr, now a forty-four-year-old businessman based in Sydney, Australia, sells his story to the *Star*, a supermarket tabloid similar to the *National Enquirer*. He portrays Ivana as an inveterate gold digger, telling the *Star*, "I can't help but think she's finally getting what's coming to her."

Ivana's moods swing from anger, depression, and self-pity to gratitude as support pours in from friends and anonymous admirers in the general public. "I think she's finally beginning to get really mad and that's good," an unnamed confidant who sounds much like Eleanore Kennedy tells the *New York Daily News*, adding that Ivana has been getting "bagloads of mail like letters to Santa Claus, Valentine's cards, lots of long letters and presents. Ivana is touched by the outpouring of sympathy for her. She feels it has changed her life. . . . But don't forget Ivana would like this thing to go away. She still would reconcile."

Ivana's socialite pal Shirley Lord Rosenthal, who is on the staff of *Vogue* magazine, then comes up with an idea designed to lift her spirits. She asks Ivana if she would like to pose for the May cover of *Vogue* down at Mar-a-Lago. Ivana thinks it over briefly and says yes.

On February 23 Donald sends his wife more mixed signals about his intentions toward their marriage. He tells the *New York Daily News* that he has "no serious relationship" with Marla Maples, that "it's all been overblown." Several days later the *National Enquirer* reports that Donald has told Marla: "It's all over. We're breaking too many hearts." Then in an interview with *New York* magazine published on the following Monday, Donald all but admits he has a roving eye. "I can't believe I'm married," he confides to writer John Taylor. "This is the prime time for me." The same week he informs *Newsweek* that his marital scandal is "pretty sad, but it's been great for business."

On February 24, having already scuttled plans to build a $200 million yacht even larger than the *Trump Princess,* Donald admits for the first time that his split from Ivana might be triggering some unanticipated financial problems. That morning he announces that he has dropped plans to make a $4.5 billion bid for Hilton Hotels and that the Alexander's department store chain, in which he and brother Robert own a 27 percent stake, is up for sale. Donald dismisses rampant speculation that the current downturn in the New York real estate market has put him in a cash squeeze. But he concedes for the first time that Trump Castle casino in Atlantic City (which had spent over $1 million dropping the apostrophe from its logo after Ivana's departure) is suffering from a cash shortage and that he might have to use personal funds to cover interest payments on Castle junk bonds due in June.

"That's not a problem," Donald assures the *News,* claiming that he has "$200 million in cash-equivalent" certificates of deposit and U.S. Treasury bills.

On March 1 the *New York Post* runs yet another front-page story on the Trump affair that is headlined DONALD MAKES A DATE WITH MARLA! According to supposedly pro-Donald columnist Cindy Adams, Marla Maples has been invited to the opening of the Taj Mahal scheduled for April 5. Adams reports that Donald is hiring an additional 150 security guards for the opening to handle what he hopes will be the "crazed media." She also asks Donald about a rumor that he has bet $1 million he can make Marla "the world's hottest name in three months." He answers with a cryptic "No comment." Adams then asks if "this whole shmear"—inviting Marla to the Taj opening—is "just a p.r. stunt." Donald replies: "Use your own imagination."

By this time even the president of the United States, George Herbert Walker Bush, is jumping on the Trump publicity bandwagon. "So I am here in New York where one of the great contests of 1990 will take place," Bush intones that afternoon in a speech on Staten Island, where Republican candidate Susan Molinari is running for a congressional seat. "A lot at stake . . . There's been a lot of money spent on both sides. . . . A lot of press . . . But I am not here to talk about the Trumps!"

The crowd roars at Bush's otherwise esoteric punch line.

If Donald appears unconcerned about Ivana's feelings toward his "date" with Marla, he does not anticipate the visceral reaction of other family members. When his father learns about Marla's invitation to the opening of the Taj, he explodes in anger: "That's the stupidest goddamn thing I've ever heard." The old man makes it clear that he and Donald's mother will boycott the Taj opening if Marla's name is on the guest list. Ten days later Donald caves in to the family pressure.

"Despite the fact that her presence at the Taj opening was considered one of the great promotional events of all time, Donald has decided to call it off," reports "a source close to Trump" in a front-page story published in the *New York Post* on Saturday, March 10. And why is Donald making such a great sacrifice? "Donald has decided it would be inappropriate to invite Marla because of concern for his family," claims the unnamed Trump intimate. "There's no way she'll be there. Donald is firm about this. . . . It's probably best at this time for her to relax and stay away."

The news catches Marla's publicist, Chuck Jones, by surprise. "Of course, she'll be there," he assures the *Post*. That evening, however, Marla decides to back out of the Taj opening as gracefully as she can. In a handwritten letter dated March 10 she informs the media: "When Mr. Trump invited me to the opening of the Taj Mahal, I was exuberant on one level yet deeply surprised on the other. I knew it would be such a 'grand' event. . . . Yet knowing how the public and his family might perceive the invitation worried me. For I know he would only want to honor his family and he would hope they would understand his intentions. But as with most issues which are considered 'newsworthy,' this event has once again been blown out of proportion and misunderstood."

On March 12, two days after Donald breaks his date with Marla, her mother tells the *New York Post* she thinks the two of them will one day get married. "They love each other," Ann Maples Ogletree declares. "There is a chemistry, a glow. You can look at somebody and know if they have that special feeling." She adds that Donald has told Marla "this publicity was going to be good for her in the long run because people are going to understand what a fine person she is. And now she has become nationally known, it would be good for her career."

The following day the *New York Post* reports that Donald's estranged wife is planning to file for divorce within the next two weeks.

Ivana breaks down and cries the moment she picks up the morning paper. In a frantic gesture of good faith, she grabs the telephone in the bedroom of her Trump Tower triplex and calls The Donald to set the record straight.

"I am not filing for a divorce!" Ivana informs her husband, struggling to choke back her tears. "I never intend to file for divorce. I want to keep my family together. I want to keep the father with his children."

For a split second The Donald is speechless. His most recent actions have demonstrated that he does not share Ivana's burning desire to save their marriage, even for the sake of the children. But for both financial and emotional reasons of his own, he does not want to end the marriage either, at least not yet. He resorts to the old standby line that has worked on Ivana in the past: "I love you, Vaska."

Donald's sweet nothings do not impress her attorney. "I will be filing something for Ivana very soon," Kennedy confirms in a March 13 interview with Liz Smith, adding cryptically, "But it won't be for divorce."

Donald does not need a mind reader to guess what might be coming. If Kennedy is not preparing divorce papers, there is only one other logical alternative for him to pursue: a lawsuit challenging the Trumps' nuptial agreement. The repercussions of such a lawsuit could be as bad as, if not worse than, those of a divorce action. Donald's personal financial status would be in limbo while the lawyers fight over what is his and what is hers. More immediately, a legal battle with Ivana could complicate New Jersey Casino Control Commission hearings on the Taj Mahal scheduled for March 29.

Donald launches a two-pronged attempt at damage control. The first phase calls for warming up to his wife, Ivana, in hope of forestalling precipitous legal action. On Saturday, March 17, Ivana spends all morning posing for *Vogue* magazine at Mar-a-Lago. Donald flies down to Palm Beach on Sunday. That night he has sex with her for the first time since the night following the confrontation with Marla Maples on the slopes in Aspen. Unbeknownst to either one of them, this will be the last time the couple has sex as man and wife. But the lovemaking session appears to have the desired effect, from Donald's point of view, of further confounding Ivana.

The second phase of Donald's damage control operation calls for him to distance himself from his mistress. Marla beats him to the punch. When Donald tries to contact her in Atlantic City following his return from Palm Beach, he discovers that Marla and Kim have departed for points unknown. For the past few weeks Donald has behaved as if he did not care what happened to Marla. "I don't give a shit about her," he told friends. "I have a dozen girls like her." Now his indifference turns to insane jealousy. Frantically he telephones Tom Fitzsimmons in an attempt to locate her.

"Come on, Tom, you've got to tell me where she is," he pleads. "Where did she go?"

As it turns out, Marla and Kim have managed to leave the country. Reports later surface in the media that the two women are somewhere in the Caribbean. In fact, they fled to Guatemala, where a college friend of Kim's happens to be working in the Peace Corps. But Marla has tired of Donald's vacillating affections and feels no compunction to call or write to inform him of her whereabouts.

While Donald wonders how to track down Marla, he is blindsided by more negative publicity about the Taj. On Tuesday, March 20, gaming industry analyst Marvin Roffman of Janney Montgomery Scott releases a letter stating that when the Taj Mahal opens, Donald "will have so much free publicity he will break every record in the books in April, June, and July. But once the cold winds blow from October to February, it won't make it. The market just isn't there. . . . Atlantic City is an ugly and dreary kind of place. Even its hard core customers aren't coming down as much."

Donald warns Roffman's boss, Norman Wilde, Jr., that he is "planning to institute a major lawsuit against your firm unless Mr. Roffman makes a major public apology or is dismissed." In response to alleged pressure from his superiors, Roffman drafts a letter of apology. The next day, however, Roffman withdraws the letter and is fired. He later files a multimillion-dollar damage suit against Janney Montgomery Scott for wrongful termination and a related civil suit against Donald.

On Thursday, March 22, the *New York Post* runs a front-page headline reporting DONALD DUMPS MARLA: GEORGIA PEACH IN TEARS AFTER TRUMP'S FAREWELL PHONE CALL. The newspaper quotes "a reliable source" as confirming that Donald has decided that he is "not going to be friends with her anymore." Marla is described as "totally devastated." According to the "reliable" source, "She told him she's never been in love like this before. She said she had never been attracted to anyone more than Trump." Now Marla is reportedly "so upset, she's virtually immobile."

The news obviously comes as a shock to Marla's publicist. "He has not cut off communications [with Marla]," Chuck Jones insists. "Some people are going to have egg on their face if they say that."

On Friday, March 23, the *New York Daily News* weighs in with an equally provocative front-page headline: MARLA HID IN TRUMP TOWER. Gossip columnist Liz Smith reports that Donald's mistress had spent five and a half weeks living in apartment 63C, right across the hall from Fred Trump Sr.'s apartment 63J, where Donald had retreated when he moved out of the Trumps' triplex on the top floors of the building.

Ivana is furious. "I am shocked and saddened that Donald could subject me and the children to such shameful behavior," she says in a statement issued through attorney Kennedy. The statement belies the emotional devastation Ivana is suffering behind closed doors. She spends the rest of the day poring over a calendar in a pathetic attempt to figure out how The Donald could have kept his mistress in Trump Tower without her knowledge.

Donald counterattacks via the *New York Post*. On Saturday, March

24, the *Post*'s front-page headline reports: MARLA'S REAL HIDEOUT—
JERSEY. The newspaper charges, inaccurately, that Liz Smith was wrong
to claim that Marla had been hiding out in Trump Tower for five
and a half weeks. According to Donald himself, she has been living
at the home of Jack and Caroline Davis at 110 South Marion Avenue
in the Atlantic City suburb of Ventnor, New Jersey. "Liz Smith is
being used by [Ivana's attorney] Michael Kennedy and [her publicist]
John Scanlon," Donald complains. "They are playing her like a fiddle. They are trying to get me to settle. What kind of man would I
be if I was sneaking [Marla] in and out, tell me that?"

On Monday, March 26, Michael Kennedy files suit in Manhattan
Supreme Court challenging the validity of the Trumps' 1987 nuptial
agreement. Ivana's complaint alleges that Donald "verbally abused
and demeaned [her] so as to obtain her submission to his wishes and
desires"—including putting her signature on their 1987 nuptial contract. She further claims that Donald concealed the true value of his
holdings at the time the couple entered into the agreement and that
he secretly intended to "engage in adulterous relationships . . .
including the notorious relationship with Marla Maples."

"This is not an action for separation or divorce," Kennedy maintains at a press conference in his Park Avenue office that morning.
"[Ivana] is a Catholic woman devoted to the idea of family. She doesn't
want a divorce. . . . This is an action to obtain rights to half the fortune, which the Trumps built together during the course of their
thirteen-year marriage." Kennedy estimates that the Trump fortune
is worth on the order of $5 billion.

Lest there be any doubt about Ivana's contribution to the couple's
financial success, the complaint quotes passages from *Trump: The Art
of the Deal* in which Donald lavished her with praise. "I like to kid her
that she works harder than I do," reads one such passage. "Last year,
when I bought my second casino from the Hilton Corporation and
renamed it Trump's Castle, I decided to put Ivana in charge. She's
incredibly good at everything she's ever done, a natural manager."

"This is the kind of greed I find contemptible," declares Donald's
attorney, Jay Goldberg. "Mr. Trump is outraged. . . . Through his
own brains he made it. She took care of the kids and did the laundry." Goldberg characterizes Ivana's lawsuit as "a low blow" and vows
that Donald "will not settle." But even as Goldberg throws down the

gauntlet, his client is being set up for another even more devastating alleged "low blow."

"DON-NULL! DON-NULL! DON-NULL!"

The man who would be Atlantic City's modern-day maharaja hears six thousand people calling his name in unison as he enters the grand ballroom of the still-unfinished Trump Taj Mahal. It is late on the afternoon of March 29. The New Jersey Casino Control Commission has just voted to grant the Taj a gaming license subject to passing routine site inspections and prescribed operational tests. The newly hired work force of the state's largest casino hotel is now ready for a celebratory pep rally.

This is Donald J. Trump's latest, greatest moment in the sun—and one of his last. His arrival is heralded by a blaze of laser lights, blaring rock music, and the larger-than-life-size video screen image of a computer-generated genie called Fabu (short for "Fabulous"). With robotic speech rhythms resembling those of the television character Max Headroom, Fabu exhorts the assembled employees to chant a series of motivational mantras whose theme is making the Taj Mahal become the "Eighth Wonder of the World."

Most of the mass media join in the cheerleading by heralding the long-awaited opening of the Taj as enthusiastically as the people on the Trump payroll. The *New York Daily News* is a notable exception. On April 1 reporter Andrew Gluck warns that the "Empire Could Strike Back." According to Gluck's sources on Wall Street, even if the Taj Mahal turns out to be a flop, it will not likely drag down the rest of Donald's "vast empire." But airline analyst Paul Turk comments that Donald may be vulnerable in a general economic recession.

"He appears not to have any major counter-cyclical investments," Turk tells the *Daily News*. "He's in airlines, which is subject to the whims of the business cycle. Casinos depend on people having discretionary income. And he's in real estate, which in a recession can't be sold or borrowed against for as much."

In an effort to dispel rumors of his impending financial crisis, Donald tells another big lie. He assures the *Daily News* that he has no less than $200 million in cash at his fingertips. (He does not mention that this is $400 million less than the amount of cash he has been telling many of his top employees he has at his disposal.) Then he predicts: "The Taj will be a monster."

Taj construction manager Tom Pippett is not so sure. The casino is scheduled to open its doors to the public on the morning of April 2, less than twenty-four hours hence, for two days of practice runs. But before it can open, the facility must go through a formal postconstruction approval survey by the Casino Control Commission, and the job site is still in a state of chaos. Donald himself is allegedly part of the problem. Since late February crews of 150 workers representing fifteen to twenty different trades have been laboring on the Taj seven days a week. But whenever Donald arrived in Atlantic City, he reportedly kept disrupting progress by conducting his unannounced site inspections and launching into tirades against managers and workers alike.

"As we got toward the end of the building, I saw a change in Donald," Pippett recalls months later. "He started lashing out at everyone, especially the people who were loyal to him and helped him attain the empire he had. He became extremely abusive. He seemed to be killing the people who helped him do what he did in life."

On the night of April 1 four Casino Control Commission (CCC) representatives tour the top two floors of the Taj with Pippett. The suites are still unpainted, uncarpeted, devoid of plumbing, and perforated with exposed electrical wires. Pippett and his crews strive to complete the Taj all through the night. Tempers flare on all floors of the building. Fistfights break out between overwrought carpenters, painters, plumbers, and electricians as they step over and on top of each other in the rush to finish their separate tasks.

But miraculously the job gets done. At 10:00 A.M. on April 2 the Trump Taj Mahal opens its doors to the public. The steel mesh security gates surrounding the casino floor rise, and thousands of cash-carrying gamblers and curiosity seekers stream into the so-called Eighth Wonder of the World.

Then disaster strikes. According to the practice day rules, patrons of the casino's 167 table games have to wager with play money. Slot machine patrons, however, are allowed to play with real coins. Among the highly touted new features of the Taj are its sparkling stations of computer-driven Mister Change machines, which promise enormous savings in labor costs by replacing traditional teller-operated change booths.

But within minutes of the opening rush the Taj Mahal's casino floor ignites in an electronic blaze of red warning lights. Almost every one of the Mister Change machines simultaneously goes on the blink. The computer-controlled devices spit out either too much change or no change at all. Would-be slot players mob the Taj Mahal's only two manned change booths, but the tellers cannot possibly satisfy the demand for coins. Since most of the casino's customers cannot get change, they cannot play the slots. Gaggles of surly, frustrated gamblers wander out into the halls and make for the exits.

Donald nevertheless finds something to crow about. The sheer volume of opening-day play at the Taj is greater than even he could have predicted. Despite the breakdown of the Mister Change stations, an estimated $5 million is wagered at the slot machines. But the unprecedented volume will in itself exacerbate another embarrassing problem that comes to light the following day.

"DON-NULL! DON-NULL! DON-NULL!"

On Tuesday, April 3, Donald hears a horde of people standing outside the Taj Mahal calling his name in unison. But unlike the casino employees who rallied inside the grand ballroom a few days before, they are jeering, not cheering. It is already well past noon on the second practice day, and the Taj has still not opened for business.

"Come on! Open up!" demands a chorus of angry customers as Trump shuttles from his limousine past the cordon barricading the front door of the Taj.

"What's the matter, Donald?" shouts one of the female bystanders. "Ain't ya got enough money?"

Moments later the crowd observes a man being carried out of the Taj on a stretcher. His name is Don Wood, and he is the casino's vice-president of finance. Amid the turmoil inside the building Wood has collapsed from nervous exhaustion.

The Taj Mahal's inability to open, however, has not been caused by a lack of money. Nor has it been caused, as Donald later maintains, by the overwhelming avalanche of cash wagered by customers on opening day. The failure of the Mister Change machines has undoubtedly contributed to the overall chaos. But the root of the problem can be traced to plain incompetence and inexperience on the part of the casino's top executives, their floor personnel, and their accounting staff.

The Taj's number crunchers simply have no accurate idea of how much money the casino took in during the first practice session or how much money is left in the change banks. In fact, the discrepancy between the estimates provided by the previous night's shift and the current day shift amounts to $2 million. Officials from the state's Division of Gaming Enforcement (DGE), led by Tony Parillo and Dino Marino, refuse to let the casino reopen until the discrepancy is reconciled.

"This is fucking crazy!" Donald storms. "I don't believe this. . . . I can't be embarrassed like this. I got celebrities coming, I got all my friends coming."

A phalanx of Trump lieutenants, including Donald's brother Robert, attorney Nick Ribis, casino consultant Al Glasgow, Trump Plaza president Jack O'Donnell, and slot machine supervisors from Trump Castle, keeps huddling with various Taj employees and the men from the DGE in an attempt to resolve the money-counting fiasco. But the Taj president, Walter Haybert, who found himself beset by a remarkably similar opening-day disaster at Trump Plaza back in 1984, is hunkering inside the master change bank, despairing of his own inability to cope with the situation.

"I don't want to get in the way," Haybert reportedly tells O'Donnell. "You handle it. I'm going to lose my job anyway, so what's the difference?"

Donald, meanwhile, keeps looking for convenient scapegoats. First, he blames the late Steve Hyde and the late Mark Etess for hiring the people "responsible" for the Taj's problems. Then, upon seeing Don Wood carried out on a stretcher, he demands that the collapsed financial officer be fired immediately. Next, he vents his rage on brother Robert, Haybert, Ribis, and virtually every other underling who dares come within shouting distance.

"I'm going to fire all you assholes," he screams at Haybert when the Taj president emerges from the master change bank. "I want pricks in here. I want people in here who are going to kick some ass."

Just as each of Donald's key executives comes under fire from the boss, each later claims individual or collective responsibility for saving the day. O'Donnell, who will provide a detailed first-person description of the Taj opening in his book the following spring, will boast that he is the one who straightened out the problems. But Glasgow, Ribis, and the hastily summoned Trump Castle president Ed Tracy, among others, will insist that they deserve most of the credit. In any event, the accounting discrepancy is eventually reduced from $2 million to $30,000, and the DGE reluctantly agrees to let the casino reopen at four-twenty that afternoon, nearly six and a half hours late.

Donald once again displays his prevaricating public relations prowess in explaining the Taj's predicament to the public. "The only problem we had," he maintains at an ad hoc press conference, "was that we made so much money we couldn't count it fast enough." Moments later he boards a helicopter bound for New York, where Ivana's attorney, Michael Kennedy, is waiting to resume negotiations over the couple's nuptial agreement.

In yet another not-so-subtle display of Trump favoritism, the state's gaming authorities back up Donald's dubious version of the Taj Mahal debacle. The reason is obvious: Atlantic City has as big a stake in Trump's success as he does. The Taj is simply too big for anyone concerned to let it fail. DGE chief Tony Parillo blames the casino's accounting contretemps on the unprecedented "ebb and flow" of cash from the opening-day hordes. According to Parillo, "It became a very lengthy process to reconcile."

Donald's helicopter touches down on the roof of Trump Castle at 8:00 A.M. on Thursday, April 5. Four of his New York-based bodyguards and Atlantic City security men Lynwood Smith and Jim Farr usher him into a waiting silver limousine that takes him from the Castle to the Trump Taj Mahal. This is supposed to be Donald's big day. That afternoon he is scheduled to give New Jersey Governor Jim Florio a personally guided tour of the Taj. That night he is hosting the Taj's celebrity-studded grand opening gala.

"Isn't this great?" Donald exults at 10:00 A.M., when the Taj opened its doors to the public for its first regular day of gambling. "Isn't this the greatest place you've ever seen?"

Donald's beleaguered subordinates try to humor him as best they can. Behind its flashy candy-colored facade, the Taj looks like a shipwrecked ocean liner. The roof leaks in several places. Many of the room keys do not fit their assigned locks. There is not enough water pressure to reach the top-floor suites. Several of the facility's most luxurious amenities, including the beauty salon, the health club, and the day-care center, are not finished. Room service is swamped, as are the first- and second-floor restaurants.

Marla Maples is not the only no-show or the most famous. For weeks the Trump publicity machine has touted appearances by such Hollywood stars as Jack Nicholson, Don Johnson, Melanie Griffith, Liza Minnelli, Brooke Shields, and Tom Cruise. None of them come. Neither does Ivana Trump. Apart from model Carol Alt, former heavyweight boxing champion Michael Spinks, and future heavyweight champion Evander Holyfield, the most prominent public figure on hand is rival Resorts owner Merv Griffin, the man who sold Donald the Taj Mahal.

The Taj's opening festivities are almost as disastrous as the previous two practice days in the casino. That night Donald joins Merv Griffin in a special VIP section in front of the white elephants guarding the Taj's main entrance to watch a fireworks show. They are flanked by Fred and Mary Trump, Robert Trump, and Donald's sisters, Elizabeth Trump and Maryanne Trump Barry. But the weather is so cold the VIPs have to wrap themselves in hastily distributed hotel blankets. Even then they cannot see the fireworks, which are shot out over the ocean from the opposite side of the building.

Donald's big night quickly turns into an embarrassment. First, the laser designed to cut a giant ceremonial red ribbon wrapped around the building slices the ribbon into shreds. Then Atlantic City Mayor James Usry, who has recently been indicted on corruption charges, appears on the podium to a chorus of boos. Several minutes later Donald rises to make a speech in which he praises the contributions of the late Steve Hyde and the late Mark Etess. But he neglects even to mention the late Jon Benenav, prompting Benenav's former fiancée, Beth McFadden, to burst into tears.

Despite the accounting problems on the two previous practice days, the DGE allows the Taj to open on April 5 for a full eighteen-hour gambling day with all 3,000 slot machines and 167 table games in operation. The casino reports an impressive, and direly needed, win of slightly over $1 million. But the DGE men refuse to issue a certificate of operation until they receive a long-term plan to get the casino's coin-changing and accounting systems in order. That night Robert Trump and Harvey Freeman propose an interim strategy. They will open on Friday with only half the slot machines in operation pending installation of more teller-staffed change booths and other improvements. According to Jack O'Donnell, DGE officer Dino Marino accepts the proposal over "the protests of his own staff."

At 8:00 A.M. on Friday, April 6, Donald summons his top executives to an emergency meeting at Trump Castle. Robert Trump, Walter Haybert, Nick Ribis, Harvey Freeman, and Jack O'Donnell cringe in anticipation of Donald's wrath. According to subsequent accounts by O'Donnell and others, he throws a profane fit about their failure to fire Don Wood. Then he rails about the proposed compromise with the state concerning the partial closing of the Taj's slot machines.

"I heard about this plan," Donald shrieks. "I can't open all my machines today. I'm not going to have all my machines this weekend. You guys are fucking crazy! I don't want it! I want every machine open this weekend!"

Haybert points out that they have no choice but to honor the deal negotiated with the DGE. But Donald will not listen.

"You're the one who fucked this place up the way it is!" he shouts at Haybert. "I never wanted you in this job. I knew you didn't have what it takes. Everybody warned me that you were the wrong guy. Now this is it. Lightning strikes twice for me. This is the same fucking thing that happened at the Plaza [casino] . . . and it was your fault then . . . and you're responsible for it now!"

Robert Trump moves to defuse his explosive brother. "Donald," he says calmly, "you know there's just no way to predict these things."

"Robert, just never mind!" Donald retorts. "I'm sure as hell not going to listen to you in this situation. I listened to you and you got me into this. . . . You think you're clean on this one? You're the one who's been down here in charge. You're the one who wanted this guy in charge of the building. You're the one who said I should do this. I thought you could handle this. I must've been out of my mind. I let you make recommendations. I'm sick and fucking tired of listening to you. . . . I'm sick of listening to all you guys!"

Robert's reaction surprises everyone. Heretofore he has been almost implacably passive, unfailingly loyal, and willing to suffer any and all abuse his brother dishes out. But Donald's diatribe, which is eerily reminiscent of Fred Trump Sr.'s humiliation of the late Fred, Jr., is the last straw. Robert immediately resigns as chief executive officer of Trump Taj Mahal Associates, packs his belongings, and boards a helicopter bound for New York.

"I'm getting out of here," he mutters, blinking his baby blue eyes. "I don't need this."

Donald watches his brother depart Atlantic City without visible regret. Later that afternoon he demotes Haybert from president to chief financial officer and names the vice-president of casino operations, Willard G. ("Bucky") Howard, the new president of the Taj Mahal. But because of a combination of mechanical glitches and money-counting discrepancies, the Taj does not open its slot machines until four that afternoon. Once they open, the slots operate so poorly they have to be shut off at nine-thirty. The state orders that the machines remain out of operation until Monday morning.

Donald spends most of the rest of the weekend fawning over singer Michael Jackson, who arrives at the Taj Mahal on Friday night, touching off a near riot. Donald seems unusually edgy. But he keeps enough wits about him to capitalize on the potential public relations windfall he missed because of Jackson's failure to accompany him on his trip to Tokyo back in February. When Jackson expresses concern about the fate of AIDS-infected Indiana schoolboy Ryan White, Donald offers to lend him the Trump jet to fly out for a visit. Jackson, in turn, invites Donald to accompany him on the trip.

Over the next few weeks the Taj Mahal struggles to recover from its opening-day debacle. The casino's slot machines are gradually put back in service several hundred at a time. At month's end the Taj reports gross revenues of $34.4 million, an Atlantic City record. That impressive figure, however, masks the underlying weaknesses in the

gambling industry as a whole and the Trump Organization in particular. It also underscores a growing anti-Trump backlash on the part
of the press and the general public.

The *New York Daily News* celebrates the opening of the Taj Mahal
by slaying some of the most sacred cows in the casino's mythology.
The *News* points out that contrary to Donald's fatuous claims, the Taj
Mahal's 120,000-square-foot casino is not the world's largest; the Riviera in Las Vegas boasts a 125,000-square-foot casino. Nor is the 1,250-
room Taj the largest hotel in the world; Bally's hotel in Atlantic City
and at least twelve Las Vegas hotels have higher room counts. Likewise, the Taj hotel tower, which Donald says is fifty-one stories high,
is actually only forty-one stories. Worse, the Taj is apparently canni-
balizing the business of its sister casinos. Trump Castle's revenues
show no increase from April 1989, while Trump Plaza's revenues
have fallen 13 percent.

Donald naturally tries to put a positive face on the negative-sound-
ing numbers. "We're going to set records every month [at the Taj
Mahal]," he boasts, adding that he is unconcerned about the slump
affecting his other two Atlantic City casinos. "They did, what, $536
million [in gross revenues] last year? So I make a few million less on
them. Who cares?"

In fact, Donald will care a great deal, and so will his casino bondholders. Gaming industry analysts predict that the Trump Taj Mahal
needs to gross $1.3 million per day, or $39 million per month year-
round, just to break even. During the period required to correct the
slot machine and accounting problems, the cost in missed revenue
amounts to several million dollars. And as time quickly tells, Donald
needs every cent he can get his hands on, especially since April 9,
1990, the beginning of the Taj Mahal's first full week of operation,
also marks the thirteenth anniversary of his rapidly deteriorating
marriage to Ivana.

Ivana Trump arrives for fashion week at the Plaza Hotel in New
York on April 10 with a stunning new look. It has been conceived by
internationally known fashion photographer André Leon Talley
expressly for the May 1990 cover of *Vogue* magazine, which is scheduled for release in less than two weeks. And it makes the former

Czechoslovakian model and ski champion look like an almost identical twin of the fabled French movie actress Brigitte Bardot.

Instead of letting her blond hair hang down, as she has done for years, Ivana wears it piled on top of her head in a sexy Bardot bun. Her recently resculpted face is powdered in lightly colored shades according to the inspiration of makeup artist Vincent Longo. Her newly tumescent lips glisten with Revlon's super lustrous lipstick in Island Pink mixed with waterproof lip shaper in Nudetones.

While her husband was struggling to get the Taj Mahal on track, Ivana gave an interview to *Vogue* writer Vicki Woods in which she implied that she was enjoying her newfound independent celebrity status as the world's most-famous woman wronged. She has already commenced talks with the International Management Group about licensing the "Ivana Collection." It will include Ivana evening wear, Ivana casual wear, Ivana baggage, Ivana shoes, Ivana lingerie, Ivana hosiery, and Ivana jewelry. There will even be an Executive Collection for businesswomen featuring Ivana briefcases, appointment books, and portfolios.

Ivana intimated to *Vogue* that her future plans would not be affected by the outcome of her legal battle against The Donald. "It's a question of upbringing," she declared. "I am Czech. Czechs are hardworking; everybody works in Czechoslovakia, women as well as men. My mother always worked; I will always work."

Even so, Ivana has developed a new attitude about fashion for the new decade of the nineties. "I no longer like the puffball look," she told *Vogue,* claiming that she now prefers "a more columnar shape." But she still favors haute couture over more down-to-earth working-women styles. "I have five pairs of blue jeans," she admits, "and I can't remember the last time I wore them." The forthcoming *Vogue* cover will picture Ivana in a sultry posture wearing an aqua blue strapless Givenchy dress, a gold-buckled Paloma Picasso belt, and jewel-encrusted Christian Lacroix drop earrings. For the five full-page photographs inside the magazine, she will be modeling smocks, gowns, and suits by Valentino, Givenchy, and Lacroix.

Ivana's appearance in *Vogue* has already been creating a favorable buzz both on and off Seventh Avenue. Because the May issue comes out just after the spring fashion shows, it is traditionally a slow month for advertising. In May 1989, however, *Vogue* reversed the trend by putting singer-actress Madonna on the cover. The magazine's advertising department has since been clamoring for a celebrity cover every May. According to one of the editors, "We were tearing our hair trying to come up with someone like Princess Di. The minute the Trumps broke up, we knew Ivana would be perfect." As with the Madonna cover, advertising sales have boomed, and so will the ensuing press coverage and newsstand sales.

When Donald gets wind of what his wife's *Vogue* photo shoot has wrought, he senses a chance to cash in on the publicity himself. On Monday, April 9, their wedding anniversary, he sends Ivana a dozen roses. The following Saturday he shows up at the house in Greenwich, Connecticut, and takes her and the children to a movie. That evening a *New York Post* photographer snaps the couple's picture as they walk out of a theater in suburban Stamford. On Sunday, April 15, Ivana hosts a children's Easter parade at the Plaza Hotel in New York. Donald shows up there, too, beaming for the bustling paparazzi and whispering in Ivana's ear.

"I love you, Vaska," he assures her again and again.

On Easter Sunday Marla Maples boards a plane in Guatemala City and flies home to Georgia. She has been in Central America with her pal Kim Knapp for more than three weeks. She and Kim have toured the countryside, seen the sights, and briefly assisted a friend of Kim's in providing Peace Corps services to Guatemalan children. Now she has decided it is time to come out of hiding.

When Marla arrives in Dalton, both her father and her mother pass along urgent messages from Diane Sawyer, co-anchor of ABC's "Prime Time Live." Sawyer wants her to do an exclusive interview. Marla calls her agent, Chuck Jones. He is opposed to the idea and convinces her to table the matter until Monday. Or so he thinks.

Not to be denied, Sawyer calls Marla's father, Stan Maples, again. He convinces Marla to speak directly to the television woman. Sawyer assures Marla she has a sympathetic ear. After all, the two share the same hairdresser, Vincent Roppatte of the Helmsley Palace salon. According to one of Marla's confidants, Sawyer also suggests that ABC will pay for a round-trip ticket to Los Angeles. Marla agrees to do the interview.

On Tuesday, April 17, Marla flies to New York and goes straight to the Helmsley Palace hair salon to keep an appointment with Roppatte. Though she wants a new outfit to wear on TV, she is still concerned with keeping a low profile amid Manhattan's den of media wolves. Caroline Davis, co-owner of Marla's former hideout in suburban Atlantic City, offers to go shopping for her at Bergdorf Goodman, where she picks out a pale yellow Gianni Versace dress.

That afternoon Marla and Caroline Davis drive down to the Davis home outside Atlantic City. Diane Sawyer and her camera crew meet them there the following day.

"Why did you decide to talk?" Sawyer asks right off.

"I think the first month [after the Trumps split], I was very much affected by what was going on in the media, and I was hoping it would die down," Marla answers. "I soon realized that it was not going to die out. My family and everyone has been so affected by this that I felt it was time I took control of the situation. . . ."

Marla claims she has declined various mass-media offers totaling a million dollars to tell her story. "I have to keep a bit of dignity," she says. "And if I were to make money off of this issue, I don't think I would be able to face myself." Marla repeatedly denies being a home wrecker or the cause of the Trumps' marital turmoil. "Only the two of them know what really went on with their marriage," she notes. "But I am not the reason for that marriage having problems."

Then, in a saccharine drawl, Marla simultaneously praises and pities Ivana for resorting to plastic surgery to change her looks. "I think she's an absolutely beautiful woman. I think she was before surgery. I—and—I mean, now, she's—she's very, very gorgeous. I think that she has the right, as anyone else does, to make the choice on how they want to better themselves."

Sawyer turns the discussion to Marla's alleged affair with Donald. "All right, here goes," she warns, telegraphing her big question about the infamous cover story in the *New York Post*. " 'Best sex I've ever had.' This one you knew about, I assume."

"Oh, it's, yeah, it's an absolute total lie," Marla replies.

"That you said it," Sawyer followed up, "or that it was."

"That I said it. That—that anything about this cover [story] has any bit of truth. . . ."

"All right." Sawyer smiles a few moments later as she presses the point. "Somebody said I should ask you, Was it the best sex you ever had?"

"Was what?" Marla giggles. "I mean . . ."

"With Donald," Sawyer interjects.

"I . . ." Marla stumbles. "This has nothing to do with why I'm here."

Sawyer then raises the issue of Donald's contribution to Marla's livelihood and career, observing that "everyone finds it so hard to believe . . . that you don't . . . take money from him."

"I think people should give him a little more credit," Marla insists as she launches into what is, in fact, a big lie of her own. ". . . I mean, he has been a married man. Is still a married man. And I think he's tried to honor his family as best he could. And he's not the type of man that would choose to support someone else while he's—while he's married—you know—to a wife that I know he has great respect for."

"Was it romance with him?" Sawyer wonders. "Do you love him?"

"I do love him," Marla admits.

"Do you want to marry him?"

"I'm taking my life day by day," Marla replies. "I am just hoping to go on. I'm hoping to continue to study. I mean, who knows what life is going to bring in the future. I—I have no control over that. Do we—do we have control?"

Marla certainly cannot control Ivana's reaction to her decision to speak out. She watches the "Prime Time Live" segment in her Trump Tower triplex on the night of Thursday, April 18, with Michael and Eleanore Kennedy. Ivana's eyes narrow as Marla concludes her remarks. "This is a pitiful woman," Ivana says.

On Monday, April 23, five days after Marla's appearance on national television, Ivana and The Donald sign a two-page agreement in the offices of their attorneys. Among other things, it allows both of them to date during their legal separation. The dating agreement is Ivana's idea. Like the Kennedys, she believes that they have The Donald in a legal vise on the adultery issue. But Ivana fears that if she is seen in the company of any man who is not known to be gay, her husband will accuse her of adultery, too.

The Kennedys warn that The Donald will find a way to turn the agreement against her. They are right. The agreement is supposed to be confidential. The next day, however, The Donald leaks it to the press. SAFE SEX, screams the front-page headline of the *New York Post* on Wednesday, April 25. DON & IVANA SIGN 60-DAY PACT TO PLAY THE FIELD.

The *Post* quotes an unnamed source "close to Trump," meaning Donald or his attorney, Jay Goldberg, who graciously offers to translate the wording of the agreement into lay terms: "Anything that would normally permit you to get a divorce, such as adultery, or sex, will not be a claim. Technically, they can have sex with other partners, and nobody can run in and say, 'You are guilty of adultery.'"

In an obvious effort at spin control, the "source close to Trump" stresses the fact that the agreement was Ivana's idea, suggesting that even though she has not formally filed for a divorce, she is the one who yearns to play around. "I assume the lady wants to get back into the social scene," the source says. "She basically is saying, 'I don't want a divorce, and I don't want to become a nun.'"

Just as the Kennedys had predicted, The Donald has made Ivana look like a fool. She plays right into his hands by panicking again. Three days after signing the agreement to date other people, Ivana insists that they scrap the deal to save her further embarrassment. IVANA DUMPS DATE DEAL, yet another front-page headline in the *New York Daily News* announces on Friday, April 27.

"Men are the last thing on my mind," Ivana tells her friend Liz Smith. "My children are on my mind, and I don't want Donald misinterpreting my going out socially with friends, or having male employees. I feared an embarrassment for some of them, and I tried to head off that eventuality. But it was a total misunderstanding. You know, I can't be remote or reclusive. I want to go on seeing my friends and living my life."

Jay Goldberg mocks Ivana's change of heart. "This is the second time this woman has attempted to walk away from an agreement that she not only signed but that she asked Donald to sign," the lawyer reminds Smith, alluding to the disputed nuptial contract the Trumps had signed back in 1987. An anonymous Trump Organization spokesman adds further insult to Ivana and the Kennedys: "Mrs. Trump and her attorneys realize that they have no case against Mr. Trump, and that the nuptial agreement is ironclad, but they recognize that they created a public relations disaster by asking for the sixty-day agreement and therefore decided to terminate it."

But unbeknownst to Ivana or even to his own lawyers, The Donald is in the midst of creating one of the greatest public relations disasters of the decade—his own.

"Donald Trump is discussing the sale or refinancing of nearly every major asset he holds, including the recently acquired Trump Shuttle," *Wall Street Journal* staff writer Neil Barsky reports in a front-page news blurb on the morning of April 27.

The story adds that Donald is also considering various deals involving the cornerstones of his empire: Trump Tower, the Grand Hyatt, and his three Atlantic City casinos. One proposed scheme calls for refinancing these "trophy" properties for $295 million. Having made his mark as a buyer of almost everything in sight, Donald has a ready explanation for why he has now become a seller and refinancier.

"What I want to do is go and bargain hunt," he tells Barsky. "I want to be king of cash."

Barsky goes on to note, however, that "others in the financial community" suspect that Donald's newfound cash fetish may signal a financial crisis caused by too much debt. In the course of a two-hour interview, Donald "vehemently and angrily" denies that his empire faces "even the hint of a cash problem," adding that he will sue the *Journal* "if any problem" with his cash flow is suggested. Donald then produces a letter from the Arthur Andersen accounting firm. The letter states that as of November 30, 1989, he has over $384 million in "cash and cash equivalents."

"There's nobody that has the cash flow that I have," Donald insists. He says that his net cash proceeds in 1989 totaled $157 million, and that he projects a net cash flow of $171 million in 1990. But Barsky does not let him off the hook so easily. He notes that Donald has to make interest and principal payments on "more than $2 billion" in bank and junk bond debts. To make matters worse, trophy properties such as the Plaza Hotel and the undeveloped West Side yards, though arguably worth more than their purchases prices, are currently cash drains rather than cash generators.

Barsky's story claims that Donald's latest efforts to liquidate a portion of his debt-loaded portfolio have run aground. On his ill-fated February trip to Tokyo, he failed to sell a 49 percent interest in the Plaza Hotel to a group of Japanese investors. Likewise, he has failed to divest himself of the faltering Trump Castle casino hotel in a proposed swap for the Waldorf-Astoria Hotel. Donald nevertheless claims he is a mogul with many options. He hints that one of those options is selling stock in the Trump Organization's vast array of properties to the general public. As he puts it, "Going public would be one of the easy things in life."

But Donald realizes that the *Wall Street Journal* story has made one of the first major dents in his well-cultivated image as a genius of modern moneymaking. Even as he talks of going public, he suddenly faces more turmoil within his tottering Atlantic City gambling empire. The same day the *Journal* story appears, Jack O'Donnell departs under pressure. Donald later claims the Trump Plaza president was fired. O'Donnell will claim he quit, informing the media, "I just got tired of working for Donald Trump."

O'Donnell's stormy departure only hints at much deeper distress within the Trump gaming empire. A few days later Trump Castle submits its regular quarterly report to the Securities and Exchange Commission. The Castle reports a loss of $6 million in 1989 and projects a cash flow of only $45 to $55 million in 1990. In June 1990, less than two months hence, the casino faces bond interest payments of $43 million. That same month the Castle will also be required to retire some $22.8 million worth of bond principal, making its total June 1990 obligations close to $66 million, or between $11 million and $22 million less than its projected cash flow.

The Castle's filing with the SEC provides the first official warning of the underlying trouble in the Trump empire. "Such requirements," the filing says in reference to the Castle's upcoming June interest and principal payments, "create cash needs that exceed anticipated annual cash flows from operations for 1990 and beyond." In other words, it does not seem likely that the Castle will make its bond payments on schedule.

All of a sudden the media smell blood oozing from the veins of the self-proclaimed "king of cash."

chapter ten
BANKRUPT
BILLIONAIRE

■ ON MONDAY, APRIL 30, 1990, Donald J. Trump strides into his office in Trump Tower, plops behind his red-lacquered gull-winged desk, and picks up the latest edition of *Forbes* magazine. His photograph is on the magazine's cover. But he does not like the banner headline plastered across his face.

HOW MUCH IS DONALD TRUMP REALLY WORTH? *Forbes* asks.

The answer, according to *Forbes,* is a lot less than Donald claims and a lot less than just about everybody else believes. Back in October 1989, *Forbes* ranked Donald number nineteen on its list of the four hundred richest Americans with an estimated net worth of $1.3 billion. But in light of a recent inquiry into his financial situation, *Forbes* says, Donald is actually worth less than half the magazine's previously published figure.

"If our estimates are substantially correct—and we think they are generous—Donald Trump's current net worth is about $500 million," *Forbes* declares. "Does Donald Trump command an impressive pile of assets? Yes. Do his assets exceed his debts by a comfortable margin? That's a different question."

Forbes claims Donald suffers from the very sort of cash squeeze he has denied in the *Wall Street Journal* with the threat of a libel suit. Though his assets may be worth as much as $3.7 billion, the magazine says, he carries $3.2 billion in bank and bond debt. According to *Forbes,* the interest payments on his bank debt alone amount to $180 million a year, but the cash flow from his airline, real estate, and Plaza and Castle casino properties yields is only $140 million a year. "That leaves Trump bleeding," the magazine notes, "at a rate of at least $40 million a year, $3 million a month, $770,000 a day."

The *Forbes* article sends a chill through the hearts of Donald's creditors. Incredibly, there has never been a complete and comprehensive independent audit of Donald's wealth. All the people who have been lending him money, from pinstripe-suited institutional executives to silver-haired casino bondholders, have been relying on not much more than his word and stacks of Trump Organization paper. Over the next several trading days the prices of Trump casino bonds fall as low as 65 cents on the dollar, representing a loss of over $350 million in market value. Behind the scenes a phalanx of nervous and numbstruck Trump bankers starts worrying that its multibillion portfolios of loans may be in danger of default.

"*Forbes* has been after me for years, consistently after me," Donald rages during a May 3 appearance on ABC's "Prime Time Live" with co-anchor Sam Donaldson. "They took properties and devalued the properties. They say the Plaza Hotel is not worth what everybody knows it's worth. . . . They include the debts of the Taj Mahal but not the income. . . . The same writer who wrote this story wrote a story for *Forbes* a year and a half ago. He wrote a story that Donald Trump lost to Merv Griffin. He got it wrong. *Business Week* got it right. . . . And for whatever reason, they *[Forbes]* have a vendetta. It makes no difference. So they say I'm worth five hundred million dollars. They say I'm worth whatever—it makes no difference. It just shows how inadequate their surveys are."

"Why would *Forbes* be out to get you?" Donaldson asks, noting that it is "a respected business publication."

"I know why, but it's going to be in my next book," Donald sniffs. "I mean, I—I can tell you why, but I'm not going to tell you now; I'm going to save it for the book. There's a very specific reason why, but I'm saving it for the book."

Donald then claims he will embarrass the prophets of his impending doom by accepting still-undisclosed offers to buy some of his most fabled trophy properties. "I will sell the *Trump Princess* for one hundred and fifty million," he predicts. In the next breath, however, he suddenly reduces the projected sales price of the yacht to $115 million, promising that whatever the final figure turns out to be, "The boat will be sold shortly for a lot of money."

Donaldson returns to the key question raised by the recent *Forbes* cover story: How much is Donald Trump really worth?

"I have absolutely no idea," Donald claims at first.

"You mean . . . Chase Manhattan banks have lent you money and you say to them, 'Look, I don't know what I'm worth, but I would like a hundred million dollars'?" Donaldson asks incredulously.

"Of course, I know what I'm worth," Donald counters. "I don't know what the Plaza's worth. It depends on what somebody would pay for it. But it's worth a hell of a lot more than this character Richard Stern [of *Forbes*] gives me credit for."

"Do the banks know what you're worth?" Donaldson asks.

"Nobody knows what I'm worth," Donald insists, "because you can't value certain properties." He nevertheless goes on to say, "Right now, I'm worth more than I ever was."

But Donald is stunned to discover that he can no longer keep fooling the financial media. A few days later the *Wall Street Journal* reports that the Trump Shuttle has suffered cumulative losses of $85 million since the day Donald bought it from Texas Air. Potential buyers of the airline abruptly back off. Then a rumored deal to sell the *Trump Princess* falls through. By mid-May the members of the Friars Club, a fun-loving national fraternity of skeptics, start laying bets on the most likely date Donald Trump will file for bankruptcy.

Donald responds with a desperate disinformation campaign. He directs his newly appointed Atlantic City gaming division chief, Ed Tracy, to announce incipient plans to sell stock in Trump Organization interests to the general public. When Tracy's trial balloon fails to float, Donald orders his public relations network to plant rumors in the tabloid press that he is sitting on a multibillion-dollar treasure trove of cash. *New York Post* columnist Cindy Adams is the first—but by no means the last—to take the bait.

"Everyone's heard tales about how poor D. T. is leveraged out, how even his Taj is up for grabs because he needs money. Bullbleep," Adams writes in her column of May 22. Alluding to the *Forbes* cover story without mentioning it by name, she declares that Donald is hardly down to his last half billion dollars. "How these august respectable financial journals overlooked certain hidden pockets in Donald's wallet, I haven't the foggiest. . . . This guy is sitting on 4 billion. Cash.

Billion with a 'b.' In terms of liquid assets, he could pour out maybe 5 billion. . . . The closest thing we've had to a semi-genius since Mme. Curie, Donald has determined that, financially speaking, it's bye-bye for the East, so he's moving his toys West. Maybe he'll buy a studio. Maybe he'll get Marla a job. And that—and only that is why he's divesting. So he can raise a few bob to invest in the Sun Belt."

Two days later rival *New York Daily News* columnist Liz Smith jumps on the Trump-is-still-a-billionaire bandwagon. "My own investigations prove Cindy is right on the button," Smith solemnly reports. "So why wasn't this on the front page? What I might add is the following. Maybe Donald is beginning to get the feeling that he has damaged himself in New York City. And as he always needs new heights to conquer, California sounds just perfect. (He is already putting up the tallest building ever in L.A. on the site of the old Ambassador Hotel.)"

There is, of course, a good reason why rumors of Donald's $4 billion cash hoard have not made the front pages of the financial journals. The rumors are not true. There is also a good reason why Donald feels it is so important to spread such rumors. He needs people to believe that they are true in order to stave off a run on his empire.

Donald is quickly reminded of the importance of maintaining his bluff when he flies down to Atlantic City with Adnan Khashoggi to witness the return of Japanese high roller Akio Kashiwagi to the baccarat tables at Trump Plaza. Trump consultant Jess Marcum, a mathematical probabilities expert who co-founded the RAND Corporation, has suggested an enticing proposition that may help Trump Plaza recover the $6 million Kashiwagi won back in February. In gambling parlance, it is called a freeze-out. The rules stipulate that Kashiwagi will start with a stake of $6 million to be wagered on baccarat at $200,000 a hand. The game will not end until he either loses the $6 million or doubles his stake to $12 million. Marcum has calculated that the odds are five to one that Kashiwagi will lose his $6 million before doubling it.

But when Donald appears on the Trump Plaza casino floor to greet Kashiwagi, he watches in horror as the Japanese high roller wins a series of $200,000 hands. Donald paces about the baccarat tables for a quarter of an hour, impolitely "sweating the action" in view of

Kashiwagi and the other patrons, then excuses himself. A few short hours later he learns that Kashiwagi is $6.8 million ahead. Donald orders Marcum to stop the game, an act that would constitute an unforgivable breach of gaming etiquette. "Be patient," Marcum urges, noting that Kashiwagi "wants to keep playing and soon the [probability] wave will run the other way."

Marcum is right. The game continues for more than five days. By the end of day six Kashiwagi has lost $6 million in cash and $4 million on credit, a total of $10 million. He now wants Trump Plaza to provide him with another $4 million worth of chips on credit so he can keep gambling. Trump gaming division chief Ed Tracy refuses. Donald later suggests that Kashiwagi return on December 7, 1990, the anniversary of the Japanese attack on Pearl Harbor. Charging that their host lacks honor, Kashiwagi and Yong, his translator, climb into a limousine and leave Trump Plaza for Caesar's Palace. They have no intention of paying back the $4 million Kashiwagi has already received on credit. As for Kashiwagi's autographed copy of *Trump: The Art of the Deal,* Yong announces that they "plan to burn it soon."

Some eighteen months later, during the weeklong Japanese celebration of New Year 1992, Kashiwagi is hacked to death with a samurai sword in the kitchen of Kashiwagi Palace. The ritual form of the murder suggests the unseen hand of the Japanese mob. Kashiwagi dies owing Trump Plaza a total of $6 million on paper, most of it in markers for gambling credit. In cash terms, Donald will be out about $1 million in his dealings with Kashiwagi, most of it in the form of hospitality expenses and chips redeemed at the casino cage for cash before Kashiwagi's final departure. As usual, Trump casino consultant Al Glasgow will offer an arch epitaph: "See what happens when you don't pay your markers."

On the morning of Wednesday, May 23, Marla Maples sashays into the Four Seasons restaurant with her lips parted in a coy smile. She is holding a press conference to announce that she has had a change of heart. She has decided to accept a deal with No Excuses after all. She will be the official representative of the blue jeans-manufacturing company with a reputation for appealing to "bad girls." The contract will reportedly pay her in excess of $500,000.

"Hi." Marla giggles as some fifty photographers rush to snap her picture. "You all look familiar. Te-hee."

Lest anyone mistakenly lump her in the same category as former No Excuses representative Donna Rice, the femme fatale linked to former presidential candidate Gary Hart, Marla announces that she will be donating $25,000, or roughly 5 percent of her No Excuses contract, to an environmental organization called the Better World Society. She will also have creative control over the advertising spots filmed for No Excuses, which, at her behest, will have an environmental theme.

"I feel that as a whole," Marla proclaims, "it is time for us to pull together in a positive way to help make people all across our planet aware of the greater issues that are affecting our world today and which may be affecting our everyday existence in the very near future if we don't acknowledge the situation and do our part."

Most of the assembled media naturally focus their follow-up questions on Marla's relationship with Donald Trump.

"Did Donald ever moan, 'Oh, Ivana'?" one of the reporters shouts.

"That's not a fair question." Marla smiles.

"Are you and Donald still together?" someone else wants to know.

"I can't comment on that," Marla replies, but admits that Donald has been "absolutely supportive" of her decision to accept the No Excuses contract. She does not reveal that he will also receive 30 percent of the proceeds under his secret contract with her.

Only the *New York Daily News* bothers to ask about her environmental concerns. "Pollution really worries me," Marla declares. "I love the ocean."

Moments after the press conference has concluded, Marla discovers that she has more to worry about than oil spills and toxic waste. A process server dispatched by Ivana's attorney, Michael Kennedy, shows up at the Four Seasons. He hands her a subpoena to give a deposition in the case of *Trump v. Trump.*

Donald quickly hires attorney Gerald Shargel, who is known for defending alleged mob figures, to represent Marla. As it turns out, Marla is never actually required to give a deposition; the subpoena is merely a Kennedy feint designed to mislead Donald's attorneys about his legal strategy. But Shargel reportedly sends Marla a bill for $10,000, which Donald advises her not to pay.

On Saturday, May 26, Ivana Trump leaves New York for Czechoslovakia. She is accompanied by her father, Milos Zelnicek, and her son Donny, who plans to go fishing with his maternal grandfather. The Donald has not seen his wife or his children for the past three weeks. Donny, who is deeply distressed by his parents' breakup, refuses even to speak with his father.

Ivana cannot help recalling, however, that the last time she had spoken with The Donald, he had posed a very curious question.

"Will you still love me," he asked her, "when I don't have any money?"

"Yes," Ivana had replied. "I already did love you when you didn't have any money. Remember?"

By the time Ivana returns to New York, she will finally get an inkling of why The Donald asked her such a question.

On the afternoon of Thursday, May 31, a platoon of twenty-five bankers and attorneys, representing Citicorp, Manufacturers Hanover Trust, Bankers Trust, and Chase Manhattan, marches into Trump Tower. They are on their way to a secret meeting with Donald. He has called them, not the other way around. The purpose of the meeting is to discuss Donald's $2 billion in current bank debt and the upcoming Trump Castle bond payments the casino has told the SEC it cannot make on schedule.

Donald ushers the bankers and their attorneys into his twenty-sixth-floor conference room. He tries to appear relaxed and confident. Remarkably there seems to be very little hostility or anxiety on either side of the table. The only glaring irony visible to all in attendance is a scale model of the stillborn TV City / Trump City project Donald wants to build on his West Side yards property.

"Everything is fine," Donald tells his bankers. "I've got these wonderful casinos, and the Taj is doing great. I've just got a temporary liquidity problem."

This "temporary liquidity problem," he explains, results from the fact that certain "capital events"—namely, the sale of the *Trump Princess* and his attempts to sell a stake in the Plaza Hotel—have been developing much more slowly than he anticipated. For that reason, he tells them, he would like to borrow enough money to make Trump

Castle's $43 million bond payment in June and a little bit extra to tide him over until he can effect the aforementioned "capital events." In other words, he wants to buy time.

At first the bankers are not overly concerned. "We need more information to construct a solution," offers a representative from Citicorp. Donald is happy to oblige. Still affecting an air of confidence, he has pastries and coffee served on the expansive mahogany conference table. He stands behind his chair with both hands on its back, cracks a few jokes, then pops in and out of the room to attend to other business. For the most part, he lets surrogates such as financial adviser Harvey Freeman talk specifics.

As the negotiations wear on into the night, however, the mood in the room grows increasingly serious. Donald insists that making Trump Castle's bond payment is crucial to maintaining confidence in the bond markets. The bankers have no problem seeing the logic of that assertion. But they will not lend him more money to pay bond market creditors until he ensures that they will also be paid back.

Donald knows that his lenders have a figurative gun to his head. They can always call in his loans, demanding that he pay up immediately. He and his bankers also know, however, that such a move could trigger his financial collapse, leaving the banks with assets they are not equipped to operate as going businesses or sell off for enough money to recoup their loans. Donald proposes a potential solution. He offers to give the banks major stakes in the Plaza Hotel and the Grand Hyatt if they, in return, will agree to reduce the amount of his debt proportionately.

The banks reject Donald's offer out of hand. As one participant later confides, they are not sure that the assets he is offering them can later be sold "for anything like what [Donald] says they are worth." The banks are also unimpressed by the capabilities of the Trump management teams and aghast at the extravagance of Donald's life-style, especially the costs of maintaining his private jet, helicopter, and yacht, which collectively total more than $2 million a year.

At 8:30 P.M. Donald departs for Atlantic City to attend a boxing match. By then it is becoming clear to everyone in the conference room that the so-called artist of the deal is in deep trouble—and so are his bankers.

"Donald J. Trump's cash shortage has become critical," the *Wall Street Journal* announces on Monday, June 4 in a front-page story by staff writer Neil Barsky. "The developer is now in negotiations with his main bank creditors that could force him to give up big chunks of his empire.

"At a minimum," Barsky continues, "Mr. Trump is likely to face a humbling change in his business and personal style, bankers involved in the talks say. 'He will have to trim the fat; get rid of the boat, the mansions, the helicopter,' one banker in the talks asserts. The banks are also likely to push for some asset sales, for some management changes and for a much more conservative operating style at Mr. Trump's principal holding company, Trump Organization.

"It remains possible that Mr. Trump can find a way to retain all of his properties," Barsky points out. "Many are quite valuable, and it is conceivable the banks could be persuaded to simply lend Mr. Trump more money, to give him time to improve his cash-flow situation on his own." But on the basis of discussions with his confidential sources in the bank negotiations, Barsky concludes: "Such a hands-off approach is unlikely. . . ."

Then there is the matter of Donald's ongoing marital battle with Ivana. "It is unclear what portion of his empire could be claimed by his wife in any future divorce action," Barsky notes. "People close to Mr. Trump say he intends to ask for a major reduction in the $25 million he previously agreed to pay his wife in the event of a divorce. She is challenging the prenuptial agreement, seeking a higher figure."

The implications of the *Wall Street Journal* story, which provides the first confirmation of Donald's banking crisis, are truly staggering. Just eight months ago *Forbes* estimated Trump's net worth at $1.3 billion; the magazine's revised estimate just five weeks ago placed his net worth at $500 million. Now the man who had claimed to be intent on becoming "king of cash" appears to be on the verge of financial collapse.

How did Donald's wealth dissipate so fast? As he and a few top-ranking members of the Trump Organization have known for years, it was never there.

On the morning of Monday, June 4, the same day the *Wall Street Journal* sounds the alarm about the Trump empire's banking crisis, a record crowd of more than three thousand people jams the Las Vegas Hilton for a Book and Author Breakfast sponsored by the American Booksellers Association. The featured speakers that morning are novelist T. Coraghessan Boyle, actress Angela Lansbury, who portrays suspense novelist Jessica Fletcher on the popular television series "Murder, She Wrote," and the real star attraction, Donald J. Trump.

"Donald Trump has literally put his name on the line with success," the former ABA president Ed Morrow informs the audience. "We also know that Trump as the author is one of the great bestsellers of our time. *The Art of the Deal*, which was published in 1987, sold over a quarter of a million copies in the weeks between Christmas and Thanksgiving. It was still a best seller the following Christmas, netting over 900,000 copies with virtually no returns. . . . The paperback was similarly a big hit.

"Mr. Trump is now ready with a new book," Morrow continues, "and I have been assured that in characteristic fashion he plans to outdo himself. *Trump: Surviving at the Top*, to be published in October by Random House, will be full of absorbing business stories, guidelines for success and revealing insights on the challenges and dangers of life at the top. All told with his inimitable verve and candor. So, join me in welcoming Donald J. Trump. . . ."

Donald takes the podium amid a crescendo of applause and speaks with what almost approaches modesty. "I am getting the worst press right now—unbelievable." He sighs. "And Joni [Evans of Random House] says to me, 'Donald, the book is going to be so hot.' And I said, 'Hot? I'm getting the worst press in the world.' And she said, 'Yeah, but that makes it hotter.' "

Donald says he asked Random House editor Peter Osnos to delay publication for at least a year, so "I'll know how good the Taj Mahal is going to be. I'll know about whether my victory over Merv Griffin was totally decisive and devastating . . . or just partially devastating." But according to Donald, the reception he has received at the ABA convention has changed his mind. He then tries to reassure the assembled booksellers of his continuing commercial appeal by treating them to an excerpt from *Trump: Surviving at the Top*, the manuscript in progress coauthored by *Newsweek* staffer Charles Leerhsen. The theme of the passage is "on toughness":

> Toughness is pride, drive, commitment and the courage to follow through on things you believe in even when they are under attack. It is solving problems instead of letting them fester. It is knowing who you really are even when society wants you to be somebody else. Toughness is knowing how to be a gracious winner and rebounding quickly when you lose.
>
> I'm never satisfied—which is my way of saying there's a great deal I still want to do and believe I should do. Some people are always saying that I can't go on like this forever, and that I'm at the beginning of the end. I'd rather see myself as being at the end of the beginning.

After reading the passage, Donald confides out loud: "I may have to end some chapters with a question mark. I may have to end the whole book with a question mark."

Back in New York City that same morning the Trump Organization releases an unusually terse statement in response to the *Wall Street Journal* article about Donald's cash crisis. It sounds as if it came from a third world debtor nation rather than from a swashbuckling American tycoon. "We are meeting with major banks," the statement says, ". . . and are confident we will arrive at a mutually beneficial solution."

Trump spokesman Howard Rubenstein adds an equally sobering statement about the impact on Donald's nuptial contract dispute with Ivana. According to Rubenstein, the money he has promised to pay her under the contract is just "too much" for him to afford at the present time. Donald has therefore requested a meeting with Ivana's attorneys to discuss a downward revision of the agreement.

Not to be left out, Marla Maples also feels compelled to make a public statement. "She is very concerned and supportive," reports her publicist, Chuck Jones.

The local and national media do not share Marla's sentiments.

Having cheered Trump's rise, they delight in jeering at his demise. On June 5, the day after the *Wall Street Journal* story about Trump's cash-flow crisis, the *New York Daily News* runs a front-page headline announcing TRUMP IN A SLUMP. The *New York Post* counters with the front-page pun UH-OWE! On the following Monday a photograph of Donald grimacing with head in hand appears on the cover of *Newsweek* magazine along with the headline TRUMP: THE FALL.

New York Daily News columnist Gail Collins takes the early lead in the media's Trump-bashing backlash. "I am only sorry that Unity Day is over," Collins writes in her paper's June 5 edition. "We are about to have one of those magic New York moments when people of all creeds, races and economic backgrounds join together in a single thought: *Hehehehehehe.*"

Interviews with average citizens on the street prove that Collins is not alone in shedding crocodile tears over Trump's financial troubles. "I am crying my eyes out for the next hundred years!" Wardell Striggles, a Bronx native who sells cassette tapes on the corner of Third Avenue and Forty-third Street in Manhattan, informs the *Daily News*. "I may have to go home I'm so upset by this terrible news!"

"I really don't care about Donald Trump and his money problems," says Robert Williams, Jr., an African-American assistant store manager. "However, I've read that his wife is running up a lot of bills that Donald must pay. That's great."

"Whatever his problems, I'd take them, including Marla Maples," says financial consultant Randolph Rawiszer. "If he needs the financial advice, he or Marla can give me a call. Actually, I'm divorced."

Donald's creditors do not take the situation so lightly. On June 5 a group of Trump Plaza and Trump Castle casino bondholders file a class-action suit accusing him of fraud and securities law violations. The bondholders allege that Donald has leaked "confidential" lists of Plaza and Castle high-roller gambling customers to the newly opened Taj Mahal in order to promote the Taj "at the expense" of his other two Atlantic City casinos. In addition to seeking an unspecified monetary damage judgment, the bondholders' suit asks that Donald be enjoined from using the allegedly invaluable customer lists to benefit the Taj.

By now Donald's no longer secret behind-the-scenes negotiations are turning grim. His bankers and their attorneys adjourn the cozy powwows in the conference room at Trump Tower and commence bitterly divisive caucuses in law firms and branch offices all over town. Donald is not invited to the meetings ostensibly because they are creditor-to-creditor negotiations. But despite protestations to the contrary, the banks are beginning to regard him as persona non grata. They now realize that their slick-talking star borrower has misled them about the true severity of his cash squeeze.

The bankers on the Trump workout teams are even more upset at their own real estate lending departments. They cannot really fault Donald for borrowing whatever he could get. But they do fault their lending department colleagues for giving so much money to him in exchange for such weak collateral. Soon heads will roll in the real estate departments of Citibank, Chase, and Manufacturers Hanover as slews of vice-presidents are fired for incompetence. In the interim the banks' workout teams are determined to attach liens to every valuable property in the Trump portfolio, including, if possible, whatever nest egg Donald stands to inherit from his old man.

Ivana Trump parades through the paparazzi-packed lobby of the Waldorf-Astoria as if she owns the place. It is precisely 6:15 P.M. on Wednesday, June 6, and she is due to be a presenter at the Fragrance Foundation awards ceremony. She wears a full-length beaded satin ball gown appropriately dyed mint green like the color of money, and she has her gold-tinted hair swept up in the Bardot bun styled for the *Vogue* cover shoot. When she reaches the Jade Room, the sound of her name echoes over the high-speed clicking of motor-driven cameras.

"Ivana! Ivana! Ivana!" shout the assembled photographers, clamoring for her to look their way.

Ivana flashes a professional smile and beckons to pear-shaped designer Arnold Scaasi. "Come on, Arnold! Pose with me! Come on!" Scaasi, who used to live in the strife-torn rent-controlled apartment building The Donald owns at 100 Central Park South, waddles over obediently. In years past Scaasi has benefited from the promotional value afforded by Ivana's patronage of his fashion lines. Now, as a woman soon to be all on her own, she needs Scaasi to stand beside her as he once needed her.

As Ivana chats with Scaasi and cosmetics queen Estée Lauder, a
CBS News correspondent shoves a microphone in her face and
asks her to comment on reports of The Donald's cash-flow crunch.
Ivana cannot believe that her husband is really going broke. She privately suspects that The Donald's sudden financial crisis is another
one of his stunts, a ploy to avoid paying her what she is due under
their nuptial contract. But she is determined to remain above the
fray.

"Donald and I are partners in marriage and in business," Ivana
tells the CBS correspondent in an obviously rehearsed reply. "I will
stand beside him through thick or thin and for better or worse."

Even so, Ivana is not about to relinquish her claims on the family
fortune. Her publicist, John Scanlon, made that perfectly clear in a
statement released to the press the previous day. "Mrs. Trump
obviously is only interested in a healthy Trump empire since she
believes she and her children are entitled to half its value," Scanlon
said. But he added that Ivana is not going to allow her husband to
renege on their nuptial contract. As Scanlon archly observed, "Not
even Donald Trump can simultaneously have a contract both res-
cindable and ironclad."

Ivana intends to fend for herself in The Donald's own tradition by
licensing the one major asset she has left: her name. After charming
the paparazzi buzzing about the Fragrance Foundation dinner crowd,
she seats herself at a table hosted by Eugene Grisanti, chairman of
International Flavors & Fragrances. It is, as Grisanti later acknowledges, "an open bulletin" that he and Ivana are developing a fragrance to be trademarked with her name. Ivana will soon commence
negotiations with the William Morris Literary Agency about writing
romans à clef loosely based on her own life story.

But The Donald still has his hooks in her. The day before the *Wall
Street Journal* broke the news of his bank negotiations, Ivana went to
the Plaza Hotel for the wedding of her fashion executive friend Martha Kramer and Sulka apparel company president Neal J. Fox. When
popular singer Neil Sedaka serenaded the bride and groom with a
new song about a lonely man who finds love, Ivana started sobbing
uncontrollably. Her table mate Paul Hallingby, president of Bear
Stearns, put his arm around her heaving shoulders. But Ivana kept
on crying. By the time Sedaka segued into his hit song, "Laughter in

the Rain," all the other women at the table—Hallingby's wife, Mai, and socialites Laura Pomerantz and Joan Schnitzer—were crying, too.

Fred Trump, Sr., is sitting in Donald's office, staring at his son in disbelief. The banks are ready to provide a bridge loan to cover Trump Castle's upcoming bond payment. There is just one hitch. In return for lending Donald more money, they want more security—to wit, a mortgage on his father's ten thousand units of rental properties in Brooklyn and Queens. Although Donald does not like the idea, he is running out of options and time. According to reports that Donald denies, he decides to ask his old man for help. But Fred Trump, Sr., refuses to get stuck to his son's financial tar baby without exacting even tougher concessions from his son than the banks will.

"I'll help you out," he tells Donald, "but only if you go back to Ivana."

Donald rejects his father's offer. He then turns to—or, rather, turns on—his younger brother, Robert, and his older sister Elizabeth. These two siblings are still living in apartments he lets them use in Trump Plaza on Third Avenue. Donald decides that their free ride should be over in light of his banking crisis.

"I want you to evict Robert and Elizabeth," he orders executive vice-president Blanche Sprague. "Make them buy their apartments for cash or I'm going to throw them out. I'm having all these financial problems. Why shouldn't Robert and Elizabeth contribute?"

Sprague refuses to carry out the eviction order. Instead she writes a memo estimating the market value of Trump Plaza units 36C and 36B, which Robert and his wife, Blaine, occupy, and units 21C and 21D, which Elizabeth occupies with her husband, Jim Grau, then wisely leaves any further action to her boss. But before Donald can act on his eviction threats, there is a breakthrough in the behind-the-scenes bank negotiations.

By Monday, June 11, it looks as if Citicorp, Chase Manhattan, Manufacturers Hanover, and Bankers Trust have reached a tentative accord. They will lend Donald $60 million, much of which will be used to make Trump Castle's $43 million bond payment due on June 15. The banks will also suspend interest payments on some $2 billion worth of loans. In return, they will get mostly second mortgages on

Trump Tower, Trump Plaza in Atlantic City, and other indebted properties. At their behest, Donald will also hire a chief financial officer from outside the Trump Organization to help put his house of cards in order.

But Donald's four lead banks cannot simply sign off on the accord by themselves. They have syndicated his loans (for which they received lucrative fees and simultaneously reduced their individual exposure) to no fewer than fifty-four other domestic and foreign banks. Each of these banks has to give its consent or the deal will not work. And by midweek several of the smaller banks start balking. First Fidelity of New Jersey, for example, has a $75 million lien on the Taj Mahal; its claim is secondary only to the first mortgage on the property held by the casino's bondholders. Under one of the big banks' proposals, all of Donald's assets would be put in a single pool with each of the banks splitting the proceeds from any future sale. But that cross-collateralization plan would only erode First Fidelity's claims on the Taj by putting it in the same boat as other creditors.

On Thursday, June 14, which happens to be Donald's forty-fourth birthday, the negotiations hit another major snag. The big banks now demand not only that he hire a chief financial officer but that he also hire a chief executive officer from outside the Trump Organization. That would effectively remove Donald from the driver's seat of his own empire. Donald lets it be known that he will not stand for what amounts to an executive coup d'etat. He then threatens to declare bankruptcy.

It is a bold ploy—and something of a bluff. Donald clearly does not want to suffer the embarrassment or run the legal risk of filing Chapter 11. But the banks are even more daunted by the prospect. If Donald were to file for bankruptcy, his empire would be put under the supervision of a trustee who would tell him and his creditors what assets to sell as well as who would get what shares of the proceeds, a scenario that would put all his lenders at the mercy of the court. The legal bills would be exorbitant, and the time involved could easily run four years or longer.

On Friday, June 15, Trump Castle fails to make the $43 million payment due its bondholders. There is still hope. The bond covenants provide for a ten-day grace period before Donald would be technically in default and faced with losing the casino to his bondholders. The official foreclosure deadline is 12:01 A.M. on June 27. But time is running out. Even though Donald's representatives and the banks continue to negotiate through the weekend, the parties make no public announcement that their talks are progressing toward a resolution.

On Saturday, June 16, Donald celebrates his forty-fourth birthday with a lavish party at Trump Castle in Atlantic City. The guests, most of whom work for the Trump Organization in some capacity, are understandably nervous about their boss's financial situation. In an effort to allay their concerns, the birthday boy rises to make a short speech.

"Over the years, I've surprised a lot of people," Donald reminds his well-wishers. "The largest surprise is yet to come."

He is right about that. One of the first surprises to emerge in the media over the next few days is the news that Donald has personally guaranteed $500 million in loans. In addition to the already highly publicized $75 million note on the Taj held by First Fidelity, the loans include $135 million on the Trump Shuttle, $125 million on the Plaza Hotel, and $60 million on Trump Palace, all of which was borrowed from Citicorp. Bankers Trust has another $100 million worth of personally guaranteed loans. In the event of default, Donald would be held responsible for satisfying the full amount of his indebtedness even if the properties were sold off for less than what he owes.

Equally surprising to many Trump watchers in the media is the news that Donald's bankers do not see a light at the end of his financial tunnel. He has tried to give the impression that the $60 million bridge loan under negotiation will solve what is merely a short-term problem and that the Trump empire will remain intact and once again become profitable. But the banks believe Donald is already on his last legs. "The misconception people have is that the $60 million would give Trump time," one participant in the negotiations tells Neil Barsky of the *Wall Street Journal*. "In fact, it is the banks who bought time to have an orderly sale of his assets."

Donald's reaction is perhaps even more surprising. Instead of churning out mounds of disinformation, as he has done in past crises, he withdraws from public view for most of the ensuing week. He spends day and night inside Trump Tower, either behind his office desk on the twenty-sixth floor or in the apartment formerly reserved for his father on the sixty-third floor. He lets his already shaggy locks grow longer and starts gaining weight from a diet of pastrami sandwiches his bodyguards picks up from Wolf's deli on Sixth Avenue.

Donald's behavior recalls the eccentric reclusiveness of the late billionaire Howard R. Hughes, whom he regards as a kind of personal hero and role model. He has isolated himself from his wife, his children, and even his old man. The only person who seems to be staying faithfully by his side is Marla Maples, who tries to calm his troubled soul by reading to him from the New Age philosophical teachings of *Emmanuel's Book*. But not even Marla can arrest Donald's downward mood swings. At one point he even talks about suicide.

"If I lose you," Donald tells Marla amid the depths of his depression, "I have nothing else to live for."

There is good reason for Donald to feel down and out. Unlike his four lead banks, the smaller domestic banks such as First Fidelity and Midlantic are not willing to join in a creditors' pool. Neither are similarly situated banks based in Japan, South Korea, Brazil, Ireland, Italy, France, and Germany, which hold first mortgages on various Trump real estate properties. They do not want to end up paying for a disproportionate share of the bad loans made by the larger banks. Finally, Citicorp Vice-Chairman Lawrence Small and Chase Manhattan Vice-Chairman Robert Douglas decide to take a cue from Donald. They use the threat of a Trump bankruptcy filing as a bludgeon to get the recalcitrant creditors in line.

By Wednesday, June 20, with Trump Castle's foreclosure date just six days away, First Fidelity and most of the other domestic loan partners agree to the asset pooling plan proposed by the big banks. Many of the foreign banks, however, are still holding out. Four of them—Dresdner Bank of West Germany and Sumitomo, Mitsubishi, and Dai-Ichi Kangyo of Japan—share portions of a $75 million first-mortgage loan on Trump Tower. They demand that Chase Manhattan, the lead bank on the Trump Tower loan, but out their first-mortgage positions so that their loans will not be tied to the uncertain fate of the Trump empire as a whole.

On Thursday, June 21, representatives of Chase Manhattan meet with representatives of the four foreign partners on the Trump Tower loan in hope of making them see the light. Once again, Chase officials raise the threat of a Trump bankruptcy, which would put all of the creditors at the mercy of a court-appointed trustee regardless of whether they hold first or second mortgages. According to one participant in the talks, Chase tries to make the foreign banks realize that "mutual cooperation is better for them, and without them the deal doesn't work."

But the four holdout banks still refuse to budge. Two more foreign banks—Yasuda Bank and Trust Company and Société Général de Financement du Québec—which share in a $200 million first-mortgage loan on the West Side yards property, decline the invitation to join the proposed creditors' pool. So do several of Citicorp's foreign and domestic partners in the Trump Shuttle, Plaza Hotel, and Trump Palace loans.

True to his word, Donald surprises everyone concerned by stepping into the breach. In his first book, *The Art of the Deal,* he outlined eleven rules for success in business and in life. Since the book's publication in the fall of 1987 he has violated almost all his own dicta, especially the one that cautions: "Protect the downside and the upside will take care of itself." Now he appears ready to heed his own advice, in particular the rules that urge "Use your leverage" and "Fight back."

On Friday, June 22, Donald breaks a weeklong public silence by announcing that he and his bankers are "very close" to striking a deal. "An overwhelming number of the participating lenders, representing both national and international financial institutions, have now joined the major banks in supporting our plan," he maintains in an official statement released by the Trump Organization.

Then, after a weekend of frustrated attempts at compromise, Donald turns on his famous charm. On the night of Monday, June 25, with Trump Castle's foreclosure deadline a little more than twenty-four hours away, he personally lobbies the recalcitrant foreign banks to cooperate with the four lead banks. His wiles work on Citicorp's partners and on Chase's partner Société Général. According to one insider, they are persuaded by "Mr. Trump's grasp of his financial situation and his confidence in turning it around."

But Donald's optimism does not impress the Dresdner Bank, the single remaining holdout. Without its cooperation the proposed $60 million bailout plan cannot work. Again, the big banks take their cue from Donald's own negotiating tactics. On Monday night Citicorp Vice-Chairman Small and Chase Vice-Chairman Douglas make personal transatlantic telephone calls to top Dresdner officials. The American bankers remind their German counterparts of the debtor-friendly nature of U.S. bankruptcy laws. More ominously they also threaten to exclude Dresdner from participation in future loans to other major customers. Faced with a potential loss of overseas business amounting to hundreds of millions of dollars, the Dresdner officials reluctantly capitulate.

On Tuesday, June 26, Donald J. Trump is born again. He and his bankers agree to a comprehensive five-year plan that is, for all intents and purposes, an out-of-court bankruptcy proceeding. The first phase of the so-called credit and override agreements calls for a $20 million bridge loan to enable him to make the Trump Castle bond payments. That loan will eventually be replaced with a $65 million loan whose proceeds will be used for working capital requirements. The banks also agree to let Trump forgo interest payments on another $2 billion in loans for up to five years.

In return for their lending largess, the banks extract some major, and rather embarrassing, concessions from Donald. Although he will not have to cede authority over his empire to a new chief executive hired from outside, his creditors remain firm in their insistence that he hire a chief financial officer mandated to trim the fat from Trump Organization operations. Donald's new CFO will be required to help the banks sell off almost all of his cash-consuming trophy properties, including his yacht, his jet, his helicopter, and the Trump Shuttle.

Finally, and most embarrassingly, the banks insist on putting Donald on a spending allowance. Under the plan, his personal expenditures will be limited to $450,000 a month for the remainder of 1990, $375,000 a month for 1991, and $300,000 a month for 1992. These spending limits, however, do not apply to upkeep and interest payments on his Mar-a-Lago estate, which total nearly $2 million a year, or to the interim maintenance of the *Trump Princess* and his Boeing 727. Also exempt from spending limits are payments on legal bills, which amount to $10.75 million for the bank bailout alone, according to Casino Control Commission documents.

On June 26 Donald spends the hours between 9:00 A.M. and 3:00 P.M. in the offices of Wachtell, Lipton, Rosen & Katz, the law firm representing Bankers Trust. During that period he signs off on more than twelve hundred pages of documents relating to his bailout agreement. When he is done, he expresses his gratitude in a statement the Trump Organization releases to the media:

> I want to thank all of my banks and lending institutions for making this complex and highly technical agreement possible. I have gained a deep respect for the banking system and those who make it work. . . . This agreement allows the Trump Organization to go strongly forward and reflects and confirms the inherent long-term value of our assets, including Trump Tower, the Plaza Hotel, the Atlantic City hotels, and the Trump Shuttle. The agreement demonstrates the confidence of the banking group in the company's ability to maximize the value of those assets.

Privately Donald can hardly contain his gloating. He believes, not without reason, that he has pulled off another coup in his bank negotiations. As he later points out in an interview, he has pioneered another trend. "I'm the only one that worked out a deal with the banks," he boasts. "You know every developer in New York, most of them, are in worse shape than I am."

Donald is not far wrong. Over the next twenty-four months several high-profile tycoons, including the Reichman brothers of the Olympic & York real estate empire, and developer-publisher Peter Kalikow will wind up filing for some form of bankruptcy protection. But unbeknownst to the banks or the general public, Donald's financial problems are by no means permanently resolved. That will become clear when the first comprehensive audit of his portfolio is completed by Kenneth Leventhal & Company in late summer. But ominous signals are already emanating from the airline branch of his empire.

On June 29, barely three days after striking his bank deal, Donald fires the Trump Shuttle president, Bruce Nobles, complaining through a spokesman that Nobles just "couldn't cut it." The facts speak to the contrary. During Nobles's thirteen-month-long tenure, the Trump Shuttle has made a remarkable turnaround, rising from a 12 percent market share vis-à-vis the Pan Am Shuttle to a 48 percent share. But because of the burden of some $400 million in debt, the Trump Shuttle has yet to turn a net profit. In fact, it shows a loss of more than $90 million.

Like the Pan Am Shuttle, the Trump Shuttle has been on the selling block for months. Prior to his dismissal, Nobles admitted to the *Wall Street Journal* that despite shows of interest, he had received no formal offers to buy the Trump shuttle. Donald was furious. "Why are you saying that?" he demanded. "Because it's true," Nobles replied. "Look, I'm trying to sell," Donald stormed. "I don't want people to think there's no interest." According to former insiders, this incident led to Nobles's departure.

Donald immediately replaces Nobles with former vice-president Richard Cozzi. The change in presidents does not change the airline's profit-making prospects. In an interview with the *New York Times,* Cozzi predicts that overall ridership on both the Pan Am Shuttle and Trump Shuttle will drop from 4 million passengers a year to 3.6 million passengers a year and blames the decline on the sagging northeastern economy. In late August, after signing final closing papers on his deal with the banks, Donald will take the Trump Shuttle off the market, claiming that the debt relief he has gotten will enable the airline to turn a profit. But by that time Iraqi dictator Saddam Hussein will be launching an invasion of Kuwait, and oil prices will be shooting up from $20 a barrel to more than $30 a barrel, imperiling the future of even the strongest air carriers.

In the meantime, Donald rushes to rewrite his second book, *Trump: Surviving at the Top,* so that it will include the outcome of his bank negotiations. As he admitted at the American Booksellers Association Convention, there are still a lot of question marks about what his future holds. This is especially true in the case of his ongoing negotiations with his estranged wife.

On July 2, just five days after The Donald announces his deal with the banks, Ivana Trump boards the Concorde in New York and takes off for London. It is her fourth trip to Europe in the past eight weeks. As one of her top associates observes, "She treats going to Europe like it's around the corner." Ivana's globe-trotting does not escape the notice of her admirers and her critics in the media. She has cut a wide swath on her previous trips abroad. This summer, in the wake of the worldwide tabloid coverage of the Trumps' marital scandal, she creates an exceptional stir.

Instead of staying at a hotel, Ivana moves into the Eaton Square home of her friend Eva O'Neill. A brassy, buxom thrice-married Austrian with three children, O'Neill reminds many acquaintances of the young Zsa Zsa Gabor. *London Daily Mail* gossip columnist Nigel Dempster describes O'Neill, rather archly, as "a blonde woman of uncertain age who lives in the right part of town but is not prominent in any way. Her friends have names like von Panz and Hohenlohe."

Ivana's association with O'Neill causes London socialites to wag their tongues in unkind ways. The two of them dash about town in designer dresses and plumed hats, posing for photographs at such highfalutin events as the horse races at Ascot and the tennis matches at Wimbledon. In between social engagements they take off for the fashion shows in Paris. But their critics dismiss them as social-climbing parvenues.

At one point, after hosting a luncheon to promote the Plaza Hotel, Ivana allegedly shoulders her way into a receiving line to shake hands with the princess of Wales. When Ivana passes through the line, Princess Di turns to a companion and exchanges disdainful glances. Sir Humphry Wakefield, a titled socialite is later accused of committing a grievous faux pas when he invites the duchess of Northumberland and several other title holders to a dinner in Ivana's honor. "Humphry will pay for this!" sniffs one of Ivana's nonplussed dinner partners.

On July 8 Ivana flies back to New York and spends four of the next five days giving depositions to attorneys in her lawsuit against The Donald. She remains in town the following week, while The Donald gives two days of depositions. In subsequent sworn testimony he will invoke the Fifth Amendment protection against self-incrimination more than seventy times, mostly in response to questions about his alleged affairs with other women, including Robin Givens, Catherine Oxenberg, Carol Alt, and Marla Ann Maples.

When the next weekend rolls around, Ivana hops aboard another jet bound for Paris, where she attends a dinner in her honor, scheduled two months in advance, at the Left Bank apartment of Emanuel

Ungaro's couture director, Catherine de Limur. Up to now Ivana has been winning points with the press and the general public by playing the wife and mother wronged. But her jaunty junkets back and forth to Europe make her seem like just another gold digger. Rumors circulate about Paris that publisher John Fairchild has informed Ungaro that Ivana is passé. When Ungaro arrives at Catherine de Limur's party for Ivana, he reportedly behaves as if the guest of honor were not there.

Back in the States, gossip columnist William Norwich of the *New York Daily News* joins the Ivana bashing with a pointed critique of her trips to Europe. Wondering aloud what "the three little Trump children are doing for their summer vacation," Norwich recalls the story of how Gloria Morgan Vanderbilt lost custody of her daughter, Gloria, because of indulging in "the sybaritic, globe-trotting life everyone rich led during the Great Depression." Norwich notes that Ivana "says these trips abroad are all about business" but warns that "a judge, the public or an irate husband may not see it that way someday." He later tells *New York* magazine writer Michael Gross, "I feel Ivana is living at risk. There was too much Ivana. It was too obvious. Her commercial endeavors are a little hard for the stuck-ups on Park Avenue to swallow."

Norwich's remarks cut Ivana to the quick. "Nothing upset her so much; it was the thing that hurt her the most," one of her confidants recalls months later. "She cried and cried over what he said about her and her children." Ivana is well aware of the subtext in Norwich's comments. He is, as she puts it, "Blaine's man," a steadfast promoter of her sister-in-law. But unlike The Donald, Ivana does not hold a grudge. Instead she starts thinking of ways to curry favor with Norwich so that she will receive more favorable mention in future columns.

In any event Ivana does not let the jealous backbiting slow her down. She flies back from Paris on July 26 and stays just long enough to repack her bags and gather up her children. On July 30 she takes off for Nice. She spends the next two weeks in the south of France, mostly at a rented summer villa in St. Jean. At night she attends parties given by the likes of socialite Lynn Wyatt, wife of controversial oilman Oscar Wyatt, who has chili and barbecue flown in from Texas aboard his private jet.

Ivana finally returns to New York on Sunday, August 12. Four days later her husband celebrates the official publication date of his second book.

In the opening pages of *Trump: Surviving at the Top,* Donald dismisses any suggestion that he has been on the financial ropes, much less on the brink of bankruptcy. "Over several weeks of very hard bargaining, my bankers and I worked out a terrific deal that allows me the time, the money, and the leeway to come out stronger than ever," he declares, hastening to add, "I see the deal as a great victory—and eventually the rest of the world will too." But Donald does confess to contributing to the cause of his banking crisis, admitting, "I got caught up in the buying frenzy myself."

In the style of his first book, Donald provides a list of rules for success. But where *The Art of the Deal* contains no less than eleven such dicta, *Surviving at the Top* offers only six. The most ironic of these is rule two: "Be honest—even if the world around you is often dishonest." The others, only slightly less ironic in their own right considering that he has recently violated each and every one of them, are: (1) "Be disciplined"; (3) "Don't think you're so smart you can go it alone"; (4) "Be reachable"; (5) "Stay close to home"; and (6) "Be flexible."

Donald's treatment of his affair with Marla Maples is similarly disingenuous. He fails to address the question that is surely on every potential reader's mind: Was it the "best sex" he or she ever had? In fact, he mentions Marla by name only twice and both times in the same spare paragraph. "Marla Maples, the beautiful young actress who bore the brunt of the hysterical publicity [about Trump's marital woes], is a terrific person," he writes, "but my relationship with her was not the cause of the trouble between Ivana and me. Marla was an easy target because of her looks. Yet if I'd never met her, Ivana and I would still be separated."

Donald allows that he is at least somewhat to blame for causing a public scandal over the breakup of his marriage to Ivana. "Ultimately, I have to confess, the way I handled the situation was a copout," he admits. "I never sat down calmly with Ivana to 'talk it out,' as I probably should have."

Donald casts more venomous aspersions on his critics in the media, his business adversaries, and various alleged "phonies." The targets of his poison arrows include *New York Daily News* columnist Liz Smith, *Time* correspondent Jeanne McDowell, rival hotelier Leona Helmsley, rival casino hotelier Barron Hilton and the so-called Lucky Sperm Club of socialites with inherited wealth, Frank Sinatra, the Rolling Stones, and the late Malcolm Forbes, publisher of the magazine that exposed his precarious financial status back in the spring.

". . . I gradually came to see [Malcolm Forbes] as a hypocrite who favored those who advertised in his magazine and tried, with surprising viciousness, to punish those who didn't," Donald writes. "I saw a double standard in the way he lived openly as a homosexual—which he had every right to do—but expected the media and his famous friends to cover for him. I can see it was only a matter of time before the family started using its magazine against me."

Among the rare, unintentionally revealing passages in *Trump: Surviving at the Top* are those that mention the few people Donald claims to admire. The most prominent female on the list is First Lady Barbara Bush, who wrote him a supportive note after she heard him "being attacked by Phil Donahue" in a TV interview. But with the exception of this "classy lady," Donald's heroes are exclusively male: former heavyweight boxing champ Mike Tyson, former business adversary Merv Griffin, controversial Saudi deal maker Adnan Khashoggi, Time Warner chief Steve Ross, Revlon boss Ron Perelman, and of course, the late Howard R. Hughes. But Donald lavishes some of his greatest praise on former President Richard Nixon.

"I've seen some real killers in my line of work, but Richard Nixon makes them look like babies," Donald gushes. He clearly wants his readers to believe that he is cut from the same quarry as Nixon. Indeed, his book bears more than passing similarities to Nixon's best-selling memoir, *Six Crises*.

Almost immediately after *Trump: Surviving at the Top* arrives in the bookstores, Donald realizes that he is starting the battle for his financial survival all over again. On August 15, 1990, the accounting firm of Kenneth Leventhal & Company sends a letter to Donald and his bankers marking the completion of the first ever comprehensive audit of the Trump holdings. That in itself is headline news. Over the past decade the nation's largest and most prestigious financial institutions have been lending billions of dollars to Donald. But until his recent cash-flow crisis, none of his banks or bondholders ever bothered to document all his assets and outstanding liabilities as they would for a home loan to an average customer. Rather, they have been lending purely on the basis of the Trump name and public image, both of which are now considerably devalued.

The bottom line of the Leventhal report contains still more sensational revelations about Donald's true financial condition. Leventhal estimates that his net worth, assuming he sold all his properties over the long term for the maximum price, is no more than $500 million, or about what *Forbes* estimated back in the spring. But according to the audit, if Donald is forced to sell his properties immediately, he will be worth less than zero. At present liquidation value, his assets are so much lower than his total debts that he would actually have a negative net worth of $295 million. In other words, the banks and bondholders have not only been lending to a self-made myth but been throwing their money down a bottomless pit.

The bad news about Donald spreads like wildfire. On August 16 New Jersey gaming authorities urge him to "break up" and "sell off" at least some of his Atlantic City assets, which include the Taj Mahal, Trump Plaza, Trump Castle, the Trump Regency noncasino hotel, and the properties he bought from *Penthouse*. According to a report by the Division of Gaming Enforcement, that is the only way Donald can avoid imminent financial collapse. But that nonbinding recommendation is not one that he appreciates—or intends to follow.

Donald believes that his book *Trump: Surviving at the Top* can become, or at least contribute to becoming, a self-fulfilling prophecy. Random House has reportedly scheduled a first printing of five hundred thousand copies and budgeted $1 million for promotion. According to documents Donald submits to the New Jersey Casino Control Commission, he anticipates net royalties to generate $1.1 million in cash. He also anticipates that the book will restore his tattered public image. Both hopes are quickly dashed.

ABC interviewer Barbara Walters hosts another segment about Donald on "20/20." But in contrast with the segment that followed the publication of *Trump: The Art of the Deal,* this is not purely a puff piece. Like many of her colleagues in the media, Walters evidently believes that Donald has betrayed her with previous false promises and hyperbole. She confronts him with a rumor that he deliberately allowed Trump Castle to miss its June bond payment in order to get better terms from the banks. Donald will not comment. When Donald declares that people are saying "[w]hat a great deal he made on the Plaza," she rejoins, "No, they're not."

"You never say, 'I made mistakes. Gee, I'm in trouble. Things are bad,' " Walters observes.

"Everybody makes mistakes," Donald replies.

"You haven't said it," Walters scolds.

"I make mistakes," Donald finally acknowledges.

In an acrobatic leap of faith Walters somehow manages to conclude her segment on an upbeat note. "Still, with all of his troubles, there's something very disarming about Donald Trump, and he possesses both courage and daring," she proclaims. "Like him or not, the man is an original, determined to survive at the top."

But despite Walters's begrudging encomiums, the sales report on *Trump: Surviving at the Top* mirrors Donald's own roller-coastering rise and demise. The book debuts at number five on the *New York Times* best seller list. The next week it shoots up to number one. Over the next five weeks the book slides to number ten, bounces back to number one, then slips back down to number ten. At the end of October it drops off the *Times* list for good. Random House winds up selling an estimated 125,000 hardback copies. Under ordinary circumstances, most publishers would consider that a substantial success. But compared with *The Art of the Deal,* which has sold more than nine hundred thousand copies, *Trump: Surviving at the Top* is an unmitigated flop. The public simply is not buying Donald J. Trump— or his books—any longer.

Neither are the mass media. Marie Brenner sets the pace for the new pack of Trump bashers in an article entitled "After the Gold Rush" in the September 1990 issue of *Vanity Fair.* She reveals that Donald is known to have received a book of Adolf Hitler's collected speeches entitled *My New Order.* The similarities between Hitler's big lie propaganda and Donald's big lies are striking. "Do people really think I am in trouble?" he asks incredulously during his interview with Brenner.

"Yes," Brenner replies, "they think you're finished."

"Just wait five years," Donald parries. "This is really a no-brainer. Just like the Merv Griffin deal. When I took him to the cleaners, people wanted me to lose. They said, 'Holy shit! Trump got taken!' Let me tell you something. It's good to be thought of as poor right now. You wouldn't believe some of the deals I'm making! I guess I have a perverse personality. . . . I've really enjoyed the past few weeks."

It is hard for anyone but Donald himself to see how or why. Having recently restructured his $2.1 billion in bank debts, he now wants to restructure the $1.3 billion in junk bond debt on his Atlantic City casinos. But a group of Taj Mahal building contractors is demanding payment on $35 million in past-due bills, and a group of Taj Mahal bondholders is organizing opposition to Donald's restructuring plans. In November the Taj bondholders will be owed a scheduled interest payment of $47 million. When Donald indicates that he will not be able to make the payment out of the casino's cash flow, the bondholders vow to take legal action.

Donald's fate is no longer entirely in his own hands. Shortly before the publication of the *Vanity Fair* piece, he was obliged to hire a chief financial officer as he promised the banks. The new Trump CFO is forty-seven-year-old Stephen F. Bollenbach, a gray-bearded veteran of the restructuring or dismantling of several once-prosperous corporate empires, including those of Daniel K. Ludwig, Marriott, and Holiday Inns. Bollenbach, who is reportedly being paid a salary of $1 million per year, has a mandate from the banks. His job is to sell off as many Trump properties as he can, specifically the *Trump Princess*, the Trump Shuttle, and the Plaza Hotel. That task will not be made any easier in light of the fact that veteran real estate executive Blanche Sprague, whom Donald described in his first book as "one of the best salespeople and managers I've ever met," has just left the Trump Organization in a dispute over salary and commission cuts.

The myth is that if the economy improves, the fortunes of Donald J. Trump will improve accordingly. In fact, the reverse is true. As long as the economy remains mired in recession, Donald will be able to maintain at least nominal ownership of his assets simply because they will not fetch prices high enough to satisfy his creditors. But once the economy improves, potential buyers will likely be willing to pay much more for those properties, and Bollenbach will be forced to supervise their timely liquidation as approved by the banks.

Whether he acknowledges it or not, Donald is truly caught between the horns of an inescapable dilemma. The time he has bought through restructuring his bank debt is working on behalf of his creditors rather than on behalf of his own personal ambitions to survive at the top. To make matters worse, there is yet another dark cloud on Donald's horizon that threatens both his own future and that of his creditors; his still-unresolved legal battle against Ivana.

chapter eleven
CHIPS OFF THE OLD BLOCK

■ MILOS ZELNICEK IS standing at a Kennedy Airport ticket counter on a warm fall day. He is about to check in for a flight back to Czechoslovakia. He is not anxious to leave. The Donald's behavior of late has so incensed him that he has threatened to punch his son-in-law in the mouth. Suddenly a man Zelnicek has never seen before walks up and shoves an official-looking sheaf of papers into his chest.

"Milos Zelnicek," says the stranger, "you are hereby served notice to appear for a deposition in the case of *Trump v. Trump.*"

Ivana's father nearly has a heart attack. Having lived his entire life behind the iron curtain, he has had no previous experience with the American legal system. Even as he watches the process server disappear out the terminal door, he is gape-mouthed and shuddering in shock.

"Are the police coming to put me in handcuffs?" he asks Ivana fearfully.

Ivana is already rushing to a nearby telephone to call her attorney, Michael Kennedy. She is almost as confused as her father and far more furious. Does this mean that he has to cancel his trip home? Will customs officials prevent him from trying to leave the country?

Kennedy assures Ivana that the subpoena is just another one of The Donald's mean tricks, a payback to them for having served Marla Maples with similar papers at the No Excuses press conference. He advises Ivana to put her father on the plane to Czechoslovakia as scheduled. He will deal with the subpoena and with The Donald.

The incident at the airport sets the tone for the next phase of the war between the Trumps. When Ivana returns to her office at the Plaza Hotel, she demands that her "dollar a year and all the dresses she can buy" compensation package be replaced by a bona fide salary. But The Donald informs her by telephone that she has been "fired."

Kennedy resists the temptation to call the tabloids. If the story of Ivana's firing is made public, The Donald will be publicly humiliated and will probably feel that the only way he can save face is to stand by his decision. Kennedy knows that Ivana is emotionally dependent on her position at the Plaza; it defines her role in marriage, business, and society. Without her job, she will have nothing to do and no place to go during the working day. She will basically be a hostage to her estranged husband's whims. At the same time the financial stakes involved are higher than anyone outside the Trump inner circle imagines.

Although Ivana has enjoyed a jet-setting life-style all summer, she is in relatively dire financial straits. Judge Phyllis Gangel-Jacob has ruled that Ivana can receive $100,000 per month in support payments from The Donald without prejudicing the outcome of her lawsuit challenging the couple's nuptial contract. But most of that money has gone to household expenses, and Ivana's personal nest egg is rapidly depleting. She has used the interest from the $100,000 certificate of deposit The Donald gave her when they were married to pay her private investigators. She is now considering the idea of selling the $1 million Harry Winston diamond ring he gave her for Christmas 1988.

Kennedy believes that it is also in The Donald's interest to keep Ivana at the Plaza. She is the one who provides the hotel with social panache and plenty of free publicity in the gossip columns, as well as daily hands-on management. He quietly negotiates with The Donald to have her reinstated at the Plaza without public notice of her firing. He further demands that The Donald raise Ivana's salary from $1 a year plus dresses to $375,000 a year. Kennedy's efforts are abetted by the Plaza vice-president Richard Wilhelm, who threatens to quit if Ivana is dismissed.

The Donald finally agrees to Kennedy's demands. He realizes that his own financial recovery depends in no small part on Ivana. She can make as much, if not more, trouble for him by dropping her suit to break their nuptial contract and insisting that it be enforced. Her legally approved place in the lengthening line of Trump creditors remains to be determined. But there is a strong possibility that she can force him to declare bankruptcy simply by demanding immediate payment of the $10 million in cash due under their nuptial contract. It makes sense to keep Ivana happy or at least at bay.

"I love you, Vaska," The Donald tells her over and over again after she resumes her duties at the Plaza.

Although Ivana melts every time she hears her husband's sweet talk, the Trump children, especially Donny, are not falling for their daddy's lines any longer. The Donald has already tried to placate his elder son by promising to stop seeing Marla Maples. But when the twosome show up together at an Elton John concert, Donny breaks down and cries, "How can you say you love us? You don't love us! You don't even love yourself! You just love your money!"

"The children are all wrecks," Ivana admits to Liz Smith. "I don't know how Donald can say they are great and fine. Ivanka now comes home from school crying, 'Mommy, does it mean I'm not going to be Ivanka Trump anymore?' Little Eric asks me, 'Is it true you are going away and not coming back?' "

The tide of public opinion quickly flows back in Ivana's favor. In early October *New York* magazine runs a cover story entitled IVANA'S NEW LIFE. Careful not to violate the still-disputed gag clause in the couple's nuptial contract, Ivana does not submit to an interview herself, but she does pose for a cover photograph wearing a two-tone pink chiffon gown and pearl earrings. "Her situation—and the dignified way she's dealt with it—has made Ivana the first great nineties celebrity," writer Michael Gross opines in his cover story. "Men cheat. Women (and some men) can relate. And Ivana makes it easy to be on her side, carrying herself with a combination of strength and vulnerability. 'Rather like Bambi,' says her friend Kenneth Jay Lane, the jewelry designer."

"I only want someone to love me," Ivana tells Boaz Mazor when he escorts her to the National Victims Center ball at the Plaza just prior to the publication of the *New York* magazine piece. "I haven't had true love in years. My heart is empty. But win or lose, I fought for what I believed in. I'll be okay."

Owl-eyed photographer Annie Liebovitz and her crew from *Vanity Fair* are fighting to keep their tongues in cheek. It is a sultry September afternoon in New York City, and they are staring at the subject of a photo shoot for the upcoming November issue, a shapely blonde in a shiny gold Donna Karan ball gown. At Liebovitz's direction, the blonde is sprawled across the foot of a red-carpeted staircase, the split of her silk taffeta skirt parted to reveal her legs in all their glory. The blonde looks almost eerily identical to Ivana Trump, right up to her swirling Bardot bun, which is exactly what Liebovitz intends. But she is not Ivana. She is the Other Woman, Marla Ann Maples.

"I believe I have a purpose and that there is a reason we're together. . . . It's a good love, it's not a harmful love. It's a really good, trusting love," Marla tells *Vanity Fair* writer Maureen Orth in an interview prior to the photo shoot.

Marla's candor about her love for Donald J. Trump signals a turning point in their relationship. A few weeks before, they decided to bring their illicit affair out in the open. (NOW THE DONALD WILL SQUEEZE HIS PEACH IN PUBLIC, the *New York Post* announced.) Marla and Donald allowed themselves to be photographed together with boxer Mike Tyson in Atlantic City and at the U.S. Open tennis tournament in New York. Donald even took Marla out to the Trump family home in Jamaica Estates, Queens, to meet his mother and father.

"It was just like going over to my grandparents'—very solid, very relaxed," Marla reports.

Marla tries to maintain an air of earthy innocence even as she poses on a roof ledge in a silver Gottex bathing suit and a a diaphanous black chiffon Fernando Sanchez robe. "I'm, like, of the soil, of the country, of a solid, firm belief in God," she says, attempting to underscore the differences between her and Ivana. "The lifestyle she's grown accustomed to is outrageous. It's outrageous spending that I can't even conceive of. It makes it difficult for normal existence when you are living at such a high level."

But Marla cannot conceal the fact that she, too, has grown accustomed to the high life. She shows Orth a braided gold Cartier "friendship ring" that Donald gave her, claiming, "It gives me my power." She also shows off her diamond-studded "tennis bracelet" whose stones represent each time Donald disappointed her, and gushes about how much she enjoys their trips to Atlantic City. "I start to relax as soon as I get into that helicopter."

As it turns out, Marla does not make the cover of *Vanity Fair*, but she makes plenty of waves with her Ivanaesque poses and with one particularly provocative comment she later disclaims. When asked to comment on Ivana's attempts to overturn the Trumps' nuptial contract, Marla allegedly replies, "She wants a billion, but we just don't have it."

Appropriately enough, the closing photo spread shows Marla standing next to a Sabrett's hot dog cart on a New York City sidewalk. She is wearing a peach-colored crystal- and rhinestone-studded gown by Bob Mackie and silver heels by Susan Bennis Warren Edwards. In the background an unidentified black man in jeans and a blue windbreaker watches with folded arms and a dour expression as Marla pretends to shove a hot dog into her wide open mouth.

"How the hell can you say something like that?" Donald rages when he receives an advance copy of *Vanity Fair*'s November issue. He is incensed by Marla's unauthorized use of the royal "we," and he hates to hear anyone say he does not have a billion dollars, especially since it is true.

"I never said that," Marla insists, claiming that *Vanity Fair* has fabricated the quote.

"You must have said it," Donald retorts, refusing to believe that anyone else could be misquoted by the media.

But Donald does not have time to dwell on his mistress's errant mouth, for his once-vaunted empire is rapidly disintegrating. Operating results for the third quarter of 1990 show that the Trump Taj Mahal suffered a loss of $14.1 million. After several rounds of heated negotiations, Donald strikes a deal with the Taj contractors, who accept $18 million in cash and a like amount in Taj Mahal bonds as payment on the $35 million due them. But Donald's attempts to strike a deal with the Taj bondholders do not go so smoothly.

On October 18 he offers to give the bondholders 20 percent of his ownership stake in the casino in return for forgiveness of the $47.3 million interest payment due in November and a reduction of future interest charges from about 14 percent per annum to about 9 percent. He warns that if the bondholders do not accept these terms, the Taj will file for bankruptcy. But the bondholders are not intimidated.

An ad hoc bondholder steering committee has hired Wilbur L. Ross, Jr., of Rothschild, Inc., to help salvage their investment. Ross, who has participated in nine of the twenty-five largest bankruptcies proceedings in U.S. history, including the dismemberment of Texaco, Inc., rejects Donald's offer, declaring, "It's a little too early for Christmas." Over the next week and a half the price of Taj Mahal bonds falls to less than one-third of face value. The American Stock Exchange finally halts trading as the Taj bonds plummet to just 26.5 cents on the dollar.

As the bottom drops out of the bond market, Donald is suddenly distracted by a family tragedy. On Sunday, October 28, he gets word that Ivana's father has died of a heart attack. That night Ivana and the children take off for Czechoslovakia. The next morning Donald and his mother decide to fly over to attend Milos Zelnicek's funeral, even though the rest of the family has begged him not to go.

"I hope their plane crashes," Fred Trump, Sr., grumbles to his very close female friend and executive assistant Amy Luersson during lunch at a Coney Island hot dog stand on Tuesday. "Then all my problems will be solved."

Ivana Trump hears a frighteningly familiar mechanical clicking as she stoops over her father's grave in a wooded cemetery on the outskirts of Zlín. Like the year-round local residents of her native town, she is used to hearing the ambient noises that emanate from the Bata shoe factory, where her father worked as an electrical engineer. But the sound she hears on the somber afternoon of October 30 does not come from the shoe factory. It comes from somewhere in the cemetery. And it sends a chill down her spine.

Ivana looks over her shoulder. She sees The Donald and his mother standing beside her mother and the Trumps' three children. Then she turns back around and sees the source of the clicking sound. A crowd of reporters and photographers is standing on the other side of the gravesite, recording the funeral for posterity. One of the cameramen snaps a touching shot of The Donald preparing to comfort his grieving wife.

"I cannot believe this!" Ivana sobs after the burial service. "He came all the way over here just to get the publicity!"

When Ivana returns to New York, she is a changed woman. As far as she is concerned, there is no longer any hope of saving her marriage. The Donald's grandstanding at her father's funeral was the last straw. She is tired of letting him treat her and the children as if they were trophy properties. On the afternoon of November 2 she calls The Donald and tells him that their life as husband and wife is all over.

"I am going to file for the divorce," she says.

The Donald explodes. He believes that the threat of divorce is merely another negotiating ploy in her attempt to overturn their nuptial contract. "If you file for divorce," he warns his estranged wife, "you won't get a nickel."

Later that same afternoon Ivana's attorney, Michael Kennedy, prepares to have divorce papers served on The Donald's attorney Stanford Lotwin, a divorce expert assisting Jay Goldberg. Then Kennedy gets an unexpected call from *New York Post* gossip columnist Cindy Adams. She has obviously been contacted as part of what appears to be a preemptive public relations strike by Ivana's husband.

"I just got word from Donald that he's filing for divorce," Adams says.

"Just say it's mutual," Kennedy replies, not bothering to belabor the fact that Ivana, not The Donald, is the one who is filing for divorce.

Three days later, on Monday, November 5, Kennedy files divorce papers on behalf of Ivana in Manhattan Supreme Court. Under New York law, there is a mandatory waiting period of sixty days before Judge Phyllis Gangel-Jacob can grant the divorce motion. But by mutual consent the parties agree to start the clock from the time Ivana filed her challenge to the Trumps' nuptial contract the previous spring. That means the divorce can be granted at almost any time.

Carl Icahn looks across his desk at Donald Trump and offers him a tuna fish sandwich. It is lunchtime on a chilly day in early November 1990. Icahn, the gaunt-faced and highly controversial corporate raider, is the chairman of TWA, one of the nation's many financially embattled airlines. Unbeknownst to the public, he is also the Trump Taj Mahal's biggest individual bondholder. The Taj Mahal's owner has come to ask him for a break. Donald wants Icahn's support for the bond debt restructuring plan he submitted back in mid-October.

"I respect you, Donald," Icahn allows. "But I bought those bonds to make money."

Icahn is likely to make money under almost any scenario. Over the past few months he has bought 18 percent of the Taj Mahal's bonds at depressed prices. Although his bonds have a total face value of $121.5 million, he paid less than $50 million to acquire them. But Icahn still thinks that Donald's offer to give the bondholders 20 percent of his equity in the Taj in return for lower interest and forgiveness of the $47.3 million November 15 payment is not good enough.

Donald leaves Icahn's office in a huff. Like Icahn, bondholder financial adviser Wilbur Ross wants him to give up 50 percent, not just 20 percent, of his stock in the Taj and to relinquish half the seats on the board of directors. Ross uses the recent bankruptcy of Resorts International for comparative purposes. He points out that Merv Griffin has just been forced to part with 80 percent of his stock. Ross's demands are echoed by Robert Miller of Berlack, Israels & Liberman, the bondholders' boyish-looking legal adviser.

Both Donald and his adversaries know that it is in everyone's interest to compromise. If the Taj is forced into involuntary bankruptcy, he could lose 100 percent of his equity in the casino, not just 20 percent. The bankruptcy court might very well allow the bondholders to exercise their first mortgage rights and take over ownership of the Taj. But Donald would still have to pay off an additional $150 million in personally guaranteed bank loans. It is not paranoia to worry that the loss of an asset like the Taj might alarm the banks into triggering an involuntary personal bankruptcy.

But if Donald and the bondholders hash out their differences, the Trump Taj Mahal can voluntarily file a so-called prepackaged bankruptcy. Such creditor repayment plans, one of which has recently been filed by the Southland Corporation, are becoming the new financial vogue of the nineties. In a prepackaged bankruptcy both the debtor and the creditors agree on the terms beforehand, thereby saving enormous amounts of time and court costs, not to mention exposure to the unpredictable judgments of a bankruptcy trustee.

But unlike Icahn, neither Ross nor Liberman has any qualms about putting the casino in bankruptcy if Donald fails to come to terms.

On the morning of November 15 Donald and representatives of the Taj bondholders meet in the offices of Berlack, Israels & Liberman. The negotiations continue into the night. At the stroke of twelve the Taj Mahal's interest deadline passes. The casino is technically in default. But it looks as if the parties are on the verge of an agreement. In return for forgiving the $47.3 million November interest payment, the bondholders will get 50 percent ownership of the Taj, annual interest payments of 10 percent, and three seats on the seven-member board of directors. The bondholders will pay Donald a management fee of $500,000 a year or 1.5 percent of the gross, whichever is higher. But in order to stay in operational control of the casino hotel, he will have to adhere to strict performance criteria, including a mandate to keep the net cash flow (gross income minus expenses) within 15 percent of his annual projections.

Then Donald raises a red flag. He insists on including an additional performance incentive. If he is somehow able to pay the bondholders interest at the original 14 percent rate in the coming months, he wants to be able to get back 30 percent of the Taj stock. Under such a scenario, his ownership stake would rise from 50 percent back up to 80 percent. The bondholders balk. They are willing to let Donald recoup 25 percent of his original stock, but not a single point more. "Okay, that's it!" Donald announces as the sun rises over the Manhattan skyline. "I'm finished. Gone. Put it in bankruptcy." Then he gets up from the table and storms out of the room.

At ten on Friday morning Wilbur Ross arranges an emergency conference call with Icahn and several of the other major Taj bondholders. Ross is inclined to proceed with the involuntary bankruptcy petition unless Donald backs down at once. But Icahn, evidently fearing for the liquidity of his 18 percent bond stake, leaps to Donald's defense. "As bondholders, you shouldn't care if Donald gets the stock so long as you get what you bargained for as bondholders," Icahn lectures. The two sides, he notes, are only five percentage points apart on a pie-in-the-sky provision. "If Donald Trump wants the 5 percent so bad he'll walk [out of negotiations]," Icahn reasons, "that shows he'll work hard to pay us off."

Icahn's logic prevails. Shortly before 11:00 A.M. Ross and attorney

Miller invite Donald back to the negotiating table. They inform him that the bondholders will give him the additional five percentage points of stock he wants under one condition: He has to put his name on the line. According to his own marketing surveys, gamblers are attracted to Trump casinos by the mystique associated with the Trump name. The bondholders want assurances that Donald will devote a "substantial" amount of his personal time to promoting the Taj. Donald, who is obviously flattered by the importance placed on his personal services, readily agrees.

At 2:15 P.M. Donald and Ross convene a press conference at the Plaza Hotel to announce they are putting the Taj Mahal through a prepackaged bankruptcy. The press conference marks the most bittersweet moment in Donald's career to date. For the first time a Trump property has officially declared itself a failure. But Donald still has reason to rejoice. The bondholders could have left him with next to nothing by triggering an involuntary bankruptcy.

"It was a long, hard negotiation," Donald tells the media, "and I think it's going to be beneficial to everyone. I think we will be able to operate the Taj successfully for years to come."

Be that as it may, Donald knows that the deal with the Taj bondholders does not guarantee the overall success of his Atlantic City gaming division. In fact, he faces a possible replay of his June 1990 banking crisis on December 15, when Trump Castle is scheduled to make another $18 million interest payment to its bondholders.

On Wednesday, November 21, Michael Kennedy strikes another blow on Ivana's behalf. Much like the Taj Mahal bondholders, he wants a kind of prepackaged settlement. He knows that a protracted court battle, besides consuming time and money, will surely consume the emotional resources of his client. Kennedy still harbors a faint hope that he can get Ivana a fair share of the Trump fortune without going to trial. But he is not about to compromise too easily.

Back in the summer Kennedy informed the media that he would not settle for "less than $100 million." In the wake of the Kenneth Leventhal audit and the Taj bond crisis, he is beginning to doubt that Donald even has $100 million, much less the billions he once claimed to have. "The most I can pay Ivana right now is $1.5 million," The

Donald maintained in their most recent closed-door negotiating session. "You'd be better off just to accept the [nuptial] agreement, or you might get little or nothing in the end."

Instead of accepting the offer, Kennedy attempts to keep The Donald from liquidating any more assets. He files papers in Manhattan Supreme Court asking Judge Gangel-Jacob to attach liens to four major Trump real estate properties: the Trump Tower triplex apartment, the apartment in Trump Plaza on Third Avenue in New York, the Mar-a-Lago estate in Palm Beach, and the house in Greenwich, Connecticut. Together, the properties are valued at upwards of $24 million.

"Donald J. Trump has stated he will consent to a divorce," Kennedy's motion declares. "[But] Donald J. Trump has refused to disclose his financial circumstances." Kennedy wants to make sure that Donald did not try to sell off any of the properties to help salvage his ailing financial empire.

Donald's attorney Stanford Lotwin protests that his client "has not taken any steps to encumber or attempt to dispose of any of the . . . properties." But Judge Gangel-Jacob is unimpressed. She issues a temporary restraining order prohibiting Donald from selling the four properties his wife wants to attach. Then she sets a hearing on the lien issue for December 4 and advises the two parties that a divorce can be granted within the next thirty days.

Just as Donald's divorce battle with Ivana appears to be coming to a head, he and Marla start fighting again. Donald blames Marla for the problems in his marriage, his problems at the Trump Taj Mahal, and just about every other problem that comes to mind. Marla is getting sick of being criticized for things they both know are not her fault. "I'm leaving, Donald," she announces, and walks out.

To her surprise, Donald does not give chase. Instead he plays the field with the help of his pal Larry Russo, who has recently joined the Trump Organization's real estate division. One of the first sex objects of Donald's attention is Rowanne Brewer, a statuesque twenty-three-year-old swimsuit model who once appeared as a contestant on the television program "Star Search." Rowanne's most recent romantic attachment prior to meeting Donald was to twenty-three-year-old white rap singer Vanilla Ice. She and Ice were photographed in the back seat of a limousine squirting honey down each other's throats.

In December Donald and Rowanne are photographed walking hand in hand to a boxing match at the Trump Taj Mahal in Atlantic City. That same month Donald takes her to the Elite modeling agency's Christmas party in New York. Rumors circulate that Donald has asked the Elite agency to arrange an AIDS test for Rowanne for the obvious reasons. According to one well-known show business celebrity who has dated Rowanne in the past, she and Donald "are not just friends."

Ivana Trump's limousine arrives in front of Manhattan Superior Court at about half past eleven on the morning of Tuesday, December 11. It is a gray day, and Ivana is wearing a gray dress. Her mother, Maria Zelnicek, still mourning her husband's death, is wearing black. There has been no public notice that today is anything special in the case of *Trump v. Trump*. Only the regular beat reporters are milling about the blue police barricades flanking the courthouse steps. Michael Kennedy whisks the two women up the steps and into the judge's chambers before most of the TV crews even have time to get their cameras rolling.

Moments later, sobbing profusely with Kennedy at her side, Ivana is standing in Judge Phyllis Gangel-Jacob's royal blue-walled courtroom. The Donald is not present, but one of his divorce attorneys, the bearish, balding Stanford Lotwin, hulks across the aisle. Gangel-Jacob, a strawberry-haired veteran jurist who seems to have little love for The Donald, looks down from the bench at Ivana and recites the divorce decrees.

"I grant you a divorce from Donald Trump on the grounds of cruel and inhuman treatment and particularly Donald Trump's flaunting of his relationship with Marla Maples," she intones.

That ends the thirteen-year marriage of Donald John Trump and Ivana Zelnicekova Winklmayr Trump. But it does not resolve the big issue: money. Donald and Ivana are still millions of dollars apart on that one, and it appears that a courtroom confrontation is inevitable in the next ninety days.

Judge Gangel-Jacob announces that Ivana will get custody of the Trumps' three children. She then informs the attorneys that all other matters—such as maintenance, child support, and the validity of the couple's nuptial contract—will be decided at trial unless the parties otherwise resolve them on their own.

Ivana leaves the courthouse the same way she came in, crying out loud all the way down the steps. As she ducks into a waiting limousine, she sniffles a parting comment to a gaggle of TV reporters who have suddenly assembled outside the courthouse: "It's very sad for me, for the children, for our families, and for everyone concerned."

It is a sad day for The Donald as well. In the past few weeks he has lost his wife, his mistress, and half his crown jewel casino in Atlantic City. He has also lost his image as the man with the Midas touch. High-ranking sources in the Trump Organization are privately telling reporters that Donald will need to borrow as much as $180 million in the next few months simply to stay afloat. The possibility that he might lose as much as half of whatever he has left in a divorce settlement with Ivana hardly bolsters the confidence of his bankers and bondholders.

Nor does it hearten the New Jersey Casino Control Commission, which commenced financial stability hearings on the Taj Mahal on December 3. Donald did not appear at the hearings. It was just as well. Try as they might, his lieutenants could not paint a rosy picture of the casino's future. For starters, the ballyhooed prepackaged bankruptcy agreement with the bondholders is not yet a done deal; it will take several more months to go through mandatory SEC and court approvals, during which time the bondholders could easily change their minds.

Until some firm settlement can be reached, the Taj will continue to wallow in the financial doldrums. The casino's gross revenues through November have averaged $34.7 million, well below the break-even mark of $39 million a month. Not surprisingly, Donald's newly hired chief financial officer, Steve Bollenbach, admits under questioning that the Taj is not financially stable. According to Trump gaming division executives, there is only one way the Taj can make future bond interest payments: by borrowing more money. To that end they say they are arranging a new $70 million line of credit.

The outlook for Trump Castle is more dire. On December 17 the Castle and Trump Plaza are scheduled to make bond interest payments totaling $34.5 million. It appears that the Plaza will be able to make its portion of the payment, some $16.1 million, with less than $1 million to spare. But according to figures submitted to the Casino Control Commission during the first week in December, the Castle has only $18 million cash in its accounts. That is not enough to cover the casino's regular monthly payroll and its December interest payment of $18.4 million.

Donald knows he is down, but he is far from out. Though he has managed to alienate or isolate himself from most of the people who were once closest to him, there is still one person to whom he can turn for help. It is the one person who has never let him down in the past: his father, Fred C. Trump, Sr.

On the afternoon of Monday, December 17, 1990, a middle-aged man in a business suit, followed by a police escort, enters the lobby of Trump Castle in Atlantic City. The man crosses the lushly carpeted casino floor followed by a police escort, and walks up to the cashier's cage, where he presents a certified check for $3.5 million. The check entitles him to buy seven hundred gray colored gambling chips worth $5,000 each. But the man does not withdraw the chips and attempt to play them at the surrounding table games. Instead he leaves the chips in the cage, gets a receipt from the cashier, and walks out of the casino with his police escort following close behind.

That same evening Trump Castle stuns the gaming industry and most of its own junk bondholders by making its scheduled $18.4 million December interest payment. "I thought it was a good thing to do," Donald tells reporter David Johnston of the *Philadelphia Inquirer,* claiming that he has made the payment "with a small infusion of cash from the Trump Organization," rather than draw on outside sources. That, as the New Jersey Casino Control Commission soon discovers, is another big lie.

For the time being, however, Donald acts as if he has gotten a new long-term lease on life. "For the last three or four years, I became complacent in the sense that I was doing really well, I was making a lot of money, and I really didn't have to work very hard," he admits in an interview shortly after making the Trump Castle interest payment. "I'm working harder now than I ever have before, or than I have since I started the company, and frankly, it's really paying off.

I relied on other people with respect to the Taj Mahal, and now I'm doing it all myself. I don't want to rely on anybody."

At the same time Donald brags about having Sunshine back in his life. Former lobbyist and real estate aide Louise Sunshine, who left the Trump Organization amid a dispute over her partnership interest in Trump Plaza in New York, recently signed on as an independent consultant. Although most of the Manhattan market remains mired in recession, Sunshine claims that the values of Trump properties have appreciated 30 percent in the preceding twelve months. She is equally sanguine about the prospects for Donald's personal recovery.

"Donald's got his act together," Sunshine says in an interview. "Now he is completely focused, regardless of what people say. I know. I get forty phone calls from him a day. If Donald stays focused, he will succeed. He will survive and be in a better position than he's ever been in."

But focus is still a problem when it comes to Donald's romantic interests. Although he openly brags about Rowanne Brewer's sexual prowess in the back of the Trump limousine ("She gives great blow jobs!" he has exclaimed on more than one occasion), he complains about her lack of conversational skills and social sophistication. "This one's as dumb as they come," he has confided to a friend. Much as he has enjoyed his newfound freedom to play the man-about-town, he remains horrified by the risk of contracting herpes or AIDS. And much as he hates to admit it, he still pines for the eternally petulant presence of Marla Maples.

"I believe Donald really gets off on fighting with Marla and vice versa," observes a mutual friend. "Both of them are control freaks."

Unfortunately Marla is incommunicado. Donald orders his security men to track her down, but they cannot find a trace of her. Then, a couple of days after the Christmas party he attended with Rowanne Brewer, Donald gets a distraught telephone call from Ann Ogletree. Marla's mother reports that her daughter has flown to Aspen, Colorado, and right into another romantic mess. One night Marla went dancing at a trendy new Aspen night spot called the Caribou Club, where she bumped into rival real estate mogul Mohammed Hadid, the Palestinian developer who is trying to build a Ritz-Carlton Hotel at the base of Ajax Mountain. Hadid, who is married and a father, allegedly kept flirting with her.

"You've got to rescue her," Marla's mother pleads.

Donald finally manages to reach Marla by telephone from New York. She tells him that Hadid is in her room at that very moment. Donald cannot control his jealousy. Hadid then gets on the phone and berates Donald for mistreating Marla. "You're a flying asshole," the Palestinian developer informs the New York developer. Marla plays the telephonic confrontation for all it is worth, believing that Donald will soon come crawling back to her, asking for forgiveness.

"The guy's in love with me," she confides to Tom Fitzsimmons after the three-way conference call. "I just know it."

She is right. Within hours of the shouting match with Hadid, Donald calls Marla and begs her to come back to New York in time for Christmas. Marla coyly agrees. Upon her return the couple starts making plans to take a post-Christmas vacation together in Colorado. But rather than go back to Aspen, they decide to try Telluride, an almost-as-exclusive ski resort on the western slope of the Rocky Mountains.

On Christmas Eve 1990 Ivana Trump attends midnight mass at St. Patrick's Cathedral in New York. The following morning she allows The Donald to pick up their three children at Trump Tower and take them out to Queens for Christmas Day lunch with Fred and Mary Trump. While the children are lunching with their grandparents, she packs her bags in preparation for another ski trip to Aspen. In light of what had happened there the year before, Michael Kennedy suggests that she might want to consider a change of vacation venues.

"No," she tells her attorney. "I will be going to Aspen."

Celebrity wedding bells ring on both sides of the Continental Divide during the days preceding New Year's 1991. Ivana cannot help hearing or reading about almost all of them. On December 15 forty-five-year-old rock and roll star Rod Stewart married twenty-three-year-old model Rachel Hunter in Beverly Hills, California. On Christmas Eve movie star Tom Cruise, age twenty-eight, married Australian actress Nicole Kidman, age twenty-three, in a rented ski chalet in Telluride.

On December 31 Ivana runs smack into another celebrity wedding in progress. Television game show hostess Vanna White, age thirty-three, is marrying forty-four-year-old Los Angeles restauranteur George Santopietro at Little Nell's, the hotel where Ivana is staying. Actor George Hamilton, Santopietro's best man, catches the garter. Ivana pops in on the White-Santopietro wedding reception just long enough to be polite. Then she celebrates her son Donny's twelfth birthday with her mother and the other children and goes to bed.

Across the snow-covered Rockies in Telluride, Donald and Marla Maples throw a small private party that lasts just past midnight. They are staying at a rustic-looking but fully modernized log cabin about fifteen miles downvalley from where Tom Cruise and Nicole Kidman got married. The place is owned by a group of architects from Phoenix, Arizona, and Donald's guests are mostly fellow real estate developers from Phoenix who happen to know the owners. Marla wears a blue, sequined, figure-flattering pantsuit. Donald wears slacks and a turtleneck.

"What do you think of Marla versus Ivana?" Donald repeatedly asked strangers he met on the ski slopes that week. He later answers his own question with typical bravura.

"You know people have said that I'm a forty-year-old married woman's worst nightmare," he says in a a subsequent interview. "I made Ivana a very popular woman. Before, she was not popular. She was mean. People didn't like her. Now everyone loves her. I told Marla, 'You know, I could make you popular by going out with Rowanne.' "

Donald appears to be in a fence-mending mood. At 9:00 P.M. the guests at his New Year's Eve party finish eating dinner and go into an adjoining room where a local rock band launches into a set of copy tunes. Donald and Marla discreetly steal away to the bedroom. Instead of making the obvious move, he picks up the telephone and begins calling various friends and foes to wish them Happy New Year. One of the people he calls is Mohammed Hadid, whose expression of stunned disbelief provides just the kind of lift he is looking for.

"Things are really going great," Donald boasts to a national magazine writer that same night. "Some press understands that, some press doesn't understand. My current deals are better than my past deals. In two years I'm going to be worth more than they said I was worth before."

Donald and Marla rejoin their guests just in time to ring in the New Year. Then, shortly after midnight, they slip out of the house and go for a drive. There is a blue moon shining full and bright in the Colorado sky, and beneath its magical glow all things seem possible, even a comeback by a bankrupt billionaire.

"You know," Donald muses philosophically upon his return to the East Coast a few days later, "it really doesn't matter what they write about you as long as you've got a young and beautiful piece of ass. . . .

"But," he adds after a pause suggesting that this is a distinction with a difference, "she's got to be young and beautiful."

On January 15, 1991, the DGE chief, Jack Sweeney, sends an official letter to Trump attorney Nick Ribis. The subject of the letter is the mysterious purchase of $3.5 million worth of unplayed gambling chips at Trump Castle shortly before the casino made its December 1990 bond payment. As it turns out, the man who bought the chips is an attorney named Howard Snyder, who was acting on behalf of Fred C. Trump, Sr. The $3.5 million Donald's father deposited in Trump Castle's cashier's cage was what enabled the casino to pay its bond obligation. That, in the opinion of DGE director Sweeney, made it the equivalent of a loan.

Fred Trump's chip purchase raises some serious legal and political questions. It is a one-of-a-kind deal, a first in the history of Atlantic City, and its behind-the-scenes history smacks of official favoritism toward the Trump Organization. Ribis notified Sweeney several days prior to the transaction that it might occur. At the time the DGE chief did not voice any specific objections to the deal. Now, nearly a month after the fact, Sweeney is singing a different tune.

According to state gaming statutes, anyone who lends money to an Atlantic City casino has to qualify as an officially sanctioned financial source. That means going through lengthy background investigations and Casino Control Commission hearings similar to those Donald faced in applying for a casino operator's license. The provision is aimed at keeping mob influences out of Atlantic City, but it applies equally to Fred Trump and everyone else. Wittingly or unwittingly Donald's old man has broken the law. That, in turn, exposes his son to penalties ranging from monetary fines to outright license revocation.

Unfortunately for Donald and the lenient-minded Sweeney, *Wall Street Journal* reporter Neil Barsky has gotten wind of Fred Trump's chips purchase. Barsky writes a story about the unusual transaction that appears in the paper's January 21 edition. Donald's critics delight in seeing him suffer the apparent humiliation of having had to ask his old man for money. But Donald senses that he is about to dodge another bullet. He cannot resist putting a favorable spin on the facts for mass-media consumption.

"First of all, people found it to be a very unique method of financing, and I think I got a lot of credit for imagination," he insists in an interview. "It's great security for my father, and I wouldn't have it any other way. I have a father who's really a good guy. He's my best friend. I've done a lot of deals for him and they've been fantastic deals. It's different when you're talking to your father than when it's someone with a less personal relationship. He didn't have to do it. And if he didn't do it, I would have made the payment anyway. But it was an easy way of circumventing—an easy way of doing something—and it worked out great."

So far anyway. Donald's father certainly does not object. As attorney Nick Ribis remarks in amazement, "Fred Trump gave us the three and a half million like it was thirty-five cents." Whether the old man, who is about to celebrate his eighty-sixth birthday, will stand up under the pressure and scrutiny of Casino Control Commission licensing hearings remains to be seen. But that is not the only dark cloud on his son's horizon.

Despite Fred Trump Sr.'s lending largess, the entire Trump gaming division is teetering on the brink of collapse. Neither Trump Castle nor Trump Plaza is out of the financial woods. If the two casinos do not immediately improve their cash flows, they will not be able to make the next round of bond payments in June. Worse, there are rumors that Carl Icahn may be balking at the deal he helped strike with Taj Mahal bondholders to put the Taj through a prepackaged bankruptcy. There are also nagging complaints coming from Castle and Plaza bondholders and a lawsuit alleging that Donald used their customer lists to promote the Taj.

Donald reacts by ordering major shake-ups in the executive ranks of all three of his Atlantic City casinos. On January 23 attorney Ribis replaces Ed Tracy as head of the Trump gaming division. Tracy's responsibilities will henceforth be confined to running the Taj, a limitation designed to mollify dissident bondholders. The Trump Plaza president Gary Selesner, who replaced the disgruntled Jack O'Donnell, is himself replaced by thirty-eight-year-old Kevin DeSanctis, a veteran of the Mirage in Las Vegas. The Trump Castle president Tony Calandra, the brother of Ivana's executive assistant, is demoted to a marketing position at Trump Plaza. He is replaced by veteran casino executive Roger Wagner, who has won praise for keeping the Claridge afloat during the citywide slump. In what promises to be the first of many cost-cutting moves, Wagner promptly lays off 190 of the Castle's 3,600 employees.

Just as Donald's casino empire begins contracting, one of his archrivals begins positioning himself for expansion. On January 29 the Hilton Hotels Corporation announces that it has applied for a casino license in Atlantic City. This is the second time at bat for Barron Hilton. He was denied a gaming license back in 1985, ultimately being forced to sell the property that became Trump Castle. In *Surviving at the Top*, Donald scorned Barron as a member of the Lucky Sperm Club. It now appears that the slur may come back to haunt him. "Hilton is waiting in the wings," predicts one Atlantic City insider. "If Icahn or the other bondholders blow the whistle on Donald, Hilton will be ready to come in and manage the properties for them."

Back in New York, Donald faces similar problems both on and off the ground. On January 17 President George Bush orders U.S. warplanes to attack Iraq. Donald feels the war's negative impact in two ways. First, there is a precipitous drop in the number of passengers riding the Trump Shuttle. Second, the war devastates the hotel trade, particularly in New York, where occupancy rates plummet. The slump could not have come at a worse time for the Plaza Hotel. According to insiders, the Plaza is already losing money at a rate of almost $2 million a month. And none of this bodes well for Donald's biggest problem on the home front: his ongoing legal battle against Ivana.

On Thursday, January 24, one week after the United States' attack on Iraq, Judge Phyllis Gangel-Jacob summons the Trumps to her chambers in Manhattan Supreme Court for a settlement conference. The session lasts three hours. But neither party gives ground.

"A deal's a deal," The Donald keeps saying, referring to his demand that the court enforce the couple's 1987 nuptial contract.

"Forget about the agreement," Judge Gangel-Jacob instructs, signaling that it will probably not be upheld if the couple's case goes to trial.

As Ivana breaks into tears under the stress of the negotiations, The Donald changes tack. He says he will forget about the nuptial contract per the judge's instructions. Instead he is prepared to offer Ivana "almost twice" the $10 million in cash she stands to receive under the nuptial contract if she agrees to settle out of court. He assures both Ivana and the judge that he can get the money despite his highly publicized financial crisis.

"That is not enough," Ivana sobs.

"That no-good bitch!" Donald screams at Ivana's attorney, Michael Kennedy. "Look at her with that fucking piece of Kleenex in her hand."

Four days later the Trumps and their attorneys return to Judge Gangel-Jacob's chambers. Now Kennedy changes tack. His independent investigations have confirmed that Donald has never been worth $100 million, much less $3 billion, as he once claimed. Kennedy informs the judge that Ivana is willing to accept the $20 million in cash Donald offered at their last closed-door conference. Donald says that he can get the money. But before he agrees to settle, he insists that Ivana meet his demands on two other issues.

First, Donald wants Ivana and the children to move out of the Trump Tower triplex within five years. Second, he insists on enforcing the gag clause in their nuptial contract. The clause prohibits her from publishing "any diary, memoir, letter, story, photograph, interview, article, essay, account, or description or depiction of any kind whatsoever, whether fictionalized or not, concerning her marriage to DONALD or any other aspect of DONALD's personal business or financial affairs . . . in any communications medium, including, without limitation, books, magazines, television. . . ."

Ivana balks on both points.

On Thursday, January 31, Judge Gangel-Jacob advises the Trumps that if they cannot agree to an out-of-court settlement, the case will go to trial on April 18. Both Donald and Ivana want to avoid the public spectacle of a trial at almost all costs. But all of a sudden the money issue becomes a problem. Donald now claims he cannot pay Ivana the $20 million he previously offered or even the $10 million specified by their nuptial contract. He says he is willing and able to pay only $8.2 million. When Ivana rejects the $8.2 million offer, Donald and his attorneys get up and walk out. Then he flies down to Florida to spend the weekend at Mar-a-Lago with Marla Maples.

A few days later Ivana gets an unexpected telephone call from Fred Trump, Sr. The old man begins the conversation by exchanging a few pleasantries. Then he asks his daughter-in-law if she would be willing to return a Rolls-Royce she recently shipped from Florida to New York, reminding her that he, not Donald, paid for the car.

"Oh, Daddy, I love that car," Ivana whines. "It was my birthday present."

"Okay, honey," the old man says. "I guess you ought to keep it then."

Fred Trump's telephone call unnerves both Ivana and her attorney, Michael Kennedy. They have no doubt that The Donald put the old man up to it. But they now worry that Donald might really be broke and unable to make good on even the $10 million payment specified by the couple's nuptial contract. The moment of truth is rapidly approaching. According to New York law, they can insist that the judge enforce the contract on March 11, ninety days after the final divorce decree. As Kennedy mulls what to do, their adversary pulls another headline-making stunt.

On the afternoon of March 5, 1990, all the major players in the future of Manhattan's Upper West Side squeeze into the Blue Room at City Hall to see and hear what none of them had thought was possible. Among the official dignitaries and community activists are Mayor David N. Dinkins, Manhattan Borough President Ruth W. Messinger, City Councilmember Ronnie M. Eldridge, State Senator Manfred Ohrenstein, and Westpride executive director Catharine

Carey, all of whom have voiced staunch opposition to the development of the West Side yards as proposed by Donald J. Trump.

Then in comes Donald himself, sporting his trademark blue overcoat, a blue Brioni suit, a pink French-cuffed shirt, a flame red tie, and, of all things, a Westpride button. The Trump entourage includes the usual complement of bodyguards, attorney Nick Ribis, his faithful executive secretary, Norma Foerderer, and his father, Fred C. Trump, Sr., nattily attired in a gray suit with a red tie and matching red handkerchief.

"Today, I have good news regarding the future of our city," Mayor Dinkins proclaims. "The city, the state of New York, Donald Trump, and a consortium of civic organizations have reached an agreement that will serve as the basis of a new plan for the Penn Yards site on the West Side of Manhattan."

Specifically, the mayor continues, the agreed-on development will include the creation of a 23-acre waterfront park on the West Side yards to be paid for by property owner Donald Trump, who will also provide free right-of-way to the city for a new elevated highway to be built east of the existing West Side Highway with funds from the state and federal governments. In return for these concessions, Donald will get a chance to fulfill one of his fondest dreams in a significantly scaled-down fashion. The new plan for the West Side yards, which remains subject to formal city and state approval and environmental review, calls for the development of 8.3 million square feet instead of the proposed 14 million square feet.

Unlike the much-ballyhooed TV City and Trump City proposals of the past, the new West Side yards project will not include "the world's tallest skyscraper" reaching 150 stories high. Donald still plans to build television and motion-picture studios and about 300,000 square feet of offices. But most of the site will be devoted to residential use, with buildings limited in height to the 30- to 40-story range. In fact, the new plan affords Donald only one million square feet more space than he could build without any zoning change. A reporter asks if the compromise is a blow to his ego.

Donald blushes uncontrollably and again turns to Mayor Dinkins. "Should it be?" he asks.

"No, it should not," Dinkins rejoins with a broad smile. "It should be a boost to your pride."

Donald rejoices in the begrudgingly favorable stories that appear in the *New York Times* and the local tabloids following the Blue Room press conference. "If half a loaf is better than none, then a downsized development project is better than what amounts to a world-class vacant lot," declares a *New York Post* editorial. "Some of his opponents revel in the fact that Trump's financial difficulties have led him to compromise on this development. They seem to forget that his business problems reflect a larger economic recession—a circumstance that has caused thousands of New Yorkers actually to lose their jobs."

Few members of the media note the irony of New York's latest alliance with Donald Trump. When Donald's financial crisis became apparent back in the summer, Manhattan Borough President Messinger proposed that city take advantage of the situation and offer to buy back the West Side yards at a fire sale price. Mayor Dinkins reacted with well-founded skepticism. "If they're selling elephants two for a quarter, that's a great bargain," Dinkins observed at the time, "but only if you have a quarter and only if you need elephants."

New York City is still short of quarters and hardly in need of more real estate elephants. The same goes for Donald Trump. It makes little sense to build millions of square feet of new buildings when tens of millions of square feet of old and recently completed structures remain vacant for want of tenants. By compromising with city officials and community activists, Donald has broken a protracted political logjam. But considering his deepening financial difficulties, it is unlikely that any of the big lending institutions will agree to back him on yet another multibillion-dollar undertaking. In fact, he openly admits that he will probably sell off pieces of the West Side yards site to other developers to raise cash.

On Wednesday, March 13, the Trumps' attorneys gather in Judge Phyllis Gangel-Jacob's courtroom for an extraordinary hearing. It is time for Donald to pay up or shut up. But his lawyer, Stanford Lotwin, delivers a stunning message on behalf of his client: Donald cannot pay Ivana the $10 million because he does not have the money, at least not at the present time. Lotwin proposes a compromise: Donald will pay $3 million on March 18, another $2 million thirty days after that, and the remaining $5 million ninety days after that.

Michael Kennedy is livid. Three months before, on the date the Trumps' divorce became final, he had asked the judge to order Donald to set aside a minimum of $10 million in cash. Donald's attorney opposed the motion. At the time Lotwin believed that the case was destined to go to trial; therefore, he claimed, the matter of making payment was moot until the court determined what Donald actually owed his ex-wife.

Kennedy says he will go along with Lotwin's proposal under two conditions. First, he wants the judge to lift the gag clause in the nuptial contract. Secondly, he tells the court, "I want Donald Trump to come in here and declare under oath that he won't declare bankruptcy before he makes payment [on the nuptial contract]."

Judge Gangel-Jacob refuses to lift the gag clause entirely, but she rules that a potential violation by Ivana cannot be used by Donald as an excuse to stop payments specified by their nuptial contract. The judge further orders that the deeds to the house in Greenwich and the apartment in Trump Plaza be transferred into Ivana's name on March 18. She also allows Kennedy to file sequestration papers on the Trump Tower triplex, preventing Donald from selling off the property or forcing his ex-wife to move out.

The next day Donald capitulates. He tells his attorneys to advise the court that he will pay Ivana the $10 million in full on March 21. Donald does not say how he is going to come up with the money he claimed not to have just twenty-four hours earlier. But it does not take long for Kennedy and the inner circle of Trump creditors to find out. Donald sends a letter to the seven biggest banks that signed the June 1990 credit and override agreements. Under those agreements the banks pledged to provide him with $65 million worth of bridge loans; so far they have released only $47 million of that amount. Donald asks them to release $10 million of the remaining $18 million so he can pay off his ex-wife.

Donald's bankers react with shock and chagrin. Early the following week attorneys for several of the bigger institutions convene a strategy session at the law offices of Wachtell, Lipton, Rosen & Katz, which represents Bankers Trust. At first most of the banks oppose the idea of lending Donald money to pay a divorce settlement. But they also know that if they do not let him have the money, Ivana may force her ex-husband to declare bankruptcy. That, in turn, would seriously imperil the banks' chances of getting back the money they have already lent Donald.

"The question is whether it's in Ivana's interest to put Mr. Trump in bankruptcy given her present situation," an unnamed bank representative tells the *Wall Street Journal*.

Donald obviously believes his bankers will see the light. On Friday, March 15, he hosts a closed-circuit telecast of the Mike Tyson-Razor Ruddock boxing match in the grand ballroom of the Plaza Hotel. In addition to a sampling of bank and bondholder attorneys, the crowd includes Donald's executive secretary, Norma Foerderer; his long-time financial adviser, Harvey Freeman; his Atlantic City gaming division chief, Nick Ribis; his personal stockbroker, Alan C. ("Ace") Greenberg; his divorce attorneys, Jay Goldberg and Stanford Lotwin; Marla's ex-boyfriend, Tom Fitzsimmons, and her publicist, Chuck Jones; his running buddy and real estate aide, Larry Russo (who arrives with model agency head John Casablancas and four leggy young females in tow); and of course, his father, Fred C. Trump, Sr.

The only notable absentee is Donald's mistress, Marla Maples. As he explains to *New York Post* gossip columnist Cindy Adams, who is seated at one of the more prominent tables, he has ordered Marla to lie low in Atlantic City. Then Donald and his divorce attorneys give Adams a big scoop: A settlement with Ivana is imminent, and he does not want to create a last-minute conflagration by being seen in public with Marla. Donald naturally claims victory as if it were a self-fulfilling prophecy. He informs Adams that Ivana is going to be paid according to the provisions of the couple's "ironclad" nuptial contract, and not a penny more.

Then, as the ballroom lights dim and the featured boxers appear on the closed-circuit TV screen, Donald sits down beside his father, Fred C. Trump, Sr., and lays his head on the old man's shoulder like a little boy seeking comfort from the storms that swirl about him.

On Thursday, March 21, Donald arrives at Manhattan Supreme Court with a $10 million check in hand. Ivana does not show, and neither does her attorney, Michael Kennedy. Donald feigns outrage as he stomps out of the courtroom.

"We had a transaction done and completed, but the other party isn't here," he tells a local television news reporter on the courthouse steps. "Perhaps they want some more cars or houses. It's ridiculous."

Judge Gangel-Jacob begs to differ. "[The case] is not settled," she informs reporters. "It was never settled. It may soon be settled." In fact, she says she scheduled the day's conference not to end the case but to see if a settlement is still possible.

The judge does not disclose that several points of dispute remain unresolved. One of them, as Donald has hinted, is Ivana's demand to keep her Mercedes convertible with the personalized license plates. Another sticking point involves the Trump Tower triplex. According the couple's nuptial contract, Donald has to pay Ivana $4 million if she vacates the apartment prior to its being sold. Michael Kennedy wants to know where Donald will get that $4 million and when.

The third and final sticking point involves the $10 million cash payment Donald will owe Ivana the day the judge orders the nuptial contract to take effect. Donald insists on paying with a personal check. Michael Kennedy insists on receiving a certified check that would be guaranteed not to bounce.

"I'd rather take a check from the Bank of Iraq than your personal check," Kennedy informed Donald the day before. When Donald allegedly refused to pay with a certified check, Kennedy claims, the judge informed both sides she was canceling the March 21 court-room conference.

But Donald has managed to pull another rabbit—in this case, a certified check—out of his debt-holed hat. Where he got the $10 million remains a mystery. But according to one well-informed insider, Donald's banks refused to lend him the money, forcing him to turn once again to his only steadfast source of funds, his father. In effect, he is planning to settle his divorce in the same way he staved off Trump Castle's creditors—with more chips off the old block.

Donald immediately sees an opportunity to do some grandstand-ing that will make his ex-wife look bad. "I'm here with what I'm sup-posed to be here with . . . a certified check," he tells reporters, displaying the check for them to see. "What more does she want? This is ridiculous. She's nickel and diming me."

Later that day Michael Kennedy releases his own statement to the media: "Contrary to the statements of Mr. Trump's lawyers, the case has not been settled and will not settle until Mr. Trump honors his obligation to Mrs. Trump and her children."

At 5:00 P.M. on Friday, March 22, Michael and Eleanore Kennedy escort Ivana Trump into the Lexington Avenue law offices of Tenzer, Greenblatt, Fallon and Kaplan, the home turf of Donald's attorney Stanford Lotwin. The parties negotiate for the next seven hours. Both sides threaten to walk out or let the case go to trial rather than concede on any of the disputed issues, which include arguments about such seemingly trivial assets as their son Eric's home computer and their daughter Ivanka's bedroom set. At one point Donald leaves the room, flies down to Atlantic City for a promotional event at one of his casinos, and flies back.

Finally, almost at the stroke of midnight, the Trumps strike a mutually acceptable deal. The terms of their settlement basically follow the letter and spirit of their 1987 nuptial contract. Donald agrees to pay Ivana the specified $10 million in cash with a cashier's check. He also pledges to pay her $350,000 a year until she remarries and an additional $300,000 a year in child support payments. Ivana will get to keep her Mercedes and the right to occupy Mar-a-Lago each year during the month of March. Donald will be trusted to pay the $4 million housing allowance specified in their nuptial contract at such time as the Trump Tower triplex is sold or she moves out.

Ivana signs the settlement papers and rushes off with Eleanore Kennedy. Despite the ongoing settlement talks, she has scheduled her annual all-female spa party at Mar-a-Lago for that weekend. She has bags to pack and a plane to catch. Donald watches them go with a sneer on his face and snide thoughts about grasping females on his mind.

"Well, I got rid of one," he remarks to Michael Kennedy, who lingers just long enough to pick up a copy of the settlement papers."Now I have to get rid of one more and I'll be free."

Then he leaves to catch a flight for Los Angeles, where Marla Maples is acting as the celebrity host for "Wrestlemania VII."

■ IT IS SUNDAY, May 5, 1991, a sparkling spring day in Atlantic City, and Marla Maples's spirits are rising even higher than the Trump helicopter she is riding in. The luxuriously appointed Super Puma is hurtling toward New York City with Marla's mother, Ann Ogletree, Marla's ex-boyfriend, Tom Fitzsimmons, and her current boyfriend, Donald J. Trump, on board.

All of a sudden Donald reaches into his coat pocket and pulls out a diamond-speckled Tiffany engagement ring he has just bought at the jewelry store in the Trump Taj Mahal.

"Marla," he asks, proffering the ring, "will you marry me?"

Marla looks at Donald with loving eyes and parted lips. "Yes," she sighs above the din of the chopper blades.

Then Marla slips on the ring and gives her fiancé a big kiss.

Donald's proposal could not have come at a better time for her. Just a few days before he and Ivana agreed on a financial settlement, the April issue of *Mirabella* magazine published a savage feature entitled "The Meaning of Marla Maples: A Social History of the American Bimbo." Feminist writer Elizabeth Kaye observed: "Like Donna Rice or Allison Stern or any of the flawless women who became the obsession of privileged men, Marla is the perfect coda to thirty years of the Women's Movement. Hers is the triumph of a retro woman with retro wiles, evidence that the more things change the more they remain the same."

Almost simultaneously, an internal power struggle erupted within the Trump Organization. Nick Ribis, the newly installed head of the

Trump gaming division, fired Atlantic City security men Lynwood Smith and Jim Farr, supposedly as part of a cost-cutting program. Marla strenuously objected to the dismissals. She had a soft spot in her heart for the two burly bodyguards who often escorted her about town in the boss's absence. When Donald refused to reinstate the two security men. Ribis commented to friends that Marla might be the next to go. Now the tables have turned. Rather than be on the way out, it looks as if Marla is at last on her way to becoming Mrs. Donald J. Trump.

But as Marla soon discovers, Donald has many things other than marrying her on his mind. He is still consumed with jealousy and bitterness toward his ex-wife and obsessed with getting back at her in and out of court by perpetuating the legal war styled as the case of *Trump v. Trump*.

On May 10, just five days after his proposal to Marla, Donald finds out that Ivana is scheduled to appear on ABC's "20 / 20," a prime-time national television program cohosted by their mutual friend Barbara Walters. That afternoon his lawyer Jay Goldberg fires off a letter to Ivana's lawyer, Michael Kennedy, charging that any interview she may give will violate the gag clause in the Trumps' nuptial contract. Goldberg warns that "unless [Ivana] takes immediate steps to see that the program scheduled for tonight on ABC is not aired, she, along with ABC, will be held accountable for substantial additional money damages."

Ivana ignores the threat, and so does ABC. At ten o'clock on the night of May 10, the "20 / 20" segment airs as scheduled. Barbara Walters begins her report with a brief recap of what has happened in the saga of Trump versus Trump over the past year and a half, culminating with a summary of their recent divorce settlement. Walters notes that at one point Ivana demanded considerably more money than she was promised under the couple's 1987 nuptial contract. She asks Ivana why she agreed to accept the contract after all.

"Well, when we started a year ago, Donald was worth billions, we were worth billions," Ivana replies. "And after seeing what was happening in last year, I knew that I could end up with absolutely nothing. I don't want to take a chance."

Then she adds: "I do believe that when we settle our case, I do believe that it was probably not last asset—because there are many wonderful assets—but in pure cash, I do believe The Donald really gave me the last of it. And I really do believe that he did want to take care of me and children."

Walters turns the discussion back to the Aspen incident, a subject allegedly under the purview of the gag clause. Ivana briefly recounts her version of the confrontation with Kim Knapp and Marla Maples at Bonnie's Beach Club restaurant. Walters asks Ivana if she thinks Donald will marry Marla. "If what makes him happy," Ivana answers in fractured English, "I think he should."

Walters asks if Ivana believes that Donald is capable of being faithful to one woman. "I don't think so," Ivana confesses. "This is why I never would want him back because I think the whole story would repeat eventually again."

Ivana goes on to admit that she does intend to marry again. She claims that she is "looking for everything but not a tycoon. . . . I have a tycoon to last me the lifetime. . . . I'm looking for love. I'm looking for somebody whom I can be with, laugh with, do things with. That's what I'm looking for."

That weekend, it suddenly appears that, as Ivana put it, "the whole story would repeat eventually again." On Saturday, May 11, the Trumps make the front page of *New York Newsday* just as in the days of old. This time the headline reads: DONALD TO IVANA: YOUR KISS-AND-TELL MAY COST YOU. The news item inside the paper reports that Donald is charging Ivana violated their nuptial contract by discussing their marriage years with Barbara Walters and may try to recoup the settlement money he gave her by means of a lawsuit.

The next day the *New York Daily News* bests *Newsday*. Gossip columnist Richard Johnson, who was one of the first members of the media to report accurately on Donald's once-secret affair with Marla Maples, reveals that Ivana has become embroiled in a secret affair of her own. In recent weeks she has been linked to a dashing cricket player from India and a real estate mogul from Iran. But Johnson reports that Ivana's new love is a semiretired inventor named Ken Lieberman. A photograph of Lieberman evidently taken at a costume ball shows a smiling late-middle-aged man dressed up as a Roman centurian; the caption reads, "IVANA'S SHINING KNIGHT."

Ivana's romance with Ken Lieberman bears striking parallels to her relationship with her late father, Milos Zelnicek, as well as to Donald's relationship with Marla. In fact, at age sixty-two, Lieberman is almost old enough to be Ivana's father. Broad-shouldered, silver-haired, and athletic, he is a chemical engineer from California who came up with a formula for a noncorrosive paint ideal for use on boat hulls. Lieberman patented the formula and pocketed enough money from its licensure that he never had to work again. By the time he crossed paths with Ivana, he was dividing his time between residences in London and Geneva and a fax-equipped yacht.

There is just one hitch: Lieberman is a once-divorced married man. He split with his first wife, who bore him three children, nearly twenty years ago and married his secretary. His second and current wife, Rosemarie, is a Swiss national who also helps oversee his financial interests. They have enjoyed a jet-setting life-style that includes Christmas trips to Aspen, spring skiing in Gstaad, and attending the tennis matches at Wimbledon.

Ivana and Ken first met at a party in London in the summer of 1990, just as news of The Donald's financial problems was hitting the front pages. At the time the Liebermans were known to be estranged, but neither had filed for divorce. Ken and Ivana started seeing each other in secret. In the spring of 1991, about the same time as Ivana and The Donald arrived at a final settlement of their divorce, the Liebermans formally separated.

Now Ivana and her new beau are ready to go public with their relationship. In the second week of May, just prior to the airing of Ivana's interview with Barbara Walters, Ken came to see her in New York. The couple dined out with friends, spent a weekend together at the Trump estate in Greenwich, and made a head-turning appearance at the American Cancer Society's annual spring gala.

On Tuesday, May 14, four days after ABC aired Ivana's interview with Barbara Walters, attorney Jay Goldberg reiterates his charge that Ivana has violated the Trumps' nuptial contract. Two days later Michael Kennedy issues a statement insisting that Ivana's "comments to Barbara Walters were fair expressions of personal opinions to which all Americans are entitled under the First Amendment to the Constitution."

That same afternoon Ivana's office issues the most surprising statement of all: "The press release given by Michael Kennedy's office today was issued without Mrs. Trump's prior knowledge or consent. Mr. Kennedy's services ended after the final divorce settlement was reached on March 22. Mr. Kennedy does not legally represent Mrs. Trump at the present time."

Neither the media nor anyone else outside the Trump inner circle know quite what to make of the apparently conflicting statements by Ivana and Kennedy. The *New York Post* leaps to the conclusion that Ivana has "fired" Kennedy. In fact, Ivana has merely succumbed to behind-the-scenes pressure from The Donald. Acutely aware that his threats still intimidate her, he allegedly promised to drop his plans to sue over the Barbara Walters interview if she issued a statement disavowing Kennedy's statement.

Ivana quickly realizes she is again being played for a fool. On May 22 Kennedy appears in front of Judge Gangel-Jacob on Ivana's behalf. Stanford Lotwin is representing Donald. That day the judge formally enters a final judgment in the case of *Trump v. Trump*. Before she does so, however, Gangel-Jacob raises the subject of the hotly disputed gag clause in the couple's nuptial contract. "I've never liked that clause," the judge declares.

"I never liked it either," Kennedy chimes.

"I'm taking it out," the judge announces, glancing over at Lotwin as she strikes the clause with her pen.

According to Kennedy's version of the judgment day story, Lotwin does not object to the judge's action but merely sighs, "All right." Lotwin, however, later denies giving his assent.

When Donald finds out what the judge has done, he erupts like an expletive-spewing volcano. As far as he is concerned, the gag clause is more important than any other part of the nuptial contract save the one limiting the amount of money he has to pay Ivana to $10 million. He orders Jay Goldberg to file an appeal of Gangel-Jacob's action with the appellate division of the New York Supreme Court, demanding that the gag clause be reinstated.

The following day Ivana sends Kennedy a "Dear Michael" note that says, "I have been very disturbed by newspaper article stating that I have 'fired' you. As you know, your services were no longer required and ended normally with the finalization of the divorce settlement. Any statements to the contrary are untrue. I have always been satisfied with your representation and would certainly engage you again, should the occasion arise in the future."

Ivana's words of praise belie a brewing schism behind the scenes. Kennedy told her he would handle her divorce case for a reduced fee, though not for free. He has sent Ivana bills amounting to about $750,000. The bulk of that billing is for the services of the law firm of White & Case, the divorce specialists who acted as Kennedy's co-counsel, and for the private investigators he hired. Kennedy's personal fee represents only $250,000. Ivana has so far paid about half the total billing of $750,000 but refuses to pay the rest.

In the interim, Ivana's former publicist, John Scanlon, submits a bill to Kennedy for $30,000 on behalf of the Daniel J. Edelman public relations firm, where he was of counsel during the media war between the Trumps. Kennedy, who has already paid Scanlon a $10,000 fee for his personal services, claims that he is being double billed and refuses to dole out another dime. Scanlon insists that Edelman did vital research work for Ivana and claims that he and the firm cut their original fee in half. He writes Kennedy a letter saying that the dispute may destroy their friendship. Kennedy replies that the cost of remaining friends is becoming "too expensive" and asks if "we can just be buddies." Scanlon immediately starts bad-mouthing both Ivana and Kennedy all over town.

"I don't know who's worse," he grumbles, "the Trumps or their lawyers."

On Friday, June 14, Donald J. Trump celebrates his forty-fifth birthday by having dinner at Marla's eighth-floor apartment in Trump Parc. The three-bedroom flat, which Marla still shares with her unemployed pal Kim Knapp, is more sparsely appointed than any room at the nearby Plaza Hotel. The living room / dining room furniture consists of a fabric-covered couch, a table, a few chairs, and a gilded mirror. There are half-packed suitcases and cardboard boxes in every corner, a sign that both women residents know they could be booted out at any moment.

Marla's apartment is a metaphor for Donald's situation as well as her own. In a recent interview with *USA Today,* Donald publicly admitted for the first time that he is in the process of "deleveraging."

That is merely a euphemism for a forced divestiture of assets accompanied by the write-off of a portion of his bad debts. Donald is now losing his trophy properties even faster than he once amassed them. Under the terms of a continually renegotiated secret accord, his bankers have agreed to release him from over $650 million of his $800 million in personally guaranteed loans. In return, he has agreed to give the banks his interest in the Grand Hyatt, his Palm Beach condominiums, his stock in the Alexander's department store chain, and the Trump Regency Hotel in Atlantic City.

In the coming weeks the banks also force Donald to part with his most expensive toys. His Boeing 727 private jet, is sold to a firm in Abu Dhabi, and the *Trump Princess* is repossessed by the Boston Safe & Deposit Company. Believing he still has the power to stand the truth on its head, Donald claims that he decided to get rid of the yacht because "I wasn't able to use it much" and that he sold it for a $15 million profit. The one major luxury item he provisionally keeps his hands on is the Super Puma, which is repossessed by the CIT Group and then leased back to one of the Trump casinos.

Donald's attempts to shore up his crumbling real estate empire have only backfired. On April 9 a front-page story in the *New York Times* announced that he was planning to convert "most of the rooms" in the Plaza Hotel to condominiums that would be sold for $1,600 a square foot, or more than three times the going rate for units in nearby buildings such as Trump Tower and Olympic Tower. Rumors have since been surfacing in the local media that Citibank plans to start foreclosure proceedings on the Plaza. Though Donald disingenuously denies the rumors, they are, for all intents and purposes, true. Citibank will agree to bide its time for a few more months. But before Donald celebrates his next birthday, the bank will demand that he part with a major stake in the landmark hotel.

Like Donald's trophy real estate properties in New York, his Atlantic City gaming division is also in legal and financial peril. On April 8 Trump Castle admitted that it had broken the law by arranging Fred Trump's purchase of $3.5 million worth of chips he never intended to gamble. The New Jersey Casino Control Commission assessed a $30,000 fine and ordered that Fred Trump, Sr., qualify for licensure as a financial source. The following week media reports revealed that Trump Castle did not expect to make its June 1991 bond payment and was trying to convince casino bondholders to accept $22.6 million worth of bonds in lieu of cash interest.

A short time later the Casino Control Commission announced its decision to move up the date of the scheduled hearing on Fred Trump's application to qualify as a financial source from June 19 to June 5. The news prompted *Wall Street Journal* reporter Neil Barsky to speculate that the rescheduling of the hearing might be a signal of more problems within the Trump empire. If Fred Trump got approved as a financial source prior to June 15, Barsky pointed out, the old man could once again be called upon to bail out his son's ailing Trump Castle casino.

Donald responded with an unusually vicious counterattack. In a *New York Post* article headlined TRUMP RIPS JOURNAL SCRIBE AS FREE-LOADER he branded Barsky's report on the rescheduling of Fred Trump's licensing hearing "an evil, vicious, false and misleading article." He claimed that Barsky, who recently won the prestigious Gerald Loeb Award for Distinguished Business & Financial Journalism for his coverage of Donald Trump, had demanded three $1,000 tickets for the April 19 heavyweight championship fight between Evander Holyfield and George Foreman in Atlantic City. After the Trump Organization obliged, Barsky allegedly demanded two more tickets and a hotel suite, which were refused. That refusal, Donald charges, is what motivated Barsky's negative story.

Both the timing and content of Donald's charges are highly suspect. According to two inside sources, Barsky is the victim of a calculated plot orchestrated by Trump gaming division chief Nick Ribis. Barsky claims that he was offered two free tickets to the Holyfield-Foreman fight, which he accepted. He says he then paid $100 for a third ticket so his father could attend the fight, only to be offered the ticket for free by the Trump Organization. Though Barsky admits it may have been poor judgment to have accepted the offer, he denies requesting additional tickets or a hotel suite. He also denies that the tickets affected his coverage of the Trump Organization pro or con.

At first *Wall Street Journal* executive editor Norman Pearlstine backs up Barsky, noting: "The fact that Donald chose to call and complain a month after the event rather than at the time suggests that he was seeking favorable coverage and is upset he didn't get it." Pearlstine adds that the *Journal* sent Donald a check for $3,000 to reimburse him for the fight tickets and insists that Barsky will continue to cover the Trump beat and will not be reprimanded. But Donald keeps planting stories in the *New York Times* and elsewhere that he plans to sue. In late June Pearlstine informs the *Journal* staff that the feud over the fight tickets has become "a source of embarrassment" to the newspaper and that Barsky is being reassigned to another beat.

The Casino Control Commission eventually approves Fred Trump, Sr., as a financial source, but not without a serious internal dispute. Division of Gaming Enforcement attorney Tom Auriemma and Trump attorney Joe Fusco claim in a statement to the commission that former Trump gaming division executives Ed Tracy and Pat McCoy and former Trump Castle president Tony Calandra were responsible for devising the casino chips loan scheme. But according to an investigation by *Philadelphia Inquirer* reporter David Johnston, Trump financial adviser Harvey Freeman thought up the idea, and Trump attorney Nick Ribis made sure it was executed.

The settlement negotiated by the DGE and Trump attorneys is even more astonishing than their version of the behind-the-scenes scenario. Trump Castle admits that the purchase of the chips by Fred Trump, Sr., constituted an illegal loan. Under Section 95 of the Casino Control Act, the prescribed penalties for an illegal loan are the return of all that money and banishment of the guilty parties from the New Jersey casino industry. But the DGE-Trump settlement merely requires Trump Castle to pay a fine of $30,000, an amount significantly less than that which a bank would have charged to lend the casino $3.5 million.

Two of the five Casino Control Commission members express outrage at the DGE's lenient settlement. "You have two standards for determining what the penalty is going to be," one for Trump interests and one for everyone else, charges Commissioner W. David Waters. "I guess what really bothers me here is the next time something like this happens it may not be between father and son," complains Commissioner Valerie Armstrong. "I think we are sending the wrong message." In the end, however, Armstrong reluctantly votes to accept the settlement because there is no sign of mob influence. Waters casts the only dissenting vote.

But more problems from the past continue to haunt the Trump gaming divisions. On August 21, 1991, the Casino Control Commission votes 4–0 to ban Trump Plaza customer Bob LiButti, the "ulti-mate" high roller, from entering New Jersey casinos because of his documented bigotry and alleged ties to organized crime boss John Gotti. The allegations of LiButti's link to Gotti arise from an incident in which LiButti allegedly tried to extort money from Taj Mahal exe-cutive Ed Tracy, who secretly tape-recorded the conversation. Despite LiButti's refusal to appear at his own banishment hearing, the com-mission also confirms that it is still investigating LiButti's charge that Donald made illegal payments to him in connection with their alleged "elaborate marketing scheme" to inflate revenues at Trump Plaza.

Amid all these dire developments, Donald has once again begun to lash out against those closest to him. One of the targets of his ire has been his younger brother, Robert. Though the two Trump boys have been maintaining a veneer of brotherly love in public, they have reportedly been feuding in private. Donald has allegedly been blam-ing Robert for the bungled opening of the Taj Mahal and for the lackluster sales of his apartment projects in Manhattan. Robert, who has suffered nearly ten years of unwarranted abuse, has apparently become fed up. He has informed his brother that he will resign his post as vice-president and leave the Trump Organization.

Robert's departure sets a disturbing precedent. Over the next sev-eral months, other top executives exit in the manner of rats jumping from a sinking ship. Among those who decide to turn in their resig-nations are real estate executives William Perseda and Larry Russo and longtime financial adviser Harvey Freeman, who reportedly earned an annual salary of $1 million. Before another year is out, chief financial officer Stephen Bollenbach, whose hiring was demanded by Donald's bankers, will also resign to take a far more prestigious position as chief financial officer at the Marriott hotel chain.

Rather than turn to his fiancée for support, Donald has been insulting and offending her, too. Having proposed to Marla in front of her mother, he seems to have left little doubt that his intentions are serious. But as the news of Marla's brand-new diamond engage-ment ring leaked out, Donald did an apparent about-face, telling the media that the ring was merely a gift of friendship, not a symbol of undying love and marital commitment. In private he and Marla have been quarreling almost incessantly over matters as trivial as the cor-rect time of day.

Marla is further dismayed by the snubs she recently received from Donald's parents. On Mother's Day, May 12, Marla invited the senior Trumps to accompany her to Sunday services at Marble Collegiate Church on Fifth Avenue. Besides being the church where Donald and Ivana were married, Marble Collegiate was the scene of at least a few illicit (and later, highly publicized) trysts between Donald and Marla. Perhaps for that reason, Fred and Mary Trump begged off.

On May 29 Marla requested a private audience with church pastor Dr. Arthur Caliandro. Unlike his predecessor, Dr. Norman Vincent Peale, Caliandro is not a best-selling author or cult figure, but he has known the Trump family for more than twenty years. Marla recently arrived at the conclusion that Fred Trump's influence was one of the obstacles to their pursuit of happiness. Caliandro reportedly confirmed that she was on the right track and suggested that Marla try to persuade Donald to come in for counseling with her.

Marla is hoping Donald's birthday dinner will give her a chance to get their marriage plans back on track. She has told friends that she is going to serve Donald's favorite meal: steak and potatoes smothered with tomato ketchup. But her own stomach is uneasy, and for good reason. That very morning an item that was covertly fed to Suzy by Trump Organization surrogates appeared in Suzy's gossip column in the *New York Post* "Word of D. Trump's new Italian girlfriend is about to break big," she reported, "leaving Marla Maples up a creek without a paddle."

Suzy is right on target. Donald recently met an internationally known fashion model on a Concorde flight from Paris. Her name is Carla Bruni-Tedeschi, and she is Marla's opposite in almost every way. Instead of being blond, buxom, and bouncy, she is mahogany-haired, flat-chested, and as sleeky smooth as a Ferrari race car. Where Marla's father is a failed Georgia real estate developer, Carla's father is an Italian composer of atonal music whose family fortune comes from an electrical cable company. But Carla and Marla do share the same taste for rich celebrities. Among Carla's more famous ex-boyfriends are rock stars Rod Stewart, Eric Clapton, and Mick Jagger. "There are only so many great men in this world," Carla reportedly told Clapton, whom she recently left for Jagger, "and I want to be with all of them."

Carla does not, however, consider Donald J. Trump one of the world's "great men." After her arrival in New York he tracked her down at the Mayfair Regent hotel and tried to ingratiate himself. Carla mischievously informed Donald that her "sister" was coming to town. He immediately offered to provide a room at the Plaza Hotel. The visitor was actually one of Carla's longtime female friends, who showed up at the Plaza with a boyfriend in tow. Carla and her friends spent the next few days ordering room service and gloating over the way they had fooled the "King of Tacky."

Marla, who is as yet unaware of all these gory details, hopes her home-cooked birthday dinner will help her win back Donald's wayward attentions. She has some grounds for optimism. The Trump Organization recently announced a dual celebration of Donald's forty-fifth birthday and the first anniversary of the Trump Taj Mahal in Atlantic City on the weekend of June 21–22. The invitations read: "Donald Trump and Marla Maples invite you to . . ." The only question in Marla's mind is how to make Donald go public with the news of their engagement so her rivals will buzz off.

Marla's cause gets an unexpected boost from Donald's estranged offspring. None of the children call to wish him happy birthday that fateful Friday night. Nor do they call on Sunday, which was Father's Day. Donald begins to realize just how alone he really is. The only constant in his strife-torn life is his strife-torn relationship with Marla Maples. And the only thing she seems to want from him is to spend the rest of their lives together.

"Okay, you've got it," Donald assures her. "I'll announce the engagement at the Taj."

On Saturday, June 22, Donald rises to the podium in the grand ballroom of the Taj Mahal with a mischievous glint in his eye. This is a party especially for the casino's high rollers, and they are out in force, attired in everything from tuxedos to designer T-shirts. The Georgia contingent is also out in force. Marla's mother and stepfather, her father and stepmother are seated at a table with Tom Fitzsimmons and some friends from New York.

Marla looks ravishing. As if in a flashback to her Ivanaesque photographs in *Vanity Fair,* she has her blond hair piled up high in a Bardot bun, and she is wearing a flame red ball gown topped with a lace bustier. Donald is dressed in his trademark blue Brioni suit with a pink shirt and red tie. He and Marla argued about the shirt on the way down from his residence in Trump Castle. She wanted him to wear white, which she considers more formal and appropriate for the occasion. He refused.

"Things are really going great," Donald advises his Taj Mahal audience, and commences on a typically hyperbolic spiel about the success of his newest and biggest Atlantic City casino. Then he turns to the Georgia contingent.

"I'd be in big trouble," he tells the assembled high rollers, "if I didn't introduce Marla's mother." He gestures toward Ann Ogletree, who smiles and waves from her chair on the front row next to her daughter.

Marla and the rest of her clan wait anxiously for what they think is coming next. But there is nothing more to come. Donald does not announce, as he promised, that he and Marla are formally engaged to be married. Instead he simply thanks the high rollers for coming and steps down from the podium.

That night Donald and Marla have a major fight in her suite on the twenty-sixth floor of Trump Castle. When Tom Fitzsimmons comes around to check on things the next morning, he finds that the door to the suite is broken off at the hinges. Marla is sitting in the living room wearing a yellow bathrobe and a tear-stained face. Donald, dressed up in a business suit, is standing over her. He turns and walks through the broken door.

"I'm taking the helicopter back to New York right now," Donald informs Fitzsimmons. "Do you want me to give you a ride?"

Fitzsimmons says he is not quite ready to leave.

"Well, then stay all week," Donald offers, and heads for the elevator.

"I can't take it anymore," Marla declares with remarkable calm as she watches Donald exit. "He's just pathological. He lies and lies and lies."

IT'S OVER! screams the front-page headline of the *New York Post* on Wednesday, June 26. "The Donald boots Marla from his East Side condo." MOVE OVER, MARLA, parries *New York Newsday* in a page one story that features a winsome modeling photograph of Carla Bruni-Tedeschi next to the headline TRUMP'S NEW PAL.

Carla is furious. She becomes even more incensed when she learns that on a recent flight to Palm Beach Donald questioned her friend Prince Dimitri of Yugoslavia about his intentions toward her. When Dimitri said he and Carla were not dating, Donald evidently felt free to start the rumor about his budding romance with the Italian model. Upon hearing this, Carla calls Trump Tower to vent her rage at Donald.

"How dare you do this!" she screams at him. "It's not true!"

"What's wrong with you?" Donald clucks. "Any girl would be pleased to have this kind of publicity."

"My parents are horrified," Carla shoots back. "They forbid me to have anything to do with you. They think you are a tacky upstart."

The same afternoon *People* magazine reporter Sue Carswell calls Trump Tower to inquire if the stories in the tabloids are true. When Donald returns her call, he identifies himself as "John Miller," a spokesman for the Trump Organization. Carswell switches on her tape recorder and asks if it is true that Donald has broken his engagement with Marla. "It was never an engagement," the mysterious "John Miller" replies.

As for Marla's ring, "Miller" claims, "That was [about] giving Tiffany some business and getting Ivana—uh, getting Marla—something that would be nice." He goes on to say, "It doesn't matter to [Donald] if Marla talks. He truly doesn't care. The biggest misconception was that Donald left [Ivana] for Marla. He didn't. He leaves for himself."

"Miller" then reports that actress Kim Bassinger had recently requested, and received, an audience with Donald. "She wanted to come and discuss a real estate transaction. And you know, she wanted to go out with him. That was the real reason she came up. . . . Important beautiful women call him all the time. . . . Competitively, it's tough. It was tough for Marla, and it will be tough for Carla."

Later that day Carswell plays the tape of her telephone conversation with "John Miller" for *New York Post* gossip columnist Cindy Adams. "There is no John Miller," Adams declares. "That's Donald." Carswell then calls Marla Maples and plays the tape for her. After hearing a few sentences of "John Miller" / Donald boasting about Carla, Marla starts crying hysterically.

"I'm shocked and devastated," Marla sniffles. "I feel betrayed at the deepest level. My friends and family have been praying for me for a long time, and this may be the answer to their prayers." Then she adds: "No matter what, I came into this for love, and I hope he finds happiness."

The very next day Marla and Kim Knapp leave their apartment in Trump Parc and drive up to Greenwich, Connecticut, where they ensconce themselves in the home of sportscaster Frank Gifford and his singer / television talk show hostess wife, Kathie Lee Gifford. Marla met the Giffords only a few weeks before at a social function in Atlantic City, but she already considers the multitalented Kathie Lee a role model and her newest best friend. Donald calls minutes after Marla arrives at the Giffords', but she refuses to talk to him.

By Tuesday, July 1, Donald is mulling over plans to fly to Italy to meet Carla Bruni-Tedeschi, even though she will publicly and emphatically deny having any romantic interest in him. But disturbing thoughts start torturing his head when he sees a photograph of Marla beside a front-page *New York Daily News* headline, A NEW TILT ON THE JILT. Inside the paper is a deliberately inflammatory story Tom Fitzsimmons and Marla's agent, Chuck Jones, have fed to Richard Johnson. "It was Marla who dumped The Donald, not the other way around," the gossip columnist reports. "And Trump is still in love with the Georgia Peach, trying desperately to get her back."

"The man is totally and completely obsessed with her," says an unnamed friend of Marla, adding that Donald has "been getting mean, crazy, wild. Because of his business dealings, he's under extreme pressure. He wants her at his beck and call, and then, when he achieves that, he isn't happy. He's insanely jealous."

That same morning Donald hops into the Trump Cadillac limousine and orders his driver to take him to Connecticut. He arrives at the Giffords' home shortly after noon. At first Marla remains firm in her refusal to talk. She is not really jealous of Carla Bruni-Tedeschi. Both she and Kim figure that the story of Carla's romance with Donald is a fiction planted by the Trump Organization publicity machine, a theory Carla herself later confirms. But Marla has run out of patience with her double-talking boyfriend.

At Donald's behest, Kim, who feels she has "a purpose on this earth" of a lofty, if ill-defined, nature, convinces Marla to give him a chance to patch things up. He makes the best of his opportunity. First, he apologizes for the John Miller stunt. Then he proposes to Marla for what she later claims is "the millionth time." This time, however, Donald offers a tangible symbol of his newfound marital zeal: He tells her he has instructed Harry Winston jewelers to set aside a diamond engagement ring that is far bigger and more expensive than the Tiffany band he gave her in May.

Marla falls for Donald's line once again. That night the couple celebrate their latest engagement at a local restaurant with their friend and intermediary Kim Knapp. "When I saw him, I could feel the truth, that we had to push it to this point to be able to truly make the commitment to each other," Marla tells *People* magazine's Karen Schneider a few days later. "Whether he did [the John Miller stunt] as a joke or as a final straw to try to push me farther away from him, it ended up bringing us to a new level. . . . When I realized I could be happy alone, it made me love him more freely. Now, instead of out of desperation, it's out of choice."

The next morning, Wednesday, July 3, Marla calls Kathie Lee Gifford and asks her to make the exclusive public announcement on the "Live with Regis and Kathie Lee" television show. Donald confirms the announcement on the air via telephone. That afternoon he and Marla play golf with Frank Gifford and former limousine magnate William Fugazy at Winged Foot Country Club in Mamaroneck, New York. Just as the group is teeing off, a messenger from Harry Winston delivers a 7.5 carat emerald-cut diamond engagement ring (estimated retail value: $250,000), which Donald presents to Marla right there on the golf course. The package also contains Marla's gift to Donald: a Harry Winston calendar watch (estimated retail value: $40,000).

The news of the Trump-Maples engagement does not create the kind of media frenzy prompted by Donald's split from Ivana back in February 1990, but the outpouring of national and international coverage far exceeds that of any other engagement announcement since Diana Spencer's engagement to Prince Charles. Marla inadvertently feeds the fire. After quelling unfounded rumors that she is pregnant, she tells *People* magazine that she does not intend to sign a prenuptial agreement. "This relationship is going to be built on trust—and that's it," she says.

The guffaws from Ivana's camp are uproarious. "If I were her, I'd get it in blood," advises Ivana's former publicist, John Scanlon. Ivana's divorce lawyer, Michael Kennedy, opines that if Marla "thinks her relationship is based on trust, I agree with her—she doesn't need a prenuptial agreement. She needs a psychiatrist."

Marla later tells reporters that her statement on the matter is "not conclusive."

Ironically, she may have more to lose by not signing a prenuptial agreement than Donald. He has already persuaded her to sign a management contract giving him 30 percent of her earnings from modeling, television, film, and theatrical jobs. She has no major out-standing debts of record. He is in hock for billions to his banks and bondholders. Indeed, many people wonder how Donald can afford a $250,000 diamond engagement ring. Although Donald will later claim to have paid for the ring in full, a Trump Organization insider insists that for the time being he is paying only the insurance pre-mium on it, estimated to cost about $5,000 a year.

Be that as it may, rumors begin to circulate that Donald J. Trump is changing for the better. The change is attributed to Marla, mostly by Marla's friends. "He's not the same person," claims Kim Knapp. "He sees the errors of his ways." Even the normally skeptical Tom Fitzsimmons is impressed. "I think we'll be seeing a new Donald, a kinder, gentler Donald," Tom tells friends.

Later that summer Donald and Marla fly to London for a vaca-tion. To her surprise, Donald actually goes out on the town with-out wearing a tie and seems to put business matters temporarily aside. The couple ends up at Annabel's, a trendy disco that Donald wanted to attract to the Plaza Hotel in New York. At Marla's behest, the "new" Donald wanders out onto the dance floor and, of all things, dances.

Ivana Trump is praying for another divorce as she boards a flight for Rome on June 5. The problem is that her new love Ken Lieber-man's estranged wife, Rosemarie, just does not want to let go. Ken meets Ivana in Rome on the night of June 7 and escorts her to a party celebrating the thirtieth anniversary of designer Valentino's career in fashion. Then they fly to London to attend four days of horse racing at Ascot, followed by a week of tennis matches at Wimbledon. Rosemarie flies from London to the south of France, where she boards the Liebermans' luxury yacht, *Mikili,* and bides her time on the Côte d'Azur until her husband's infatuation ends.

That does not take long. Ken quickly discovers that playing around with Ivana is more wearing than working for a living. He is not accustomed to coping with the swarms of paparazzi that buzz about Ivana wherever she goes. Nor is he accustomed to serving as the drone of a social queen bee. And unlike The Donald, he has a lot more than $10 million to lose in the event of a divorce. Rosemarie has been at his side as a true business partner for more than two decades. She can easily lay claim to half his entire fortune.

On July 9 *New York Post* gossip columnist Suzy breaks the news that Rosemarie and Ken have reconciled and are back in London together. Ivana flies into a schizophrenic rage. Night after night she goes to bed crying and moaning over Ken, only to wake up the next morning full of *joie de vivre* that lasts until nightfall. Ken's return to Rosemarie is a humiliating defeat, a blow to Ivana's pride and sense of self-importance. During the jealousy-fraught fortnight following their final rendezvous at Wimbledon, she keeps asking herself and her friends the same question over and over again: "How can I get him to leave his wife?"

One evening in London Ivana decides to make a move. She and her friend Eva O'Neill go out on the town with a mission both woman would, if ever confronted about it, deny to their dying breaths. Their objective is to track down Ken Lieberman. They find him at Annabel's. Ken is sitting at a table with Rosemarie, beaming, as one friend observes, "like he had just won the Academy Award for returning to his wife." Ivana walks over the Liebermans' table and, right in front of Rosemarie, asks Ken if he would like to dance.

For a few fleeting seconds it looks as if the three-way encounter at Annabelle's might turn into an equally embarrassing replay of Ivana's confrontation with Marla Maples on the slopes of Aspen. But it is not to be. Ken rises to his feet in keeping with gentlemanly protocol and politely declines Ivana's invitation to dance. Then he sits back down beside Rosemarie.

Ivana returns to her own table, collects her purse and composure, and leaves. She refuses to waste the rest of her summer pining over Ken. Instead she flies to the French Riviera, where she rents a Mediterranean villa called L'Oiseau Bleu (The Blue Bird). As in years past, she spends most of July and August playing mother to her children and partying with a coterie of international jet-setters such as her Houston socialite friend Lynn Wyatt. "I think I'm too old for her," Lieberman tells London gossip columnist Nigel Dempster, adding, "Old men should be left with their memories."

As it turns out, Ivana already has another man in her life who is younger, more debonair, and far more handsome than Ken Lieberman. His name is Riccardo Mazzucchelli, and he is a forty-eight-year-old construction tycoon from Rome who has an aquiline nose, what one writer will describe as "ice-blue Siberian-wolf-dog eyes," and a passion for scuba diving. He also has a twenty-five-year-old son from a previous marriage, two flats in London, a condominium in the Swiss Alps, an apartment in Prague, and a powder blue Rolls-Royce.

Unlike The Donald, Riccardo, the son of a mining magnate, is not obsessed with making money. At age twenty-two he started a construction firm called ASCO and moved to Africa, where he claims to have made his first million by the age of twenty six. Over the next twelve years ASCO reportedly completed $3 billion worth of construction projects in Africa and the Middle East, ranging from sewer systems to bowling alleys. But along about 1982 Riccardo had a kind of mid-life crisis inspired by reading the works of Erich Fromm. He stopped undertaking massive construction projects, started exploring environmentally oriented business interests, and began showing up on the London party circuit.

Riccardo and Ivana first met at a London dinner party at Claridge's during Ascot Week in the summer of 1991. The next day he started sending her flowers. Then he followed her to the French Riviera, spent a few weeks there, and flew her to Italy, where he escorted her to the Save Venice Ball. By this time the paparazzi were hot on the trail. On September 24 a *New York Post* photographer snaps a picture of Ivana and Riccardo strolling down Fifth Avenue hand in hand.

Shortly after Ivana returns from Europe, The Donald counters her public display of affection for Riccardo by terminating her position as chief executive of the Plaza Hotel. Then he denigrates her performance with four-letter words, accusing her of costing him money by failing to turn the hotel into a profit maker. As if to prove that chivalry is not dead, Riccardo picks up the phone and lets The Donald have a piece of his mind.

"Ivana is a wonderful woman," Riccardo declares. "She doesn't deserve to be spoken to that way."

A few days later Riccardo gives Ivana the equivalent of a "friendship" ring symbolically similar to the one her ex-husband gave Marla Maples prior to the Trumps' divorce. But The Donald is too preoccupied with the alleged infidelities of his former mistress turned fiancée to give the gift a second thought.

One night that September Donald takes Marla and Kim to the Taj Mahal in Atlantic City to attend a Michael Bolton concert. Bolton, a popular singer with long golden locks and a handsomely chiseled chin, has specialized in redoing old soul music tunes. He now has a hit song near the top of the music charts entitled "Time, Love, and Tenderness." Kim asks Donald to take her and Marla backstage after the concert to meet Bolton. Besides having a crush on Bolton, Kim claims she wants to interview him for a book she and Marla are writing about "the unhappy lives of successful men." But Marla also has a budding crush on the singer—and a plan to make her groom-to-be jealous.

"I'm about to meet the love of my life," Marla swoons as Donald leads the two women backstage. "Isn't he the sexiest man you've ever seen?"

Marla proceeds to flirt with Bolton backstage as if she meant just what she said. Much to Kim's chagrin, she then takes it upon herself to ask Bolton to give an interview for "their" book the following day. Donald is furious. "If you talk to him again," he bellows, "we're divorced!"

A few days later Donald strikes back. He takes Marla to the 1991 Miss America Pageant in Atlantic City, where he proceeds to flirt with the eventual winner, a buxom brunette from Hawaii named Carolyn Sapp. Now Marla is furious. In a reversal of her confrontation with Ivana in Aspen, she walks up to Sapp and demands, "What are you doing flirting with my fiancé?" Marla later claims that she was "just teasing." But things go quickly downhill from there. When the finals of the beauty pageant begin, Donald and his male friends keep making ungentlemanly comments about Sapp.

"They were sitting around saying, 'She's got a great body!" and 'It's about time they got a good-looking one!' " Marla later complains to *People* magazine. "He still thinks it's cool to act like a ladies' man. But I don't think it's very respectful. I deserve better than that."

Marla decides that the "new" Donald still needs to come to terms with the "old" Donald. Over the past weekend he has, on separate occasions, introduced Marla as Ivana and Ivana as Marla. She begs him to go for counseling with Dr. Caliandro. He refuses. Then, like Ivana before her, she begs him to go see a psychiatrist. Finally he agrees, though he continues to behave as if he were not the one with a problem. "I'll do it," he says, using almost identical words he once used with Ivana, "if it will make you better."

On Tuesday, September 17, Donald and Marla dine with evangelist Billy Graham, who is in town to give a sermon in Central Park. Like Graham, Marla keeps endorsing the value of religious and psychological counseling. Two nights later, however, Donald and Marla quarrel in public once again during intermission at *The Will Rogers Follies* on Broadway. After the performance they return to his sixty-third-floor apartment in Trump Tower, where their fight rapidly escalates. The issue is no longer his behavior at *The Will Rogers Follies* or hers. It is the whole past, present, and future of their relationship.

"You want to know what's wrong with you?" Marla screams at one point. "You want to know why you're so messed up?" She goes over to a side table, picks up a photograph of Fred Trump, Sr., and shoves the photograph in Donald's face. "This is why!"

"That's it. I've had it. I can't take this anymore," Donald storms. Then he picks up the phone and calls security. "Come get her," he orders, "and get her out of here."

On Sunday, September 22, the *New York Daily News* runs front-page photographs of a scowling Donald and an openmouthed Marla next to the headline HERE WE GO AGAIN . . . TRUMP DUMPS MARLA. "Marla is just a wonderful, beautiful woman, very talented, with a terrific future as a model or actress," Donald tells columnist Richard Johnson. "I want to remain good friends with her. But it's time to step aside and look in other directions." An unnamed "source close to Trump" adds that no decision has been made about the 7.5 carat diamond ring Donald has given Marla.

Donald wastes no time sampling life without Marla. On Friday, September 20, he goes to a private party in the East Side penthouse of nightclub owner Jerry Brandt and meets a raven-haired beauty wearing a baseball cap emblazoned with the logo Alley Cat. Her name is Kim Alley, and she is a twenty-one-year-old Wilhelmina model from Richmond, Virginia. They leave Brandt's party in his limousine, drive to a nearby night spot called the China Club, then head downtown to the Roxy. Alley later provides some salacious details to the *New York Post,* which runs yet another front-page story on Donald's love life.

While Donald tangles with his Alley Cat, Marla removes her diamond engagement ring and spreads her wings. On Tuesday, September 24, two days after the *New York Daily News* story about her latest breakup with Donald, she and Chuck Jones take off for Los Angeles. The official purpose of Marla's trip is to tape a segment on the CBS television series "Designing Women." The slot, which was scheduled before her recent breakup with Donald, calls for her to appear as herself in the role of a bride-to-be. The script is quickly rewritten to reflect the new developments in her life.

After finishing the CBS taping, Marla flies up to Yakima, Washington, where Michael Bolton is giving a concert at the Central Washington State Fair. Word of their romantic rendezvous makes headlines in the *New York Daily News* the following Tuesday, October 1. "We're not surprised," says an unnamed source in the Trump Organization. "Marla is trying to hurt Donald because he left her." But Donald realizes that the newspapers are making it look as if Marla left him for Bolton, whom one gossip columnist describes as "a new beau, younger and hunkier than Donald Trump."

Donald scrambles to save face by getting Marla back. He invites her mother, Ann Ogletree, to New York, and puts her up in the Presidential Suite at the Plaza Hotel. Then on Thursday, October 10, barely two and a half weeks since the news of their breakup hit the press, he crashes a luncheon Marla is having with a pair of publicists at the Russian Tea Room. That weekend he takes Marla out to Bridgehampton, Long Island. They play golf at the newly opened

Atlantic Country Club. Then they stop by Pumpkintown in nearby Water Mill, where she selects a pair of Halloween pumpkins. But the very next week their romance hits the rocks again.

On Monday, October 14, CBS airs the "Designing Women" episode in which Marla makes a guest appearance. The dialogue in her main scene borders on the risqué. It starts when one of the female characters on the show tries to commiserate over Marla's recent, highly publicized breakup with Donald. "That's what happens when you go out with someone who has a big ego," Marla sighs. "You wind up getting the short end of the stick."

There is a pregnant pause. "Oh," says her fictional soul mate on the program, interpreting Marla's line as a thinly veiled Freudian pun, "so that was the problem."

The "Designing Women" episode infuriates Donald. So does a report by *New York Post* gossip columnist Cindy Adams that Harry Winston not only expects him to pay for the ring but has sent him a still-unpaid bill. Then Marla's roommate, Kim Knapp, informs her mother and several friends of a startling discovery: evidence of a possible break-in attempt. Although the ring is still safely tucked away in its hiding place, a packet of nude photographs Donald took of Marla is missing. Kim claims that she found a mysterious surgical glove inside their apartment.

Kim's "discovery" sets off a new round of furious speculation by the Trump and Maples inner circle. Is Donald really trying to steal back the ring? If so, how could someone crafty enough to pick the Medeco lock on the apartment door be clumsy enough to leave a glove behind? If Donald is not behind the alleged break-in attempt, are Marla and Kim plotting to switch the real ring for a zircon replacement? Or could another insider be up to no good?

Whatever the case, Donald keeps begging Marla to take him back. By mid-October their friends are predicting that he and Marla are going to elope. On the weekend of October 18 he accompanies her to Dalton, Georgia, where she is crowned the Whitfield High School football homecoming queen. That night they fly to Atlantic City, where they are joined by Marla's mother and stepfather. But no reengagement, elopement, or nuptial is forthcoming. Instead Marla plays coy. She keeps seeing Donald. And she also keeps seeing Michael Bolton.

Ivana keeps replaying her own version of the Trump saga with industrialist Riccardo Mazzucchelli. In mid-November, after sending Simon & Schuster the ghostwritten manuscript of her *roman à clef For Love Alone,* she appears in a cameo role on the six thousandth episode of the daytime television soap opera "One Life to Live." That same week Riccardo accompanies her on a trip to Alberta, Canada, where she joins former British Prime Minister Margaret Thatcher in a three-day seminar for top stockbrokers at the Mackenzie Financial Corporation. Ivana gives a forty-five-minute speech on motivating people to achieve results.

Upon returning to New York, Ivana and Riccardo tape a personality profile with independent producer Daphna Barak for CBS television. In one segment Ivana attempts to show off her cooking skills by preparing a lunch of Hungarian goulash. She manages to get the steaming dish to the table without incident. But after she and Riccardo down their helpings of goulash, they both get sick. Riccardo recovers sufficiently by the next taping session to give CBS a sensational scoop: His intentions toward Ivana are as serious as they can possibly be. "I know what I want," he declares. "Yes, I am going to propose. Give it a little time and . . ." His voice trails off.

Ivana is still a little leery. "I am very romantic," she says. "Still, I need some time before I get married again." Ivana claims that she has learned some important lessons from her tumultuous years with The Donald. Foremost among these lessons is that "a woman is not supposed to bring home her career problems. Before, with Donald, I used to mix business with my private life. It wasn't healthy. A woman should be tough in business, but feminine at home. That's what I'm doing now."

In December Riccardo gives Ivana a 10 carat yellow diamond ring. Rumors of an impending engagement fill the London gossip columns. But Christmas and New Year's pass, and no announcement is forthcoming. In late February 1990 Ivana and Riccardo go out to dinner with Ken Lieberman and his wife. "I want to show the people that we are all the friends," Ivana tells *Vanity Fair* writer Bob Colacello. "You know, just friends. Not the *friend,* like the people think."

It is early on the morning of Wednesday, February 12, 1992, and Donald Trump is talking on the telephone. The voice on the other end of the line belongs to former world heavyweight champion Mike Tyson, who has just been convicted by a jury in Indianapolis, Indiana, of raping nineteen-year-old Miss Black America contestant Desiree Washington. Tyson is still out on bail awaiting sentencing and has reportedly called Donald to seek his advice and support. According to an exclusive story he gives Cindy Adams, Donald proposes that Tyson offer to set up a fund to benefit rape victims.

"If Mike Tyson sits in jail and his earning power is curtailed, it is punitive to him but beneficial to no one," Donald declares. "What has happened to him, the conviction, is already punitive. The victim has had the satisfaction of humbling him and being vindicated. Now, we could go further. This is what I told Mike. I am willing to be the go-between and to act in his behalf."

The money at stake is considerable. If Tyson can stay out of jail, he can earn up to $30 million by beating reigning heavyweight champ Evander Holyfield in an already scheduled bout. According to widely circulated reports, Tyson's promoter, Don King, previously offered the victim $750,000 to drop the rape charges. She refused. But Donald apparently believes she might change her mind if he helped up the ante.

"All I'm willing to do is, I am willing to call this lady," Donald tells Cindy Adams. "I am willing to approach her on Mike's behalf. I am willing to make a strong statement to her. I am willing to see if this arrangement that I have envisioned can be worked out."

Unbeknownst to Adams, Donald's sympathy for Tyson may be based on his own personal experience. It is conceivable that Ivana could bring rape charges against Donald if she goes public with her version of what he did to her in Trump Tower following his ill-fated scalp reduction operation in the fall of 1989. But like many other average citizens, Adams finds Donald's proposition objectionable on its own merits. "The fact that this may well be a quality lady who might never have been bought off simply does not occur to these people," Adams observes. "In the way 'they' think, everyone has a price."

Whether Donald seriously believes his proposed fund for rape victims has a chance of being acceptable to the victim and the Indiana authorities is open to debate. But there is nothing surprising about the short-term repercussions. On February 13, the day after he broaches the proposal to Tyson, Donald is once again the subject of front-page headlines in the *New York Post*. Donald's proposal, as outlined in Cindy Adams's exclusive story, is picked up by many of the major news services, which circulate it nationwide. Indiana authorities, however, are not impressed. Tyson is eventually sentenced to six years in prison.

The Tyson rape fund proposal is both a measure of Donald's character and a measure of how far he has fallen. The only relatively unencumbered asset he seems to have left is the ability to generate self-promoting publicity. Back in the good old days, he could do that all by himself. Now he is often forced to piggyback on the successes or the misfortunes of other people whose names have become household words, including his own mother.

On October 31, 1991, a sixteen-year-old white youth playing hooky from school attempted to mug seventy-nine-old-Mary Trump in a Queens shopping center. The fragile Mrs. Trump suffered a broken hip and broken ribs in the attack. The alleged assailant was later charged with robbery and assault and released on $25,000 bail. Donald leaped to his mother's defense in the media.

"I think it's a disgrace when someone commits this kind of crime and is allowed out again," he declared with words sharply contrasting with those he later uses on behalf of Mike Tyson. "This guy almost killed someone. I am incensed that he is free to do as he pleases— while my mother is lying in the hospital."

Donald could not resist the temptation to exploit the public relations value of the incident. A forty-four-year-old black bystander named Lawrence Herbert managed to apprehend Mary Trump's alleged assailant as he tried to escape with her purse and held him down until the police arrived. Two weeks later Donald invited Herbert to have dinner with him and Marla at the Plaza Hotel. A truck driver by trade, Herbert was reportedly working two jobs in an effort to prevent a bank from foreclosing on his home. Donald did not mention anything about helping Herbert out financially, but he did pose with the good Samaritan for a three-quarter-page photograph that was published in the next day's edition of the *New York Daily News* alongside a three-quarter-page photograph of Marla.

On November 18 anonymous sources close to Donald leaked word to the media that he had recently jumped out of his limousine to break up a streetside confrontation between a man wielding a bat and an unarmed bystander. On November 19, a date that coincided with an appearance on CNN's "Larry King Live," Donald announced that he was inviting basketball star Magic Johnson, who had tested positive for the AIDS virus a few weeks earlier, to come to New York for a press conference intended to raise public awareness about AIDS. Johnson later backed out of the press conference.

Two days later Donald testified before a House panel in Washington, D.C. He urged Congress to levy higher taxes on the wealthy and create incentives for them to reinvest in job-creating ventures rather than in certificates of deposit. He claimed that the Tax Reform Act of 1986, which eliminated such incentives, proved to be a disaster, especially for the real estate industry.

With the dawn of the New Year it appeared that Donald became more desperate than ever to capitalize on celebrity-driven publicity opportunities. In January 1992 he agreed to appear in a movie being filmed at the Plaza Hotel with child star Macauley Culkin of *Home Alone* fame. He had later arranged for Calkins to have a play date with his daughter, Ivanka, an event that prompted yet another dribble of media coverage. In February 1992, just prior to broaching his Tyson rape fund proposal, Donald got into a highly publicized shouting match with New York talk radio station WFAN host Don Imus, whom he had praised in *Trump: The Art of the Deal* for raising money to help farm widow Annabel Hill. The two men eventually made up, but only after their "Battle of the Dons" had generated a week's worth of free cross-promotional publicity in the local tabloids.

The "Battle of the Dons" and the Tyson rape fund proposal are quickly followed by the strange "Case of the Stolen Caddy." While Donald, Marla, and singer John Denver are eating at a Greenwich Village restaurant late one night, their chauffeur reportedly leaves the Trump Cadillac parked by the curb with the keys in the ignition. An unidentified thief comes along and takes the limousine for a joyride. The Cadillac is found undamaged about two hours later in lower Manhattan. The *New York Post* reports the theft in a front-page story on Wednesday, February 26, then gets second thoughts. The next day, the newspaper's "Page Six" gossip section runs a cartoon showing Donald talking to a porcupine-haired hood as he dines with Marla.

"Here's twenty bucks," reads the quote bubble streaming from Donald's mouth. "Park it on Broome St., then call the press."

Donald's next media gambit, however, is a true testimony to his enduring art of the spiel. On March 9, 1992, two of his Atlantic City casinos, Trump Plaza and Trump Castle, formally file prepackaged bankruptcy petitions. Since Trump Plaza has not defaulted on any bond payments, Donald is not forced to relinquish a portion of his ownership stake. But in order to raise more capital to continue operations, Trump Plaza takes on additional new long-term debt and issues four million shares of preferred stock. In the case of Trump Castle, which has defaulted on its bond payments, Donald is forced to hand over 50 percent of his ownership stake to the casino hotel's bondholders; in exchange, the bondholders forgive a portion of Trump Castle's debt and allow Donald to pay them a lower interest rate. About the same time the Taj formally emerges from its Chapter 11 proceedings. But just ten days later rumors circulate that Donald has agreed to give Citibank a 49 percent interest in the Plaza Hotel in exchange for reducing his personally guaranteed debt by $125 million. The following month U.S. Air announces that it is taking over operations of the Trump Shuttle.

For anyone other than Donald J. Trump, these developments could be interpreted only as a sign of continuing decline. But Donald is somehow able to put a positive spin on the news of his most recent debt-for-asset deals. In the issue dated March 23, 1992, *Business Week* magazine runs a story headlined TRUMP: HE'S BA-AK! The gist of the story is that Donald has positioned himself to make a startling financial comeback. It is an amazing thesis, as well as one that defies standard principles of accounting and elementary arithmetic.

Business Week notes that Donald has parted with a dozen major assets over the past two years. In addition to the Trump Shuttle and the rumored relinquishment of a 49 percent interest in the Plaza Hotel, they reportedly include the newly completed Trump Palace apartment building in New York, Trump Plaza of the Palm Beaches, his stock in Alexander's, his yacht, his helicopters, land parcels in Atlantic City, his 50 percent interest in the Grand Hyatt, and 50 percent interests in two of his Atlantic City casinos. Like Donald, the magazine makes much of the fact that in the course of divesting himself of these trophy properties, he has also reduced his total personally guaranteed debt from nearly $900 million to $115 million.

So what is the bottom line on the Trump fortune to date? *Business Week* provides a handy chart showing that Donald has assets of $1.116 billion, and debts of $2.495 billion. That works out to a negative net worth of minus $1.379 billion. What *Business Week* fails to note, however, is that rather than improve his financial status during the months since his banking crisis became public knowledge, Donald has actually gone deeper in the hole. Back in the summer of 1990, just after his financial crisis became public knowledge, the Kenneth Leventhal & Company audit showed that under a worst-case scenario Donald had a liquidation value negative net worth of minus $295 million. In other words, he is currently worth $1.084 billion less than he was worth eighteen months earlier, primarily because his properties have suffered the nationwide deflation in real estate values.

But *Business Week* does not even mention the Leventhal figures, much less attempt to reconcile them with its own. Instead the magazine falls for Donald's claim that once the U.S. economy improves as a whole, so will his own financial condition. "You'll never see me sitting on the corner sucking my thumb," *Business Week* quotes Donald as saying. "The name Trump will be hotter than ever."

In fact, there may be some truth to Donald's prediction, but it is a most ironic one. If the economy improves, the value of the properties he still holds, which include the West Side yards, the commercial space in Trump Tower, Mar-a-Lago, 51 percent of the Plaza Hotel, and interests in his three Atlantic City casinos, may also increase. But it is likely that his banks will seize such an opportunity to liquidate still more of his real estate assets so they can recoup their loans. And if the name Trump increases in value, it may well be because of his ex-wife, not Donald himself.

In the week of April 6, 1992, photographs of Ivana Trump appear on the covers of *Vanity Fair, People, Lear's,* and *Penthouse* magazines. The same week Ivana herself appears on "The Oprah Winfrey Show," the "Sally Jessy Raphael Show," HBO "Entertainment News," ABC's

"Good Morning America," ABC's "Live with Regis and Kathie Lee," and CNN's "Larry King Live." She also gives interviews to *USA Today,* "Entertainment Tonight," the *Washington Post,* and the *Boston Globe* and signs books at stores in New York City; Levittown, Long Island; Stamford, Connecticut; Arlington, Virginia; Boston, Massachusetts; and Palm Beach, Florida.

All this is part of a campaign coordinated by Ivana's personal assistant and publicist, Lisa Calandra, to promote *For Love Alone,* the novel Ivana has produced with ghostwriter Camille Marchetta. *For Love Alone* is part of a three-book package for which Pocket Books has paid a $1.5 million advance. The publisher is reportedly releasing a first printing of five hundred thousand copies, a sign that Pocket Books believes the book is destined for the best seller list. In the next thirty days Ivana will travel to thirteen cities in the United States and Canada before taking off for an extensive European tour.

Set amid the social whirl of New York, London, Aspen, and the French Riviera, *For Love Alone* bears intentional similarities to Ivana's own story. Names of real-life friends such as designer Carolina Herrera, tennis star Martina Navratilova, and investment banker John Gutfreund are sprinkled throughout the 532 pages. On the acknowledgments page Ivana even does some real-life social and political fence mending by thanking gossip columnist William Norwich, whom she once privately regarded as her rival sister-in-law Blaine's "man," for "coming to me two years ago with the idea of writing a book." But the book is hardly, as The Donald will allege, a thinly veiled fictional version of the true Trump saga.

The heroine of *For Love Alone* is a Czech beauty and athlete named Katrinka. Her background and early life are much like Ivana's. Unlike the author, however, Katrinka has an illegitimate child whom she gives up for adoption; later Katrinka defects from Czechoslovakia by skiing across the border. Katrinka goes on to become a self-made businesswoman with a small but classy hotel in Switzerland and starts a long and frustrating search for the child she gave up for adoption. Then Katrinka meets and marries a handsome American shipping tycoon named Adam Graham with whom she has such titillating adventures as "mile-high sex" aboard a jet.

The only things Adam Graham has even superficially in common with Donald Trump are a fondness for publicity ("We're going to be in the papers a lot, Katrinka," he boasts) and an unbridled ambition. Adam comes from a wealthy WASP family based in Newport, Rhode Island, not from Queens; his domineering mother traces their ancestry back to the American Revolution. As in the case of Ivana and The Donald, Katrinka becomes both spouse and business partner, adding a chain of high-class hotels to the Graham marine dynasty. And as in the case of the Trumps, their competitive marriage ends in divorce. There is even a southern-born femme fatale named Sugar Benson some readers will claim is based on Marla Maples; she is described as a "sexual athlete" who runs a high-class brothel.

But Sugar Benson is not the cause for the failure of Katrinka's marriage to Adam. Nor is she Adam's next fiancée. In fact, the central story line is not even about Katrinka's relationship to Adam, though that occupies a fair portion of the total narrative. The book is really about Katrinka's own search for happiness—and for the child she gave up for adoption in her youth. In the end she finds both a new husband and her long-lost, now fully grown-up son. The narrative closes with a passage that in no way describes the not-so-happy and never-ending battle of *Trump v. Trump*. "Here now, surrounded by all the people she loved most in the world, for this moment, however brief, she had it all."

When advance copies of the book make their way to media reviewers, The Donald strikes back. An anonymous "source close to Trump" tells the *New York Post* that Ivana is trying to cash in on the Trump name. "He had two bestsellers himself," the source reminds. "This is merely a thinly veiled attempt to get Donald into the act because he sells." The source, who sounds suspiciously like The Donald himself, opines that the book is a violation of the still-disputed gag clause in the couple's nuptial agreement. Then the source takes a swipe at Ivana.

"When Donald met Ivana, she didn't have 10 cents in the bank, and was doing very poorly," claims the unnamed Trump confidant. "Donald had her simply manage Trump Castle, and later on, the Plaza Hotel. She was overbearing. She used her power far more than she should have."

Ivana, by contrast, takes the high road. When asked about the similarities between *For Love Alone* and her real life, she insists that the book is truly a work of fiction, not a thinly disguised exposé of her marriage to The Donald. She refuses to say anything about those years while the appeal of the gag clause is pending. When Oprah Winfrey asks her about The Donald on the air, she refuses to attack him or complain about his continuing attacks on her. "He's the father of my three children," Ivana says softly but firmly, "and I wish him the best."

"What a woman . . . what a woman . . . what a woman!" Oprah exclaims as the audience thunders applause.

Four days later Donald comes out from behind the smoke screen of a "source close to Trump" and fires his reply via Cindy Adams. "This book is not even thinly disguised," he tells the *New York Post* gossip columnist. "The only reason [Ivana is] even trying to deny it is because my lawyers are chomping at the bit to sue her ass off. Everyone laughs when she claims it's made up fictional stuff. Sure, with a Czech heroine, a Southern mistress, and you as the rotten lousy columnist."

Before Donald can unleash his "chomping" lawyers, however, he must wait for the appellate division judges to rule on the trial judge's decision to strike the gag order from the Trumps' nuptial contract. If the appellate justices decide that the gag clause must be reinstated, he may have grounds for a lawsuit, provided, of course, that he can also prove that *For Love Alone* is actually a rehash of his marriage to Ivana. But if the appellate justices decide not to overturn Judge Gangel-Jacob's action, he will have no legal leg to stand on.

"This Phylliss Gangel-Jacobs [sic] who presided in our lawsuit, she's a woman's judge," Donald complains. "Her court is stacked in favor of women. She's known to rule in favor of women. It's why she won't be upped to the Supreme Court. Men oppose her nomination. She's unfair to them."

Donald claims he included the gag clause in the nuptial agreement to "protect the kids," even though the original and still-unchanged version was written before the Trumps' first child was born. "I paid $25 million for this clause," he rails. "And from an agreement already agreed to and signed to by both parties, this judge arbitrarily, on her own strikes out only this one clause, after I hand over the check. . . ." Donald goes on to predict that the justices will overturn Judge Gangel-Jacob's ruling. "When I win this," he says, "I'll make a determination exactly what to do [about Ivana's book]."

Easter Week 1992 descends gloomy and dank upon Donald J. Trump. The weather is unseasonably bad, and so is his press. The week begins with U.S. Air converting the Trump Shuttle into the U.S. Air Shuttle. Already workers are rapidly removing the name Trump from the road signs around La Guardia, Logan, and National airports and from the fusilages of the shuttle jets. At midweek there are inaccurate reports that the Trump children will be spending Easter with Ivana when they are actually going to Palm Beach with their father. The week will end with reports that the banks are about to foreclose on Donald's embattled apartment building at 100 Central Park South.

But on Holy Thursday, April 16, 1992, Donald J. Trump suddenly rises from the dead, not like Jesus Christ but rather like Glenn Close wielding her knife as she rises out of the bathtub in the film *Fatal Attraction.* That afternoon the justices of the appellate division of the New York Supreme Court rule 5–0 that Judge Gangel-Jacob erred in striking the gag clause from the Trumps' nuptial contract. The trial court exceeded its "limited authority to disturb the terms of a separation agreement," the judges conclude, adding that the terms of the Trumps' settlement do not "offend public policy as prior restraint on free speech."

Donald is ecstatic. As he departs New York for the holidays on Thursday afternoon, he gives a car phone interview to Cindy Adams. His three children, Donny, Ivanka, and Eric, are by his side. "This is total victory. . . . An absolute 100 percent total fucking victory," he gloats. "I'm really happy about this. Hey, let's face it. *Any* ex-wife of mine could write a book and have a guaranteed bestseller."

Donald's attorney Jay Goldberg has already indicated that serious legal action against Ivana is in the offing. According to Goldberg, they may sue her for the royalties from *For Love Alone,* they may withhold $350,000 a year in alimony payments, and they may try to recoup the $10 million divorce settlement she has been paid. But before the case of *Trump v. Trump* resumes in court, Goldberg's client has one more knife to throw at his ex-wife.

"I'm going to sue her," Donald vows, "for custody of the kids."

TIME WOUNDS
ALL HEELS

■ ON A SULTRY day in July 1992, Chuck Jones marches through the pink-marbled lobby of Trump Parc and takes the elevator up to Marla Maples's eighth-floor apartment. Although he is only six months shy of his fiftieth birthday, married, and the father of two school-age girls, Jones looks like an overgrown Dennis the Menace with his gleaming gray eyes and his boyishly long brown hair balding in front. But on this particular day Jones's customary mischievous smirk is missing.

"You've got a bad image," Marla told him a few days before. "You're the press agent mixed up in the scandal."

Jones strides right up to unit 8A and, without bothering to knock, extracts a set of keys from his pocket and unlocks the door. He is impressed by what he sees. The formerly half-furnished three-bedroom flat that Marla used to share with her pal Kim Knapp has recently been transformed into a Trumpian pleasure palace. The renovation work took a good six weeks and probably cost upward of $100,000.

The living room now features an aqua suede chaise longue set guarded by a pair of rust-colored faux marble columns. Kim's old room has been made into an office / workout space equipped with a computer and free weights. One of the extra bathrooms has been converted into a steam room. The master bedroom has been elevated with a platform so that Marla can see out the picture window overlooking Central Park; the walls and furnishings are decorated in purple and white, her so-called magical colors.

Jones eyes the scene more than a little wistfully. For the past six years he has devoted his life to Marla, acting as her publicist, personal confidant, and chief protector, providing her with acting jobs, advice, and sympathy, and even lying to the media for her, throughout the turbulent times before, during, and after the Trump marital scandal. He has also held a mysterious paid position as a "consultant" to Donald Trump on the West Side yards project. Now, with Marla set to make her Broadway debut in *The Will Rogers Follies* in just a few weeks, it sounds as if she wants to let him go.

"I really feel like killing myself because of this thing with Marla," Jones told their mutual friend Tom Fitzsimmons earlier that summer. "I just can't believe she'd abandon me after all the things I've done for her."

Jones roams through the bedrooms, noting that Marla's closets are filled with a colorful assortment of designer pumps and exercise shoes. This is good news. Last summer Marla lost a packet of photos of Donald and her nude and at least a dozen pairs of expensive shoes. Then Kim found a suspicious surgical glove lying on the carpet. Marla believes the glove was left there by a burglar who stole her shoes, but so far no culprit has been found. Donald thinks it is all just a ploy to get him to buy her more high heels. He keeps comparing Marla with the shoe-hoarding former first lady of the Philippines.

"What are you," Donald fumes, "another Imelda Marcos?"

Jones can't help smiling. If Donald and Marla only knew the truth, they both would be shocked. Jones has been in Marla's apartment like this many times before. He later claims that the purpose of his visit is an innocent one. In any event he does not expect Marla to walk in on him and demand an explanation. He knows that she is busy rehearsing for *The Will Rogers Follies*. What Jones does not know is that he is being videotaped by a newly installed Trump security camera.

On the morning of July 15, 1992, Jones gets an unexpected telephone call from Trump security man Dominick Tezzo, who asks him to come to the Plaza Hotel to assist with a press conference. Jones rushes right over, only to find Marla, her mother, Ann Ogletree, her friend Janie Porco, and Trump security chief Matt Calamari waiting for him in Tezzo's office. Calamari immediately confronts Jones with a still photograph taken off the videotape made by the hidden camera in Marla's apartment and accuses him of stealing dozens of pairs of Marla's shoes as well as the missing photographs of her and Donald nude.

Jones vehemently and repeatedly denies that he is the thief. Calamari is not satisfied. According to Jones, the Trump security chief holds him hostage at the Plaza for the next eight hours, grilling him about the items missing from Marla's apartment. As the long afternoon wears on, Marla starts to believe that Jones may be innocent after all. But Calamari wants to check out one more hunch.

"Okay," he orders Jones. "Take me to your office."

Jones accompanies Calamari and the rest of the group to the eighth floor of an apartment building at 150 West Fifty-first Street. His office comprises an outer room, consisting of a purple carpet, a couch, a mirrored wall, and a kitchenette, and an inner sanctum, equipped with a banker's desk, a computer workbench, and a closet containing half a dozen file cabinets and a safe. Jones asks Calamari and the others to wait in the outer room while he confers with Marla in the inner sanctum. Moments later they hear a shriek.

"Those are my shoes!" Marla cries.

Calamari rushes in to find Marla staring at the file closet. It and surrounding nooks and crannies are allegedly stuffed with thirty pairs of Marla's shoes (some with slits cut in the back), photocopied excerpts from Marla's diaries, and a family photo album reported missing from Ann Ogletree's suite at the Plaza. When Jones refuses to open the safe inside the closet for further inspection, Calamari allegedly wrestles him to the floor so that Ann can snatch his keys. Calamari then unlocks the safe and allegedly finds a pornographic magazine called *Spike* and three unregistered handguns—a vintage 1912 .25-caliber Browning semiautomatic and two nineteenth-century antique pistols.

Evidently feeling that he has seen and heard enough, Calamari calls the police. The cops allegedly subject Jones to further questioning without allowing him to call a lawyer. Finally Jones is able to telephone Tom Fitzsimmons, who promises to get him legal counsel. At 8:00 P.M. attorney R. Emmett Heaphy calls Jones's office. The cops inform Heaphy that they plan to take Jones to the Midtown North Station for booking.

"This is not in your best interest," Heaphy warns Marla. "It'll be in all the papers tomorrow. You ought to let him go."

"Yeah, you might be right," Marla reportedly replies. "Let me see what happens, and I'll call you back."

Moments after Heaphy hangs up Jones's wife, Lynn, calls to ask Marla to let her husband go. But Marla apparently thinks that the matter is already out of her hands. She tells Lynn Jones that she has to run, that she and Donald are expected to join New York Governor Mario Cuomo at Madison Square Garden for the closing night of the 1992 Democratic National Convention. The cops haul Jones off in a transport van and throw him in jail for the rest of the night.

On Thursday, July 16, the *New York Daily News* banners the news of Jones's arrest across the top of its front page. MARLA: HE'S A HEEL, screams the headline. PUBLICIST ADMITS FETISH, HAS BEEN STEALING HER SHOES FOR YEARS. The story inside reports that Jones is suspected of stealing more than shoes. "Stuff had been disappearing for years," claims an unidentified "friend" of Marla's. "Little by little—shoes, underwear, books, photographs, notes. It was driving her crazy. People didn't even believe her after a while. Everyone thought she was losing her mind."

At 7:00 P.M. Jones is arraigned on charges of burglary, criminal possession of stolen property, and criminal possession of a weapon. Jones, who is now represented by attorney Herald Price Fahringer, pleads not guilty to all three charges, claiming that he has had his own set of keys to Marla's apartment and was simply there to "recover some of his own property." Bail is set at $5,000. Since Jones does not have enough cash to make bail, he is removed to the Tombs. That night he gives an exclusive jailhouse interview to *Daily News* gossip columnist Richard Johnson.

"I failed Marla, I failed Donald," Jones sobs, adding that his shoe fetish simply became overwhelming. "The more it developed, the more fearful I got. It's a problem I have to deal with. I'm just scared out of my mind."

On Friday, July 17, Lynn Jones comes up with $5,000 in cash, and her husband is released from the Tombs with a hearing date set for October 20. The following Monday Marla appears at the Manhattan district attorney's office wearing a brand-new pair of gold satin Charles Jourdan pumps and cream-colored slacks. She spends three hours identifying items the police have gathered from Jones's office. On Thursday, July 23, the district attorney's investigators raid Jones's office with a search warrant. They later search Jones's home in Greenwich, Connecticut, but fail to come up with Marla's diaries or the missing nude photographs.

Behind the scenes Jones is already blaming Marla and Donald for going public with the story of the shoe caper rather than handling the matter in private. He is especially upset by media reports suggesting that he stole "panties and bras" from Marla's apartment as well as shoes, insisting that any women's clothing found in his office belongs to his wife. He hints that if and when he is cleared of the criminal charges against him, he may file a civil suit against Donald Trump and his security men.

Marla, on the other hand, claims that Jones's refusal to seek psychiatric counseling left her no choice but to call in the police. "I don't want what happened to me to happen to anybody else. I also want [Jones] to admit needing help and get it," she says that evening on the television program "Entertainment Tonight," adding, "It was really sad to find out who it was. I would've hoped it was a stranger. [Jones] was always trying to convince me that he was the one person who would never do anything to hurt me."

On Monday, August 3, *New York Daily News* gossip columnist Richard Johnson reports a "new angle" on the missing photographs. An unidentified source who sounds like Tom Fitzsimmons claims that there are photos of Donald showing that "he's shaped like a bowling pin and he has a cottage cheese butt." The source adds that Donald has reason to be concerned about Marla's missing diaries, which supposedly contain passages about her relationships with Michael Bolton and "some Arab guy in Aspen," presumably Mohammed Hadid.

That evening Marla makes her long-awaited debut in *The Will Rogers Follies* on Broadway. In subsequent interviews producer Pierre Cossette admits that his old golfing buddy Donald deserves to "share credit" for getting Marla the part, though he also insists that Marla's association with Donald "worked against her because everyone assumed she'd be a dog." Cossette claims that after meeting Marla at a dinner party at Frank and Kathie Lee Gifford's house, he sent her to work with an associate who determined that "she can sing and she can dance." Marla later auditioned for a creative braintrust including Tommy Tune, Peter Stone, Cy Coleman, Betty Comden, and Adolph Green, who concluded that she could handle the part. In any event Marla's potential for generating free publicity is not lost on Cossette, who decorates the door to the Palace Theater with life-size photos of the show's newest cast member.

Predictably Marla's performance has already been panned in advance by *New York* magazine critic John Simon, who charges that she "surely cannot hold a candle" to her predecessor, former Tony nominee Cady Huffman. But Marla winds up doing much better than the naysayers expect. *New York Newsday* reviewer Jan Stuart notes that Marla is "capable" playing the part of "Ziegfeld's favorite," a role that calls for her to act as "a curvaceous prop who slinks on [stage] . . . with next to nothing on [to] provide a butt for Rogers' off-the-cuff innuendo. In short, a cheesecake with a wink." According to Stuart, "Marla looks too much the overripe Georgia-cheerleader type to convey the joke. On the other hand, she doesn't embarrass."

After the performance Donald hosts a party for Marla at the Plaza Hotel. Her mother, Kim Knapp, Janie Porco, Tom Fitzsimmons, Frank and Kathie Lee Gifford, and just about everyone else who has been important to her life and career are on hand—except, of course, Chuck Jones. The only blemish on the evening is a run-in with La Toya Jackson, who shows up with her ubiquitous boa constrictor. La Toya wants to pose for a photograph with Marla, but Marla whispers to Donald that she does not want to be shot in the same frame. La Toya overhears Marla's comment and heads for the door in a huff.

The next day Donald sends La Toya a bouquet of flowers, and Marla calls to apologize. "Let's go shopping," she suggests in an effort to patch things over with the help of her boyfriend's credit card. La Toya declines the invitation. But in the days that follow, La Toya claims she keeps hearing that Marla is bad-mouthing her all over town. Finally, she telephones Marla, and vents her rage. "You think I'm just some black bitch," La Toya charges. "Well, you're a racist who stole a husband. Kiss my ass." After La Toya slams down the phone, Marla tries to call her back but cannot get through. She later blames La Toya's outburst on prompting by her estranged publicist, Chuck Jones, who is now representing La Toya.

Marla and Donald are further distressed by the fallout from the shoe-stealing episode. Over the next few weeks they hear unconfirmed reports that Jones and / or Knapp are trying to sell the missing nude photographs to the *National Enquirer*—stories both deny. There is also a wild rumor that Jones, who by now is seeing a psychiatrist, wants to kill Marla, a story he also strenuously denies. Even more upsetting from Marla's point of view is that public sympathy seems to favor Jones, who is seen by many as yet another victim of her publicity-seeking boyfriend, Donald Trump.

On Thursday, September 10, Donald meets with Jones and attorney Herald Price Fahringer in Trump Tower. Jones, who claims to have mortgaged his home to pay for some $50,000 in legal fees, later reports that Donald is trying to blame everything on overzealous Trump security chief Matt Calamari. He says Donald wants him to sign a waiver promising not to sue the Trump Organization if Marla drops her complaint. Although the Trump Organization makes no official comment, one unidentified source tells reporters, "The peace talks have begun."

Ivana Trump raises her champagne glass with anything but peace on her mind. It is Tuesday, May 19, 1992, months before the exposure of the Chuck Jones caper but only a few weeks after her ex-husband's Holy Thursday court victory on the gag clause issue. Ivana is hosting a luncheon at Le Cirque for her author friend Sugar Rautbord. As fellow writer Joan Juliet Buck, CNN talk show host Sonya Friedman, porcelain dynasty heir Lady Jean Wedgwood, and half a dozen other socially prominent ladies look on, Ivana proposes a toast to Rautboard's newly published novel, *Sweet Revenge.*

"I love the title," Ivana declares with a naughty twinkle in her eye. "Maybe I'll use it in reality."

In fact, Ivana has been trying her damnedest to do just that. She has already taped a series of soon-to-air television commercials for Clairol shampoo in which she coyly observes, "Beautiful hair is the best revenge." Even sweeter is the fact that her own first novel, *For Love Alone,* is on the *New York Times* best seller list and has been optioned by CBS for a television miniseries. Having debuted at number six in late April, the book will remain on the *Times* list for a good six weeks. That is no match for the forty-seven-week run enjoyed by her ex-husband's first nonfiction book, *Trump: The Art of the Deal*, but it is a more than respectable sales performance for a first novel. And it is enough to infuriate The Donald.

"He can't stand that I divorced him," Ivana confides to her luncheon companions. "He can't stand that I didn't lie down and die. He can't stand that I have a wonderful man in Riccardo [Mazzucchelli] and that my book is a best seller."

Ivana is not just paranoid. The day before the luncheon the front page of the *New York Post* announces the news: TRUMP'S SUING IVANA! SAYS SHE AND HER PLAYBOY LOVER ARE . . . LIVING IN $IN. The *Post's* exclusive story, which is written by The Donald's favorite gossip columnist, Cindy Adams, features quotes from affidavits by Trump employees attesting that Ivana and Riccardo recently traveled together to Rome, St. Moritz, Paris, Venice, Aspen, Houston, San Francisco, and Los Angeles and spent more than three weeks at Mar-a-Lago in Palm Beach. Besides giving money to the Trump children for such items as baseball cards and a pet turtle, Riccardo reportedly joined Ivana and the kids in, of all things, raking leaves at her house in Greenwich.

"I mean this guy is with her in houses I paid for," Donald complains to Adams, "eating in kitchens I paid for, sleeping in beds I paid for, and I'm still supposed to pay for it?"

Of course, as Adams duly notes, The Donald has more at stake in filing suit against Ivana than his macho ego. Under the terms of the Trumps' nuptial contract, Ivana must move out of the Trump Tower triplex once she marries or starts "cohabiting" with another man. If cohabitation is established, Donald still owes her a $4 million move-out allowance, but he can stop paying some $700,000 a year in spousal support, child support, and household maintenance.

In late June Ivana retains a new attorney, Neil Papiano of Los Angeles, who has represented the likes of Elizabeth Taylor and Joan Collins. Papiano promptly files a point-by-point rebuttal of The Donald's cohabitation allegations. The next day Cindy Adams fires back with an exclusive account of a statement by Minna Laputina, Ivana's recently terminated former personal assistant. Laputina claims that

Riccardo is Ivana's "constant lover and companion" and that he has given her $500,000 to decorate a house at 16 Cadogan Square in London. Laputina also claims Ivana stated that she would delay marrying Riccardo so she could continue receiving support payments from The Donald.

"Let that bastard pay me for another year," Laputina quotes Ivana as saying.

Thanks to The Donald, Ivana remains on the defensive for the rest of the summer. On July 1 the New York Court of Appeals declines to review her appeal of the gag clause ruling, stating that "no substantial constitutional question" is involved. Noted appellate expert Floyd Abrams, who is spearheading Ivana's legal team, vows to seek a rehearing. But his efforts are destined to be in vain. In the fall the Court of Appeals will deny Abrams's plea to review the gag clause. That will leave Ivana with only one remaining avenue of appeal, the United States Supreme Court.

In the meantime, The Donald presses his advantage. On July 28 he sues Ivana for $25 million, the estimated gross cash and asset value of their financial settlement. He claims that her best-selling novel *For Love Alone* violates the gag clause in their nuptial contract and charges that she has committed "fraud" by revealing details of their marital relationship in the guise of her *roman à clef*. He demands an accounting of all her book profits and the return of all moneys he has paid out to her under their divorce agreement.

Amid her fight with The Donald, Ivana wages a series of other postdivorce battles. She still has not settled her dispute with former attorney Michael Kennedy over his unpaid legal fees, and Kennedy has not settled the related dispute over former publicist John Scanlon's bills. On August 4 Ivana loses to yet another creditor. Investigative Group Inc. (IGI), which Kennedy retained to spy on The Donald, is suing her for failing to pay $225,000 worth of bills. Although Ivana's attorney Gary Lyman terms the IGI bill "outrageous," Manhattan Supreme Court Judge Shirley Fingerhood eventually rules in IGI's favor and orders Ivana to pay up.

As in recent summers past, Ivana also cuts a rather wide swath through European high society. On June 8 she attends an Oscar de la Renta fashion show at Claridge's in London and commits the double faux pas of entering and leaving the room before Her Royal

Highness Princess Margaret. Word of Ivana's miscues makes it all the
way across the Atlantic, where the tabloids report that she suffered
the further embarrassment of writing Princess Margaret "a note of
groveling apology." Two days later, while touring Ireland to promote her novel, Ivana and her aides create an impatient ruckus in
the waiting room of a Dublin radio station while the talk show host
finishes interviewing eighty-two-year-old anti-Nazi heroine Christa-
bel Bielenberg. Upon emerging from the interview room, Bielenberg
confronts Ivana and her party, demanding, "And where is this Mrs.
Plump?"

In late July Ivana arrives in Paris for the couture, claiming that the
airline has lost her luggage. She calls on designer Valentino to come
to her rescue. Valentino obligingly rushes a new wardrobe to Ivana's
hotel so she will not have to give up her front-row seat beside the
runways. A few months later *People* magazine nevertheless names Ivana
to its 1992 Ten Worst Dressed List, a dubious distinction she shares
with Roseanne Arnold, Monica Seles, and La Toya Jackson. The
magazine notes that she has access to "a cadre of big-name designers
from Versace to Ungaro to Thierry Mugler" but always seems a bit
"off." The reason, according to image consultant Susan Bixler: "She
doesn't understand understatement."

By summer's end Ivana resumes her ongoing battle against The
Donald with a pointed legal offensive. On August 26 she announces
that she has made a 10 percent down payment on a $2.8 million town
house at 10 East Sixty-fourth Street in Manhattan, signaling that she
is at last ready to move out of the Trump Tower triplex. She then
demands that The Donald pay her the $4 million housing allowance
stipulated in their nuptial contract. Her attorney Neil Papiano also
announces plans to ask the court to cite The Donald for contempt
because of his refusal to pay Ivana her 1992 alimony.

Ironically, Ivana may be better able to secure her own financial
future than The Donald. Like show business stars Cher and Madonna,
she lets it be known in charitable and commercial circles that she is
dropping her married and maiden names and solely using her first
name, which she perceives to have greater social and marketing cachet
than ever. According to longtime aide Lisa Calandra, the new president of Ivana, Inc., she plans to market a line of Ivana jewelry in

time for Christmas 1992, followed by Ivana skin products in the spring of 1993 and Ivana clothing in the fall of 1994.

But Ivana may have an even greater coup in store. By late September it is an open secret that Citibank is becoming increasingly anxious to have The Donald sell the Plaza Hotel for any reasonable offer. The rumored trigger price is $425 million, or roughly the principal amount the bank lent on the hotel. Although The Donald and Citibank have reportedly rejected a $370 million bid as too low, several major hotel firms continue to express interest in buying the Plaza. The kicker is that at least one of those potential buyers has privately approached Ivana to see if she would be interested in coming back to run the hotel. "It would be a brilliant marketing move," claims one former Plaza executive familiar with the behind-the-scenes talks. "There are lots of people who worked for her in Atlantic City and New York who are dying to work for her again."

Be that as it may, Ivana continues to show that she is as maladroit in American politics as she seems to be in the company of British royalty. In mid-November she flies to Little Rock to attend a benefit sponsored by the Arkansas Multiple Sclerosis Society. She quickly discovers that Bill Clinton's home state is not as hospitable as she imagined. First, Ivana tries to pay a call on the president-elect at the Governor's Mansion, only to be turned away by the Secret Service. The day after the benefit she gets into another embarrassing flap at the Capitol Hotel when she refuses to pay her bill for $235. Ivana claims that her expenses are supposed to be covered by the MS Society, but the incident only adds to her growing reputation as a first-class deadbeat.

At the same time Ivana is pleasantly surprised to find that Trumpian politics can indeed make strange bedfellows. During the week preceding her ill-fated trip to Little Rock she appears at an AIDS benefit sponsored by the Fashion Accessory Industry Together for Health (FAITH). The benefit, which is held at the trendy bistro Cité, features Ivana and a cast of other New York celebrities modeling pajamas. After the show Ivana is greeted backstage by an unexpected admirer, the notorious Chuck Jones.

"I just wanted to congratulate you on a fine show," Jones ventures, noting that the paparazzi are noting the two of them standing together.

"Thank you very much," says Ivana. Then, as the cameras start to click, she leans over and busses Jones on the cheek.

Donald Trump strides into Marla Maples's newly renovated apartment in Trump Parc preparing to lower the boom. It is early October 1992, and their love is on the rocks for the umpteenth time. After a spat earlier in the summer Marla pulled off her Harry Winston diamond engagement ring and threw it at him. Donald has never given it back. In mid-September Marla created a public row at a party at Tavern on the Green when Donald left her in the wings to go chasing models with former Mets star Keith Hernandez. Now Donald is at the end of his rope.

"I'm sick of your possessiveness," he tells her. "It's over, Marla."

"You're damn right it's over," Marla retorts. "You deserve all those mindless bimbos."

On October 14 the *New York Daily News* banners the Trump-Maples breakup on the front page: SPLITSVILLE—NEW YORK'S FUN COUPLE CALLS IT QUITS . . . AGAIN. Not to be outdone, *New York Post* columnist Cindy Adams reports that she has seen the split coming ever since she accompanied Donald on a trip to Atlantic City in September. "I only know that whatever happens to us I will have no guilt," Donald supposedly told Adams. "Marla's doing well. I have given her career a boost. I've made her famous."

Although Marla does not issue a public statement, she is clearly prepared to go it alone. Her new exercise video, *Journey to Fitness,* is coming out in a few weeks, and she has done a good job on Broadway. According to the producer, ticket sales at *The Will Rogers Follies* are up 20 percent since she joined the cast. She has even made a guest appearance on "Loving," the television soap opera she unsuccessfully auditioned for when she first came to New York; as if to attest to her celebrity, she plays herself and conducts a *Journey to Fitness* exercise class.

"I don't need Donald's help anymore," she tells friends. "I can make it on my own."

Marla starts showing up around town with Richard Fields, her would-be manager and the proprietor of a comedy club called Catch a Rising Star. Fields even closes down the club to host a birthday party for her nine days after Marla's split from Donald hits the front pages. The catch is that Fields's star is hardly rising. It turns out that he has recently put the club in Chapter 11 after promising his landlord to pay $25,000 in back rent.

Donald wastes no time in letting the media know that he is enjoying his newfound freedom. He enlists the aid of a long-haired designer / party organizer named Milan to promote his night life and allows himself to be photographed in the company of fashion models Frederique Van de Wall, Angelica Bollinger, Anna Nicole, and Eva Herzigova, as well as with Miss Universe, Michelle McLean, and Miss USA, Shannon Marketic. Then he gives a Halloween party at Mar-a-Lago for which John Casablancas flies down no fewer than twenty Elite models, and he invites "Entertainment Tonight" to come into the mansion and film the scene. "Mrs. Post is turning over in her grave," Donald says with a grin.

But for all his outward swagger Donald is hamstrung by his own fears. Though he boasts about his nocturnal conquests, he never seems to connect with any of the women he meets—or take them home to bed. According to his male pals, this is partly due to his social ineptitude and partly due to his abject terror of contracting AIDS or some other sexually transmitted disease. In fact, by early November, only a few weeks after their breakup, Marla confides to friends that he is calling her again every day. Donald tries to squelch such stories, informing Cindy Adams, "I'm no wimp."

At the same time Donald is well aware that public perceptions of his professional life are even less favorable than those of his private life. Back at his birthday party in June, he introduced former Middle East hostage Joseph Cicippio to his other invited guests, then startled all in attendance by comparing his financial ordeal to Cicippio's ordeal in Lebanon. He now determines to change the perception that he is on a slow road to personal bankruptcy by declaring that he has already made an astonishing recovery.

On the evening of Saturday, November 7, a throng of elegantly attired guests, murmuring with excitement and wonder, files into the grand ballroom of the Trump Taj Mahal in Atlantic City. At the far end of the room there is a giant paper screen emblazoned with newspaper stories announcing Donald J. Trump's financial comeback. Suddenly the sound system strikes up the theme from the movie *Rocky*.

"Let's hear it for the king," screams an announcer.

On cue, a familiar figure bursts through the screen, punching the paper aside with a pair of bright red boxing gloves. It is none other than Donald J. Trump himself, clad in a black tuxedo with a red satin boxer's robe draped over his shoulders. Following in the lyrical style of former heavyweight champion Muhammad Ali, Trump gaming division chief Nick Ribis celebrates his boss's appearance by reading a specially composed poem.

"He was tough and resilient, and he had no fear. He made the comeback of the year," Ribis rhymes. "Against all odds his opponents buckled with a thump. The winner was Donald J. Trump."

The party becomes still more surreal as the guests find their tables. Each place setting comes with a life-size mug shot of Donald at the end of a wooden stick and a disposable camera that the partygoer can use to take snapshots of everyone wearing the Don-on-a-wand mask. After munching a meal of lobster-covered veal, the diners are entertained by Marilyn Monroe and Elvis Presley impersonators, who serenade the host / guest of honor. Then there is a Trump-produced video commemorating the opening of Donald's three Atlantic City casinos.

"What he has achieved is almost a miracle," claims gaming industry analyst Marvin Roffman, who has recently won a wrongful termination suit against his former employer, Janney Montgomery Scott, and reconciled with Donald out of court despite his initial negative forecast for the Taj. "Trump casinos had the best year-to-year improvement of any of the casinos in Atlantic City.

"This has been maybe the best year of my life," Donald later proclaims in an interview with a New Jersey newspaper.

While some may debate that, Donald has certainly had an interesting week. On Monday *New York* magazine celebrates his supposed comeback with a cover story headlined FIGHTING BACK: TRUMP SCRAMBLES OFF THE CANVAS. In the course of taking writer Julie Baumgold on a guided tour of the Trump empire, Donald announces that he is already working on a third book tentatively titled *Trump: The Art of the Comeback*. But instead of hiring another ghostwriter, he is dictating the narrative into a tape recorder. "I learned that I'm the toughest bastard around," he says of his financial crisis, later adding, "New York was dead for a while, the deals were almost finished. When Trump is back, New York is back."

But it is far from certain that either one is "back." On the very same day that the *New York* magazine article hits the stands, the Plaza Hotel files a prepackaged bankruptcy plan in federal court. Under the plan, Citibank and three other banks agree to restructure Donald's $300 first-mortgage loan on the Plaza Hotel and to release him from his personal guarantee on the hotel's $125 million second-mortgage loan. In return, Donald officially gives up a 49 percent ownership stake to the banks. The Trump Organization claims that Donald will continue to operate the Plaza and retain a right of first refusal on any buyout offer. But his bankers privately insist that they now "control" the Plaza as the hotel's general partners and that they have first and final say on any buyout.

Three days after the Plaza Hotel bankruptcy filing, Boston Safe Deposit agrees to give Donald a five-year extension on a $9 million loan on Mar-a-Lago. With that announcement, a previously proposed plan to have his father, Fred Trump, Sr., guarantee the loan is shelved. But Donald is hardly home free. Though Boston Safe pledges not to foreclose on Mar-a-Lago unless Donald defaults on his interest payments, the bank insists on holding the deed to the Palm Beach estate. In order to make good on his part of the restructuring, Donald must pay the bank more than $1.1 million a year to cover back interest and current interest on the loan.

Donald's ability to make those and other debt-related payments is far from certain. Unbeknownst to the media and the general public, the banks have abandoned the idea of keeping him on the personal spending allowance announced with his original June 1990 debt restructuring. ("We've basically forgotten about all that crap," says a Citibank source. "It just didn't work. Donald is basically going to do what he wants to do with whatever money he makes.") As a result, Donald continues to enjoy a multimillion-dollar annual income stream provided by the recent restructuring of the bond debt on his casinos. According to documents filed with the Casino Control Commission, the Taj Mahal is paying him more than $1.5 million a year in "management fees," while Trump Castle pays him a little over $1 million a year.

"What happened to Trump is a testament to a breakdown in the nation's bankruptcy system," the *Washington Post* declares in a November 29 Sunday feature piece, noting that Donald's personal financial situation is far better than it would have been if the banks had forced him into Chapter 11. The same cannot necessarily be said for the banks and boldholders holding the restructured debt on his fabled trophy properties in New York and Atlantic City. While a protracted bankruptcy court proceeding might have further eroded the potential returns for Donald's creditors, they have collectively lost well over half a billion dollars in unpaid bank and bond interest already, and hopes for a truly dramatic turnaround remain dim.

Despite their highly publicized "comeback," the Trump casinos have by no means put themselves on solid financial ground. As Donald repeatedly points out, all three have indeed enjoyed impressive year-to-year increases in gross revenues. In October, for example, the Taj grossed over $35.7 million, up more than 20 percent from October 1991. Gross revenues at Trump Plaza and Trump Castle were up 23 percent and 29 percent respectively. But according to Trump casino consultant Al Glasgow, much of these gains are part of citywide increase in gross revenues attributable to the advent of twenty-four gambling and to changes in slot machine jackpot accounting rules and increased coin giveaways.

Relatively little of the Trump casinos' improvement in gross revenues makes it to the bottom lines. In fact, the gross operating profits for the Taj and the Plaza for the three months ended September 30, 1992, are actually down roughly $2 million and $1 million respectively from the same period in 1991. Only Trump Castle shows an increase in gross operating profit of roughly $2.5 million. Perhaps even more significant, all three casinos are still burdened with enormous debt. Trump Plaza appears to be in the best shape with roughly $300 million in bond and preferred stock obligations. But in order to repay the bond debt on the Taj Mahal, Donald would have to sell the casino for over $800 million. He would have to realize over $329 million in asset sales to repay Trump Castle bond and bank indebtedness.

Back in New York City, Donald's real estate empire is also beset with serious problems. In late September he reports that broker Carrie Chiang has recently sold fifty-three condominiums in Trump Palace on Third Avenue for $43 million, but that impressive sales figure disguises the fact that the units are selling for millions of dollars below the prices listed in the allegedly fraudulent prospectus he submitted to Citibank to get a loan on the property. That same month Donald leaks word to *New York Post* columnist Cindy Adams that Princess Diana might build a $5 million apartment for herself in Trump Tower. Apparently unaware that Donald circulated an identical false rumor back in the mid-1980s, Adams gives full-page play to the story despite Buckingham Palace's denial.

Meanwhile, Donald continues to wage a bitter legal battle against the Pritzkers, his partners in the Grand Hyatt Hotel. REFCO, the Pritzkers' corporate operating entity, is demanding that he pay for half of what they believe to be a direly needed $34 million renovation of the hotel. The dispute is in the hands of an arbitration panel that generally seems to judge REFCO's claims as meritorious. "The Grand Hyatt stands out in the marketplace as the one hotel which is neither new [n]or newly renovated," the REFCO complaint maintains, charging that Donald's refusal to pay his share of the costs represents "nothing more than the desperate attempt of a struggling business-man to escape from an agreement." To make matters worse for Donald, the REFCO suit is apparently stalling a previously announced plan for him to transfer his half interest in the Grand Hyatt to Bankers Trust in order to reduce his outstanding real estate debts.

The one glimmer of hope in Donald's troubled portfolio of trophy properties is the West Side yards. In late October the City Planning Commission unanimously approves a scaled-down version of his Riverside South project. According to the revised plan, Donald will be allowed to build only 7.9 million square feet on the site, instead of the proposed 8.3 million square feet, and will have to contribute millions of dollars for subway and infrastructure improvements. But he also gets some major concessions from the city. In most instances the city grants developers only three years to complete the shell of the first building on a development site. Donald is given six and a half years to complete the shell of Riverside South's first building, an extraordinary grace period he hopes will increase his leverage with the banks and potential buyers.

Even so, there are nasty undercurrents surrounding Donald's latest development proposal for the West Side yards. A few weeks before

the City Planning Commission vote City Council President Andrew
Stein, a longtime Trump political ally, takes a poll asking residents of
the Upper West Side if they would be more inclined to support him
in a mayoral race against incumbent David Dinkins if he opposed the
Riverside South project. Donald naturally interprets Stein's poll as
evidence of betrayal. "A nuclear bomb is waiting to drop on Stein,"
he tells *New York* magazine writer Baumgold. An anonymous source
later hints to *New York Daily News* columnist Richard Johnson that
Donald may have some tape recordings that could cause Stein considerable embarrassment.

On December 17 the City Council convenes to cast a final vote on
Riverside South. As it turns out, Stein's position is irrelevant, for he
can vote only in case of a tie, and the vote is not even close. Significantly, six of the ten members of the Manhattan delegation vote against
the project; all six represent districts on the West Side. They are joined
by two councilmembers from Brooklyn. But a total of forty-two other
councilmembers vote in favor of Riverside South. One of those who
votes in the majority, Councilman Charles Millard of Manhattan's
Upper East Side, expresses some of the doubts and ambivalences of
his colleagues by composing a takeoff of the poem " 'Twas the Night
before Christmas." Millard's verse reads, in part:

> Because to build here will be so costly it might be a goof
> To think there'll be built even one little roof.
> In the meantime this gift to The Donald is passed
> As he tries to put bankruptcy talks in his past.
> For while all this might be built in a year or in ten
> We could well be dealing with this site again.

There is more than a grain of truth in Millard's doggerel. In order
for Donald to develop Riverside South himself, he would have to
secure hundreds of millions of dollars in additional bank financing
above and beyond the $213 million debt the property already carries.
It appears far more likely that banks will make him sell off chunks of
the property to other developers who would be bound by the same
newly passed zoning regulations. But as if to prove that he has not
lost his sense of timing or his talent for manipulating the media, Donald's public relations machine delivers some rather intriguing news

to the *New York Times* just prior to the City Council vote on Riverside South.

TRUMP'S BACK AND MAY BE BANKABLE, declares the headline of a *Times* business section lead story by Diana B. Henriques on November 16. The Gist of the story is that the Trump Plaza casino plans to sell $375 million worth of new bonds. Donald claims that the proceeds of the bond issue will be used to retire $300 million worth of existing Trump Plaza debt, leaving some $75 million for him to use to buy back portions of his bank debts at a discount. "In two years, I will be stronger than I ever was," he predicts in a subsequent exclusive interview. "And it will be real strength—not just smoke and mirrors."

The optimistic tone of the *New York Times* article, which is buttressed mostly by quotes from unidentified bankers, brokers, and lawyers, conveys a sense of déjà vu. Back in 1976, when Donald was putting together his first bid deal for the Grand Hyatt, a flattering but unsubstantiated *New York Times* article by the late Judy Klemesrud helped lay the foundations for the Trump myth. Now history seems to be repeating itself as the *Times* helps lay the mythological foundations for Donald's comeback.

"Is this 1976 all over again?" a reporter asks after the vote on Riverside South.

"I hopes so," Donald says with a smile.

The banks' scenario for Donald J. Trump's future, however, is not nearly so rosy. By their estimates, his current net worth is still considerably less than zero, possibly as low as minus $400 million. Donald's bankers privately maintain that he may have only $30 million worth of equity in Trump Plaza casino, not $75 million, and possibly another $15 million worth of equity in the Trump Tower apartment units he still owns. That is hardly enough to repay the $165 million in personally guaranteed debts he owes above and beyond the more than $800 million in debt still mortgaged against his New York real estate properties. Earlier in the fall, when asked point-blank by an analyst if Citibank would lend Donald more money to develop his West Side yards property, bank chairman John S. Reed replied with an unequivocal no.

Donald is, at least in the view of his bankers, playing an end game. The banks believe that even if he liquidates all his major assets by the time the grace period provided by his June 1990 restructuring expires in June 1995, he will still be in the hole to the tune of $100 million in personally guaranteed debt. And what will happen if Donald is unable or unwilling to make up the $100 million shortfall out of his own pocket? "We'll go after him," says one banker.

Donald's only major potential avenue of escape from such an embarrassment—turning to his old man for more financial aid—appears to have been narrowed, if not completely closed off. In the summer of 1992, while Donald was starting to circulate rumors of his impending comeback, Fred Trump, Sr., turned over management of his estate, estimated to be worth in excess of $150 million, to Donald's younger brother, Robert. Although Donald denies being at odds with his brother, according to some family friends that move did not go down well with Donald. A few weeks later Robert reportedly nixed a pending plan to have Fred, Sr., guarantee the $9 million loan on Mar-a-Lago, a clear sign that he is determined to keep his older brother's hands out of the family cookie jar.

"Robert and Donald won't see eye to eye," Fred, Sr., keeps complaining to family friends, his voice cracking with emotion.

Despite reports of encroaching senility, the old man seems to grasp the tragicomic nature of Donald's fate far better than Donald himself. Until the banks and bondholders sell his trophy properties out from under him, he can still parade about town pretending to be an unbowed former billionaire in the midst of a remarkable comeback. He is still able to generate self-serving headlines in the national and local tabloids and sometimes even in the *New York Times.* He is still asked to make cameo appearances in daytime soap operas and television miniseries. There is even talk of a Broadway show tentatively titled *Trump: The Musical.*

But in almost every other way Donald J. Trump has become the lost tycoon of the late twentieth century. He has already lost many of his most glittering trophy properties, including his yacht, his plane, his airline, and half of his largest Atlantic City casino. Over the next two years, barring a financial miracle, he stands to lose virtually all the rest of his best real estate assets and at least one, if not all three, of his casinos. He has alienated his ex-wife, his ex-mistress, and most of his former top-ranking business associates, not to mention his brother and his father. And if he still retains his beguiling charm and a certain uncanny populist appeal, he has lost both his credibility and his once-storied image as the master artist of the deal.

And yet it seems that the more things change in the life of Donald J. Trump, the more they remain the same. On the advent of the Christmas / New Year holiday of 1992, the third anniversary of the now-infamous three-way confrontation on the ski slopes of Aspen, Ivana takes off for Switzerland, where she plans to be photographed in the company of men other than Riccardo in hopes of drawing attention away from her ex-husband's cohabitation suit. Marla suddenly returns to New York from her exercise video promotional tour amid rumors that Donald is once again begging her to marry him. And Donald prepares to fly to Aspen with his children in tow, dauntlessly returning to the scene of the crime that triggered his vainglorious fall, beating against the current, and trying to defy the truth of F. Scott Fitzgerald's axiomatic observation in *The Last Tycoon*, "There are no second acts in American lives."

NOTES

The purpose of these notes is to credit previously published and unpublished sources not fully identified in the text. Author's interviews and other communications to the author are generally not included in the notes.

PAGE   1. DON OF A DECADE

1   "I've never met a successful man . . .": This and other quotations in this chapter attributed to *Playboy* are from Glenn Plaskin's interview with Donald J. Trump published in the March 1990 issue.

14   "I think what attracts us so much is the energy . . .": Ivana Trump quoted from Norma King, *Ivana Trump: A Very Unauthorized Biography* (New York: Carroll & Graf, 1990), p. 65.

15   "The worst thing a man can do . . .": Donald J. Trump statement to Mark G. Etess quoted in John R. O'Donnell, *Trumped!: The Inside Story of the Real Donald Trump—His Cunning Rise and Spectacular Fall* (New York: Simon & Schuster, 1991), p. 67.

20   "It's not going to be a big fight . . .": Donald J. Trump statement quoted ibid., p. 189.

21   "Call my lawyers . . .": Cartoon dialogue from G. B. Trudeau, *Give Those Nymphs Some Hooters: A Doonesbury Book* (Kansas City: Andrews and McMeel, 1989), p. 7.

21   "Dear Mr. Trumps [*sic*] . . .": Letter excerpted in *New York Daily News*, October 9, 1989.

23   "If Donald were married . . .": Ivana Trump quoted in *Time* (January 16, 1989).

23   "I run my operations . . .": Ibid.

25   "Lions and fawns . . .": *Fortune* (April 11, 1988).

28   "I always stand by the man . . .": Ivana Trump quoted in King, op. cit., p. 170.

28 "I think it's upsetting ...": Ivana Trump quoted in Michael Shnayerson, "Power Blonde," *Vanity Fair* (January 1988).

2. LIFE IS CHEAP

37 "These two guys are my experts ...": Donald J. Trump quoted in *New York Daily News,* October 11, 1989.

38 "I just hope I'm still young ...": Stephen Hyde quoted in O'Donnell, op. cit., p. 191.

38 "Donald Trump, Steve Hyde and I ...": Mark G. Etess quoted in *New York Daily News,* October 11, 1989.

39 "I can't wait ...": Mark G. Etess quoted in Donald J. Trump with Charles Leerhsen, *Trump: Surviving at the Top* (New York: Random House, 1990), p. 17.

40 Dialogue between Donald J. Trump and Stephen Hyde quoted ibid., p. 17.

41 Details of helicopter crash and rotor blade defect based on National Transportation Safety Board, Alan J. Yurman, "Factual Report: Aviation," March 29, 1991.

42 Telephone calls between Donald J. Trump and Jeri Hasse, Trump and CBS News reporter quoted in *TRUMP: Surviving at the Top,* p. 18.

43 "For an instant, as they were walking ...": Ibid., pp. 17–18.

43 "Life is fragile ...": Ibid., p. 19.

43 "It cheapened life to me ...": Donald J. Trump quoted in John Taylor, "Trump: The Soap Opera," *New York* (March 5, 1990).

43 "Can you believe they rode ...": Donald J. Trump quoted in O'Donnell, op. cit., p. 197.

44 "Boy, wouldn't the competition ...": Ibid., p. 197.

45 "This has been a horrible experience ...": Ibid., p. 197.

46 "God, that was an incredible thing ...": Ibid., p. 200.

56 Trump Taj Mahal estimated cost overruns cited in ABC News interview with construction manager Tom Pippett, November 14, 1990.

57–58 Account of Trump Plaza deal with Rolling Stones and press conference based in part on O'Donnell, op. cit., pp. 234–42, 325.

59–60 Account of Donald J. Trump trip to Chattanooga based in part on "Caught: Trump & His Mistress," *National Enquirer,* May 1, 1990.

3. QUEENS REX

67 "The most important influence ...": Donald J. Trump with Tony Schwartz, *Trump: The Art of the Deal* (New York: Random House, 1987), p. 65.

68 Donald J. Trump claimed his grandfather "came here from Sweden": Ibid., p. 66.

68 Value of Fred Trump estate based on probate court records, Queens County, New York.

69 Account of Lehrenkrauss bankruptcy based in part on Wayne Barrett, *Trump: The Deals and the Downfall* (New York: HarperCollins, 1992), pp. 33–39, 102.

70 Account of Shore Haven and Beach Haven deals based in part on Jerome Tuccille, *Trump: A Biography* (New York: Donald I. Fine, 1987), pp. 28, 35–36; also, Barrett, op. cit., pp. 46–58.

71 Account of Trump Village scandal based in part on Tuccille, op. cit., p. 47; Barrett, op. cit., pp. 59–70.

74 Account of mob influence over New York City concrete industry based in part on Selwyn Raab, "Irregularities in Concrete Industry Inflate Building Costs, Experts Say," *New York Times,* April 26, 1982, and other articles by Raab, Michael Orestes, Leslie Maitland, and Arnold H. Lubasch in *New York Times,* 1982–1987.

78 Ted Levine statements quoted from his interview with ABC News, July 22, 1990.

78 Colonel Ted Dobias's statements quoted from his interview with ABC News, summer 1990.

81 "all the good [real estate] properties . . .": *Trump: The Art of the Deal,* p. 94.

82 "Don't tell me what the law is . . .": Nicholas von Hoffman, *Citizen Cohn: The Life and Times of Roy Cohn* (New York: Doubleday, 1988), p. 380.

83 Trump campaign contributions to Hugh Carey reported in Barrett, op. cit., p. 122.

84 Victor Palmieri's assessment of Trump net worth cited in his interview with ABC News, summer 1990.

84 "Whatever Donald and Fred want . . .": Abraham D. Beame statement and account of David Berger role in Penn Central deal based on Barrett, op. cit., pp. 94–114; also Penn Central Transportation Company bankruptcy records. Philadelphia, Pennsylvania.

85–86 Account of convention center dealings based in part on Tuccille, op. cit., pp. 107–18; Barrett, op. cit., pp. 104–07, 125–26; and Penn Central bankruptcy records.

87 "Buying the Commodore . . .": Fred C. Trump, Sr., quoted in *Trump: The Art of the Deal,* p. 121.

89 "make sure that this . . .": Michael Bailkin statement quoted from his interview with ABC News, August 2, 1990.

92 "When he was working on the Commodore . . .": This and all subsequent statements attributed to Neil Walsh quoted from his interview with ABC News, August 2, 1990.

93 Account of Fred C. Trump Sr.'s arrest based on author's interview with the Prince Georges County housing authority arresting officer, Joe Healy; Barrett, op. cit., pp. 81–82.

4. CZECH MATE

96–97 Account of Ivana Trump's youth based in part on King, op. cit., pp. 18–26, and author's interviews.

97–102 Account of Ivana Trump's relationships with George Syrovatka and George Staidl based in part on author's interviews with Ladislav Staidl; also King, op. cit., pp. 26–46, and Bob Colacello, "Ivana Be a Star," *Vanity Fair* (May 1992).

104 Account of Donald J. Trump's conversations with Audrey Morris and Yolande Cardinal based on King, op. cit., pp. 70–79.

105 Account of battle over first and subsequent Trump nuptial contracts based in part on records in Manhattan Superior Court.

111–12 Account of Commodore Hotel closing based in part on Von Hoffman, op. cit., p. 383, and Barrett, op. cit., pp. 129–32.

112–13 "Hey, let me know if . . .": This and all subsequent statements attributed to Ralph Steinglass quoted from his interview with ABC News, July 9, 1990.

115–18 Account of Trump Tower deal based in part on *Trump: The Art of the Deal,* pp. 145–93.

118 "Galanos—I just ordered . . .": Ivana Trump quoted in Tuccille, op. cit., p. 155.

119–20 Account of Donald J. Trump's entry into Atlantic City based in part on Alan Lapidus interview with ABC News, July 2, 1990; also sworn testimony and affidavits filed in connection with *Daniel Sullivan and Stavan Industries v. State of New Jersey, et al.*

120 Account of Bonwit Teller demolition and Trump Tower tax abatement controversy based in part on sworn testimony by Daniel Sullivan, Albin Lupinski, and others in *Henry J. Diduck, et al. v. Kaszycki & Sons Contractors, Inc., et al.;* also Edward I. Koch, *Mayor: An Autobiography* (New York: Simon & Schuster, 1984), pp. 293–59, 297.

124 Account of "John Baron" role in Bonwit Teller artwork episode based in part on Tuccille, op. cit., pp. 163–64.

125 Account of 100 Central Park South battle based in part on ABC News interview with John C. Moore III, summer 1990, and author's interviews with Moore and other participants.

126 "Our family environment . . .": This and other Donald J. Trump statements to *Playboy* in this chapter quoted from his interview with Glenn Plaskin, *Playboy* (March 1990).

5. TRUMP TOWERS

130 Account of Trump Tower construction based in part on Jonathan Mandell, *Trump Tower,* with photographs by Sy Rubin, (New York: Lyle Stuart, 1984).

130 Account of mob involvement in Trump Tower construction and role of John Cody based in part on Raab, et al., *New York Times* articles, supra, and Barrett, op. cit., pp. 193–201.

134 Account of Donald J. Trump financial status based on New Jersey Division of Gaming Enforcement report of October 16, 1981.

134 Statements attributed to Tom Pippett here and on subsequent pages quoted from his interview with ABC News, November 14, 1990.

135 Statements attributed to John Allen here and on subsequent pages quoted from his interview with ABC News, summer 1990.

136 Account of Donald J. Trump diet drug treatments based in part on copies of Trump medical records and other information published in John Connolly, "Just Say 'Please,' " *Spy* (February 1992).

138 "The enormous success of Trump Tower . . .": Quoted from N. J. Perry, "Presenting: A Trump / Tisch / Davis Production" *Fortune* (April 11, 1988).

138–40 Account of Donald J. Trump professional football venture here and on subsequent pages based in part on Jim Byrne, *The $1 League: The Rise and Fall of the United States Football League* (New York: Prentice Hall, 1987).

141 "Cowboys? We don't want cowboys . . .": Ivana Trump quoted in William Geist, "The Expanding Empire of Donald Trump" *New York Times Magazine,* April 8, 1984.

143 "a congress of oddities": Al Glasgow, *Atlantic City Action,* Atlantic City, New Jersey, June 8, 1984.

147–48 Account of Conrad Stephenson's role in Trump bank loans based in part on Barrett, op. cit., pp. 299–317; also author's interviews with former Trump Organization executives.

148–61 Account of Trump Castle purchase based in part on *Trump: The Art of the Deal,* pp. 225–48, and John Connolly, "All of the People All of the Time" *Spy* (April 1991); also author's interviews with Al Glasgow and others.

155 Account of Donald J. Trump's relationship with Joe Weichselbaum here and on subsequent pages based in part on Manhattan real property record, records in United States District Court for the Southern District of Ohio, and author's interview with Weichselbaum.

156–57 Trump campaign contributions to Andrew Stein, Jay Goldin, and Ed Koch reported in Barrett, op. cit., p. 326.

161 Account of Donald J. Trump purchase of Holiday Inns' interest in Trump Plaza based in part on Connolly, op. cit.

161–62 Account of Donald J. Trump dispute with Louise Sunshine based in part on Marie Brenner, "After the Gold Rush," *Vanity Fair* (September 1990); also author's interview with Sunshine.

6. HOUSE OF CARDS

163–64 Account of Marla Maples audition for television program "Loving" based on May 1986 audition tape.

164–65 Description of Dalton, Georgia, based in part on Art Harris, "The Hometown of the Killer Blondes," *Washington Post,* February 19, 1990, and Fred Grimm, "2 Blondes Brighten 'Carpet Capital,' " *Miami Herald,* February 27, 1990.

167–68 Account of Marla Maples's relationship with Jeff Sandlin based in part on the *National Enquirer,* April 17, 1990, confirmed by author's interviews with informed sources.

170 "The place settings were astronomical . . .": Von Hoffman, op. cit., p. 378.

172 Account of Donald Trump's relationship with Mario Cuomo based in part on Barrett, op. cit., pp. 376–86.

175 Statements by Annabel Hill and Frank Argenbright quoted from interviews with ABC News, July 1990.

176 "Trump had sized up the competition . . .": O'Donnell, op. cit., p. 30.

176–77 Figures for Trump casino revenues here and on subsequent pages quoted from various issues of *Atlantic City Action,* 1986–1992.

178–79   Account of Donald J. Trump stock deals based in part on Connolly, op. cit.;
         also author's interview with Alan C. Greenberg.
185–87   Account of Ivana Trump's performance in Atlantic City based in part on
         O'Donnell; also author's interviews with Al Glasgow and other sources.
   188   Account of Donald J. Trump's complaints about Ivana's expenditures based
         in part on ABC News interview with Jerry Argovitz, summer 1990.

7. THE DEALS THAT MADE NO SENSE

201–3   Account of Donald J. Trump's relationships with Mike Tyson, Robin Giv-
         ens, Ruth Roper, and Don King based in part on Montieth Illingworth, *Mike
         Tyson: Money, Myth, and Betrayal* (New York: Birch Lane Press, 1991).
204–6   Account of Donald J. Trump's dealings with Merv Griffin and purchase of
         Taj Mahal based in part on Connolly, op. cit., Pippett, author's interviews
         with Al Glasgow, and accounts in the *Philadelphia Inquirer* by David Johnston
         May 27, 1990, and April 24, 1991.
   207   "Ego. That's probably the only way . . .": *Trump: Surviving at the Top*, p. 108.
   225   "Ivana was attempting" quoted in O'Donnell, op. cit., pp. 121–22.
   228   "It's inconceivable that . . .": Donald J. Trump quoted in Bill Barol, "Trump
         Ahoy," *Newsweek* (July 18, 1988).
   231   Account of "DJ Trump" episode based in part on O'Donnell, op. cit., pp.
         136–39.
   232   Description of wealth in United States based in part on Kevin Phillips; *The
         Politics of Rich and Poor: Wealth and the American Electorate in the Reagan After-
         math* (New York: Random House, 1990).
236–37   Account of Ivana Trump's citizenship ceremony based in part on King, op.
         cit., p. 166.
   240   "I don't fire people . . .": Ivana Trump quoted in Shnayerson, op. cit.
   242   Account of Donald Trump battles with Leonard Stern based in part on Edwin
         Diamond, "The Unmaking of a Documentary," *New York* (September 4, 1989).
   247   Marla Maples "putting a strain on the accommodations" quoted in O'Don-
         nell, op. cit., p. 151.
   247   Donald Trump comment about Marla Maples quoted ibid., p. 154.

8. THE ASPEN INCIDENT

   257   Account of Donald J. Trump confrontation with Ivana Trump based in part
         on Michael Gross, "Ivana's New Life," *New York* (October 15, 1991).

9. THE KING OF CRASS

287–88   Accounts of Akio Kashiwagi gambling at Trump Palace here and on subse-
         quent pages based in part on David Johnston, *Temples of Chance: How Amer-
         ica Inc. Bought Out Murder Inc. to Win Control of the Casino Business*, (New
         York: Doubleday, 1992), pp. 1–8, 235–42.

284–   Account of Taj Mahal employees gathering and opening problems based in
 306   part on O'Donnell, op. cit., pp. 267–96.

10. BANKRUPT BILLIONAIRE

318–19   Account of Marla Maples press conference based in part on *New York Daily News,* May 24, 1990.

320–22   Account of Donald J. Trump negotiations with bankers on this and subsequent pages based in part on various articles in the *Wall Street Journal* by Neil Barsky, spring and summer 1990; also various articles in the *Philadelphia Inquirer* by David Johnston, spring and summer 1990.

323–24   Account of American Booksellers Convention based on transcript of videotape made by ABC News, June 4, 1990.

326–27   Account of Ivana Trump appearance at Fragrance Foundation dinner based on Brenner, "After the Gold Rush," loc. cit.

327–28   Account of Ivana Trump appearance at Fox-Kramer wedding: based on Gross, op. cit.

335–38   Account of Ivana Trump's trips to Europe based in part on ibid., and William Norwich column, *New York Daily News,* August 7, 1990.

11. CHIPS OFF THE OLD BLOCK

346   "How can you say you love us?": Donald J. Trump, Jr., quoted in Brenner. "After the Gold Rush," loc. cit.

350–52   Account of Donald J. Trump meeting with Carl Icahn based in part on reporting by David Johnston of the *Philadelphia Inquirer.*

12. TRUMP V. TRUMP

378–80   Account of Casino Control Commission action on Fred Trump, Sr., chips purchase based in part on Johnston, *Temples of Chance,* loc. cit., pp. 288–95.

382–83   Carla Bruni-Tedeschi quoted in Bob Colacello, "La Dolce Carla," *Vanity Fair* (November 1992).

390–91   Account of Riccardo Mazzucchelli's background and business career based in part on Colacello, op. cit.

ACKNOWLEDGMENTS

This book is based on more than two and a half years of research, scores of primary and secondary sources, and over five thousand pages of court documents and other records. The author has met and spent varying amounts of time with all the principal characters, including Donald J. Trump, Ivana Trump, Marla Maples, Fred C. Trump, Sr., and Robert Trump. Donald Trump granted three formal interviews. Ivana Trump declined to grant an interview because of the still-disputed gag clause in the Trumps' nuptial contract. The author also benefited enormously from the input of many present and former members of the Trump inner circle.

Very special thanks are due researchers Christina Oxenberg, Anna Tipton, and Judy Lewenthal, Bob Dattila of the Phoenix Literary Agency, and Starling Lawrence of W. W. Norton & Company, without whose patience and diligence this project could not have been completed.

The author would also like to thank the following for their invaluable support and encouragement: Dr. Joel Aronowitz, Alexander Auersperg, Wayne Barrett, Alison Becker, Patricia Birch, John and Carlyon Bransford, Marie Brenner, Dominique Browning, William D. Broyles, Jr., Linda Buckley, Candace Bushnell, Joseph Carruth, Julie Chwatsky, Rob Clark, Pat Cook, Laurin Copen, Jennet Conant, Theodore B. Conklin III, John Connolly, George Crile III, Sam Donaldson, Laurie Durning, Morgan Entrekin, Molly Ferrer, John Fielding, George Finckenor, Tony Freund, Dr. Jamshid Ghajar, Tom Greene, Sheldon Greenhut, Marc Grossberg, Charles Grubb, Larry and Maj Hagman, Richard Halstead, Elizabeth Hamilton, Beth Henley, Michael Hirschorn, David Hirshey, John Hoffman, William R. Hurt, Margaret B. Hurt, Fred Huvar, Christopher Isham, Heyward and Sheila Isham, Nima Isham, Ralph and Ala Isham, Todd Jacobs, Nancy Jay, Peter Jennings, Doug Johnson, David Johnston and Jennifer Leonard, Gilbert Kaplan, Maura Kiely, William Kornreich, Steve Kroft, Nicholas B. Lemann, Patrick and Candace Malloy, Ruth Mandel, Terry and Joannie McDonell, Maxine Mesinger, Pete McAlevey, Marilyn Morris, Alice Murphy, Pat Oliva, Anne D. Owen and Hal Pontez, Harrell Hays Perkins, Dorothy H. Price, Al Reinert, Bart Richardson, Jordan Rogers, Judd Rose, James Savoca, Sheila Sculley, Dr. Fiona Shalom, Dean Smith, Dorrance Smith, Nancy Smith, Price Topping, Alexander and Sandra Vreeland, Dan Wicker, Nancy Weinberg, Jay Weiss, Richard G. Wells, Dirk Whittenborn, and Beverly Xua.

INDEX